AT WIT'S END

# At Wit's End

**THE DEADLY DISCOURSE ON THE JEWISH JOKE**

*Louis Kaplan*

FORDHAM UNIVERSITY PRESS   NEW YORK 2020

**Frontispiece:** Book cover for Alexander Moszkowski, *Der jüdische Witz und seine Philosophie* (The Jewish joke and its philosophy), designed by Lucian Bernhard (Berlin: Dr. Eysler, 1922). Collection of the author. The first version of this extremely popular joke book entitled *Die jüdische Kiste* (The Jewish box) was published in 1911 with the same Jewish jack-in-the-box caricature and with its cover signed by Bernhard. The earlier version serves as the basis for the cover of this volume.

Copyright © 2020 Fordham University Press

All rights reserved. No part of this publication may be reproduced, stored in a retrieval system, or transmitted in any form or by any means — electronic, mechanical, photocopy, recording, or any other — except for brief quotations in printed reviews, without the prior permission of the publisher.

Fordham University Press has no responsibility for the persistence or accuracy of URLs for external or third-party Internet websites referred to in this publication and does not guarantee that any content on such websites is, or will remain, accurate or appropriate.

Fordham University Press also publishes its books in a variety of electronic formats. Some content that appears in print may not be available in electronic books.

Visit us online at www.fordhampress.com.

Library of Congress Cataloging-in-Publication Data

Names: Kaplan, Louis, 1960– author.
Title: At wit's end : the deadly discourse on the Jewish joke / Louis Kaplan.
Description: First edition. | New York : Fordham University Press, 2020. | Includes bibliographical references and index.
Identifiers: LCCN 2019057420 | ISBN 9780823287550 (hardback) | ISBN 9780823287567 (trade paperback) | ISBN 9780823287574 (epub)
Subjects: LCSH: Jewish wit and humor — History and criticism. | Jews — Humor.
Classification: LCC PN6149.J4 K63 2020 | DDC 809.7/98924 — dc23
LC record available at https://lccn.loc.gov/2019057420

Printed in the United States of America

22 21 20    5 4 3 2 1

First edition

*To my father, Leon, for all his words of wit and wisdom*

Contents

Introduction: The Joke and Its Questions   1

1   Secondary Moves: Arthur Trebitsch and the Jewish Joke   24

2   Of Caricatures, Jokes, and Anti-Semitism: The Case of Eduard Fuchs   60

3   Of Watchmen and Comedians: Jewish Jokes and Free Speech in Weimar Germany   95

4   "Far from where?": Erich Kahler and the Jewish Joke of Exile   119

5   Of Jokes and Propaganda: The Mobilization of the Jewish Joke in the Nazi Era   153

6   Jewish Joke Reparations and Mourning in Post-Holocaust Germany   182

Conclusion: Final Thoughts and Last Laughs   219

Afterword: The Jewish Joke in Trump's America   224

ACKNOWLEDGMENTS   231

NOTES   235

INDEX   299

AT WIT'S END

# Introduction
## The Joke and Its Questions

> Deep. Deep like so many Jewish anecdotes. They offer an insight into the tragicomedy of contemporary Judaism.
> — HEINRICH BERMANN IN ARTHUR SCHNITZLER,
> THE ROAD INTO THE OPEN

In 1909, the Berlin-based commercial illustrator, caricaturist, and writer Edmund Edel (1864–1934) published what is considered to be the first monographic study that examines the Jewish joke in the German language.[1] In contrast to Sigmund Freud's psychoanalytically inclined *Jokes and their Relation to the Unconscious* (*Der Witz und seine Beziehung zum Unbewussten*, 1905)[2] where the Jewish joke figures into a larger schema about the way in which the human mind functions in general, Edel appears to be less interested in making universal claims about the joke and its nature. Written in the hybrid style of the feuilleton between literary criticism and artful journalism, Edel's *Der Witz der Juden* (Jewish wit) not only recounts and analyzes numerous Jewish jokes but also offers astute observations about the meaning and function of Jewish wit in modern culture (fig. 1). From the outset, Edel is keenly aware that theoretical speculations about wit and humor are the best way to ruin the laughter. This initial observation is not to be taken lightly; it is a lesson lodged in the unconscious of the studies that comprise this investigation considering the variegated discourse on Jewish wit and humor that emerges with these two writers and others at the beginning of the twentieth century, when the Jewish joke became a subject of serious inquiry and when it inserted itself as a rhetorical figure into the larger cultural and political debates among Jews and Germans in the German-speaking lands against the sobering and ideologically

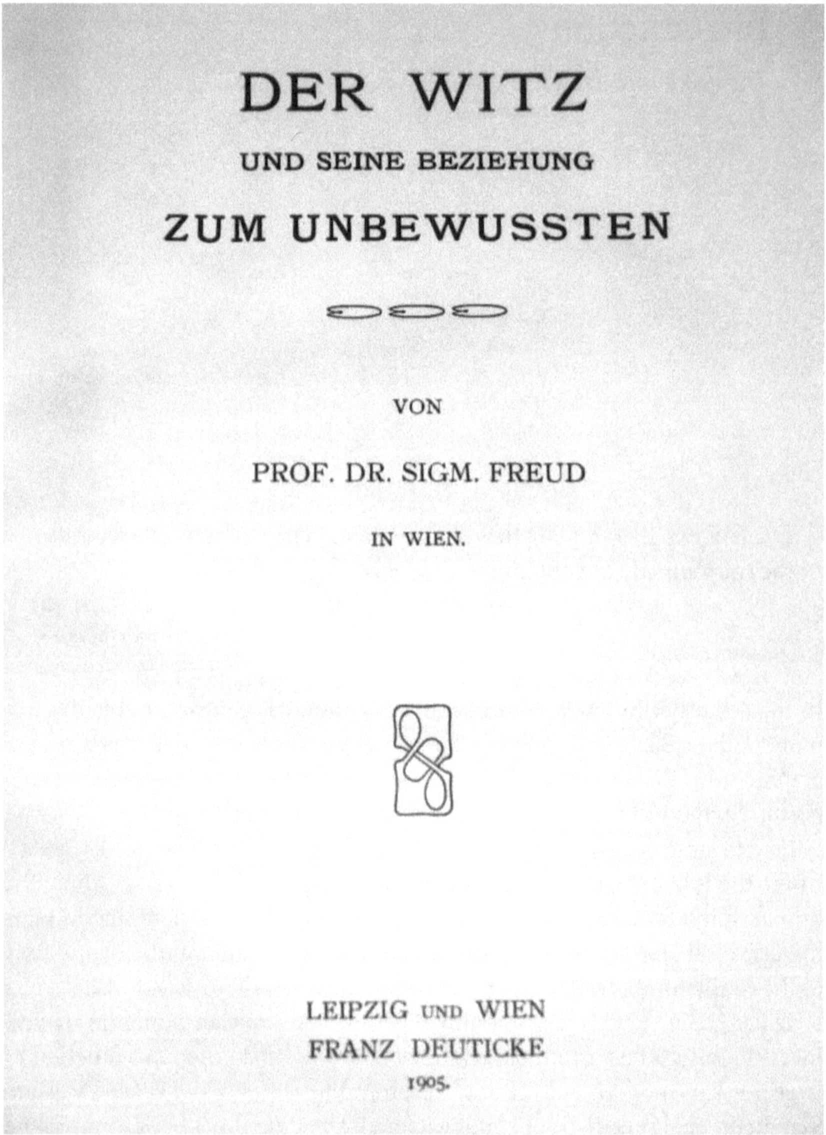

# DER WITZ
## UND SEINE BEZIEHUNG
# ZUM UNBEWUSSTEN

VON

PROF. DR. SIGM. FREUD

IN WIEN.

LEIPZIG UND WIEN
FRANZ DEUTICKE
1905.

Figure 1. The twentieth-century discourse on the Jewish joke begins with Sigmund Freud's *Der Witz und Seine Beziehung zum Unbewussten* (1905) and Edmund Edel's *Der Witz der Juden* (1909).

# Der Witz der Juden

von Edmund Edel.

1909
Berlin
Verlag von Louis Lamm.

charged backdrop of religious, economic, and racial anti-Semitism and the so-called Jewish question. In what might be viewed as an archetypical Jewish self-ironic gesture that pokes fun at his own serious endeavor, Edel previews the fettered perils of "Jewish joke science" in the following manner: "It is impossible to laugh about laughter — it is difficult to write a theoretical treatment or discourse [Abhandlung] about a joke. All commentaries spoil the punch line — the ball on the chain hinders free striding."[3]

## It's a Thin Line: Between Jewish Self-Irony and Anti-Semitism

Edel takes up the subject of Jewish self-irony as an important characteristic of Jewish wit later in this work. In this regard, he finds himself on the same page with Freud who famously pointed to "self-criticism" as central to Jewish humor and who stated that he did "not know whether there are many other instances of a people making fun to such a degree of its own character."[4] In this way, the Viennese psychoanalyst and the Berlin writer set the tone for the repeated use of this self-directed trope as the distinguishing marker of Jewish wit in modern times.[5] But what is even more striking about the following excerpt is the way in which Edel implicitly understands that Jewish self-irony cannot be extricated from the rhetoric of anti-Semitism whether it serves as a response to or as a provocation for such animosity. In this first sense, Ruth R. Wisse argues in her study *No Joke: Making Jewish Humor* that the Jewish joke (whether self-ironic or outer-directed) was often a response to anti-Semitism and provided a way for the Jews to "channel their humiliation into laughter."[6] Meanwhile, Sander Gilman's recent essay dealing with "Jewish Humour and the Terms by Which Jews and Muslims Join Western Civilization" moves the matter of joke appropriation in another direction — "an argument could be made [for Jewish humor] that the antisemitic image of the Jew is the enemy's weapon now used by the Jews."[7] In *Jewish Comedy: A Serious History*, Jeremy Dauber also discusses this "particularly discomfiting type of Jewish comedy of anti-Semitism" that features "an internalization of some of the charges" made against the Jews by anti-Semites and that often leads to accusations that these Jewish jokers practice "a kind of Jewish comedy that is frequently called 'self-hating.'"[8] On the other hand, the Jewish joke cannot be situated in a space that is somehow free and uncontaminated from its potential appropriation or recuperation by the enemies of the Jews and their desire to disseminate hate speech by means of cruel laughter. The potential consequences posed by Jewish self-irony as it both responds to and opens up the risks of anti-Semitism will be a key concern for this study as our analysts navigate the ambiguous and vacillating space of the Jewish joke. While Edel notes in the following excerpt that this risk is unfortunate, it is also unavoidable. It goes along with the turf of Jewish self-mockery and the turning of its tables so that what the Jew jokingly says about himself may be used against him. As Edel observes:

> The Jew not only loves to make fun of others, but also does not shy away from ironizing his own personality at every opportunity. This self-irony of the Jews has created a huge mass of excellent observations and jokes. In the times of the great anti-Semitic movement, these products served the opponents as sharp weapons unfortunately, but, just the same, from the perspective of religious Jews, one cannot quite approve of this type of self-spoofing either because these give a rather lopsided picture to other faiths missing the subtleties of our tribe. You will have to admit that this very ironizing of one's own weaknesses has produced wonderful pearls.[9]

In pointing to "the times of the great anti-Semitic movement," Edel presumably looks back to the Berlin anti-Semitism conflict (*Berliner Antisemitismusstreit*) that was inaugurated in 1879 with the German historian Heinrich von Treitschke's infamous remark, "The Jews are our misfortune!"[10] Such anti-Semitic rhetoric would continue over the course of the next decades and eventually move from a religious to a racialist brand. As the historian of caricature Henry Wassermann writes, "The appearance of anti-Semitic political parties in the 1880's and 1890's was accompanied by the dissemination of overtly anti-Semitic caricatures and malevolent representations of Jews that were precursors of the *Stürmer* tradition."[11] In other words, there was no shortage of how Jewish humor was taken up in an anti-Semitic fashion in the jokes and caricatures of illustrated humor magazines such as the Viennese *Kikeriki*, the Berliner *Kladderadatsch*, or the Munich-based *Fliegende Blätter* during that period.[12] Given that political anti-Semitism lost some of its popular appeal in the decade preceding World War I or at the time when Edmund Edel published his book, one notices that he uses the past tense when referring to this "great anti-Semitic movement." But this turned out to be a rather short respite with the outbreak of World War I in 1914 that would lead to military defeat, the loss of territory, and the reparations demanded by the Treaty of Versailles. Such events would rekindle an ardent German nationalism and concomitant anti-Semitism turning the Jews into scapegoats for the downfall of the Second Reich in Germany and the Hapsburg Empire in Austria in 1918. (It is then and there that my study really takes off with Arthur Trebitsch's use of the Jewish joke to bolster his own Viennese brand of anti-Semitic diatribe.) Edel's analysis also highlights how such self-mocking and self-spoofing is less appealing to religious Jews as well because of the relentless capacity of these jokes to desacralize and to poke fun at that which is deemed holy in the Jewish religion. The religious Jews fear that these iconoclastic jokes produce only superficial and negative stereotypes that give the Jewish minority such a bad name when viewed from the dominant Christian perspective. In this way, Edel frames Jewish humor as a modern phenomenon found primarily among secularizing and urban Jews. Interestingly, the historian and literary scholar Mary Gluck addresses this same point in *The Invisible Jewish Budapest* stressing the ironic worldview of Jewish wit that serves as the defining feature of Edel's analysis: "For the defining feature of *Judenwitz* [Jewish wit/joke] was not the affirmation of any particular social, political, or moral agenda but the ironic deflation of all such agendas. *Judenwitz* was the voice of the disengaged individual who saw the world in absurdist terms. It gave rise to a relativistic and modernist state of mind that reflected the instability of human experience and the fragmentary nature of human identity."[13]

There is a great deal of ambivalence in Edel's commentary on Jewish self-irony because the Jewish joke is the site of an intense ambivalence and instability. Is the type of self-irony that is expressed in such Jewish jokes and its exposure of Jewish weaknesses a good or a bad thing for the Jews? It is certainly a good thing for Jewish humor. But are we dealing here with self-irony or self-hatred? On the one hand, Edel affirms how Jewish self-irony has "produced wonderful pearls" and "created a huge mass of excellent observations and jokes." On the other hand, there is the serious concern that the unfortunate consequence of these self-inflicted barbs is to give the anti-Semites something that can be used against the Jews. Edel's reference to Jewish jokes as "sharp weapons" exposes the fear that this already self-directed weapon might backfire if placed in the wrong hands. Thus, a well-intentioned and self-mocking Jewish joke in one context would be converted into "hate speech" in another context depending on the aims of the joke teller.[14] According to Markus Patka, Edel "observes shrewdly" that Jewish self-irony functions as an "explosive force inside and outside of Judaism."[15] It is a ticking time bomb that can blow up quite easily in the face of the one who wields this weapon. On the inside, religious or self-defense organization leaders, such as Alfred Wiener of the Central Association of German Citzens of Jewish Faith (Centralverein deutscher Staatsbürger jüdischen Glaubens), sought to defuse the bomb before it went off. Their goal was to limit or even censor this type of self-mockery that they deemed to be a form of self-hate speech.[16] Even the cultured Jew (*Bildungsjude*) Erich Kahler, who appreciated the value of what he called the Jewish *Galuthswitz* (the joke of exile), was concerned that a certain strand of frivolous Jewish self-deprecation would lead to justifiable anti-Semitic attacks (pursuant to Dauber's point; see chapter 4). On the outside, the anti-Semites — as shown in the case studies of the self-hating Jew Arthur Trebitsch (see chapter 1) and the Nazi propagandist Siegfried Kadner (see chapter 5) — were more than happy to twist these Jewish jests to their own ends in order to get as big a negative charge out of them as possible. They sought to take the Jewish weaknesses exposed by these jokes and to reframe them as anti-Semitic and racialist proofs of Jewish inferiority or degeneration.

The question as to whether or not Jewish self-irony was good or bad for the Jews also troubled the young Gershom Scholem shortly after the end of World War I. In seeking out the sources of the Jewish joke, the renowned scholar of Jewish thought speculated that its mockery and subversive mix-ups took the earnest Talmudic analysis and interpretation of the biblical canon for comic spins so that "the Jewish joke developed through the systematic mix-up between the canon and the transmission of tradition." Scholem continues in this diary entry dated December 23, 1918, with a serious and profound reflection on Jewish self-irony (or, as he put it, when the Jewish joke "is turned ironically against itself"): "In which case the Jewish joke would conceal within itself an unmistakable symbolic reference to the deepest danger of what is Jewish, namely, the deep strata of self-accusation."[17] For Scholem, Jewish self-irony exposes us to what is the deepest danger and threat posed by Judaism to itself even before the external threat of anti-Semitism.[18] Digging ever deeper, self-irony transforms into self-accusation. Scholem's penetrating analysis of the symbolic significance of Jewish self-irony also provides us with a rationale and framework for a deeper understanding of the Jewish anti-Semite Arthur Trebitsch who published *Geist und Judentum* (Spirit and Judaism) at the same time. In other words, Trebitsch was so fascinated by the Jewish joke because the deeper that he delved into its self-ironies, the more he revealed and reveled in this mode of self-accusation that complemented (and contributed to) this "Aryan" convert's intense persecution of himself (or of his former Jewish self).

Nevertheless, the Jewish joke had its defenders who argued that the actual purpose of igniting such Jewish joke bombs was to defuse and deflect anti-Semitism and to bring the laugher over to one's side. Reviewing the history of the oppression of the Jews in Europe, this more positive interpretation underscores the reason why the joke was sometimes cast as "the last weapon of the defenseless" as it sought to disarm the anti-Semitic enemy through laughter.[19] Meanwhile, the renowned Berlin comedian and cofounder of the Kabarett der Komiker (KadeKo; Cabaret of Comics) Kurt Robitschek, among others, insisted during the heyday of the Weimar Republic that free speech must be protected at all costs and that any collateral damage that came along with offending certain Jews or even stirring up anti-Semitic sentiments was well worth the price if that was what it took in order to uphold democratic values.

Inversely, the German Marxist cultural historian Eduard Fuchs argued that Jewish self-irony was not necessarily a sign of weakness but rather a sign of strength—and that it often served as the feint and the pose of a self-confident people (see chapter 2). Fuchs's view is related to one of Sander Gilman's major contentions that self-ironic Jewish humor offered the Jews the terms by which they were able to join Western civilization after Jewish emancipation by showing the Gentile world that they could take a punch(line). Gilman asks this rhetorical question in order to explain the rise of Jewish self-irony (or Jews telling jokes about Jews) at this particular historical moment: "Or is it to show that as civilized people they can take jokes told about themselves?"[20]

The Jewish folklorists of this period who collected Jewish jokes and anecdotes, such as the prolific Hassidic Rabbi Chayim Bloch (1881–1973), argued for the maintenance of a distinction between two categories of jokes. To recite Bloch's formal distinction: "In fact, there are two genres of the joke—the Jewish joke [*Judenwitz*] and the Jewish '*Lozale*' [crude jokes] referred to by [the Jewish religious leader in Vienna] Dr. Joseph S. Bloch as the 'Jewish anti-Semitic joke.'"[21] But such a dichotomy ignores the close ties—sometimes too close for comfort—that bind the self-mocking Jewish joke with anti-Semitic discourse. In *Der Witz*, the German joke scholar Lutz Röhrich argues against this dichotomy by noting the impossibility of preventing the recasting of the "authentic" Jewish joke as an anti-Semitic weapon: "The problem of the Jewish joke lies above all in the fact that in becoming a weapon [*Kampfmittel*] of anti-Semitism, the Jewish joke will have been reminted into the Jew joke."[22] As part of the Jewish Renaissance movement, these folklorists reclaimed "jokelore" as an important part of a living Jewish tradition and a means for social bonding. Thus, these editors, compilers, and translators constructed the Jewish joke book as a folkloric object of study. However, their insistence on the "law of genre" and their search for Bloch's authentic and uncontaminated Jewish joke blinded them to a more nuanced approach that would acknowledge the inherent anti-Semitic risks to which every Jewish self-ironic joke is exposed. Indeed, such classification into two fixed categories did not allow for the consideration of the transformation of historical circumstances that could alter the social perception of the same self-ironic "Jewish joke" and whether or not it should be told. Even though it might seem harmless in a more tolerant moment, it could fan the fires of anti-Semitism at another point in history.[23]

At times, even the Jewish community disagreed as to how to classify certain Jewish jokes. For example, whereas the KadeKo comedians in Weimar Germany believed that they were telling self-ironic Jewish jokes,[24] the Centralverein led by Alfred Wiener interpreted them as morally depraved material akin to Jewish anti-Semitic jokes in Bloch's sense. The same contentiousness goes for a Jewish joke book published during the Weimar Republic with its pseudonymous authorship mocking the Nazi party leader (fig. 2). The book *Jüdische Witze* (1927) is attributed to H. Itler in a provocative act of Jewish self-irony and in what is assumed to be an attempt to defuse anti-Semitism. While this satirical gesture may have relieved anxiety about Hitler's threat at the time, it also lends itself to becoming a weapon in the hands of anti-Semites. After all, here is "H. Itler" making (anti-Semitic) jokes about and against the Jews. One doubts whether this same gag would have been made six years later even when leaving the question of Nazi censorship aside.

In the same manner, the earlier cabaret theater of the Brothers Herrnfeld on Berlin's Kommandantenstrasse also staged a contentious brand of comedy as it played the line between Jewish self-mockery and the charge of anti-Semitism. There was an interesting incident that deserves recounting that took place just one year before Edel published his book and at a time when "it has long been considered uncouth to be anti-Semitic; on the contrary, tolerance is quite in fashion now."[25] The author of this article with the Parisian-inflected *nom de plume* of Flaneur laments and attacks "The Anti-Semitic Brothers Herrnfeld" in a citation that is worth quoting at length:

> This makes it all the more unpleasant that in Berlin, of all places, a most pernicious and unpleasant remnant of the old anti-Semitic hooliganism still holds on tenaciously. I have in mind the Theatre of the Brothers Herrnfeld, which for years has been at pains to defame Judaism and the Jewish character in the crudest manner imaginable, and to present the entirety of German Jews as rubes [*Trottel*] or vagabonds [*verlumpte Kerle*]. . . . Even a spoof on Jewry [*Verulkung des Judentums*] can be harmless, self-irony and persiflage being deep-seated features of the Jewish character; and all the delightfully corny jokes (which the excellent Manuel Schnitzer has now collected in two superb volumes) generally involve harmless ribbing [*harmlose Verspottung*] of our own character and our own mistakes. But what is so disturbing over on the Kommandantenstrasse is the hateful one-sidedness with which Jews as a whole are presented as wretches [*Wichte*] and cretins.[26]

For Flaneur, Jewish "self-irony and persiflage" had been pushed too far with the theater of Herrnfeld Brothers to the point where it became "hateful one-sidedness" and outright anti-Semitism. Nevertheless, in hindsight, Centralverein leader Ludwig Holländer nostalgically viewed the Herrnfeld Brothers' entertainment as relatively palatable when compared to the next generation's the KadeKo gags and in the different historical context of the

Figure 2. H. Itler, *Jüdische Witze* (1927). Cover art by Friedrich Kurt Fiedler.

Weimar Republic, thereby providing another example of the protean nature of the Jewish joke and the wavering border between Jewish self-irony and its anti-Semitic appropriation (see chapter 3). The Berlin-based designer Lucian Bernhard's startling caricature of a Jewish jack-in-the-box with an outstretched right arm serves as another example of shifting historical interpretations and thin lines (see frontispiece). As the cover of Alexander Moszkowski's extremely popular *Die jüdische Kiste* (1911) and *Der jüdische Witz und seine Philosophie* (1922), the clownish figure was not consciously associated with anti-Semitism.[27] One hundred years later, the cover will be misread as a Jewish joker making a self-denigrating Nazi salute thereby transforming into an anti-Semitic anachronism.

This ambivalence of the Jewish joke (and the mutual imbrication of Jewish self-irony and anti-Semitic discourse) subverts any essentialist attempt to distinguish them as modes of cultural production. In each case, the instability of the border between Jewish self-irony and anti-Semitism parallels the mutually imbricated terms of Germanness (*Deutschtum*) and Jewishness (*Judentum*) that cannot be separated but which several major Jewish joke analysts (specifically, Erich Kahler, Siegfried Kadner, and Arthur Trebitsch) sought to maintain. It is important to deconstruct such essentialist gestures that prop up the concept of a fixed Jewish or German national or racial character. The reintroduction of the Jewish joke book after the Holocaust offers another case of slippage. When Salcia Landmann revived the Jewish joke book as a folkloric object, she insisted in her introduction that it was always possible to differentiate between "self-critical and anti-Semitic jokes." As she wrote, "It is very easy: only the real Jewish joke accuses the Jews of their real faults and sins, and not invented ones."[28] Ironically, the Viennese writer Friedrich Torberg launched a critique of Landmann's project that focused in part on the great difficulty of maintaining such a hard and fast distinction (see chapter 6). Indeed, Torberg accused many of Landmann's "real Jewish jokes" of reinforcing classic anti-Semitic stereotypes.

Arthur Schnitzler's novel *The Way into the Open* (also published in 1908) is pertinent to this introductory excavation of the thin line between Jewish self-irony or self-criticism and anti-Semitism. This final case study offers a variant on the KadeKo controversy with another Jewish joking twist. The Jewish dramatist in the novel, Heinrich Bermann, recounts the classic joke of the two Jews on the train, one of whom relaxes by putting his legs up on the seat across from him upon learning that he is riding with a modern co-religionist who has revealed his Jewishness by asking him about the timing of the Yom Kippur holiday that year.[29] Bermann proceeds to lash out at the Jews for their lack of respect and for their failure to master the so-called "ordeal of civility."[30]

Bermann concludes, "For all emotional relationships take place in an atmosphere of familiarity, so to speak, in which respect is stifled."[31] Bermann's disrespectful interpretation also provides the reader with a wonderful example of self-reflexive speculation that offers a snapshot of the discourse on the Jewish joke at that time. His critical reading of the joke and what it represents leads him to conclude negatively that Jews are incapable of respect. After hearing this diatribe, his Christian friend Georg von Wergenthin laments: "'Do you know what I think,' Georg remarked. 'That you are a worse anti-Semite than most Christians I know.'"[32] We are left on the wavering border between what the Jew thinks he is expressing (i.e., legitimate Jewish self-criticism about a beloved self-ironic Jewish joke) and how his speech is perceived by a sympathetic Christian observing from the outside (i.e., Jewish self-hate speech that is akin to anti-Semitism).

## Ideological Prisms and Contemporary Currents

What does the discourse on the Jewish joke (which is always concerned with questioning and with the questionable) have to contribute to an understanding of the Jewish question in this crucial period of Jewish and world history? This book explores the complex cultural trope of *der jüdische Witz* (as both Jewish wit and Jewish jokes) and how it can help us further illuminate German-Jewish intercultural relations and their breakdown in the German-speaking lands—from the end of World War I to the rise of national socialism and the controversy surrounding the reintroduction of the Jewish joke into the public sphere after the Holocaust with the publication of Landmann's Jewish folkloristic collection in 1960. It paradoxically demonstrates how giving thought and earnest reflection to the meaning and significance of the Jewish joke (as well as to its provocative laughter) provides an unusual and unique perspective by which one can gain insights into this deadly serious historical moment occupied with the Jewish question. The historian and literary scholar Mary Gluck has grasped the connection between the Jewish joke and the Jewish question by turning to the anthropologist Mary Douglas and her work on jokes: "Douglas's insight that jokes were the expressions of contradictions within the social order suggests inescapable connections between *Judenwitz* and the Jewish question. Indeed, it could be argued that the two were mirror images of each other, reflecting the ideological crisis of Central European modernity that thrust Jews into the epicenter of the conflict. Surprisingly, little is known about the theoretical and empirical interconnections among *Judenwitz*, the Jewish question, and modernity."[33] By examining the discourse on the Jewish joke and its social and political ramifications from the Weimar Republic to the Holocaust and beyond, *At Wit's End* is in part an attempt to fill some of the gaps in knowledge that Gluck has pinpointed.

Reviewing this critical and traumatic moment in modern German-Jewish history through the complex and sometimes deadly discourse on the Jewish joke, I divided my multidisciplinary study into three chronological periods — the Weimar and Austrian Republics (1918–1933), the Third Reich (1933–1945), and the period after the Holocaust (1945–1964). Chapters 1 and 2 are devoted to the immediate aftermath of World War I (focusing on texts by Arthur Trebitsch in Vienna and Eduard Fuchs in Berlin); chapters 4 and 5 are devoted to the first years of the Nazi's reign of anti-Jewish terror (examining the work of Erich Kahler in Munich and later in exile and Siegfried Kadner in Berlin); chapter 3, bridging the two spheres, looks at the KadeKo controversy in Berlin during the middle period of the Weimar Republic; and chapter 6 explores the post-Holocaust revival of the Jewish joke in Germany in the era of reparation (*Wiedergutmachung*) and the controversy surrounding the phenomenal success of Landmann's *Der Jüdische Witz* first published in 1960. My premise is that the Jewish joke was mobilized in strikingly different ways in light of its protean nature which is why I review the claims made about the Jewish joke by notable writers and thinkers (both Jewish and German) from a variety of ideological perspectives and cultural subject positions. Each chapter offers a different lens or prism on the meaning and the significance of Jewish wit, focusing on a key text to illustrate how this rhetorical figure refracted differently according to the investments and desires of each Jewish joke analyst. These ideological perspectives and cultural positions include the Jewish anti-Semite and early Nazi sympathizer Arthur Trebitsch, the German Marxist cultural historian and collector Eduard Fuchs, the Jewish diasporic historian and literary scholar Erich Kahler, the Jewish cabaret impresario Kurt Robitschek, and the Nazi literary and cultural propagandist Siegfried Kadner, among others. These protagonists are joined by an array of figures who wrote and speculated about the meaning and significance of the Jewish joke in this same period, including the Zionist philosopher of education Ernst Simon, the Viennese psychoanalyst Theodor Reik, and the Berlin satirist and "jokologist" Alexander Moszkowski.

In hindsight, these literary and cultural critics, psychologists, historians, philosophers, and others who engaged in the serious adaptation of Jewish joke materials to suit their particular rhetorical and ideological ends engaged in a process that I call "dejokification." This polyphony of voices recorded the views of Nazis and satirists, Jewish anti-Semites and German socialists, secular and religious, diasporic Jews and Zionists with each joke analyst seeking to master Jewish wit and its meaning. Therefore, this study operates on a level of reading and interpretation that foregrounds the strategies and the staging necessary for the construction of cultural arguments that rely upon "Jewish wit" as a key concept as well as on the analysis of particular Jewish jokes in order to make their mark.

There has been a renewed interest in Jewish wit and jokes over the past decade in both popular culture and in academic circles. I have mentioned already the recent publications on Jewish wit by leading North American scholars such as Sander Gilman, Ruth Wisse, and Jeremy Dauber. The German symposium "Der jüdische Witz: Zur unabgegoltenen Problematik einer alten Kategorie" ("Jewish Wit: On the Unsettled Problem of an Old Category"), organized by Burkard Meyer-Sickendiek (Berlin) and Gunnar Och (Erlangen) at the Free University in Berlin in May 2013,[34] focused on "the question of the cultural and historical impact of the Jewish joke."[35] A number of the presentations looked at key German-Jewish literary figures such as Heinrich Heine, Ludwig Börne, and Karl Kraus and the role of Jewish wit in their literary productions. The brochure for the conference specifically mentions Salcia Landmann's collection and her debate with Friedrich Torberg in the 1960s when the Jewish joke was revived after the Holocaust (see chapter 6).[36] The conference also featured a presentation by Micha Brumlik related to his publication on the German neo-Marxist visual cultural historian and collector Eduard Fuchs who is the subject of chapter 2.[37] In addition, the Viennese curators Markus Patka and Alfred Stalzer also participated in the Berlin symposium. Their massive exhibition and catalog *Alle Meschugge?: Jüdischer Witz und Humor* opened at the Jewish Museum in Vienna in spring 2013.[38] All these examples attest to the renewed interest in Jewish wit and Jewish jokes in Germany and Austria as an object of study (and fascination) for historians and literary scholars as well as an object of display for museum institutions over the last decade.

In addition to such scholarly interest, there is the enormous pop cultural appeal of our ticklish subject and the provocative issues that it raises often by means of an angst-filled laughter. The success of contemporary cultural phenomena such as Sacha Baron Cohen's satirical films (whether *Borat* or *The Dictator*), *Heeb Magazine*, and Jon Stewart's *The Daily Show* all point, in Sander Gilman's words, to "this post-modern, post-Zionist age of self-consciously Jewish appropriation of anti-Semitic images."[39] Georg's anti-Semitic accusation in *The Way into the Open* is revived when confronted with this brand of outrageous Jewish wit that seeks rather self-consciously to be mistaken for anti-Semitism. Borat's satirical song, "In My Country There is a Problem" (also known as "Throw the Jew Down the Well") offers a twenty-first century example of Jewish humor that both parodies and provokes anti-Semitism. This double-barreled example of self-ironic and tendentious wit makes fun of the anti-Semites while also making fun of Jews in making believe that it is an anti-Semitic provocation. For this reason, Baron Cohen received a stern letter of warning from Abraham Foxman and the Jewish Anti-Defamation League citing that the general public might not grasp Borat's satirical message.[40] In chapter 1 of his erudite book on *Jewish Comedy* aptly titled "What's so Funny About Anti-Semitism?," Jeremy Dauber writes how Baron Cohen "takes *his* transgressive delight in displaying a hidden or not-so-hidden seam of anti-Semitism in famously tolerant America."[41]

Similarly, the graphic artist and self-professed Jewish diasporic gadfly Eli Valley has created stinging satirical cartoons that take aim at politically conservative Jewish and Israeli targets (from Foxman to Netanyahu to Jared Kushner) and that warn of their complicity and collusion with anti-Semites in the Trump era.[42] Valley's vicious cartoons also attack the so-called alt-right movement (e.g., the American president's former political adviser Steve Bannon) to expose the new face of American anti-Semitism and neo-Nazism and its satirical scapegoating of the Jews. The current wave of anti-Semitic attacks instigated by the alt-right upon Jews in the media in particular replete with Holocaust jokes and the mockery of Jewish names recall the smear tactics instigated by Nazi propagandists Joseph Goebbels and Siegfried Kadner during the Third Reich (see chapter 5). But while some have argued that the ascendancy of the alt-right demands aggressive and cutting political satire (in the style of Chaplin's *The Great Dictator* or Mel Brooks's *The Producers*) to make today's neo-Nazis look ridiculous, others warn to the contrary that such conspicuous Jewish humor empowers the alt-right by putting them into the spotlight even further and that such exposure can produce even greater harm. Even while leaving themselves open to the charges of "self-hate" speech as in the Weimar antics of the KadeKo (see chapter 3),[43] the comic examples of Baron Cohen and Valley take today's audiences to the edge of appropriateness and good taste. They constitute new variants of the ways in which self-ironic Jewish humor "takes back" anti-Semitic hatred and converts it into laughter even while being exposed to its toxic risks.[44] They also lead us to the speculation that one might be able to take on controversial political issues and questions today only by means of this extreme and edgy type of comedy rooted in the tradition of biting Jewish humor and its self-mocking defense against anti-Semitism even if such a strategy oversteps the limits set by so-called "political correctness."

## *Witzenschaft*: Reviewing Jewish Joke Science

A little over two hundred years ago, the first Jewish joke books appeared in the German language. In 1810, Solomon Ascher published a book of Jewish anecdotes entitled *Der Judenfreund* and signed it ironically with the pen name "Judas Ascher" to mark its ambivalence and betrayal of Jew-friendliness. Ascher's early collection provides us with a prime example of the wavering border between Jewish self-irony and anti-Semitism at the origin of the Jewish joke book.[45] But the most famous joke book of that era edited and introduced by then–Chief Rabbi of Berlin Lippmann Moses Büschenthal was published two years later.[46] Coincidentally, the year of its publication coincided with Jewish Emancipation in Prussia so that the birth of the modern Jewish citizen and of the modern Jewish joker run parallel with each other. Sander Gilman sees this as no accident arguing that such joke books "provided Jews with one means of joining a newly evolving German civil society."[47] Interestingly, Rabbi Büschenthal saw the humor of the Jews as a direct response to their status as an oppressed people and he thereby put into print the popular hypothesis that Jewish humor involves the transformation of Jewish suffering into laughter: "But that the Jews are so witty in general, we believe must be attributed to their oppression suffered over the centuries." From this perspective, laughter was not only to be viewed as offering relief from Jewish suffering but also as a direct response to and necessary effect of such suffering. Then the Berlin rabbi went on to address issues of gender and class in relation to these Jewish joking matters: "Distress and weakness—this the female sex teaches us—give birth to deception, and deception is the mother of wit. One therefore encounters this much more frequently among persecuted and poor rural Jews than among rich ones."[48] Büschenthal's introductory comments illustrate the desire of the compilers of joke collections to make sense of Jewish wit and its significance from the start.

A decade after the publication of Rabbi Büschenthal's compilation, the discourse on Jewish wit would take center stage in the realm of German literature and journalism with the interventions of three major post-emancipation Jewish satirists: Heinrich Heine (1797–1856), Ludwig Börne (1786–1837), and Moritz Saphir (1798–1858). Jefferson S. Chase has traced the discourse on *Judenwitz* (Jewish joke or wit) as a stereotype and as a strategy in German literary culture from 1820 to 1850, and his work serves as a precursor to this present study. Through the mocking lens of the *Judenwitzler* (Jewish joker), Chase details "the association of Jewishness and destructive, satiric laughter in nineteenth-century Germany."[49] Moreover, Chase insists upon this "association of Jewishness with destructive humor" as "a particular German phenomenon" (4) whose development was favored by Germany's own emerging sense of nationalism. Chase situates the sarcastic and "malicious laughter" of *Judenwitz* as a discourse of outsiders in direct opposition to the positive and dominant discourse on German *Humor* that was characterized with "empty buzzwords" such as benevolence, imagination, and *"Gemütlichkeit"* (coziness) rooted in "the cultural achievements of Goethe and Schiller" (2–3).[50] From Chase's perspective, the rise of a literary and cultural discourse deploring Jewish wit as a destructive force and affirming German humor as a positive force served as a rallying point and unifying motif for both nationalist and anti-Semitic sentiments. He writes "The reaction to the three writers established links between mainstream and antisemitic views of German cultural history. Although the vast majority of nineteenth-century Germans did not think in terms of ethnic absolutes, the *Judenwitz* discourse represented a point of literary- and cultural-historical convergence between mainstream nationalism and the lunatic fringe of antisemitism" (16).

Chase argues that "the perceived antithesis between Jewish and German modes of discourse, between *Witz* and *Humor*," established itself as an inescapable figure in the study of German literary and cultural history and indeed it managed to reach the status of a "literary-historical legend" (17). He concludes, "By the end of the nineteenth century the assumption of what I will henceforth term *Judenwitz* had become standard in literary and cultural history, and its influence would continue unchallenged up until 1933 and into the Third Reich" (2). From this perspective, *At Wit's End* begins where Chase leaves off given that the book traces the discourse on Jewish wit and jokes from Sigmund Freud and Edmund Edel through the Weimar years and into the toxic rhetoric of the Third Reich. Indeed, the rhetoric in the writings of the Nazi propagandist Siegfried Kadner and his racist book *Rasse und Humor* follows Chase's schema to the letter as he divides the world into destructive Jewish cynics and life-affirming German humorists (see chapter 5). But this same neat binary opposition (that I want to problematize) also impacted other Jewish thinkers on the subject whether Erich Kahler or Sigmund Freud.[51] Indeed, Chase insists upon Freud's familiarity with this binary opposition and his fascination with and unwavering defense of *Judenwitz* in his study haunted by the ghost of Heinrich Heine: "That Freud, sensitive as he was to issues of Jewishness, should have been as fascinated by *Witz* is hardly accidental — as his own choice of examples shows, he was writing very much in the wake of Heine and the controversies described throughout this book" (9).

We may go even further than Chase here in insisting that Freud sought to convert the discourse on *Judenwitz* into scientific knowledge (*Wissenschaft*) via psychoanalysis. In this manner, the discourse about the Jewish joke took a more formal turn at the end of the nineteenth and beginning of the twentieth century as investigators in the cultural sciences immersed in the process of the rationalization and systemization of human phenomena analyzed the Jewish joke's cultural and philosophical significance and brought it into the province of modern knowledge.[52] Exemplified in the career of Sigmund Freud, the attempt to study the joke in a "scientific manner" was part of the larger process whereby subjects that were formerly rejected and marginalized now became acceptable and legitimate objects of study. Whether investigating dreams, human sexuality, or jokes, things that had been considered taboo or trivial now became the provenance of the emerging fields of psychoanalysis, anthropology, sociology, cultural history, and folklore.[53] At the same time, this legitimation of the Jewish joke also opened up the possibility for more popular intellectual speculation as witnessed in Edmund Edel's study or in the remarks of the fictional character Heinrich Bermann when he commented that these "deep" Jewish jokes "offer an insight into the tragicomedy of contemporary Judaism."[54] From folklorists to psychoanalysts, from cultural historians to literary critics, from philosophers to educators, the Jewish joke (and Jewish wit in general) was now considered a source of knowledge as well as wisdom and therefore worthy of systematic study. At this critical juncture, it just was not funny (or witty) anymore. Or it was not *just* funny. The Jewish joke was no longer just a part of an oral tradition of folklore passed on from generation to generation. In the words (and word play) of Paul Mendes-Flohr, the Jewish joke had moved from the level of "lore" to the level of the "law." The Jewish joke was no longer to be viewed as a transient triviality of everyday life or a flight of whimsy aimed solely at an explosion of laughter. Moreover, it was meant to be something more than a mode of amiable exchange at social occasions. At this moment of its intellectualization, the Jewish joke had become a rhetorical figure that was embedded in something that was much larger than itself. It was positioned and inserted into a highly charged political and ideological debate with serious import. At home in a semantic field connoting a war of words, the Jewish joke functioned as a loaded weapon in the crossfire between Jews and Germans as they discussed and debated their cultural and political present and future. At this self-reflexive level of a second-order discourse, the Jewish joke shifted from being a direct means of self-defense or of giving offense employed by (or against) the Jewish minority to one of the figural means by which to gain further insight into the Jewish question and the cultural crisis of the Jews in twentieth-century Germany. It was now something to be used to construct a larger argument about the nature of culture and society or about the relationship between *Deutschtum* and *Judentum*. The common and folksy joke had assumed an air of reflectiveness and importance by which it entered the halls of cultivated discourse. For some of our writers, this was also when the joke was put into the service of a body of knowledge or when the joke became a trope in the formation of a discourse that claimed to have a scientific status. In the strange case of Arthur Trebitsch and his deadly serious anti-Semitic discourse, the Jewish joke was appropriated as a totalizing metaphor for the secondary and inferior quality of the Jewish mind and Jewish character in general.

This was when *Witz* became subject to *Wissenschaft*, forming the neologism in the German language — *Witzenschaft*. A red-letter date for the beginning of this discursive phenomenon was June 22, 1897, when the young Sigmund Freud wrote to his friend Wilhelm Fliess about his collection of Jewish jokes in process: "I must confess that for some time past I have been putting together a collection of Jewish anecdotes of deep significance."[55] The keyword here is *deep*, the same word that the fictional character Heinrich Bermann uses in Schnitzler's novel. The consideration of Jewish jokes as something deep or, as Freud tells Fliess in another letter, as "so much profound and often bitter worldly wisdom,"[56] sets them up as an appropriate object for psychoanalytic study. These Jewish anecdotes would form the nucleus of Freud's attempt to constitute his joke science in *Der Witz* eight years later.

But even as the Jewish joke is transformed into a trope and these joke fragments becomes exemplary vehicles for writers such as Freud, Kadner, Kahler, Fuchs, Trebitsch, and others to say something grand and eloquent about the Jewish character, the Jewish mind, and the Jewish question, there remains a level of resistance that derives from the Jewish joke itself. In other words, there is something funny going on here. This "something funny" brings with it the lingering skepticism regarding the very presumption to take these Jewish jokes so seriously or to assume that they are of profound significance. *At Wit's End* needs to be attentive to this level of joking resistance to being taken so seriously that trips up these discursive and theoretical claims leaving only laughter in its wake. This laughter marks the return of the repressed (whether as irony or absurdity) that mocks this meaningful enterprise. To return to Mary Gluck's point, "For the defining feature of *Judenwitz* was not the affirmation of any particular social, political, or moral agenda but the ironic deflation of all such agendas. *Judenwitz* was the voice of the disengaged individual who saw the world in absurdist terms."[57] I would argue that such doubt about the Jewish joke's significance also haunted Freud's confession to Fliess when he admitted that he wanted to make a second-order discourse out of these jokes in the service of psychoanalysis. This joke collector's confession (signaled in the opening, "I must confess") springs from an aspiring scientist's guilty conscience (or unconscious) that he is doing something frivolous or unseemly in preoccupying himself with something as trivial, transient, and superficial as jokes. Therefore, this study is also interested in registering how the joke is always ready to flip things over (in line with the Jewish comedic figure of the *Dreh*, or "spin") in order to become "a collection of Jewish anecdotes of shallow insignificance." The dialectical tension between profound wisdom and total joke opens up the space for this interpretive reading that returns to the unstable root of German-Jewish joke tradition as *schwankhaftig*, or vacillating, in its character and to the literary form of the *Schwank*, or droll story or farce.[58] This is closely related to the Jewish joking technique of the *Dreh* — the comic turn or inversion that takes things for a spin and that allows one to see things from the flip side. Edmund Edel was well aware of this driving force of Jewish wit and character when he wrote: "This is the Jew. He will always give (himself) a spin."[59] Throughout its musings, this book will lend an ear to the laughter generated by the incessant plays of the Jewish joke vacillator as it resists these various attempts at cultural or philosophical appropriation. In direct response to the discursive call of "It's just not funny anymore," there will come the insistence of a resistant laughter and its mocking retort, "They must be joking!" In this manner, the repressed *Witz* returns in order to wreak havoc amid the wisdom and the *Witzenschaft*.

## *At Wit's End*: Laughter Through Tears

Why *At Wit's End*? Why choose an idiomatic expression that typically implies being at the limits of one's sanity or mental capacity as the title for a book that reviews the debates surrounding Jewish wit and jokes during the first half of the twentieth century in Germany and Central Europe? The phrase certainly resonates because it depicts a world that had gone mad and delirious (*meschuggene* in Yiddish) with the Nazi rise to power and with the implementation of a state-sanctioned anti-Semitism and the genocidal Final Solution of the Jewish question. The rabble-rousing Adolf Hitler was himself not averse to using this expression in reference to the Jews and the anxious and unhinged frame of mind in which he wanted to put them. Götz Aly recalls the fierce anti-Semitic rhetoric of Hitler's speech on July 24, 1930 to the Nazi Party assembly in Nuremberg: "Hitler also announced that the time was coming when people would no longer believe 'the Jew.' He thundered; 'Then he'll be at his wit's end. The time is already at hand when he'll be treated as he was treated hundreds of years ago.'"[60] The political and cultural climate around this legally enforced state of persecution (and state of emergency) produced an agitated Jewish population in dire need of the distraction and release provided by Jewish jokes in order to lighten its heavy burden. In this paradoxical situation, one can argue that being and living "at wit's end" demanded some comic relief often in the form of morbid and macabre Jewish jokes in order to ease the pain and suffering. In other words, the literal state of being "at wit's end" helped to generate the production of a mordant Jewish wit as both a necessary response and a coping mechanism.

At Wit's End also illustrates how Jewish jokes moved from being a mere jest to something that was taken quite seriously as they became a legitimate part of the human and social sciences in this period. With the rise of the discourse on Jewish wit, people believed that Jewish jokes could say something meaningful and profound about German-Jewish social, cultural, and political life. More pointedly, At Wit's End offers an elegant way to signal the crossing of the line that is at the core of this study. If and when Jewish self-irony moved too much in the direction of anti-Semitism, it ran the grave risk of creating an unstable political situation that was not funny anymore for the Jews—when the cries of "hate speech" arose that sought to censor and to limit these provocative Jewish jokes that were viewed as contributing to a climate that was favorable to Jew-baiting and anti-Semitic persecution. In such circumstances, the discourse on Jewish jokes became literally deadly. This was especially so for the historical trajectory from the Weimar Republic to the Third Reich to the Holocaust. In other words, this project cannot help but find itself "at wit's end" in terms of its chronology in telling the story of how the living cultural tradition of Jewish wit and humor in Eastern and Central Europe reached its terminus in the mass destruction of European Jewry by 1945. In the context of the Nazi's deadly discourse against the Jews and their jokes, we are reminded of one of Joseph Goebbels's grim statements at the time of the Final Solution of the Jewish question in his *Diary* on March 27, 1942: "The Jews have nothing to laugh about."[61]

Nevertheless, in the postwar era of *Wiedergutmachung* and its "Jewish joke reparations," Jewish wit experienced a post-Holocaust revival and afterlife (see chapter 6). This Jewish joke survivor would not be extinguished so easily. Indeed, there is something about the function and the necessity of Jewish wit that makes its every potential or presumed ending yet another opening for another round of its inextinguishable laughter. Barring the total destruction of Jewry (or humanity for that matter), this makes any exterminating phraseology of "being at wit's end" both a deceptive and an untenable one. Thus, the apocalyptic pronouncement of being at wit's end gives way to its (eternal) renewal and recurrence as part and parcel of humankind's mortal condition—a paradoxically living tradition that chooses to laugh in the face of death. Modern Jewish wit and humor has always been cognizant of this type of limit experience because it has been designed to laugh itself out of the clutches of persecution and the imminence of death that this condition foregrounds. Therefore, the other leading idea to account for the importance of Jewish jokes from Rabbi Büschenthal to the present has been "laughter through suffering" or "laughter through tears." As Edmund Edel writes in this sensitive passage: "Tossed around for thousands of years in world history, [the Jew] had to endure the scorn and the ridicule of people and it was perhaps his only satisfaction when he came to his peers in the ghetto with a joke in order to shake off all of the unpleasantness that had seized him outside."[62] Naturally, this was an even more attractive argument to make in the face of mounting persecution in the Nazi era as well as after the Holocaust when Salcia Landmann reiterated it in her own compilation of Jewish jokes. Simply put, living at the end of one's wits — as one of the hallmarks of the Jewish diasporic experience as described by Edel — demanded and required laughter through suffering and tears.[63]

In explaining Jewish jokes by means of "laughter through suffering," one is reminded of the Yiddish phrase "Woe is me!" ("*Oy vey!*," or "*Ah waih!*") — a phrase that served as the punch line for a number of Jewish jokes (as well as for Torberg's critical attack on Landmann). Subject to comic exaggeration, this exclamatory utterance provides a direct and literal way of turning the pain and suffering of persecution into laughter. One such joke was included in Calman Levi's collection of *Jewish Jokes* published in the 1910s.[64] The two Jewish comic characters in the anecdote, Rosenduft (Rose-scent) and Veilchenduft (Violet-scent), meet each other on the street and the first Jew sees that his friend has gotten a thrashing by the authorities. Rosenduft wants to know why the other has received such blows; he wants to understand why his friend is in pain. In a game that resonates with the famous skit of the American vaudeville comedians Abbott and Costello about the players on a questionable baseball team ("Who's on first?"), Veilchenduft takes every question literally and he does not tell his friend the reason that would explain the cause of his woes. Perhaps this Jewish joke ironically points out in an oblique manner our inability to find a causal basis or rationale at the root of anti-Semitism thereby marking its arbitrariness or radical contingency.[65] For the joke concludes this way. The angry Rosenduft: "I ask you, what have you done?" To which Veilchenduft replies, "Well, I've screamed 'Woe is me!'"[66] After a string of five questions, Rosenduft still does not get the answer he is seeking. But the final answer that he receives — the exaggerated scream of an "*Oy vey!*" — points to the Jewish joking strategy of "laughter through suffering." It is an open question as to whether this joke should be viewed as merely a series of questions that do not get Rosenduft anywhere or whether it ought to be viewed as a profound meditation on anti-Semitism and the Jewish question that illustrates how Jewish wit and "laughter through suffering" offered the Jews a coping strategy and a release valve in modern times for something that was extremely difficult to comprehend. By the way, the joke is entitled "Die Judenfrage" in Levi's volume,[67] and it therefore appears to be thinking self-reflexively and providing its own ironic commentary about the Jewish question—or about the Jewish joke and its questions. Was this some meaningful coincidence? Was this some wisecracking joke?

# 1
# Secondary Moves
*Arthur Trebitsch and the Jewish Joke*

In 1923, the Austrian-Jewish novelist Joseph Roth published *Das Spinnennetz* (*The Spider's Web*) about the anti-Semitic and anti-Communist World War I veteran Theodor Lohse who becomes a spy for a secret right-wing terrorist organization in the early years of the Weimar Republic. Along the way, he encounters one of the group's notorious leaders, a certain Dr. Trebitsch, who conceals his Jewishness and who serves as the author of anti-Semitic pamphlets for the ultranationalist organization.[1] This thinly-veiled fictional character is based on the life of the virulent Viennese Jewish anti-Semite, Arthur Trebitsch (1880–1927) (fig. 3). The son of a successful Jewish silk merchant, the independently wealthy Trebitsch published more than twenty books in which he set down his racialist theories, his love for the German Volk with whom he identified completely, and his hatred for all things Jewish which he disavowed completely. The messianic — and fortunately blonde-haired — Trebitsch saw himself as another Christ figure who could overcome his Jewishness and lead the Aryan race. In his anti-Semitic polemic and self-loathing confession *Geist und Judentum: Eine grundlegende Untersuchung* (Spirit and Judaism: A fundamental investigation, 1919), Trebitsch denied his Jewish identity whether present, past, or future with the following exclamatory declaration: "I am not a Jew, I never was one, and I never will be one!"[2] Given his Judeophobia, it is not surprising to learn that Trebitsch was an early supporter of the National Socialist Party under Adolf Hitler providing it with generous financial support in the early 1920s and he "figured prominently in the development of the Austrian Nazi movement."[3] As perverse as it may sound, Hitler had great respect for Trebitsch and his writings and he even flirted with the idea of appointing him as the official Nazi Party ideologist in 1925. Eight years after Trebitsch's death, the Führer endorsed his work in the following imperative manner: "Read each sentence he wrote. He has unmasked and exposed the Jews as no one else did."[4] Like his fictional double, Trebitsch firmly believed that an international Jewish conspiracy was responsible for the outbreak of World War I as well as for Germany's resounding defeat (the so-called "stab in the back") and he went on a lecture tour in 1918 to warn the German people of the imminent Jewish danger.[5] According to Sander Gilman: "[*Geist and Judentum*] is a historical and philosophical exposé of the basic nature of the Jews and their conspiracy. Needless to say, Trebitsch was welcomed with open arms by the growing anti-Semitic movement that developed at the close of the nineteenth century and flourished after Germany's defeat in 1919. Here was the Jew who bore witness to the truth of the accusation that it was the Jews who caused Germany's defeat."[6]

What is less known about *Geist und Judentum* is that Trebitsch turned to the Jewish joke in this book as a rhetorical figure in order to concoct a convoluted argument about Aryan superiority and Jewish inferiority regarding matters of mind, spirit, and character. To continue Hitler's figure of speech, Trebitsch takes up the role of demystifier in order to expose how the Jewish joke functions as one of the many deceptive and diversionary masks by which the Jew conceals his true self. In this way, the Jewish joke enters into a seminal text in the protohistory of the Nazi movement and plays a key role in mounting its racist and anti-Semitic attack. Trebitsch's book spans a time of enormous political and social upheaval—from the Great War to the abdications of the Emperors and the break-up of the Austro-Hungarian empire, to the foundation of the Weimar and Austrian republics.[7] Trebitsch was not at all pleased with the leftist turn in the politics of his native city and its new status as "Red Vienna" with the Social Democrats in power for the first time after the collapse of the Habsburg dual monarchy. As Theodor Lessing recalls, "The collapse of Austria and the revolution drove Trebitsch into a state of hopeless rage."[8] Indeed, this was an intense period of mobilization and rapid transformation, so it is no surprise to learn that the figure of mobility (*Beweglichkeit*) turns out to be a crucial one that functions as a source of anxiety for Trebitsch in *Geist and Judentum*. The goal of this chapter is to review exactly how and why the Jewish joke plays such an important role in Trebitsch's text and the often absurd contradictions and ridiculous paradoxes that this infamous author unleashes when making his ideologically loaded arguments that contribute to the anti-Semitic discourse on Jewish wit during and after World War I.

In *Geist und Judentum*, Trebitsch subjects the entirety of Jewish cultural and historical experience into the neat packaging of the "secondary-mobile spirit" ("*sekundäre-bewegliche Geist*") in contrast to the primary fixation of the

Figure 3. Portrait of Arthur Trebitsch, 1926.

Aryan spirit.[9] Deploying a stereotypical pop psychology that masquerades as a scientific theory of perception and that mimes models of racial biology itself, Trebitsch divides the world of seeing subjects and their grasping of reality into those who embody fixed views (*"den festen Blick"*) and those who possess fleeting glances (*"den 'flüchtigen', den 'fliehenden' Blick"*) (36–37).[10] Trebitsch's typology and its primary privileging casts a petrifying gaze upon the horrors of mobility in all its forms. In terms of Trebitsch's own obsessive fixation upon fixation, *Beweglichkeit* becomes a synomyn for this convert's inability to deal with the nomadic and diasporic aspects of the European Jewish cultural experience and the figure of the wandering Jew. But it is not the main focus of this essay to speculate about Trebitsch's specious scheme and overarching binary opposition. Instead, our investigation will focus on one particular aspect of its grand design — namely, how the Jewish joke becomes an accomplice to this totalizing scheme of things to the extent that Trebitsch uses it as part of his larger argument about the Jewish spirit as secondary, fleeting, and mobile. This demands a close analysis of chapters 15 and 16 in *Geist und Judentum* that undertake this overt act of appropriation whereby Jewish wit becomes one of the means by which to validate Trebitsch's theoretical claim about the secondary spirit of the Jews.

But even as the concept of the Jewish joke and selected examples are mobilized into exemplary vehicles to say something grand and eloquent about Jewish spirit (*jüdische Geist*) or Jewish character (*jüdische Charakter*) in the texts of Trebitsch, there is a degree of "push-back" that takes place in the staging of the argument itself. It is as if the joke materials were talking back or even laughing at the author's polemic thereby subjecting Trebitsch himself to some comic unmasking. At strategic points, the reader encounters a variety of ironies and paradoxes that tie up the Trebitschean text in performative knots whether these are viewed as internal contradictions, double binds, laughable paradoxes, or outright absurdities. In spite of the author's dichotomizing desire to side with the primary against the secondary spirit, things have a way of getting crossed up to the extent that Trebitsch even circulates his own jokes at certain points in a return of the (Jewishly) repressed. The *Beweglichkeit* that Trebitsch locates as the moving center of the Jewish joke comes back to haunt him and the internal structure of his own theories as they become subject to these same comic effects. We will review how these "secondary moves" get the better of their author and his primary intentions so that his texts come to resemble the object of study. In other words, it may be said that Trebitsch deploys the strategies of the Jewish joke in spite of himself, or perhaps, to spite himself.

This spiting (and splitting) of the self raises the specter of Jewish self-hatred (*jüdische Selbsthaß*). This theoretical construct and conceptual framework has guided the reading of Trebitsch by placing his life and work in the context of the larger problematic of those who accepted and internalized the dominant cultural discourse and its conception of a Jewish other as a rejected or an accursed part.[11] However, the focus of this essay will be to shift the terms of analysis from the realm of emotional affect and the psychological drama around the tortuous concept of Jewish self-hatred to one that traces the paradoxical and internally contradictory effects that generate or are generated by this subject position on the rhetorical (and performative) level of a mobile and nimble space of language and its articulation of wit in speech and writing. This plays out and resonates with the French psychoanalyst Jacques Lacan's insistence (in contrast to Freud) that "everything relating to wit takes place on the vacillating level of speech" and, "if it weren't there, nothing would exist."[12] In contrast to Trebitsch's racist polemic, Lacan's analysis insists that it is not the secondary-mobile or vacillating spirit of Judaism at the root of these jocular effects but rather "the vacillating level of speech" that is activated by Jewish jokes, by everything relating to Jewish wit.

## Lessing's Return of the (Foolishly) Repressed

The present approach and its focus on the "secondary moves" should be contrasted with the most important study in Trebitsch's critical reception that has been cited a few times already. In 1930, Theodor Lessing published *Jüdischer Selbsthaß* (Jewish self-hatred), a book that includes a chapter that has served to immortalize Trebitsch as the Jewish self-hater par excellence. Moreover, Lessing referred to Trebitsch as "the most furious persecutor of the Jews" of his generation. In this biographical portrait, Lessing pathologizes the life of his subject by invoking a medico-psychiatric mode of narration. He refers to Trebitsch's life as a "medical history" (*Krankengeschichte*) that requires critical treatment.[13] He states a little further on that his is the "textbook example" (*Schulfall*) of Jewish self-hatred that demands pedagogical study and from which lessons are to be learned.[14] Even more dramatically, Trebitsch's story is a tragedy that elicits respect and reverence, but where the rest is silence. As Lessing concludes: "We stand before a tragic fate. It is befitting of a respectful silence."[15] Over the years, Lessing's approach has been criticized for its own appropriation of the terms of a racial-biological definition of Jewish identity.[16] While this critique is valid for its revelation of the double bind that accompanies any essentialist argument based on racialist biology, it is more to the point of this chapter and its pursuit of Trebitsch's "secondary moves" to uncover the comic underside that clings to Lessing's selection of tragedy as his preferred narrative genre for studying Trebitsch's life. For in staging Trebitsch as a psychopath and madman, Lessing also provokes a nervous and titillating laughter in his readership who will be only too happy to laugh at someone considered outside the pale of reason (or, as they say in Yiddish, someone who is a *meshuggener*). In this way, Trebitsch's story becomes a black humorous science fiction tale about a man who believed that invisible electromagnetic rays were beamed at his cranium by the super-scientists of a secret Jewish organization ("Alliance Israelite") and who were trying to drive him mad and assassinate him.[17] By foregrounding Trebitsch's persecution complex and paranoia (*Verfolgungswahn*), Lessing seeks to discredit his thinking and to cast him in the role of the ridiculous man. For all his tragedian's rhetoric to the contrary, Lessing's account also advances the comic underside of Trebitsch's story thereby branding him as a (mad) fool. From this perspective, the rest is laughter rather than silence.[18]

Trebitsch was the author of one of the strangest of autobiographical confessions — *Die Geschichte meines "Verfolgungswahns"* (The story of my "paranoia").[19] One notes how the quotation marks placed around "*Verfolgungswahns*" in the title function as a distancing device by which Trebitsch tries to bracket the delusionary term and to keep it away from himself even as it is modified by the possessive (and therefore possessed) pronoun of autobiographical attribution (*meines*). This book reviews a paranoid episode in his life between April and June 1919 — or during the same year as the publication of *Geist and Judentum* — when he believed that he was being pursued by a "secret society" (*Geheimbund*) of Jewish persecutors. Not unlike the confessions of Judge Daniel Schreber, Trebitsch felt that poisoned electric rays were being beamed at him by a superior Jewish force.[20]

Although one can dwell on the specific psychohistorical details of this bizarre confession and its conspiracy theories, our goal is more pointed here. It is rather to consider how this paranoid delusion (*Wahnvorstellung*) and its attendant associations put Trebitsch in connection with the role of the madman and the fool. Even Lessing underscores Trebitsch's ridiculousness and laughability (*Lächerlichkeit*).[21] In line with Sven Brömsel's account, there is a way to read the delusional history of Trebitsch in this period as the story of someone who made a real fool out of himself (a *Narr*), and thereby as someone who played the *schlemiel* character straight out of Jewish folklore.[22] In what appears to be a lucid moment or, perhaps, in a fit of extreme paranoia, the author emphasizes that he is being made the butt of a Jewish joke. This statement is but the flip side of Trebitsch's desire to ingratiate himself to non-Jewish society by making fun of the Jews. The point does not have to be stressed, but Trebitsch does it anyway: "That Judaism will take care that all my activities at explanation (*Aufklärungstätigkeiten*) are laughed at, joked about, and held in contempt does not need to be stressed at all."[23] In this citation (and in the next anecdote), one notices the proffering of the word *Aufklärung*. It is the magical incantation that provides the means by which Trebitsch seeks to attest to his clarity and sanity amid the accusations of madness and the mockery attendant with such a conjecture.

But this laughable situation repeats itself in a close encounter of the Aryan kind as well. His own story is taken to be a Jewish joke or at least a joke in which the Jews have converted him into a foolish and delusional figure. When Trebitsch visits one of his idols, the racist historian and philosopher Houston Stuart Chamberlain, to warn him that the Jewish conspiracy is after him and that his own incipient paralysis can be explained by the fact that death rays are being targeted at his Aryan cranium in the same way that they had been aimed at Trebitsch,[24] the response is a knowing and patronizing smile. Whether he knows it or not, Trebitsch plays the part of the anti-Semitic court jester in his audience with Chamberlain at Bayreuth. Far removed from the realm of Freud's *schadchen*, or marriage broker, the polite and tolerant Chamberlain is made to believe that he is hearing a different kind of lame joke.

> And when I sought out the honorable man myself in the years following and when I tried to warn this scholar of higher learning in the natural sciences of the true causes of his condition which could no longer be doubted on my part, I noticed then how all the explanations that I delivered were opposed at once, and that either dyed-in-the-wool narrow-mindedness and a know-it-all manner or rather the activities of the secret conspiracy had taken care of it that the lame man listened to my explanations with the mild smile of one who lends his ear to a little foolish folly [*närrischen Phantasterei*] with polite toleration.[25]

As the story concludes, Trebitsch acknowledges not only that his theory has fallen upon deaf ears but also that it partakes of foolishness — that, for the other, it is a flight of fantasy with no objective basis. Subject to the effects of mobility, the comedic undertones repressed in Lessing's biographical account of Trebitsch come to the surface and find their expression in the autobiographical narration of this bizarre and delusional episode that pursues its biographical subject at and to the end of his wits.

Finally, Lessing's narrative avoids any linkage between the concept of "Jewish self-hatred" and the question of Jewish humor. Ever since Sigmund Freud, joke researchers have asserted that ethnic humor told by a minority group about itself provides a means to channel (and to defuse) its own hostility against itself and to identify with the majority. To this end, there is a common strategy among Jewish anti-Semitic writers to utilize comic forms (e.g., jokes) through which to mock other Jews not only to release this hostility via comedy but also in the hope of becoming better accepted by the dominant culture. This theory would help to explain the large number of self-critical Jewish jokes that appear in *Geist und Judentum* as Trebitsch plays the role of the anti-Semitic court jester. However, Trebitsch believes that he is telling these Jewish jokes in the guise of the unbiased cultural scientist in pursuit of knowledge and a proper understanding of the Jewish psyche. This oscillation in role playing is on full display in our next allegorical scene.

## The Jewish Question on the Trebitschean Mirror Stage

Trebitsch's *Geist und Judentum* begins before a mirror.[26] The looking glass functions as the site where the book casts its reflections and projections onto Judaism and its spirit. The basic binary oppositions of the book as well as the distinct possibility of their flipping (and "flipping out") are already on view. What magically evokes this mirror image or what brings it into play is something resembling a joke—an anecdote that recalls the remarks made by some unidentified witty fellow—someone with whom the narrator identifies on the surface—at the expense of someone identified specifically as a Jewish scholar—someone with whom the narrator disidentifies upon first glance.

> And as a quick-witted man posed the question to a Jewish scholar—who had come to the conclusion that one could not put forward one single essential criterion to confirm what constitutes "Jewishness" as based on the most penetrating historical, phrenological, psychological, and biological research into the Jewish question—if he had not had a look in the mirror, so we too want to look straight into the countenance of our time and the people of our closest acquaintance in order to unlock all the essential answers from such reflections upon the question! (13–14)

Not surprisingly, this narrative indicates that the witty man and the Jewish scholar hold different opinions about the Jewish question in Germany. On the one side, there is Jewish scholarly denial propped up by science. Based on his fourfold scientific investigations, the Jewish scholar has been led to conclude that there is no such question at all since he has been unable to find any essential criterion that constitutes Jewish difference. But since he has already been identified and branded as Jewish from the start, and since the contested criterion has already been bracketed off as "Jewishness," it does not seem that this particular point of view holds much weight in Trebitsch's tautological narrative so that the argument that poses similitude—if not assimilation—already has been lost. On the other side, there is an affirmation of the Jewish question that relies solely on physical appearance. But, in asserting this position, the quick-witted man (the one who is not identified as a Jew) does something identified as quite Jewish nonetheless when he answers the Jewish scholar with a question—a question that directs the other's gaze to the mirror and to his perceived image.[27] By posing this rhetorical question to the scholar that asks him to look into the mirror and, to all appearances, to be identified as a Jew and as other, the quick-witted man (*geistreiche Mann*) works in the service of difference and "dissimilation" in the reintroduction of the Jewish question.

This anecdote is also unusual because Trebitsch does not invoke a body of knowledge to support his views vis-à-vis race and culture. Throughout the rest of the book, Trebitsch assumes the subject position of the Jewish scholar in this anecdote as he enlists support for the distinction between primary and secondary spirit (*Geist*) and as he presents evidence from these same sciences and modes of inquiry. But here, the Trebitschean scholar gives way to the Trebitschean joker (*Witzbold*) in the figure of the "quick witted man." Taking exception to the observation that Trebitsch always cast his rhetoric in terms of the emerging scientific languages of the day,[28] the recitation of this anecdote is set against any and all scholarly disciplines that would seek to prove or disprove that there is such a thing as "Jewishness." Instead, Trebitsch's witty invocation is aligned to the commonplace anti-intellectual critique of Jewish intellectualism. In making the Jewish scholar the butt of the joke, the punchline appeals to the racist doxologies of a common sense designed to move things away from the lofty realms of the hyperintellectualized *Luftmensch* (literally, "man of air" or contemplative person) and to bring things back to a more concrete level — to the stereotypical matter of physical appearance as *the* essentialist criterion for Jewish differentiation and inferiority.

The punchline of this joke is thinly veiled in its anti-Semitic content. For it goes without saying that the look into the mirror in this anecdote will have yielded to the illustrated stereotypes of Jewish caricature as an object of mockery and derision found in the satirical journals of the day such as *Die Fliegende Blätter* or *Kikeriki*.[29] In particular, the verbal joke cited by Trebitsch might be compared with an anonymous caricature from around 1890 derived from the anti-Semitic Viennese comic newspaper (*Witzblatt*), *Kikeriki* (fig. 4).[30]

Entitled "*Die Socialdemocratie im 'Spiegel der Wahrheit'*" ("Social democracy in the 'mirror of truth'"), this satirical image depicts an underlying rapacity replete with money bags at the heart of a Jewish social democratic consciousness and its support of the working class when this political program is held up before the mirror. Above the ironic caption of *Adlerrace* ("eagle race"), the stereotypical Jew is depicted with the conventional negative visual stereotypes of long nose, rapacious gaze, and forked beard. Although this image goes well beyond the matter of physical appearance in terms of its vicious political satire, it illustrates how the figure of the mirror could serve as a means by which to project anti-Semitic sentiment with a racist virulence as well as to

Figure 4. Anonymous, "Die Socialdemocratie im 'Spiegel der Wahrheit,' dargestellt vom Kikeriki" (1890; Social democracy in the 'mirror of truth,' displayed by Kikeriki). Reprinted in Fuchs, *Die Juden in der Karikatur*, 195.

demonstrate how Trebitsch's one-liner about the look into the mirror would evoke such negative images in its readership raised on this type of racially slurring caricature.

But what is most bizarre about this mirror staging lies elsewhere. It is only when one begins to unpack Trebitsch's division between primary Aryan and secondary Jewish spirit that one begins to sense the profound ironies that haunt this witticism. For if Trebitsch wants to identify the secondary-mobile Jew as fleeting ("*flüchtig*"), then how can he imagine that the Jew (as the perpetrator of mirages) could be captured in this mirror reflection? This logic of a Jewish refusal to cast a fixed reflection needs to be placed in connection with the horror-laden figures of the vampire and the ghost that regulate not only *Geist und Judentum* but Judeophobic discourses in general.[31] Inversely, if the Jewish scholar will have allowed himself to be captured in the mirror image, then he will have partaken of the primary Aryan spirit—the spirit that fixes and seizes in its gaze. A similar contradiction can be located in the fact that, in a book entitled *Geist und Judentum*, the quick-witted and spirit-rich ("*geistreich*") man is not the one who is identified as a Jew. Such a personification seems to contradict Trebitsch's dichotomy that always puts the Jewish spirit on the side of nimbleness of mind in terms of its *Beweglichkeit*.

There is the unconscious suspicion that the mirror placed at the outset of the text provides Trebitsch with the chance to project his own disavowed position in relation to the construct of Jewish identity. It is this "self-image" against which he spent a lifetime in engaged opposition. There is more than meets the eye here when we recall Trebitsch as a Jewish self-denier par excellence. In this scenario, it is Trebitsch who would experience a return of the Jewishly repressed when facing the "mirror of truth" and it is the Jewish scientist (rather than the non-Jewish joker) who forces him to experience this mirror image distortion of himself. From this warped perspective, Trebitsch would have to be viewed as the Jewish scientist of this jest who stares into the mirror, who is forced to acknowledge that he is (still) Jewish, and who, therefore, has all the more reason why he has to deny virulently that there is any type of resemblance. The split scene of Trebitsch's (dis)identification with Judaism helps to explain the motor of an inverted dialectic that is often unintentionally comic and that turns Trebitsch into an anti-Semitic writing machine, driven to produce his more than twenty treatises. This haunted corpus constitutes a ceaseless exercise in Jewish exorcism, and it features a series of rants and raves against Judaism during his entire adult life. Thus, the opening mirror stage of *Geist und Judentum* displays an intricate series of projections (and rejections) regarding the identification of a Jewish self and its other where it becomes difficult for each party to this dialectical deal to keep its own image straight.

Returning to the rhetorical level, this trade-off helps to explain why Trebitsch concludes with the paradoxical image of looking at his own age straight in the face—yet only with the help of a mirror that thereby functions as a mediator. For, as he says, Trebitsch seeks to unlock all the essential answers from the reflections or, quite literally, the mirror images (*Spiegelbilde*) cast by the (Jewish) question. But, given the mirror's logic of the split (and splitting) image, one senses that this rhetorical strategy provides the devout Jewish anti-Semite only with further cracked reflections.

## "Das ist echt jüdisch": The Search for Joking Authenticity

In a chapter entitled *"Die Abtrünnigen"* ("The apostates") from a classic collection of Jewish jokes, Alexander Moszkowski includes a variant of a popular baptism joke (*Taufenwitz*) of those assimilatory times. The sophisticated and transformative logic of this witty exchange points to an authentically inauthentic Jewish experience and locates an aspect of Jewish identity in its very antithesis:

> "Have you already heard? Dovidl Bramson wants to get baptized."
> "That's a really Jewish [*echt jüdisch*] thing to do!"[32]

This joke relays a conversion experience in the sense that it makes the act of exiting from Judaism into an authentically Jewish rite of passage, into something that is *"echt jüdisch."* Naturally, the comic case study of Dovidl Bramson has a cosmic precursor in the primary example of Jesus Christ. But it also resonates with the life experience of Trebitsch—who formally resigned from Vienna's central synagogue in 1909 (at the age of twenty-nine) and who would come to identify with the Messianic Christ to the extreme.[33] Trebitsch's career as a renowned Jewish anti-Semite was marked by logical contradictions that parallel the case history of the comic Dovidl Bramson. Upon hearing of his incessantly obsessive raving (and *kvetching*) against all things considered Jewish, one would be tempted to reply using the inverted logic of a Jewish joke that this was a really Jewish thing for him to do.[34] Indeed, the historian Walter Laqueur repurposes a Freudian concept from *Moses and Monotheism* and speaks of Trebitsch's "militant anti-Semitism" and "individual psychopathology" as an extreme case of being "badly baptized." Laqueur writes: "Freud called them 'badly baptized' [*schlecht getauft*]. In its extreme manifestation, when the self-loathing turned to militant anti-Semitism among individuals such as Trebitsch, an early Jewish Nazi, or Otto Weininger or Maurice Sachs in France, it was a problem more for individual psychopathology than for historical or cultural analysis and generalization."[35]

But it appears that the comic jargon of (in)authenticity and the self-mocking self-reflexivity expressed in the Dovidl Bramson anecdote had no impact on Trebitsch and his own serious pursuit of the authentic Jewish joke. Thus, Trebitsch concludes his joke analysis with a prescriptive formula that cuts to the core and that stifles the mobility — that is, what resists the stability of authentication — that he attributes to the Jewish joke. If and when one can demonstrate how a particular joke partakes of the overarching structure of the secondary mobile spirit, then one partakes of an essential and authentic Jewish joking experience: "If therefore the core of the Jewish joke and essence is recognized in the secondary-mobile mode, then, of course, we will be right in calling other such jokes 'authentic' where other examples of this special modality of relating to the world and to the host folk appear. Thus, either the secondary spirit itself or rather the character of the Jewish secondary individual is illustrated and represented in the Jewish joke" (81–82). But Trebitsch is not only concerned with defining what makes a Jewish joke authentic. In this search for authenticity, this compulsive dialectician also constructs a binary opposition that provides the means by which to differentiate between the real thing and the rank imitation: "To what little extent the essence of the Jewish joke has been recognized and understood until now is shown in the pleasure that comes in increasing the value of the joke through a Jewish intonation. This is applied everywhere even where it has no place because not every 'Jew-ified' [*gejüdelte*] joke should be called a 'Jewish' [*jüdischer*] joke necessarily" (76). Trebitsch here insists that his scientific research into the Jewish joke has little in common with those unsophisticated and simple-minded anti-Semites who believe that all one has to do is to stick in a few Yiddishisms here and there or alter one's vocal inflection in the delivery in order to come up with an authentic Jewish joke. Always the conceptual purist, Trebitsch refuses to accept any emphasis placed upon linguistic performance (i.e., the use of intonation, accentuation, or jargon) as the defining characteristic of the Jewish joke. Indeed, Trebitsch's strict form-content distinction refuses to consider the level of narration as a part of the meaning. To Trebitsch's way of thinking, it is not Jewish intonation that makes a joke authentically Jewish. Rather, it is the strict conformity of the joke to the ideal typology of the Jewish spirit that he has constructed and its complicated inversion of norms. Presumably unnoticeable to himself, Trebitsch changes intonation in the following exclamatory utterance when he underscores this very point: "Thus we can grasp with complete certainty that a real 'Jewish' joke and not just a joke narrated in a Jewish manner exists in every case and only there where the secondary has become the first, and where the primary has become the supplementary, inconsequential, and unnoticeable secondary!" (81). Helping to elucidate the quotation marks placed around *"echt"* (authentic) in a previous quotation, Trebitsch has been led to the twisted conclusion that the authenticity of the Jewish joke lies in its inversion of values—or the way in which it ruins or betrays the primacy of experience that clings to something like the concept of authenticity in the first place.

Another extended irony arises when one realizes that the anti-Semite's search for the authenticity of the Jewish joke parallels other contemporary attempts by philo-Semitic folklorists to define the difference between the authentic and the inauthentic Jewish joke in terms of binary oppositions. Ironically, Trebitsch's insistence on the *"echt jüdisch"* connects him with a larger (Jewish) discourse tracking the authenticity of the Jewish joke. Nevertheless, Trebitsch's delineation differs greatly from these Jewish folklorists who argue that the presence or absence of anti-Semitic content provides the means by which to institute the dividing line between the imitation and the real thing. In his introduction to *Das Jüdische Volk in der Anekdote*, Chaim Bloch writes: "In fact there are two species of these jokes—the Jewish joke [*Judenwitz*] and the Jewish '*Lozale*', referred to by Dr. Joseph S. Bloch as the 'Jewish anti-Semitic joke.'"[36] In *Jüdische Schwänke*, Siegfried Schmitz begins his afterword with the very same distinction: "In the first place, speculation about the essence of the Jewish joke leads to a distinction in order to avoid mistakes. There are Jewish jokes and there is the Jewish joke [*es gibt jüdische Witze und es gibt jüdischen Witz*]."[37] As he elaborates further, the goal of Schmitz's project is to set up strict border controls between an authentic and essential Jewish joking experience and an inauthentic one— "that wants to distinguish itself on the one hand from the '*Lozelach*' [Yiddish: amusing and scornful anecdotes] of the common Jewish joke [*landläufigen Judenwitzes*] and that, on the other hand, wants to express the intensely fixed essence of the Jewish folkloric joke [*jüdischen Volkswitzes*]."[38]

However, the blindspot in these binary accounts lies in an active forgetting of the vacillation at the heart of the Jewish joke wherein Jewish self-irony or self-criticism and Jewish anti-Semitism (or German criticism of Jews and German anti-Semitism) play off each other and even exchange places at times.[39] Indeed, in the very same paragraph that Schmitz argues for the stable distinction between the two forms, he also recalls "the fluctuating characteristics of the Jewish joke [*die schwankhaften Charakteristika des jüdischen Witzes*]" and thereby refers both to the tradition of the *"Schwank"* as a comic genre and to the vacillations contained in these stories.[40] In a sense, this last point of fluctuation serves the same function as Trebitsch's *Beweglichkeit*. The perverse fact that the Jewish anti-Semite Trebitsch tells these perfectly authentic Jewish jokes in order to stir up hatred against the Jews in *Geist und Judentum* also helps to illustrate the difficulty on the part of these philo-Semitic folklorists to support their claims to Jewish joke authenticity and purity and to resist potential contamination. The important point here is not the specific response that a folklorist gives to the question of what constitutes an authentic Jewish joke. Rather, it is to question the essentialist desire at the root of such overarching considerations and to underscore how such an approach suppresses the site-specificity that adheres to telling and laughing at Jewish jokes and the ways in which they induce unstable effects. In other words, the policing strategies of writers such as Schmitz and Bloch — as well as Trebitsch — and the search for "the authentic Jewish joke" ("*der echte jüdische Witz*"[41]) smothers the laughter that relies upon the localized effects of a panoply of joke occasions and performances.

## At Home in the House of Language

The history of ideas makes for strange bedfellows. Who would have thought that Jewish émigré and diasporic litterateur George Steiner would have something in common with Trebitsch and, moreover, that this connection would be drawn by way of a reference to Heinrich Heine? In "Our Homeland, the Text," Steiner writes: "Heine's phrase is exactly right: '*das aufgeschriebene Vaterland.*' The 'land of his fathers,' the *patrimoine* is the script. In its doomed immanence, in its attempt to immobilize the text in a substantive, architectural space, the Davidic and Solomonic Temple may have been an erratum, a misreading of the transcendent mobility of the text."[42] Ironically, Steiner's battle cry for upholding the deterritorializing textual tradition of diasporic Judaism resembles Trebitsch's opening salvo as he begins his analysis of the five jokes that he has selected to support his argument of the Jewish joke in the service of the secondary mobile spirit. Trebitsch begins: "Those who are at home in the realm of words — but only there." This is an odd grammatical construction whose dash marks his reservations thereby limiting the Jew's proper place in the world. In fact, this remark displaces the feeling of "at homeness" from the realm of the world to that of the word. However, even though the "textual homeland" may be a common trope for both these writers, their valuations are quite antithetical. In contrast to Trebitsch's avid negation, Steiner affirms the figure of mobility as a positive component of Jewish literary space. His distinction also includes a stark contrast between any misguided immobilizing of the Temple Mount in contrast to the positive mobilization of the textual apparatus.

Meanwhile, Steiner's argument also lacks the peculiar epistemology and metaphysics of language that Trebitsch attributes to the Jewish spirit. According to Trebitsch, the Jewish joke stages a simple inversion of language that substitutes knowledge of the word for the thing. It is on account of this joking inversion that puts words first—or that puts the signifier in the place of the referent—that leads Trebitsch to the belief that the Jewish spirit acts secondarily. To recite a typical expression of this radical reversal, "Thus the typical Jewish joke is only and solely something that corresponds to the spirit in which the fact regarding 'knowledge of the word' comes to expression in a convincing manner before 'knowledge of the thing'" (76). The dead seriousness of Trebitsch's convinced appraisal assumes the Jewish joking strategy of the *Dreh*, or "spin," as it offers the proof for the way in which language operates according to the Jewish spirit. Unfortunately, Trebitsch never considers the possibility that the language operates in this way only on account of and according to the dictates of a joke practice that depends upon a comic inversion of linguistic conventions. In taking things (or, in this case, words) too seriously, Trebitsch loses track of the joke's playful and parodic possibilities.

Trebitsch's first joke analysis focuses on what he sees as this basic turnaround that posits the primacy of language over lived experience. It is a classic joke in the period that can be found in many variants, and Trebitsch's version is rather clipped in its narration.[43] It is a philosophical joke that looks deep into the soul of the animal kingdom in posing its epistemological inquiry. Indeed, another variant of the joke is entitled "*Die Tierseele*" (The animal soul): "The scholar goes for a walk with his student. A loud barking dog springs at them and the two of them take flight. Thereupon, the student is astounded: 'But, Rabbi, don't you know that dogs that bark do not bite?' And the answer: 'You know that, I know that, but do I know if the dog knows it?'" (76). This joke is part of the subgenre that foregrounds unknowing or "nonknowledge" on the part of an actor to achieve its comic effect. In this case, it is the antianthropomorphic doubt expressed by the Rabbi that the third party (a nonhuman actor or a barking dog) would happen to know the one about "dogs that bark don't bite." But Trebitsch sees much more in this particular joke. He links its epistemological doubt to a lost relation between reality and language. The secondary Jewish spirit has lost faith in the primacy of experience or even that the linguistic idiom reflects experience. In this alienated world of words or of being at home only in the house of language, the Jewish spirit doubts to what extent the reality of experience has a place anymore: "Those who are home in the word—but only there—have already lost the conviction everywhere (so here as well) that the path of the intellect leads from experience and observation to the word and the 'idiomatic expression.' He possesses words and idioms as his real and essential thinking material, and thereupon he doubts to what extent reality lets itself be guided by the idiomatic expression" (78).

Trebitsch's structural inversion of word and thing as an explanation for the joke (wherein the idiomatic expression exchanges places with the world of experience) also refuses to consider the allegorical significance of this joke in terms of concrete historical experience. This offers another interpretation of the joke that is deeply rooted in the history of anti-Semitism. This oversight becomes even more glaring when one considers the central place that anti-Semitism occupies in the writings of Trebitsch. In this reading, the story of the barking dog without the bite rivals the "white dog" stories of the American South in its racist overtones.[44] In the section entitled "Anti-Semitism" of their popular Jewish humor compendium, William Novak and Rabbi Moshe Waldoks elicit the following associations in the joke that take Trebitsch's anti-Semitic rhetoric to its extreme logical and historical conclusions. In this manner, Trebitsch's persecution complex of being pursued by a Jewish conspiracy comes back in an inverted form as the Nazis let slip the dogs of war in their persecution of the Jews: "Dogs that bark (and even dogs who do not bark) denote the anti-Semite in these stories. For urban dwellers, dogs were not loveable domestic animals, but a part of the enemy powers. During the Nazi era, dogs were employed for the purpose of ferreting out Jews who had hidden themselves."[45] Rather than losing themselves in the epistemological uncertainties unleashed by a dog's foreign mode of reasoning (i.e., not knowing if the dog knows or not) or in a search for a proper relationship between language and reality or experience, Novak and Waldoks take the dog as a double-edged symbol. The dog is both an anthropomorphized metaphor for the anti-Semitic persecutors and a terrorizing weapon in the service of the anti-Semites.[46] As the Jewish joke about the barking dog moves from epistemological doubt to a metaphysics of language to an allegory for the history of anti-Semitic persecution, this folkloric artifact exerts an interpretative agility that appears at home in a multiplicity of contexts.

## *"Auf der Ka-lauer"* — Being on the Lookout

According to Trebitsch, the secondary spirit's inversion of word and thing is linked to a proclivity for the pun (*Kalauer*) in Jewish wit.[47] The overall devaluation of the pun as a low and degenerate form of contrived humor that depends only on a similarity of sound to generate easy word plays fits with Trebitsch's overall rhetoric to devalue the wit of the Jewish secondary spirit.[48] Sander Gilman summarizes his position: "For Trebitsch there is a specific Jewish 'wit,' which is manifested in the Jews' love for wordplay, for an undermining of the surface meaning of the word and an emphasis on the word rather than on the thing that it represents. It is this love for wordplay that characterizes both the nature of the Jews' wit and their misuse of language in general."⁴⁹ Otherwise known as the sound joke (*Klangwitz*), the pun stages a concatenation of significance based on the similarity of its sonic materials. This linguistic perversion subjects the nature of things to the sound of the words that constitute them. The pun acts as if an accidental similarity in the seme makes sense by necessity.⁵⁰ It is another example of a perverse focus on the level of the signifier instead of the signified meaning. For Trebitsch, the pun demonstrates how the mobile mind goes with the flow of word plays and follows the acrobatic chains of associations on the level of the similitude of the signifying materials at the expense of their divergent meanings: "On account of his mobility, he often will perceive the similarity of the words unimpeded by the discrepancies of their natural values [*Wesenwerte*], and thus he will show a peculiar interest for the pun [*Kalauer*] that remains almost incomprehensible to those for whom seeing differences in things are more important than listening to sonic similarities" (75).

As hysterical as it may sound, Trebitsch's theory suggests that the inability on the part of non-Jewish culture to get homonymic Jewish jokes has led to mutual disharmony and the breakdown of German-Jewish intercultural exchange and dialogue.⁵¹ Talking at cross-purposes about one and the same joke, the angry non-Jew hears nonsense and stupidity while the laughing Jew hears profound comedy. Trebitsch expounds, "To non-Jews who are not suited to this secondary mode, the profound comedy of the 'Jewish joke' will remain hidden quite often because they only overhear the 'nonsense' and the rubbish which aggravates and angers them without stimulating any laughter" (79). Returning to Jefferson Chase's analysis, Trebitsch's distinction here contrasts the secondary spirit of *Judenwitz* with the primary spirit of German humor. But if non-Jews cannot understand the profound comedy of the Jewish joke, then one begins to wonder, who is the audience for whom Trebitsch has written this Jewish joke analysis? Certainly, not many Jewish readers — who would get the joke — wanted to listen to him on account of his virulent anti-Semitic stance. Perhaps, this peculiar situation helps to explain Trebitsch's ongoing complaints about his lack of readership on both sides of the binary divide.⁵² However, it is also possible to read Trebitsch's position on joking separatism as a reaction to the high degree of German-Jewish social contact and intimacy at the time, underscored by the large number of ethnic jokes circulating in what seemed to be an intercultural space of porous and permeable borders.

According to Trebitsch's black and white scenario, when the Germans who privilege the "thing over the word" meet the Jews who privilege the "word over the thing," mutual misunderstanding is the logical outcome. Trebitsch's reading suggests that one cause of anti-Semitic antagonism is derived from the fact that the Jews have been overindulging in the pun as the lowest form of humor or that they have been telling too many bad and corny jokes. The result of this communication breakdown was a large degree of "discontent and provocative boredom" on the part of the German listening public. Of course, any look at the statistics of the thriving cabaret scene in Trebitsch's own Vienna in the interwar period featuring numerous popular Jewish comedians would go a long way to problematizing the following joke speculations:[53] "This explains specifically the predilection for word play [*Wortwitz*] in the airy mental regions of the secondary spirit, but also the discontent and the provocative boredom that it prepares for the primary spirit! Therefore, this Jewish way of thinking likes to be — a funny image within the image! — on the lookout for the pun [*auf der Ka-lauer*], a search party that remains completely alien to living-thinking [*Lebendig-Denkenig*]" (76).

There is something most peculiar in Trebitsch's choice of words in the previous excerpt. At this juncture in an argument that condemns the secondary spirit for its frivolous punning and its predilection for the word over the thing, Trebitsch, recognized as the world's leading authority on the nature of the primary spirit,[54] appears to fall into a secondary trap himself in the form of a pun. Operating on a metalevel of experience, this self-reflexive witticism stages a double play because it literally makes a pun about the pun. In its abysmal logic, it is "a funny image within the image" — as he himself is forced to confess — and one that he cannot resist using and indulging. It should be underscored that in a chapter that is supposed to illustrate the pun as a central Jewish joking device, this is the one and only example. While Trebitsch provides no reference for the source of this witticism, it is most likely that he has imported this turn of phrase directly from Freud. *Der Witz* relates an unusual anecdote about a scientific friend with a tendency to expose himself to some pretty frivolous and nonsensical behavior in his spare time. Risking the indulgence of another pun, one might take the liberty of calling him a *Witzenschaftler* (humorist-scientist). Freud recalls:

> There are some people who, when they are in high spirits, can, for considerable periods of time, answer every remark addressed to them with a pun. One of my friends, who is a model of discretion where his serious achievements in science are concerned, is apt to boast of this ability. When on one occasion he was holding the company breathless in this way and admiration was expressed for his staying power: "Yes," he said, "I am lying here *auf der Ka-lauer*." And when he was finally begged to stop, he agreed to on condition that he was appointed "*Poeta Ka-laureatur*." Both of these, however, are excellent jokes of condensa-

tion with the formation of composite words. ("I am lying here *auf der Lauer* [on the lookout] for making *Kalauer* [puns].")⁵⁵

While Freud certainly had another Viennese colleague in mind, it is tempting to make a referential substitution here and to cast Trebitsch in the starring role. For all his serious scientific intentions to the contrary, the Trebitschean pen slips out of the realm of "living-thinking" and he joins the rank of the punsters as the Jewish self-denier refers to this abysmal experience of "a funny image within the image" with an exclamation point. Nevertheless, it is not necessary to judge Trebitsch on his own terms regarding this "secondary move" — that is, to see this only in terms of a relapse into the secondary spirit. For one can say just as easily that he has been taken advantage of by means of a linguistic play. For all his vaunted vigilance and his being on the lookout, Trebitsch has fallen prey to a language that has gotten the better of him — what one cannot always master and about which one might have to laugh. In other words, the *"Ka-lauer Kalauer"* stages for Trebitsch the return of the repressed on the level of language and the revenge of the materiality of the signifier.

## Almost Ghostwriting Freud

For all his self-professed antipathy toward the new science of psychoanalysis which he deemed to be a Jewish provenance,⁵⁶ it is clear from the two joke chapters and other excerpts from *Geist und Judentum* that Trebitsch studied and even borrowed from Freud's *Witz* book. Already one probable instance of borrowing has been witnessed in Trebitsch's secondary appropriation of the *Ka-lauer* joke. This is not surprising when one considers that Freud's text was the most important book on "joke science" at the time. In the first footnote of chapter 16, Trebitsch pays tribute to his Viennese contemporary by name — but in a manner that refuses to acknowledge Freud's specific contribution to the study of the Jewish joke. Trebitsch generalizes the terms of the psychoanalytic contribution to the study of wit by focusing on its discovery of pleasure saving devices in an unconscious psychic economy: "In particular, it is necessary at this point to mention Freud's substantial work. In it, he tries to acknowledge the pleasurable moment [*Lustmoment*] of saving or economizing [*Ersparnis*] as essential to the joke" (73). Nevertheless, this footnote on Freud is placed amid a self-congratulatory proclamation that prior to Trebitsch, no researcher had said anything about the essential foundation of the Jewish joke because no one has been able to link it to the underlying principles of the Jewish secondary-mobile spirit.⁵⁷ In this way, Trebitsch shifts the emphasis from a dynamic psychical economy to a permanent psychological structure. This section reviews two other examples where Trebitsch's jokes intersect with Freud's *Witz* book. Whether Trebitsch borrows from Freud directly or whether these are coincidental convergences in their object of study, a comparison of their joke treatments yields interesting results and obvious ideological differences.

The first case that matches the wits of Trebitsch and Freud is a *schadchen* or marriage broker joke. As a traditional comic figure in the Jewish joke arsenal, the schadchen operates and negotiates in a rhetorical gray area that may bend the truth at times to achieve the desired end of striking a match and bringing couples together. Indeed, there is something about the meddling metier of the schadchen as mediator (*Vermittler* in Freud's text) and the ongoing shuttle diplomacy that recalls Trebitsch's inconstant analysis of the Jewish mobile character (with its unethical undertones) as the spirit that swings back and forth like a pendulum (*"hin und her pendelnde Geist,"* 70). Meanwhile, there is also the possibility that Freud himself identified with the position of the schadchen in the *Witz* book on account of the broker's critical stance in many of these jokes that serve to demystify this traditional Jewish cultural practice.[58]

This particular schadchen joke serves as Trebitsch's fifth and final example. It is a grotesque jest that establishes the thrust and conviction of its argument based upon pseudo-logic and through the hyperbolic assistance of the arts of persuasion. Its hypothetical argument is based upon a large dose of hypochondria. By the end of the twisting and turning and bone-crunching rhetoric, the schadchen nearly leads one to believe that the accidental risks to the healthy are much greater than the assurances of the lame. And with this verdict in sickness rather than in health, the case is closed.[59] In contrast to Freud who narrates the joke as a dialogue between the schadchen and the hypothetical bridegroom, Trebitsch tells the joke through the distancing mode of indirect speech.[60]

> A marriage broker offers a girl to someone who is seeking marriage. However, after he has seen her, the man rejects the girl because she limps. Thereupon, the marriage broker [*Vermittler*] begins with a passionate torrent of words and exercises the arts of persuasion to convince him of the advantages of the girl with the most detailed arguments—that a healthy woman could be traveling in a wagon one day, that the wagon could topple over, and that the consequence would be a broken leg, a long hospital stay, all the accompanying expenses, and, in the end, the limping gait. After similar possibilities are represented in the most insistent manner, he ends his exposition with these words: "All of this can happen with a healthy girl, but here you've got yourself a closed case! [*fertige Sach'!*]" (77–78)

Even though it is not necessary to review all the nuances of their respective readings, it is important to examine where the critical languages almost touch upon one another and the significance of the near miss that makes one word drop out of Trebitsch's interpretation. Freud places this schadchen joke in tandem with the classic joke about the rabbinical *Kück* (look) — the story about the *Wunderrabbi* (wonder rabbi) who did not actually see what was happening in a faraway village but whose telepathic gaze was wondrous in any event. In both cases, Freud pinpoints the meaning of the joke in the logical error that *almost* equates the realm of the real with the realm of possibility. Freud explains: "The faulty reasoning common to the last two examples is here undisguisedly admitted. The value of phantasy is exalted unduly in comparison with reality; a possibility is almost equated with an actual event."[61] But, in Trebitsch's version, the word *almost* (*fast*) drops out completely. His schadchen joke ought to be taken at face value as a case study regarding how Jews think and act — but certainly not how they play. According to Trebitsch: "[This joke] develops the triumph of the word over reality to perfection in that the possibility — or more precisely the ability to convince someone of an outcome — is equated with the reality of a given thing, and the advantages of a fictive 'accomplished fact' are taken into serious consideration prior to any of the transformations that are no longer viewed as necessarily disagreeable in their consequences! This equation of possibility and reality is only fully comprehensible for the secondary type" (81). The positing of the total equivalence of the real and the possible as an attribute of the Jewish secondary spirit becomes Trebitsch's own closed case (*fertige Sach'*) or the means by which the schadchen joke trips him up.

The rationale behind this world of difference and the absence of this one word is quite obvious. For Freud, the schadchen joke dwells in the world of sophistry. As he introduces the story, it is framed as inhabiting a rhetorical space that shadows philosophical reflection: "We find another piece of sophistry in the following marriage-broker story."[62] The artistry and sophistry of the schadchen joke occurs in an "as if" universe whose subjunctive posing and positing opens the space for play.[63] In contrast, Trebitsch takes the joke literally as a true expression of the secondary mind and its mode of operation. Yet, in the attribution that equates possibility and reality within the joke, Trebitsch reveals his own confusion instead. The analyst of equivalence forgets completely the matter of joking mobility — or how the joke in its vacillation operates in the gap of an "as if" that consciously plays off possibility and reality to achieve comic effects.

The need to take the Jewish joke seriously and to view it as an accurate indicator of the Jewish secondary spirit forms part of a recurrent pattern in the

Trebitschean text that demands further debunking. Because Trebitsch considers the Jewish joke as an expression of a particular state of mind, he systematically excludes the joking possibility that this second-order discourse inhabits a parodic space. He further ignores the possibility that the joke serves a parasitic function as a dangerous supplement that cannot stand on its own and that it does so to expose the limits of all primary orders.[64] In his obsessive pursuit of capturing the essence of the Jewish secondary spirit, Trebitsch can only insist that the moral to be gleaned from the barking dog joke is that "the secondariness of the resulting word has become the primary possession of thought" (78). Nevertheless, this particular joke and its raising of epistemological doubt suggests how the Jewish joke plays with the subjunctive possibility of radical and counterintuitive reversals. Such comic inversion posits what the world might be like if words and things were to flip places with each other thereby affording a playful, fanciful, and counterfactual space in which to laugh.

The other joke that Freud and Trebitsch have in common takes place on a train. This staging belongs to another standard category in the situation comedies of Jewish jokelore. These jokes describe the misadventures of mobile Jewish diasporic subjects and their being in transit. Furthermore, they possess a self-reflexive quality because of their exchange among Jewish tradesmen on the move as a means to pass the time in their long journeys across Europe.[65] This particular joke does not appear in the two central chapters devoted to the analysis of "*der jüdische Witz*." Rather, it is deferred to part 2 where it serves as a negative example to demonstrate the so-called "secondary-mobile character [*sekundär-bewegliche Charakter*]." This joke mocks the indiscrete behavior of the Eastern Jew (*Ostjude*) from the superior vantage point of the civilized Westerner (whether German or German-Jew).[66] It belongs to a large class of period jokes that focus and deflect the aggression directed against the immigrant invasion of the unassimilated Eastern Jew into the Western lands.

> On the occasion of the presentation of the "Jewish joke," we have mentioned the category of the character joke that arises from the [Jew's] behavior in the (new!) environment. A significant example may be recited here: A Jew in Eastern dress sits in a railway car for a long time in a perfectly anxious posture across from a man who is dressed genteelly. But then this man asks him suddenly, "When do we have Yom Kippur?" Before he even imparts the requested information, the Eastern Jew first lets out an "*Esoil*" (Ah, so!) and, now feeling "relaxed," he stretches out his feet onto the free seat opposite him! (103)

Trebitsch immediately follows the telling of the tale with a character analysis. To Trebitsch's way of thinking, this particular joke masks a meditation on abjection and a Jewish inferiority complex. In short, he interprets the bad manners and uncivil behavior of the passenger as symptoms of the "Jewish's own inferior self-valuation."

> Now here we find something that is brought to expression convincingly in this most unconscious of all character anecdotes that takes as a given what is happening to the Jew psychologically in relation to the host nation and to his fellow tribesmen. And if anything in the world were to give the most unmistakable proof for an inferiority based on the Jew's own inferior self-valuation — in short, for the most public display of former slave behavior [*Entsklavungsverhalten*] — then it would be this "joke"! (103)

However, the fact that Trebitsch reaches this conclusion is quite surprising for two reasons. First, it is a strange reversal when one considers that Trebitsch first sets up the joke in the context of the naturalizing circumstances of the postemancipation process with an explanation of how the joke springs from the Jew's relationship to his new environment. Given this seemingly cultural relativist assumption, one might expect that the joke analysis would proceed to explain the Eastern Jew's behavior in the train as reverting back to the way in which he would have acted if he found himself in his old shtetl environment — as an enactment of the intimacy of shtetl culture where "life-is-with-people" and where all borders are lacking between public and private space.[67] Second, Trebitsch's joke interpretation overlooks the proper behavior of the assimilated Jewish passenger who passes as a civilized mensch and who does not betray any sort of inferiority complex in the story.

But what is even more extreme about Trebitsch's conclusion is that it is exactly the opposite from the one reached by Freud when analyzing the same joke. Freud's comments arise at that critical juncture when he makes his astute observation that self-criticism functions as the definitive Jewish joking strategy. But this ability to laugh at oneself is not viewed as a symptom of self-deprecation that leads to an inferiority complex. Rather, the liberally minded Freud argues for the Jewish joke as the great leveler that recognizes no differences between master and servant. Freud's joke interpretation makes light of the contentiousness and lack of discipline of such a mode of thinking, and instead stresses the Jewish joke's deflation of pretensions and its democratic spirit.

> Incidentally, I do not know whether there are many other instances of a people making fun to such a degree of its own character. As an example of this, I may take the anecdote, quoted on p. 80f., of

a Jew in a railway train promptly abandoning all decent behavior when he discovered that the newcomer into his compartment was a fellow-believer. We made the acquaintance of this anecdote as evidence of something very small. It is meant to portray the democratic mode of thinking of Jews, which recognizes no distinction between lords and serfs, but also, alas, upsets discipline and co-operation.[68]

Having reached these opposite conclusions on the meaning of this particular joke on the move, it is not my purpose to legislate this ideological debate. There is no desire to play schadchen at this point and to engage in shuttle diplomacy in order to find a compromise solution between Freud's democratic mode and Trebitsch's inferiority complex. Instead, my more limited goal has been to consider mobility (*Beweglichkeit*) not as an attribute of the Jewish spirit, but rather as an emblem for the process of reading and interpreting Jewish jokes. The pendulum swing between Freud and Trebitsch is a rather extreme example of how the joke lends itself to such fluctuations. It is only when this instability is acknowledged as part and parcel of the joke's packaging that one is placed into a position to be moved by these Jewish jokes.[69]

## Otto Weininger as Trebitsch's Joke Writer

Over the last decades, Trebitsch's indebtedness to Otto Weininger and his pre-suicidal volume *Geschlecht und Charakter* (Sex and Character, 1903) has been documented extensively.[70] Weininger was Trebitsch's schoolmate and childhood friend and they were both members of the intellectual circle around Houston Stewart Chamberlain. One anonymous essay argues that Trebitsch did not possess one original thought and that all his stereotypical ravings against Jews and women can be traced back to Weininger's diatribes. Although that author traces many of the jargon words in Trebitsch's repertoire back to Weininger's text, he/she forgets to include a possible Weiningerian derivation of the term *Beweglichkeit* which plays such a key role in Trebitsch's joke analysis. This reference can be found in direct connection with the nature of the Jewish spirit in the infamous chapter 13 on "*Das Judentum*" where Weininger offers a descriptive catalog of Jewish clichés and stereotypes including "the great talent of the Jews for journalism, the 'mobility' [*Beweglichkeit*] of the Jewish spirit, [and] the lack of any rooted and original way of thinking."[71] Weininger also writes about the question of humor here and subscribes to the stereotypical dichotomy of the destructive *Judenwitz* vs. congenial national humor (whether English or German). The anti-Semitic and misogynistic Weininger believed that both women and Jews are humorless and that they possess only a talent for satire and mockery. Weininger insists, "Jews and women are devoid of humor, but addicted to mockery."[72] This binary opposition and Jewish character assassination programs Trebitsch's thinking in *Geist und Judentum* and it is also at the heart of the Nazi propagandist Siegfried Kadner's *Rasse und Humor* (1936). Weininger also underscores the Jewish aptitude for self-irony and for smut. The Jew "is ready to be witty only at his own expense or on sexual things."[73] Elliott Oring summarizes Weininger's position: "Because Jews have no transcendental inclinations and lack the creative freedom of the will, they have no true humor; they are addicted rather to mockery, satire, and irony."[74]

In reviewing what is at the core of this relationship of dependency of Trebitsch on Weininger, it is curious to observe that the anonymous author of "Jewish Self-Hatred and the Contempt of Women" has recourse to a joke. The essay begins with an excerpt from Hermann Swoboda's posthumous study, *Otto Weiningers Tod* (Vienna, 1911) and then delivers an unambiguous and damning thesis about the writings of Trebitsch: "Hermann Swoboda believes, 'There are jokes even into the uppermost regions of human thinking. Massive works of philosophy are sometimes built upon one single joke.' In fact, Treibtisch's entire work appears to us to be based upon one single joke — Weininger's definition of 'inner ambiguity [*innere Vieldeutigkeit*]' found in *Sex and Charakter*."[75] According to our anonymous source, there is a clear-cut relationship between these two writers. In a sense, it suggests that Weininger can be understood as Trebitsch's original joke writer. Weininger's writings supply the primary source material that the secondary Trebitsch elaborates and works up in his own writings. Without a doubt, Trebitsch would have never consented to this analysis and its conclusion. The man who believed that he had understood the Jewish joke better than anyone else on account of its relationship to the secondary mobile spirit never would have admitted that the analytical tools which he deployed to understand Jewish jokes were either jokes themselves or somehow appropriated from Weininger as their primary source. Even as one follows Trebitsch's joke analysis and its damning of the Jewish spirit, the risk of risibility raised by this anonymous essay must be kept in mind.

Trebitsch introduces the concept of "inner ambiguity" at the point in *Geist und Judentum* where he makes the distinction between the fixed (primary) and the fleeting (secondary) gaze. After the introduction of this term, Trebitsch does acknowledge his source (and roots) as follows: "Here we can anticipate that root of the Jewish spirit whose outcome and 'flowering' Otto Weininger has already grasped in what he shows to be the 'inner ambiguity' of the Jewish spirit" (43). In turn, when one looks at Weininger's introduction of the term, one finds a variant upon the contrast between the steady and fleeting gaze in regard to their range of perceived possibilities. Indeed, Weininger's binary opposition between (Jewish) inner ambiguity (*innere Vieldeutigkeit*) and (non-Jewish) naiveté (*Einfalt*) contains Trebitsch's distinction between secondary mobility and primary fixation in germ. Here are a few snippets that illustrate Weininger's distinction: "The Jew always has yet another opportunity, still plenty of opportunities, whereas the Aryan, without being poorer in his glance, actually decides and selects. . . . This inner ambiguity, this lack of unmediated inner reality of any psychical events. . . . Inner ambiguity, I repeat, is absolutely Jewish, and naiveté and simplicity (*Einfalt*) is absolutely un-Jewish."[76] Trebitsch's appropriation of inner ambiguity even goes so far as to incorporate Weininger's comments regarding a tendency toward uncertainty when discussing Jewish facial physiognomy in *Geist und Judentum*. Without due respect, the traditional stereotyping of the Jewish nose spreads to the corners of the mouth and leads to the Jewish smile (*"das jüdische Lächeln"*). From Jewish joke to Jewish smile, this generates a skeptical theory of facial expressions which is halfway on the path to laughter. Trebitsch casts a backward glance toward his master Weininger in fixing the fleetingness of a smile for eternity: "This mode of skepticism is comprehended in the most profound way by those who have glimpsed the Jewish smile, as Weininger has described it so masterfully: 'It is not a spiritual or a painful or a proud or a contorted smile, but rather [it is] this indefinite facial expression (the physiognomic correlate of inner ambiguity) that betrays a readiness to enter everything and lacks all reverence [*Ehrfurcht*] for humanity'" (120–121).

There are many ways to problematize the construct of "inner ambiguity." Of course, the most obvious one would be to show how this idea projects Trebitsch's and Weininger's own inner ambiguity about their Jewish roots onto the Jewish joke (and the Jewish spirit) in general. In other words, "inner ambiguity" tells the reader a lot more about the mobile discourse of so-called "Jewish anti-Semites" living in Vienna at the time than anything else.[77] In addition, one could offer sociocultural analysis that would externalize and explain this concept as well. For example, inner ambiguity can be understood as the result of the split situation of assimilating Jews during the period after emancipation being caught between two social and cultural worlds. Finally, it is possible to question the assumption that "inner ambiguity" is a particularly Jewish problem and point to its multiethnic dimensions when one begins to study the function of humor across a variety of cultures. From these sociological and multicultural perspectives, all jokes may be seen as a group's attempt to stage and to come to terms with its own inner conflicts and inner ambiguities.[78] Indeed, it is on account of the fact that jokes attempt to negotiate a moving field of ambiguities — and to release the tensions that these engender via laughter — that one can locate the source of their comic effect and effectiveness.

Trebitsch also adopts Weininger's views about a Jewish relation (or nonrelation) to skepticism. According to an amusing paradox set forth by Weininger, Jewish disbelief is so overwhelming that it lacks the conviction even to believe in skepticism. Weininger phrases this point quite succinctly: "But the Jew also does not believe in knowledge. And yet, he is in no way a skeptic on account of this fact because he is as little convinced by skepticism."[79] Trebitsch's adaptation of this particular point of view leads to the positing of yet another dichotomy between an authentic and primary form of skepticism and an inauthentic and secondary form of skepticism. While the former doubt springs from a deep sense of devoutness and piety, its evil twin is frivolous and unproductive. Although the first can be sublated in a search for a solution, the second cannot be transformed in this manner because the secondary mobile spirit knows no place from which to take and stake out a position.[80] Again, Trebitsch incorporates the rhetoric of the diasporic subject and the wandering Jew into his definition of a secondary skepticism as it hovers over the abyss. This leads Trebitsch to the pictographic positing of these terms to express the essential difference between these two doubts. The dichotomy in doubts divides the questioning subject who is split into two ("*Zwei-fel*") from the questionable subject marked by and as an indeterminate and unknown variable ("*X-fel*"). With these slick mathematico-linguistic gestures, Trebitsch again slips into word play on the level of the letter and finds himself on the verge of the dreaded (and dreadful) *Kalauer*.

> Whosoever smiles, thinks, and doubts in this way does so even before all reservations [*Bedenken*] about the world, whose skepticism is not a counterattack against belief, and thus, never to be understood as in true skepticism [*die wahre Skepsis*] in relation to a previously deep faith [*tiefer Gläubigkeit*]. It would be represented best in contrast to the true "*2-fel*" [doubt] that also can be expressed mathematically — as an "*X-feln*" [doubt]. In this way, it achieves only an *x*, an eternal indefiniteness and questionability, and it never leads to a solution or to clarity in the way that is often possible with productive skepticism. (121)

It is against this skeptical backdrop that one turns to the presentation of Trebitsch's third Jewish joke. It raises the question of skepticism in that it features a doubter in the starring role. While Trebitsch does not mention it, this particular joke belongs to the *Apikoires* (the Jewish free thinker) category.[81] A direct product of the process of emancipation and under the sway of secularization, the *Apikoires* assumes the role of the skeptic who questions the traditional dogmas of religious belief in all forms. What follows here is a lengthier version of the story as an *Apikoires* anecdote under the appropriate title of *"Der Freigeist"* (The free spirit) that appeared in a Jewish joke compilation in 1921. It is the story of a doubt-obsessed shoemaker named Effze Zentnerschwer. He is the man of the heavy-duty "perhaps" since that is the English translation of the Yiddish word *"effze."* In the anecdote, Effze aims his nature-based sarcastic and biting critique at the supernatural powers advocated by the Rabbi of Brody. The free spirit asks for the miraculous proof of a divine intervention that would defy the natural cycle of the seasons.

> **"The Free Thinker"**
> The shoemaker in Brody, the scourge of the Talmud teachers on account of his lust for doubting, is a virulent free thinker. God and his creation form the standing object of his critical observations.
> 
> One winter day, he goes for a walk with the Rabbi who enjoyed conversing with him. As always, the holy man speaks of the wonders of the world-creator in order to bring the doubter back to the right path.
> 
> As they are walking across the frozen pond, the Rabbi says:
> 
> "Clarify something for me, Effze. Why are we now able to go across the water?" "That's a joke!" Zenterschwer laughs, "It's frozen. A sheet of ice lies over the water."
> 
> "And who has made this covering, Effze? Think it over! Who has made this covering over the water?"
> 
> "Who should have made it? . . . The frost made it."
> 
> "And who has made the frost, Effze?"
> 
> "Do I know?" Effze states uncertainly.
> 
> "God has made it, you fool!" The Rabbi announces. "God is the one who has let the water freeze over!"
> 
> "Well," states Efze calmly, "if God can let the water freeze over, he should do it sometime in the summer."[82]

In comparison, Trebitsch's version refuses to acknowledge the free-thinking context of this anecdote. His joke is no longer a lively and extended dialogue that is a contest of wit and wits between the rabbi and the free thinker. Instead, Trebitsch converts "Effze" into another type of character in Jewish jokelore—the unthinking *Am Ha-Aretz* who plays the part of the ignorant simpleton.[83] When the religious teacher tries to convince his nameless pupil of the supernatural source of nature's wonders, Trebitsch's character dismisses the wonder with a wave of the hand and a commonsense utterance: "A teacher goes for a walk with his pupil. As they stand before a roaring stream, he tries to prove to the boy the omnipotence of God. He tries to demonstrate the power of the Creator in terms of the river which freezes into ice if the Lord commands it. Whereupon the lad dismisses this with a supercilious smile and a wave of the hand. Some stunt (*Kunststück*), in winter!" (77). It is important to review the transformations in Trebitsch's presentation of this witticism and to see how they fit into his overarching scheme. The main character is no longer a doubting old shoemaker but a superciliously smiling student. The story does not end with a challenging rhetorical retort about the other season, but with a cynical exclamation about the same season. The playful pose of the free thinker has been replaced by the dismissive Am-Haaretz who takes things as given or what Trebitsch refers to as the "self-evidently given" ("*Selbstverständlich-Gegebenen*"). It is in part on account of these devaluations that Trebitsch is able to put forth the dubious argument that the character in this story partakes of what he describes as the bad form of doubt. As in his other joke commentaries, Trebitsch links the joke to a metaphysics of language as professed by the wandering Jewish spirit wherein the word has been converted into his primary experience and possession: "And so this joke therefore also possesses such a deep power of disclosure because we sense where this quite specific disbelief and impiety has its origin. It is not in the 'doubt' about the meaning and meaningfulness, but rather quite simply about what is 'self-evidently given' that everything here on earth might have for somebody for whom the word was experience and possession long before the (fleetingly examined) fixation" (80). Trebitsch's attribution of abysmal doubt (*X-fel*) to the simpleton pupil leads to his cynical and nihilistic utterances in opposition to his wonder Rabbi in this Jewish joke — or even in contrast to the hidden sources of Aristotelian philosophy that always begin in wonder. In this way, an *Apikoires* joke with its radical doubt cast upon the Jewish Creator has been stripped of its blasphemy and its heady existential affirmation of being in a world without God. In Trebitsch's hands, "The Free Thinker" joke ends up as the emblem of a Jewish being at home in the word (rather than in the world) and devoid of any relation to fixed reality or lived experience.

## Joking Business, Questionable Practices

Two of the five jokes analyzed by Trebitsch as archetypically Jewish in Chapter 16 deal with questionable business practices. This is not surprising when one considers that a large number of Jewish jokes and caricatures in the humor magazines and books of the period foreground the negative stereotype of a dishonest relationship between Jews and money.[84] For Trebitsch, the connection between Jewish business practices and what is questioning and questionable (in the sense of immoral conduct) must be understood as an essential part of the Jewish spirit. Through a chain of associations, Trebitsch argues that the concept of "mobility" (*Beweglichkeit*) explains the necessary link between Jewish economic life and an interrogative mode of being. Both the questioning and the questionable are linked to Jewish commercial life wherein the fluctuations and variables of the price of commodities matters more than the actual and fixed worth of the thing (in) itself. Ironically, Trebitsch's ideas and theories about a Jewish financial model reflecting the secondary mobile spirit resonate with the Marxist distinction between exchange value and use value.

> Because they who are driven by trade (i.e., by the spirit that compares and oscillates back and forth) will approach everything and anything mainly from the perspective of purchasing [*Kauf*] and appraisal [*Bewertung*] and they will do so with doubting and questioning gestures and with the appropriate voice intonation. For those to whom everything achieves its value from the first through the variable of "price" which in turn leads to setting a thing's value rather than through the fixity and solidity of experience (with things!), everything will seem "questionable" ["*fraglich*"]. And from the "questionable" and dubious value of the world, there comes the "questioning" tone ["*fragende*" *Ton*] and the typical Jewish intonation and expression. (69–70)

As the all-encompassing argument progresses, Trebitsch goes so far as to draw a direct relationship between the questionable worth placed upon things in the commercial world and the questioning tone that is found in Jewish speech patterns. In this way, the discussion shifts from nurture (i.e., bad habits or acquired patterns of behavior) to nature in the attempt to locate mobility at the deepest core and essence of the Jewish secondary spirit. While excluding himself from the present company, Trebitsch accentuates the sing-song variable in the following manner: "It is equally necessary to stress here that the sing-song in their speech is by no means to be understood as merely a bad habit, but rather as the deepest core of this human species [*Menschenart*] therefore just as indebted to the secondary spirit of mobility!" (69).

The terms of analysis applied by Trebitsch to the vacillating and questionable nature of Jewish commercial trading practices are the same terms as those applied to the analysis of the Jewish joke. The "'questioning' tone and the typical Jewish intonation and expression" that characterizes business bargaining runs parallel to the way in which Jewish jokes are told and, at times, exaggerated when parodied in the "'Jewified' joke" ('*gejüdelte*' *Witz*, 76). The spirit that oscillates back and forth ("*hin und her pendelnde Geist*") possesses those driven by business and it also serves as a parallel to the mobilizing machinations implicit in Trebitsch's authentic Jewish joke. Similarly, Trebitsch's financial argument that privileges price fluctuations over the value of the thing itself offers another variant of the joking technique that places the primacy of the word and its associations over the thing itself. Therefore, Jewish jokelore and Jewish commercial practices offer parallel universes and structural similarities that enable Trebitsch to posit variations upon the theme of the Jewish secondary mobile spirit.

One business joke serves to illustrate Trebitsch's thesis by foregrounding the questionable rhetorical practices of an agent who wants to talk an unwitting consumer into buying something that he really does not need. For Trebitsch, this joke exemplifies "the trade activities that we have described already in their secondarily driven zeal in regard to selling, extolling, and peddling goods" (78–79). Trebitsch sees the joke as both a confirmation and a commentary upon the Jew as a slick business operator who is too overbearing and pushy in his wheeling and dealing. Nevertheless, the agent in the story (also referred to in the intermediary form of *Vermittler*) serves as a counterpart to Trebitsch himself as one who is engaged in a process of persuasion in an attempt to win the reader over to his Jewish joke theories.

This classic witticism takes place near a body of water whose (relative) worth seems to shift with the currents.[85] As the punchline is mobilized in response to a flood of controversy, the proximity of the "so close" exchanges places with the distance of the "so far."

> An eager salesman extols the virtues of a villa that lies on the shores of the Dnjepr—its advantages in the summer when one can bathe, its advantages in the fall when one can fish and go canoeing, its advantages in the winter when one can enjoy ice skating and the journey across the frozen river. All this is described in the most glowing colors with the repetition of the refrain: "There is the villa and then there is the Dnjepr!" However, in response to the anxious question of the client as to how things will be in the spring when the floods might endanger the house with the garden to some extent, the salesman speaks these words of dismissal in his overzealousness to extol its virtues: "Where is the villa and where is the Dnjepr!" (77)

Trebitsch's analysis points to the amusing contradictions that occur when the business negotiations and the stress on "patience of the words" instigated by this rhetorical agency gain precedence over the fixed or singular value of the thing in and of itself that has been left speechless. Trebitsch reviews this reversal by means of which the secondary gains the upper hand without the slightest protest on the part of what should be primary: "Thus, his power of fixation will be devoted to the selling, suggesting, and peddling of the (excellent) goods, and this can lead to such amusing contradictions [*heiterer Gegensätzlichkeit*] with the 'patience of the words' that do not 'protest' like things in their unambiguousness [*Eindeutigkeit*]" (79). But while Trebitsch locates these amusing contradictions at the point where the rhetoric of the word detaches itself from the fixity of the object, the present interpretation locates how Trebitsch's joke analysis — subject to the rhetorical effects of joking mobility (*Beweglichkeit*) — produces laughable results as the relative distances between primary and secondary are subject to alteration, and as the self-professed primary thinker engages in secondary activities in spite of himself.

The other comic inversion in this category involves a purchasing agent rather than a sales agent, but the same questionable business practices seem to be operative. This is the one about the purchaser who convinces his boss that he needs more money to buy the best dachshund around — only to end his negotiations with a question that asks for the meaning of the object to be had in the first place with his newly won purchasing power.

> A count commissions his Jewish servant to buy him a pair of dachshunds and he will supply him with 100 gulden for this purchase. The hired Jew replies passionately, professing that it is impossible to get hold of dachshunds — in so far as they should be impeccable — for less than 300 gulden. After a long period of back and forth negotiations [*längerem Hin- und Herhandeln auf den Preis*], the two men settle upon the price of 200 gulden. The Jew gives his parting wishes, but then turns around at the door, and asks in a sudden recollection, "A propos, my dear Count, just what are dachshunds anyway?" (77)

This joke is one of the more commonly repeated stories in the Jewish joke books of Trebitsch's era. Richard Raskin reviews eight different variants of the joke published in the German language between 1907 and 1928.[86] If one performs a content analysis of these versions and compares them with Trebitsch's narration, there is one striking detail that stands out here. While all the jokes describe the increase in the amount of money that the purchasing agent secures from the count, only Trebitsch's joke portrays this aspect as a bargaining process between the two men. In his version, the agent raises the bid to 300 gulden, and they eventually settle on the price of 200 gulden at the end of the negotiations. The inclusion of this long bargaining process is a clever device that enables Trebitsch to connect this Jewish joke to his larger theory regarding the essential vacillation of the Jewish spirit as the "*hin und her pendelnde Geist*" (70) that fluctuates back and forth.

In all of this joking business, Trebitsch's question-finding mission confounds intellectual and spiritual attributes for a particular historical situation. Instead of focusing on the Jewish joke as an emblem for the questionable nature of the Jewish spirit, it is necessary to redirect our attention to the Jewish joke as participating in the overall process of questioning that typified this period wherein traditional Jewish beliefs and "transmitted values" were put into question on account of the process of secularization that began with the Enlightenment. This historical explanation and its "putting into question" puts the Jewish question itself into a very different light. From this perspective, the Jewish joke provided a popular means to give expression to the *problematization* process that was part and parcel of modernization. Therefore, it is no coincidence to discover that the literary genre of the Jewish joke book published in the German language runs parallel to this process of secularization. What Stéphane Moses has pointed out in relation to the black humorous literary texts of Franz Kafka can be applied to the Jewish joke book as well: "But this crisis of Jewish tradition has to be understood at the same time as part of the general putting-into-question [*Infragestellung*] of transmitted values that indicates the ongoing process of secularization of European culture since the Enlightenment. It is certain that this crisis took an especially acute form in Judaism."[87] When the joke work is viewed as a part of this overall interrogation of received ideas in an age of crisis and in terms of a specific historical moment, the two aforementioned stories on "joking business" may be viewed as symptoms of Jewish and European cultural modernity and its relativization of values expressed on the level of Jewish folklore rather than displaying essential negative traits of the Jewish spirit as found in Trebitsch's anti-Semitic polemicizing.[88]

## Postscript: Fallen into the Viennese Strudel

The vacillating experience of the following joke amid the apple strudel and the ice cream, amid the racial and the religious anti-Semitism, induces something approaching vertigo:

> As it swings back and forth between religious hatred and racial hatred without ever deciding for either one of the two methods, anti-Semitism virtually threatens — to become a Jewish joke! Because such a way of thinking truly bears comparison with the Jew in the restaurant who orders an ice cream that he exchanges for a piece of apple strudel in a sudden "on second thought." Then, when it comes to paying and

in order to avoid this annoying procedure, he points out that he has surrendered the ice cream for the apple strudel, but indeed—he has not eaten it?! (211)

On the one hand, one is astounded by the fact that anti-Semitism could be taken so lightly by Trebitsch—that it can be reduced to a coffee house witticism, that it can be taken as a Jewish joke. On the other hand, one is astounded that a joke—and especially one that Jacques Lacan once called "the silliest story"[89]—could assume such serious import that it could be mobilized as a means by which to think through the essential problem of anti-Semitism. In staging this witticism, Trebitsch leaves behind the heavy baggage of the pseudo-scientific discourse that has framed his analysis of the Jewish joke. Amid the table conversation of a presumably cultivated Vienna coffee house, he turns to a Jewish joke to make a rather crass analogy about the current status of anti-Semitism and its two attack modes. Given the framing of this analogy, the intent of the joke is clearly anti-Semitic in pointing to the Jew's deceitful restaurant practices when it comes to picking up (or, in this case, leaving behind) the check.[90] But the clipped manner in which Trebitsch appropriates and interprets this joke indicates that he is less concerned about its actual dynamics than its metaphorical status. While the joke relates an inherently unequal series of transferences that depend upon money as the missing unit of exchange, Trebitsch insists upon all things being equal when he represses the economic factor completely in his subsequent mathematical formula in the next paragraph that posits this oddball analogy—apple strudel to ice cream as religious anti-Semitism to racial anti-Semitism.[91] However, the joke suggests that the exchange of ice cream for apple strudel depends upon a refusal of payment by the evasive Jewish consumer and this has dropped out of Trebitsch's version.

In Trebitsch's recounting of the joke, one is struck on the grammatical level by the dash as a form of hesitation or dramatic pause that appears immediately before the exclamatory announcement of the Jewish joke. In this way, Trebitsch prepares the reader for the shock of the analogy or the revelation that contemporary anti-Semitism is structured like a Jewish joke. Now it is not only that the taunts and pranks of anti-Semites—Jewish or otherwise—utilize comic forms to make a mockery of all things Jewish. For Trebitsch, the structure of contemporary anti-Semitism itself partakes of the same vacillating structure as the Jewish joke and Jewish spirit (*"hin- und her pendelnde Geist"*) as it goes back and forth in its antipathies between a religious and a racial variant of hatred.[92] (One assumes that this pendulum swing between religious and racial could also be applied to Trebitsch's own Jewish self-hatred.) In this confounding manner, the reader is confronted by the staging of an argument that is at odds with the content of the argument itself. Trebitsch's anti-Semitic argument condemns the secondary Jewish spirit — and yet it is staged in an analogy to and by means of a Jewish joke — one of the hallmarks of the secondary Jewish spirit. Trebitsch's binary opposition claims that only the secondary spirit vacillates — and yet, here, the fixed primary spirit of anti-Semitism is wavering as well. Taken as a final rhetorical instance, the case of the Vienna strudel provides yet another opportunity to witness the internal contradictions and "secondary moves" that take Trebitsch's mobilization of the Jewish joke for a spin.

It is a bitter and perverse irony of history that an Austrian Jew was one of the first and foremost patrons of the Nazi party. In reality, this remains Trebitsch's sickest anti-Semitic joke of all. Of course, Trebitsch did not live to see the end of the vacillations sketched above and the triumph of racial over religious hatred (and thus the triumph of the ice cream over the apple strudel) in the years that followed his death from tuberculosis in 1927. For it is common knowledge that the same Nazi party that Trebitsch supported in its fledging days would grow in political power in Germany and Austria to the point where it was able to make anti-Semitism the law of the Third Reich and to decree the mobile discourse of the Jewish joke as the cultural product of a degenerate race.

# 2
# Of Caricatures, Jokes, and Anti-Semitism
*The Case of Eduard Fuchs*

At a time when graphic novels, animated cartoons, and political caricatures are not only ubiquitous in contemporary culture but also serve as appropriate subjects for both popular and academic studies, it is difficult to remember a bygone era when such visual media were marginalized and not taken seriously. The German neo-Marxist visual cultural historian and art collector Eduard Fuchs (1870–1940) was one of the first to recognize the significance of caricature as an artistic medium and to understand the important role that it played in modern European societies. By understanding caricature as "a form of illustrated social history,"[1] the prescient Fuchs was part of a larger movement in the human sciences that began to take objects of study seriously that had been formerly considered as trivial or marginalized forms of knowledge. According to Walter Benjamin's astute historical materialist reading in his extended essay "Eduard Fuchs: Collector and Historian" (1937), Fuchs ventured into zones considered to be taboo or too insignificant for conventional art histories of his era: "He was a collector who strayed into border disciplines such as caricature and pornographic representation. These border disciplines sooner or later meant the ruin of a series of clichés in traditional art history."[2] Fuchs's unconventional visual cultural path began with the publication of the monumental *Die Karikatur der europäischen Völker* (*Caricatures of European Peoples*) in 1902.[3] Benjamin recalls in a footnote to his essay that this two-volume work was followed by many other projects covering specific topics in the field of caricature as "Fuchs dedicated special works to the caricature of woman, of the Jews, of the World War."[4] His three-volume *History of Erotic Art* (begun in 1908) was a huge popular success and it built upon an initial study, *The Erotic Element in Caricature* (1904). In addition, Fuchs published numerous studies on Honoré Daumier, the leading French caricaturist of the nineteenth century who held up bourgeois society to ridicule and with whom Fuchs identified.

Benjamin composed his insightful essay on Fuchs while they were both in exile in Paris during the 1930s. The revered German-Jewish literary and cultural critic attests here to the importance and relevance of Fuchs and his body of work to German social, political, and cultural life in a career that spanned almost five decades. Even if Benjamin's essay contains a number of points that mark Fuchs's intellectual shortcomings including his embrace of a practice of cultural history lacking in some of the nuances of dialectical thinking (to be discussed later in this chapter), he still admired many aspects of Fuchs's approach to material culture and his contributions to a Marxist theory of art. Benjamin begins the essay by praising Fuchs's pioneering spirit: "As a collector Fuchs is primarily a pioneer. He founded the only existing archive for a history of caricature, of erotic art and of the genre picture [*Sittenbild*]. More important, however, is another, complementary, circumstance: because he was a pioneer, Fuchs became a collector. Fuchs is a pioneer of a materialist consideration of art."[5] Benjamin believed that Fuchs's major innovations for the study of art history were found "in the interpretation of iconography, in the contemplation of mass art as well as the examination of techniques of production" and that all these areas challenged "traditional conceptions of art."[6] In these ways, one might look to Fuchs as a trailblazer in the field now known as visual cultural studies.

Benjamin also reviews how this young Social Democrat got involved in the business of caricature and how his big breakthrough came with the *Süddeutsche Postillion* (South German Courier) in the late 1880s. While working as a bookkeeper, Fuchs was asked to help out on an issue of this "socialist magazine of political humor" with some of his own lampooning contributions. The great success of that issue led to the request for more input and he eventually became the "editor of a magazine devoted to political satire."[7] However, the successful use of caricature as a political weapon in this humor magazine (*Witzblatt*) would lead to Fuchs's arrest and imprisonment at the age of eighteen. On two occasions, in 1888 and 1889, he was jailed for five months on the charge of slandering Emperor Wilhelm II. In his editorial capacity, the autodidactic Fuchs learned as much as he could about the history of caricature and he also began to collect such material in an acquisitive manner. Benjamin recalls the paradox of Fuchs's life in terms of how this lifelong Social Democratic activist and later founder of the Berlin Communist Party became a wildly successful popular author, a fabulously wealthy art collector, and the proud owner of a villa in the exclusive Berlin-Zehlendorf District designed in part by the Bauhaus architect Mies van der Rohe: "[His] pride and expansiveness lead him to bring reproductions of his collection onto the market for the sole reason of being able to appear in public with his collections. That in consequence he becomes a rich man, is again a Balzacian turn."[8] But while the left-leaning Fuchs may have been an innovator in understanding how and why caricatures mattered and how its political satire could be used in the service of revolution at certain historical moments, he was not a pioneering spirit when writing about the related subjects of Jewish caricature and Jewish jokes. Unfortunately, his adherence to Marxist ideology brought with it stereotypical anti-Semitic baggage that shut him up in an iron cage of historical and theoretical premises out of which he could not be liberated — not even by means of a liberating laughter.

Fuchs is well-known for his important study on the history of Jews in caricature, *Die Juden in der Karikatur: Ein Beitrag zur Kulturgeschichte* (1921; Jews in caricature: A contribution to cultural history),[9] and, therefore, the study of a satirical mode of visual humor that consists predominantly of non-Jews making fun of Jews and with close links to anti-Semitic discourse. Nevertheless, it is hardly mentioned in the critical literature that he devoted the last chapter of this book to the investigation of the phenomenon of Jewish self-irony and particularly as it related to literary satire and verbal wit. Fuchs takes notice of a range of media as sites for Jewish self-irony including joke books, humor magazines, novels, caricatures, and theatrical farces. He begins the chapter by offering high praise for this joke "collaborator" as he takes up the phenomenon of Jews laughing at themselves: "The satire of the Jews has a principal collaborator [*Hauptmitarbeiter*] that may not remain anonymous in a book such as this one — the Jews themselves. This collaborator is characterized by the fact that a very huge part, and a part of the very best, emerged from his mind necessarily whereby Jewry was glossed satirically throughout the ages and in different countries. To summarize in one short sentence: the best jokes about the Jews come mostly from Jews" (303–304).

Although *Die Juden in der Karikatur* has received much critical attention in the world of German-Jewish scholarship over the past years, little or no attention has been paid to Fuchs's thinking as it pertains to the Jewish joke or to Jewish self-irony.[10] My goal in this chapter is to provide a close reading of Fuchs's "Die jüdische Selbstironie" (Jewish self-irony) and to examine his arguments about the nature of Jewish self-mockery. I am particularly interested in Fuchs's view that Jewish self-irony comes from a position of strength and self-confidence and I contend that this position blinded him to some extent to the negative potential of this type of Jewish wit in conjunction — or in collaboration — with anti-Semitic discourse. The Jewish jokes that he selected and the intellectual sources from which he drew to support his views expose the latent anti-Semitism that adheres to his position at the beginning of the Weimar Republic.

Fuchs's ideas, even though opposed to nationalist anti-Semitism (e.g., the conservative views of German historian Heinrich von Treitschke), are also tied to negative and stereotypical presuppositions about the Jews, money, and capitalism derived from his reliance on the ideas of Karl Marx's "On the Jewish Question" (1844) and Werner Sombart's *The Jews and Modern Capitalism* (1911).[11] According to Liliane Weissberg, this latter reference enables "the substantiation of scientific claims in his *Juden in der Karikatur*."[12] Disputing Max Weber's idea that it was the Protestant work ethic that was the motor for the rise of capitalism, Sombart argued that the responsibility for capitalism rested with the Jews and Judaism in a review of their contributions to modern economic life. Ironically, Sombart sets up this connection via a rhetorical question that contains an uncanny reference to the (Jewish) joke: "What is the meaning of this parallelism in the fundamental ideas of the Jewish religion and capitalism? Is it mere chance? A bad joke perpetrated by fate?"[13] Weissberg goes further by suggesting that "Sombart's *The Jews and Modern Capitalism* becomes a book about money and the Jews in caricature for Fuchs."[14] I will examine how Fuchs's anti-Semitic stereotyping comes into play in his analysis of a joke about the Rothschild's fortune and in his analysis of a number of caricatures that made the Rothschilds the tendentious object of their visual satire. In the process, I explore the latent "anti-Semitism of the Left" embedded in Fuchs's ideological position as one begins to read between the lines of his analysis of Jewish jokes and caricatures to reveal how he reproduces the contradictions of Marx and Sombart on the Jewish question.[15] This is what Micha Brumlik has referred to as "the tragedy of good intentions" in Fuchs's work.[16]

The German-Jewish studies scholar Sander Gilman is another contemporary thinker who has taken up the complex case of Fuchs, comparing and contrasting the avid German collector of caricatures with the Jewish joke collector and psychoanalyst, Sigmund Freud: "Fuchs, like Freud, is a compulsive collector of comic material."[17] In the same way that Sigmund Freud took the Jewish joke seriously with the publication of his book on jokes and their relationship to the unconscious, Fuchs took Jewish caricatures as both a significant object of scientific analysis and aesthetic admiration in his dual capacity as cultural historian and compulsive collector. For the sake of engendering a better contrast with Freud, Gilman begins by referring to Fuchs's preferred medium as jokes only to quickly change gears when he pronounces "caricatures rather than jokes as his primary source." Nevertheless, my study, with its focus on Jewish self-irony, suggests that Fuchs had some important things to say about Jewish jokes too. In the overlooked final chapter (11) of his book on Jewish caricature, Fuchs joins Freud in his assessment that he knows of no other nation that makes fun of itself to such an extent. Fuchs follows Freud to the letter when he refers to Jewish self-irony as "this significant intellectual entity [*Wesenheit*] of the Jews that is found in a similar fashion in no other nation"[18] (307). In this way, the Berliner Marxist cultural historian and the Viennese Jewish psychoanalyst find common ground in their valorization of Jewish wit as self-deprecating and self-mocking.

## The Anti-Semitic Roots of Caricatures and Jokes about Jews

In *Jews in Caricature*, Fuchs senses the tensions that arise in the formation of caricature. Using a weather analogy, he expresses this point in a socially determined manner: "In the same way that there have to be specific tensions and resistances in the air for the emergence of a thunderstorm, very specific social tensions are the necessary precondition for the formation of every caricature" (3). Simply put, according to Fuchs, each caricature serves as the reflection or the mirror of social tensions and conflicts. The idea of social conflict at the root of caricature is deeply influenced by and fits quite nicely with the Marxist conception of historical materialism as expounded during the period of the Second International that looks for the tensions and contradictions that result from the class struggle that exists between labor and capital. Extending the weather analogy of caricature as a social barometer to the study of history, Fuchs argues that one can understand the political climate of a past age by looking at its caricatures: "Given the greater or lesser rancor of anti-Jewish caricatures published at a certain time, one also can read [*ablesen*] the degree to which the existence of the masses was and is threatened by the upheaval in question. One can further read [*ablesen*] from caricatures which sections of the population were particularly affected" (109).

Given these assumptions, it is not surprising to learn that Fuchs believed that any attempt to comprehend the Jewish question would be enhanced by the study of Jewish caricature (as the visual form of comic expression) and Jewish jokes (as the verbal form of comic expression). In this way, the question of what to do with the wandering Jews of Europe and the intense debate motivated by this question is reflected in the pictorial means of caricature as a visual mirroring device or the literary means of jokes as a verbal mirroring device. To employ the theoretical assumptions of traditional Marxist analysis as deployed by Fuchs, artistic and cultural products (such as caricatures and jokes) occur as part of an ideological superstructure that mirrors or reflects the social and economic tensions of the base. Fuchs spells out the relationship of the base and the superstructure: "Therefore the uncovering of social tensions and contradictions which have generated anti-Jewish caricatures for hundreds of years in almost all European countries (and are generated anew every day) must be the basis of all my explanations" (6). This same logic would apply to Jewish jokes generated as a response to or as an outlet for social tensions and contradictions. The discovery of social tensions and contradictions led Fuchs to investigate the pivotal role played by the Jews in the origin and the growth of capitalism as well as the economic resentment that this caused in the masses whose animosity was given vent in the cultural sphere via the production of anti-Jewish caricatures and jokes.

However, Fuchs's ideological presuppositions (following Marx and Sombart) overlook the intrinsic nature and structure of jokes and caricatures which rely on tensions, contradictions, and paradoxes to produce their comic effects. This alternative approach that is more attuned to the deconstructive potential of Jewish wit begins with the assumption that the object of study itself—the excesses and instabilities of caricature (occupying a space that destabilizes the truth) and the protean nature of jokes—play an important role in bearing responsibility for the shifting borders and internal contradictions that one encounters in examining Fuchs's attempts to comprehend *Jews in Caricature*. From this perspective, the tensions and vacillations played out in jokes and caricatures are none other than wit's excessive revenge on this thinker who sought to package caricature and wrap up its history for mass consumption. It recalls that caricatures and jokes work (and play) on the basis and the release of tension, on the basis and the exposure of contradiction. This is how and why we laugh. Such an explosion and backlash of laughter mocks the historian of caricature's system building or inscribes his stalwart efforts as something overburdening (and, after all, this is the way that caricature works). It challenges and questions Fuchs's attempt to subject an exaggerating, distorting, and openly dishonest medium to a discourse of truth and to wipe out its difference (i.e., caricature's difference from the truth) with a concept such as "the truth lies in the extreme." The truth is that, speaking light-heartedly or even slanderously, caricature and jokes may not be speaking the truth at all. And, if that is the case, then its truth always lies elsewhere.

There is no denying that Fuchs locates and condemns anti-Semitism as the root cause of the vast majority of Jewish caricatures and Jewish jokes. As Fuchs writes in the chapter whose title is worded on the verge of a Jewish persecution complex, "Warum sind die Juden von aller Welt gehasst?" ("Why are the Jews hated by the whole world?"): "Unfortunately, the most atrocious forms of hatred of the Jews belong not only to the past, but, on the contrary, to the present day.... To explain the roots and the contexts of this hatred of the Jews [*Judenhaß*] through the centuries—which is clearly the most fertile breeding ground for the majority of all Jewish caricatures ever published—is the assignment that I have set for this chapter" (76). Again, one sees in Fuchs's analysis how social tensions that are expressed quite viscerally in anti-Semitism serve as the motivating source for satirical production whether as Jewish caricatures or jokes. Fuchs draws a similar connection between anti-Semitism and the production of verbal jokes directed against the Jews in the following passage, and he discusses the joke format as a particularly modern phenomenon that has replaced the maxim and the epigram of the Renaissance period.

> To cite a single example, let me remind you of the almost innumerable Jewish jokes that have been made and published in the most diverse countries year after year, and that are still produced day in and day out without interruption.... To be sure, the Jewish joke [*Judenwitz*] is the satirical realm in which both private and politically organized anti-Semitism has long manifested itself at its most unruly, and that is because this satirical form of expression reflects the modern psyche as much as the proverb [*Sprichwort*] did from the fifteenth to the seventeenth centuries. (277)

In this section, Fuchs also discusses the publication of satires during the early nineteenth century wherein "the strong anti-Semitic stream of the [eighteen] thirties found its literary reflection" (280).

For Fuchs, the target and the trigger at the basis of such anti-Semitism is the figure of the Jew as capitalist. As in many other points in the book, Fuchs denies here that the source of Jew-hatred lies in racial difference: "In this connection, it must be pointed out with all clarity that it is absolutely not the racial difference between the Orientals and the Europeans that establishes the hatred against the Jews at its core; on the contrary, it is only the Jew as capitalist who triggers hatred. Each historical verification of this matter (of racial hatred) proves that the other race is hated if and only if it appears as a dangerous economic competitor" (80). In this excerpt, Fuchs adapts Werner Sombart's views of the central importance of financial instruments and money lending for the enabling of capitalism and the crucial role that Jews played in this endeavor (see "The Rothschild Joke" in this chapter).

Yet, one of the ways in which Fuchs defines caricature leaves much doubt as to whether he really believes that anti-Jewish caricatures and jokes are only the product of the lies of anti-Semites who vent their hatred against the Jews in visual form. These doubts begin to surface in Fuchs's maxim about caricature as the art that demonstrates how "the truth lies in the extreme."[19] According to this paradoxical logic, the exaggerations of caricature become its means of getting at the truth. Rather than focusing upon the distance from the truth of this distorting medium, Fuchs appropriates caricature to a discourse of truth. He loses track of the medium's lies and distortions or what would disenable his theoretical apparatus on this issue. Fuchs explains, "Thus caricature is one-sided due to these various circumstances, but it is exactly on account of its one-sidedness that it is a valuable source of truth about the past—because the element of caricature consists in the exaggeration of the essence of a phenomenon, the essential appears in caricature in its most obvious manifestation" (6).[20]

The concept of caricature as "source of truth," the idea that it contains a "kernel of truth," and even the incredibly naive view that Fuchs articulates at the conclusion of the *Die Karikatur der Europäischen Völker* that caricature always stands on the side of progress, "on the side of the beautiful and the good,"[21] becomes quite problematic if and when one is dealing with a topic like the anti-Semitic representation of the Jew in visual and verbal satire. On the one hand, Fuchs's concept of caricature as "source of truth" might be interpreted to mean in a neutral sense that the truth that it reveals is the fact of anti-Semitism. However, this can also mean that the truth that caricature reveals is the "truth" that lies at the core of anti-Semitic representations of Jews. For Micha Brumlik, Fuchs holds to this latter view unfortunately: "Fuchs's further analysis shows how much he is imprisoned from today's perspective in the anti-Semitic assumptions of his time, assumptions that he does not criticize fundamentally but accepts in substance and only reinterprets for moral reasons" (27). But how is one to explain the origin and the function of the self-ironic and self-mocking impulse that is also an important feature of Jewish jokes and caricatures? Is it somehow a response to these same anti-Semitic impulses as well despite its apparently Jewish sources?

## Understanding Jewish Self-Irony

Interestingly, Fuchs begins his analysis by looking at and taking issue with the presumed understanding of Jewish self-irony through the lens of contemporary anti-Semitism. Naturally, this sets up a binary opposition that divides us from them and it underscores how Fuchs did not see himself as tainted by anti-Semitic rhetoric in any way. For Fuchs, the anti-Semitic argument as promulgated by right-wing German nationalists and racists focuses on the simplistic stereotyping of a number of negative attributes of Jewish character in a superficial manner. For example, the iconoclastic and "spineless" Jews are alleged to hold nothing sacred or holy—not even themselves—and this attitude lends itself to the production of self-directed wit. According to Fuchs, the anti-Semitic position frames and defames the Jewish self-ironist in a vilifying and demeaning comparison with a shameless prostitute and this leads to the accusation of their shared cynicism. With a nod to a classic Jewish joker, Fuchs then distances himself from this simplistic interpretation and what he sees as crude name-calling and reactionary vitriol:

> Anti-Semitism has a very simple explanation for this well-known phenomenon. It derives this [self-irony] from the alleged internal groundlessness and instability [*Haltlosigkeit*] of the Jews, their superficial feelings, and especially from their peculiar lack of character and even spinelessness [*Charakterlosigkeit*] for which nothing is at all sacred. For these reasons, they do not flinch from making fun of themselves before the whole world in the most cynical way just like a street prostitute who likewise exposes herself to the whole world in a shameless way. But things are not as simple as that. The self-irony of the Jews, which is reflected in thousands of astounding proofs and which found its most classic representative in Heinrich Heine, has much deeper causes (304).[22]

In fighting against this reactionary brand of anti-Semitism, Fuchs is directly at odds with the ideas of the German nationalist historian and politician Heinrich von Treitschke and his derogatory assertions regarding "the peculiar Jewish rudeness and bad habit of self-derision" ("*die sonderbare jüdische Unart der Selbstverhöhnung*").[23] Beginning in 1879 when he launched the Berlin Anti-Semitism debate with the infamous one-liner, "The Jews are our misfortune!," Treitschke took to the offensive against what he saw as corrupting Jewish and radical influences on German culture. From Treitschke's racist perspective, the Jews are nothing more than "German-speaking Orientals" whose use of Western language is, according to Sander Gilman, "merely a mask to disguise their Oriental wiles."[24] Fuchs cites Treitschke's chapter on radicalism and Judaism ("Radikalismus und Judentum") from his massive *German History in the Nineteenth Century* (1885). In the following excerpt, Treitschke applies this Jewish Orientalist argument to his interpretation of "nimble Jewish jokes" as he discerns a tragicomic situation that foregrounds "the absurdity of the contrast between their Oriental nature and their Occidental form." Treitschke also focuses on the Jew's lack of political sovereignty and alludes to the figure of the "wandering Jew" in order to further underscore the gap between their parasitic language and customs and those of their host nation Germany:

This people without a state, who are scattered widely throughout the world and who accepted the language and customs of other nations but without giving up their own, lived in an eternal contradiction which seemed just as much tragic as it was comic according to how one presented it. The nimble Jewish jokes [*behenden jüdischen Witze*] could not escape the absurdity of the contrast between their Oriental nature and their Occidental form. Therefore, the European Jew has been accustomed to mock himself with the utmost ruthlessness for a long time.[25]

One can attempt to laugh off "the absurdity of the contrast" and "the eternal contradiction" at the heart of Jewish jokes (and especially self-ironic ones). But the German nationalist historian refuses to fall victim to the Jewish joker's comic stratagems. Instead, he also sees this situation as something tragic and in need of serious repair. In Treitschke's case, this is linked to his call for an immediate and total assimilation of the Jews in the German-speaking lands as the only way to close the gap and to eliminate this contradiction from which this pernicious form of Jewish wit springs.

However, Fuchs sees Treitschke's analysis as "absolutely superficial" and as something that does not get to the root cause of "Jewish self-irony." One senses the leftist's resentment at the authority and influence carried by this right-wing historian-politician of an earlier era. For Fuchs, Treitschke's essentialist analysis does not get us beyond the "existing fact" that there is Jewish self-irony and that it is a part of Jewish nature rather than offering a more sophisticated analysis that would trace the original sources from which it springs and how it is nurtured in society. While one may accuse Fuchs of anti-Semitic and even racist assumptions about the Jews in certain respects, this does not apply to his historical materialist argument that Jewish self-irony (as embodied in caricatures and jokes) serves as the reflection of social tensions. Fuchs responds, "This so-often parroted quotation remains absolutely superficial because Treitschke never went to the deeper connections of things and this is indeed not surprising. It is much more a confirmation of the existing fact, rather than an exploration of the primary sources from which Jewish self-irony inevitably flows" (304). Interestingly, Fuchs's citation leaves out the next few sentences of Treitschkean invective that are also damning in their condemnation of Jewish self-deprecation. Indeed, the final sentence of the above citation does not end at this point but continues through the use of a semicolon to amplify further points of Treitschke's anti-Semitic diatribe as it is directed against Jewish self-mockery: "For a long time, the European Jew therefore was accustomed to mock himself with the utmost ruthlessness; the cruelest that has ever been said about the Jews comes from Jewish lips. The racial pride of the chosen people in contrast to the non-Jews [*Goyim*] was certainly rooted so deeply that it could not be shaken by the most shameless self-mockery [*frechste Selbstverspottung*]."[26] It is possible that Fuchs decided not to quote Treitschke in full because he did not want to be contaminated by the anti-Semitic historian's overtly racist framing of Jewish self-irony as self-confident. For Treitschke's argument insists on the "racial pride of the chosen people" in contrast to the historical materialist viewpoint that Jewish self-mockery is "an outpouring of a well-founded sense of self and justified self-esteem" in direct response to the "many centuries of their constant oppression" (306).[27]

Fuchs then turns to another attempt at the analysis of the Jewish joke that he considers to be more profound but that is still wanting in certain respects. The source is the German-Jewish language philosopher Eduard Engel and his popular book *Deutsche Stilkunst* and specifically Engel's chapter 17, which deals with humor, wit, and irony.[28] Fuchs recalls Engel's view of the joke as a weapon of the weak and the oppressed and its consequent "overgrowth" among the rhizomatic Jews of the diaspora. Like Treitschke, Engel also situates Jewish wit as the product of the loss of national sovereignty and state power: "Fritz Engel penetrates much deeper in his book on German style when he says: 'The joke is a good weapon, but one more for the weak than for the strong, more for the oppressed than for the ruling class. Therefore, that overgrowth of the joke among the Jews . . . the Jews polished the subtle weapon of wit but only after they were wrested from the coarser one of state power'" (304).[29] Note the presence of an ellipsis in this excerpt. Interestingly, an examination of the original text by Engel shows that Fuchs has excised the language philosopher's pointed criticism of the Berlin Jewish satirist Alexander Moszkowski and his exaggerated claims about the place of the Jewish joke on the world stage. In the original source, Engel downgrades Moszkowki's attribution of any world historical significance to the Jewish joke as follows: "One of our most knowledgeable masters of wit, Alexander Moszkowski, was misled to the audacious statement: 'The Jewish joke is the foundation and the crown of all jokes.' The crown, perhaps, but the foundation, hardly: the Jews polished the subtle weapon of wit but only after they were wrested from the coarser one of state power. The Greeks from Homer to Aristophanes onwards were funnier than the Jews of the Bible."[30] Here, Engel appreciates the humor to be found in ancient Greek epic and drama and he finds no equivalent in the Jewish Bible stories. Interestingly, Fuchs's book was published in the same year that Moszkowski delivered his important lecture on the Jewish joke and its philosophy where he sought to assimilate and universalize Jewish humor in order to link it to the humanistic tradition of Western philosophy that begins with the ancient Greeks.[31]

What Fuchs does not mention, however, is the important fact that Engel also authored *Sprich Deutsch!* (Speak German!) and that this book called for a German language purified of foreign words.[32] In mounting this attack against the invasion of foreign linguistic elements (*Fremdwörter*) into German, Engel took aim at both Yiddish (as German-Jewish dialect) and *mauscheln* (as the Jewish accentuation of German) as modes of corruption of the German language and its purity.[33] In doing so, Engel sought to eradicate (for better and worse) key aspects of Jewish jokes as told in the German language given that these jokes were full of Yiddishisms (*Judendeutsch*) and *mauscheln* for their comic effect and impact. In this way, this "language purifier" shared many assumptions with the anti-Semites about the inferiority of the Jew on account of a corrupt language.[34] In light of this agenda, it may seem ironic that Fuchs turned to Engel as an authority on Jewish wit. Nevertheless, Fuchs echoes Engel's linguistic concerns when he writes of how "the satirical application of Jewish jargon in which one has a corrupted German [*verdorbenes Deutsch*] in front of him became a chief tool [*Haupthilfsmittel*] for the purpose of the most successful satirical mockery [*satirischen Verhöhnung*] of the Jews" (280). He goes on to relate how this tendency played itself out in the 1830s with the satirical works of Itzig Feitel Stern authored by the Christian anti-Semite Heinrich Holzschuher who struck the pose of Jewish self-irony in the adoption of this pseudonym.[35] Fuchs continues: "Literary satire made use of this remedy with particular preference. The numerous pamphlets of the anti-Semitic publisher von Goedsche in Meissen where the strong anti-Semitic stream of the thirties found its literary reflection are consistently written in Jewish jargon" (280). While Fuchs calls attention to how "Jewish jargon" pervades these anti-Semitic satirical publications, it remains rather ambiguous as to whether the real culprit in this conflict is for him the jargonized Jew who must no longer speak a corrupt German language or the "unruly" anti-Semites who must stop making the Jew a satirical scapegoat for the tensions and contradictions of capitalism.

## Jewish Self-Irony as Defense Mechanism

Although Fuchs accepts Engel's analysis of the Jewish joke as the preferred weapon of the weak and the oppressed, he is not fully satisfied with it because Engel reads self-irony as the means by which to fight one's enemies when one has been deprived of state power. Fuchs sees Jewish self-irony as even more subtle and crafty in its ways. Paradoxically, Jewish self-irony is to be viewed as a weapon that offers a diversionary tactic in order to defuse hostility or to avert conflict. When the Jews walk away from a fight, they leave their enemies laughing in stitches. The following scenario sketches a radical reversal as the Jews trump their enemy's anti-Semitic aggressions in a witty manner. This strategy serves not to deny or argue against anti-Semitic discourse but to exaggerate it and to defuse it through laughter ("yes, yes, you're right!") To deploy Freud's conception, the Jew hereby wins the laugher over to his side by heaping further comic abuse upon himself. In this ambivalent manner, the abject Jewish joker performs an act of resignation that functions at the same time as an act of self-liberation. Fuchs reviews this complex strategy of self-mockery in the following excerpt:

> But even with that, the decisive factor is not fully told yet, because Jewish self-irony, which is active in the form of the joke, almost never serves the fight against the opponents of the Jews, but much more frequently illustrates the renunciation or the abandonment of a fight. In my opinion, what reveals itself in Jewish self-irony is the resignation of one who does not want to fight. Jewish self-irony is to be regarded as the form of self-liberation through which the Jew always redeems himself anew from the oppressive pressure of social humiliation [*lastenden Druck des gesellschaftlichen Erniedrigtseins*]. In this way, the Jew gets out of the way of the fight, he disarms the opponent in that he trumps him in an ingenious and witty [*geistreicher*] manner, and, even more striking than this, he is capable of proving: "Yes, yes, you are right!" (304–306)

Taking a closer look at Fuchs's nuanced reading of Jewish self-irony, we find a sociological (and social psychological) understanding of its causes and function in modern German culture. In line with a Marxist analysis, Fuchs argues that the famous Jewish self-irony at the root of Jewish humor is not a racial trait but one that is socially and historically constructed and that depends upon the social position of the Jew as an outsider. For Fuchs, Jewish self-irony functions as the defense mechanism of an oppressed and persecuted minority. That is why he stresses the need for the Jew to redeem himself constantly from "the oppressive pressure of social humiliation."[36] Furthermore, self-irony serves as a form of self-protection for those who do not wield a club or a flail. If the Jew is perceived by the anti-Semite as a money-lending profiteer and a money-grubbing capitalist, then Jewish self-deprecation plays up and exaggerates this or whatever negative stereotype in order to make fun of himself (and of the stereotype) in a strategy designed to flip the anti-Semite's anger and hatred into laughter. This again highlights the strategy of the spin or the reversal that is endemic to all modes of comic inversion.[37]

Nevertheless, Fuchs invokes intellectualism and mobility of mind as explanatory mechanisms for Jewish joking in a way that is reminiscent of the categories of the Jewish anti-Semite Arthur Trebitsch's essentialist analysis as Fuchs touches upon the slippery constructs of "nature" and "predestination" and as he treads closer to an analysis of Jewish characteristics as either acquired through inheritance or rooted in a typology of race in this and several other passages in the book.[38] Here, Fuchs's analysis of Jewish self-irony owes much to Sombart's chapter on "Jewish Characteristics" in *The Jews in Modern Capitalism* that also stresses the stereotypes of Jewish intellectualism and the mobility of the Jewish mind specifically.[39] Fuchs comments:

> There is no finer or better form of self-protection [*Eigenschutzes*] that is known if one has no club with which to hit the opponent's skull at the appropriate time and insofar as this latter method contradicts the very nature of the oppressed in question. And both are the case for the Jews. For thousands of years now, they have had no state power in their hands, and likewise their highly cultivated intellectualism [*gezüchteten Intellektualismus*] bred over thousands of years ago does not answer the robust argument with the flail. Added to this was the agility and mobility [*Beweglichkeit*] of their minds that literally predestined them to be virtuoso players with words and ideas. (307)

In continuing with his argument of Jewish self-irony as a mode of "self-protection," Fuchs includes mimicry as a particularly Jewish mode of adaptation: "In these circumstances, there had to develop formally among the Jews the ability and the desire for self-ironization [*Selbstironisierung*] during the many centuries of their constant humiliation as a specifically Jewish intellectual characteristic [*jüdischen Geisteseigenschaft*]—like the mimicry of a particularly weak animal surrounded by a great many enemies" (306). Fuchs draws upon evolutionary biology to situate Jewish self-irony in connection with that type of self-protection found in nature undertaken by a particularly weak and defenseless animal against its predators. In this way, Fuchs plays at pop biologist in order to situate Jewish self-irony as a mode of self-defense or the protective mimicry that takes place when organisms are able to avoid encounters that would be harmful to them by tricking or deceiving their enemies into treating them as something else. To apply this sophisticated strategy of evolutionary biology to Jewish humor, the Jews are able to avoid encounters that would be harmful to them through their use of Jewish self-irony that mimes the rhetoric of the anti-Semites at the same time that it convinces these enemies to treat them as harmless, ridiculous, and laughable. Unfortunately, the negative stereotype of the Jew as a deceiver and trickster as deployed in anti-Semitic rhetoric makes use of this same strategy as well. In this context, Jay Geller reminds us that anti-Semites used the metaphor of mimicry and adaptation as a means of disparaging assimilating Jews and that this rhetorical figure was rampant by the beginning of the Weimar Republic: "By the 1920s, mimicry became the hallmark of the Jewish menace to German identity."[40] Such mimicry also helps to explain the Jewish proclivity for acting (and overacting) that Fuchs speaks about in another passage. In invoking the figure of the Jew as a mimic and actor, Fuchs joins the popular Weimar discourse on the performance of identity.[41] Fuchs foregrounds "self-mockery" as a Jewish rite of passing in the "theater of social comportment" (to use Steven Aschheim's phrase) but one whose mimicry highlights not so much "the self-protective need to blend in" but rather the rendering of his difference as both enjoyable and harmless.[42] All in all, Fuchs's adoption of mimicry and adaptation in the context of Jewish self-irony is not so innocent and it recalls a passage from Werner Sombart's chapter "Jewish Characteristics" in *The Jews in Modern Capitalism* that is rife with stereotypical anti-Semitic overtones about Jewish masquerade and dissimulation that can be traced from ancient Jews who "play dead" to postmodern ones such as Woody Allen's comic character Zelig who functions as a human chameleon. "How mobile the Jew can be is positively astounding. He is able to give himself the personal appearance he most desires. As in days of old he was able to defend himself through simulating death, so now by color adaptation or other forms of mimicry."[43]

After this ambivalent analysis of mimicry, Fuchs engages in one more flip that ironically follows the structure of a Jewish joke and that turns Jewish self-irony from a "proof of weakness" into a sign of strength for the Jews. While Fuchs does not go so far as to invoke the stereotype of the "chosen people" that inhabits the rhetoric of Treitschke, he does speak of the Jews as having a sense of "justified self-esteem": "But a further aspect has to be mentioned here. Even though self-irony expresses the resignation of active struggle very frequently, it is not necessarily a proof of weakness, but very often its opposite. The ability and the desire to make jokes about oneself, to reveal one's own weaknesses to the world with one's own mouth, are just as much an outpouring of a well-founded sense of self and justified self-esteem [*Ausfluß von begründetem Selbstgefühl*]" (306).

In all these considerations of Jewish self-irony, Fuchs never situates this characteristic as a potential problem. Like the subversion of hierarchies in a Jewish joke, the jocular revealing of one's weaknesses before the world is converted into an assertion of self-esteem and thereby taken to be a Jewish strength for Fuchs. There is no concern that such self-directed humor leaves itself open to the charge of further anti-Semitic criticism nor that it internalizes anti-Semitic stereotypes. Even when Fuchs's discussion of mimicry involves taking on anti-Semitic abuse, this serves as a means for Jewish self-protection rather than as a potential means for harm in any way. Fuchs's naively positive spin on all of these points goes as far as to proclaim that "all intellectually active" Jews derive pleasure even from the anti-Semitic jokes that are made about them as long as these are "good" ones (whatever that means).[44] In the following excerpt, Fuchs raises the specter of anti-Semitism only to conclude by praising Jewish self-irony's transformative power to convert weakness into an assertion of self-confidence: "Furthermore, the general approval that even directly anti-Semitic jokes find — if they are good — in all intellectually active Jews — and which is not explained by the saying: 'the Jews are naturally the best experts, they know their errors better than all others' — is also not a sign of weakness, but something much more about an unshakeable self-confidence and self-importance [*Selbstbewußtsein*]" (307).[45]

Even if Fuchs's estimate of "unshakeable self-confidence" was accurate here (and there is much evidence to the contrary starting with the infamous case of the Brothers Herrnfeld in 1908),[46] this situation would change drastically in the next few years with the 1925 campaign undertaken by Alfred Wiener, Ludwig Holländer, and the Centralverein and their stern objections to the rise of anti-Semitic jokes (whatever the source) in Berlin cabarets and joke books that will be the subject of chapter 3. Clearly, these "intellectually active Jews" did not share Fuchs's positive opinion of the "general approval" to be accorded to "directly anti-Semitic jokes."

## The Rothschild Joke: From Jewish Word Play to a Critique of Capitalism

In an odd lapse of bibliographical exactitude, Fuchs includes an unmarked citation in "Jewish Self-Irony" in the context of a section that argues for the pun and wordplay as central to Jewish wit and that elaborates further upon the idea of the Jews as "virtuoso players with words and ideas" (307). Fuchs writes, "From this, it is the case that the Jewish joke moves primarily in puns; 'he literally plays with words, as a skillful acrobat plays with knives and swords, so that one marvels, admires, and cheers him on'" (306). The original source of this punning judgment is the late nineteenth-century Austrian rabbi and scholar Adolf Jellinek. Rabbi Jellinek devoted a chapter to the Jewish joke in his *Der jüdische stamm in nichtjüdischen sprichwoertern* (The Jewish tribe in non-Jewish proverbs, 1881).[47] Seen in context, the passage provides us with a better understanding of Jellinek's views about why the pun must be viewed as the major modality of the Jewish joke: "Above all, the Jew wants to show his intellectual superiority, gain approval [*Beifall*], appreciation, and admiration, and he does not set out to hurt someone deeply with the weapon of the joke. How the audience will judge him and his wit [*Esprit*] is the main purpose for him; it is not the wound that he inflicts upon the object of his joke. So it is that the Jewish joke moves in puns for the most part."[48] Thus, Jellinek stresses the Jew's desire to avoid conflict with his witticisms and how this tendency toward conflict avoidance privileges puns and wordplay over aggressive and tendentious jokes.

Immediately after reciting this mysterious quotation, Fuchs provides an example of a Jewish joke that relies on wordplay. This turns out to be a Rothschild joke of which there are hundreds in the annals of Jewish joke-lore. Fuchs recounts a magnificent spoonerism that relies upon the deliberate wordplay of a morphological switch in order to make its witty mark (and remark): "To quote just one such pun [*Wortwitz*], I refer to the following: 'What is the difference between Napoleon I and Amsel Rothschild? Napoleon had a life rich in activity [*ein tatenreiches Leben*] behind him, and Rothschild had a rich dear father [*reiches Tatteleben*]'" (307). Fuchs then goes on to comment: "This joke is certainly harmless in its irony, but its solution is overwhelming such that we admire to a certain extent the author who wants to achieve self-irony" (307).

Fuchs claimed that he chose this particular joke only to demonstrate the prevalent use of wordplay in the Jewish joke. But even as he offers this reason, it is obvious that Fuchs could have chosen any number of other Jewish jokes to demonstrate the presence of wordplay in Jewish humor. For example, there are a number of such jokes in Jellinek that he could have recounted whereas the Rothschild joke is not included there.[49] However, the fact that this quite recent Communist Party member under the sway of both Marx and Sombart chose this particular joke is not an accident in terms of its content (regardless of any formal considerations) and this is due to the fact that this class-conscious witticism takes the Rothschilds as the tendentious object of its ridicule thereby satirizing them as the face and the symbol of Jewish finance capital. Indeed, the Jew as capitalist insider is embodied in the figure of the Rothschild banking family in light of their alleged dominance over European financial markets.

How does Marxist rhetoric creep into Fuchs's argument as he adapts the ideas of the half-Jewish economic anti-Semite Karl Marx on the Jewish question? Even if mediated by more contemporary sources (e.g., Werner Sombart, August Bebel, and Franz Mehring[50]), *Die Juden in der Karikatur* is grounded in Marx's essay "Zur Judenfrage" (On the Jewish Question, 1844). In this unflattering essay that is riddled with the anti-Semitic tropes of its day, Marx equates modern Judaism with the worship of the secularized deity of money. To recall Marx: "What is the secular cult of the Jew? Huckstering. What is his secular god? Money."[51] Thus, Marx interprets capitalism as a secular form of Judaism. In response to this situation, Marx argues for a socialist state that supports "not the social emancipation of the Jews but the emancipation of society from Judaism"[52] and therefore its emancipation from capitalism. In this manner, the Marxist and anti-Semitic views of the world begin to intersect.

But we also need to remember the importance of Fuchs's reliance on Werner Sombart in forging a version of economic anti-Semitism. One of the cornerstones of Sombart's argument regarding the Jewish contribution to capitalism involves the innovation of moneylending and the taking of interest since such usurious activity was prohibited to Christians. According to Sombart, "The money-lending activities of the Jews were thus an objective factor in enabling the Jews to create, to expand, and to assist the capitalist spirit."[53] In paraphrasing Sombart's hypothesis, Fuchs incorporates this stereotype into his analysis as well: "This sense has made the Jews locate the most rewarding side of the financial economy — moneylending. . . . Capitalism is born out of money-lending" (30).

For Fuchs, the Rothschild caricatures that he reproduces in his books possess a core of truth that sounds strangely anti-Semitic in character: "Among the most important and sometimes even the best caricatures of this period belong those that are directed against the financial coffers of Amsel Rothschild who ruled all Europe at the time. . . . [They] strike the core of the problem [Kern des Problems] in a most descriptive way and reveal a truly grand style" (227–228). What is the core of the problem to which Fuchs refers here? It is the Marxist equation of the Jew with unethical capitalist exploitation and the revolutionary ideal that the capitalist mode of production as well as the society and the religion that promotes such inequalities must be surpassed. Fuchs pinpoints his critique: "For the characteristic of the total power of money, its unlimited domination of the world, and its unscrupulous greed. . . . Rothschild still remains the prototype" (233). From Marx to Fuchs, the condemnation of capitalism is colored by an undertone of anti-Semitic rhetoric such that the visual anti-Semitism rampant in Die Juden in der Karikatur insinuates itself into Fuchs's textual commentary as well.

With this conceptual background in place, we can situate the "wordplay" joke in the context of the anti-Semitic caricatures devoted to the Rothschilds in Jews in Caricature. For instance, Fuchs was drawn to the infamous caricature of 1845 entitled Die Generalpumpe (The general pump) which depicts Mayer Amschel Rothschild as an international financial backer in the mechanical form of a money pump that makes the world go around.[54] As the arm

Figure 5. Julius Bohmer and H. Delius, *Die Generalpumpe* (ca. 1845). Lithograph with watercolor depicting German banker Mayer Rothschild as a water pump dispensing money to various German rulers from a large bag of gold at his feet. Reprinted in Fuchs, *Die Juden in der Karikatur*, 120.

cranks are turned, the money flows into circulation through this Rothschild banking network (fig. 5). In volume 2 of the *History of European Caricature*, Fuchs discusses this particular image and demonstrates how he accepts the terms of Rothschild's financial power before its subjection to caricature. This description supplies an inversion of the Jew as an underprivileged outsider as Fuchs recounts Rothschild's rags-to-riches story. The Rothschild family rises from the "dirtiest Jewish alleys" (in a phrase that resonates with the racial slur of the "dirty Jew") to the financial control of what is often disparaged as dirty lucre: "This is the broadsheet with which the most powerful of the powerful on earth, the absolute Count in the realm of finance, Rothschild, has been awarded his best monument in the realm of caricature. He is a 'general pump' to whom all are subject. He is the chief of the great financial dynasty that came out of the dirtiest Jewish alleys of the world. However, the cash flows now descend to both the just and the unjust alike so long as this only yields profits (*sofern es nur profitablen Gewinn einträgt*)."[55] Fuchs expresses this last thought in the most exaggerated form possible in the original German as he overemphasizes the taking of profits as a noun (*Gewinn*, profit), as an adjective (*profitablen*), and as a verb (*eintragen*, to profit).

OF CARICATURES, JOKES, AND ANTI-SEMITISM 79

The figure of the globe as visual embodiment of Rothschild's power returns again half-a-century later in Charles Lucien Léandre's color caricature *Le Roi Rothschild* that served as the cover illustration for *Le Rire* on April 16, 1898 (fig. 6). In this cartoon, the old Baron has the whole world in his hands or rather his vampiric tentacles (208–209). With his golden crown topped by a laughing golden pig and a golden halo, the long-beaked Rothschild is depicted as the Jewish Pope of the secular god of money. The ironic Latin

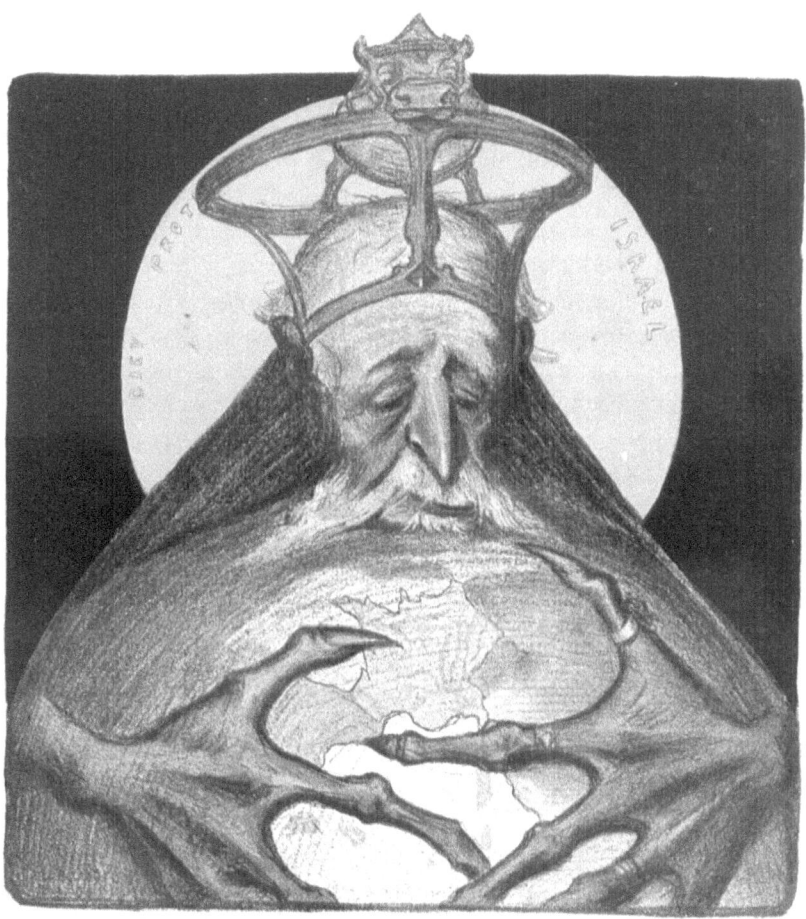

Figure 6. Charles Lucien Léandre, *Le Roi Rothschild* (King Rothschild) on the cover of the French humor magazine, *Le Rire* (April 16, 1898). Reprinted in Fuchs, *Die Juden in der Karikatur*, 208.

caption might be translated as "Israel's Protecting God." The motifs expressed in this illustration became a recurrent trope in anti-Semitic caricature.[56] Moving along this anti-Semitic path, one wonders how far it is from accepting the negative Jewish figurations depicted in these Rothschild caricatures to the infamous anti-Semitic Protocols of the Elders of Zion positing an international Zionist monetary conspiracy aiming at world domination and whose book cover utilized the same style of caricature when published as *Le Peril Juif* in France at the time that Fuchs was in exile in Paris during the Third Reich.[57]

Another Rothschild illustration from the nineteenth century (and the era of the young Marx) is entitled "How Amschel Rothschild travels through the world—harnessed up to vulturous bankruptcy" (fig. 7). Fuchs's analysis of this caricature locates the problem of capitalist exploitation as both a moral failing and a loss of feeling on Rothschild's part: "The lack of compassion with which capital (as embodied in Rothschild) exacts its demands throughout the world is so clearly written on the face of the old Rothschild in this caricature that the dullest glance must recognize it" (228). In taking the moral high ground, Fuchs's analysis overlooks the intense racism implicit in this particular caricature and its dehumanization of Rothschild into a monkey man in line with the linkage made between Jews and blacks as inferior races in the popular scientific thought of nineteenth-century Germany.[58] The insider capitalist is now transformed into a dehumanized outsider given the inversion and subversion of hierarchies found in the exaggerated realm of caricature. The failure to acknowledge the racial dimension of this particular caricature is not an isolated incident in Fuchs given the ideological biases of his neo-Marxist class analysis and I will return to this glaring blind spot in a later section of this chapter.

### The Metajoke: How Jews Laugh

Fuchs also proceeds to tell a rather truncated version of one of the most renowned jokes in the canon of Eastern European Jewish wit. Entitled "How They Laugh," it is a joke that revels in self-mockery while making fun of non-Jews at the same time. In its full version, the joke introduces the learned Jewish folklorist Immanuel Olsvanger's Yiddish compilation *Rosinkess mit Mandlen* (Raisins and almonds) originally published in 1920 (one year before Fuchs's book) and that would be translated into the German language as *Jüdische Schwänke* some years later.[59] Three groups of non-Jews are featured in this particular joke—the peasant, the landowner, and the policeman—with the level of ridicule meted out according to a ranking system that is based on each group's relationship to the Jewish joke. But in the end, the joke turns out to be on the Jew as well. To recount Olsvanger's version:

Figure 7. Anonymous, "How Amschel Rothschild travels through the world—harnessed up to vulturous bankruptcy" (Frankfurt, ca. 1845). Reprinted in Fuchs, *Die Juden in der Karikatur*, 112.

When you tell a joke to a peasant, he laughs three times, once when you tell it to him, the second time when you explain it to him, and the third time when he understands it.

The landowner laughs twice. Once when you tell it to him and again when you explain it, because he never understands it.

The policeman laughs only once when you tell it to him, because he doesn't let you explain it, so he never understands it.

When you tell a Jew a joke, he says, "I've heard it before. And I can tell it better."

Paradoxically, the self-mocking punch line of "How They Laugh" turns out to be directed against the Jew (as the joke know-it-all or *Besserwisser*) who does not laugh, but who tells a better version of the same joke. In addition, the fact that the Jew interrupts the joke teller instead of politely waiting till the end of the joke highlights and pokes fun at another Jewish stereotype of bad social comportment. Ruth Wisse's analysis of the joke (in *No Joke*) also focuses on the self-ironic punch line wherein the Jew does not laugh: "If the Jew fails to laugh, it is not, God forbid, because he missed the point of the joke but because he has exhausted the fund of laughter."[60]

Fuchs's reference to this "very witty" Jewish joke comes more in the form of a proverb that misses certain nuances that one finds in the full-fledged version in Olsvanger. Fuchs discusses this joke in a passage about the Jew's ability not only to get the joke but also to enjoy self-deprecating Jewish humor. This leads to the question of what constitutes a good Jewish joke. The answer is Fuchs's encapsulation of the "How They Laugh" joke in the form of a wise saying:

> It is an indelible consequence that Jewish self-irony is supplemented by a general understanding of Jewish jokes on the Jewish side. Not only does a good joke at the expense of the Jews often have a Jew as its author, but in fact it also does not have a more grateful public than the Jews themselves. A nice saying about what is a good Jewish joke expresses this very wittily: "The mark of a good Jewish joke is that every Jew already knows it and a *goy* does not understand [*Das Kennzeichen eines guten jüdischen Witzes ist, daß ihn jeder Jude bereits kennt und ein Goj nicht versteht*]". (307)

It is probable that Fuchs derived his version from Alexander Moszkowski who once composed this short and witty verse to dramatize the difference in reactions to the Jewish joke: "A Jewish joke with a Jewish accent: What a Goy does not understand and what a Jewish always already knows."[61] Following Moszkowski, the subtle differentiation of the three types of non-Jewish recipients is reduced to the blanket and generic Gentile (*goy*) who does not understand the joke in contrast to the Olsvanger version where at least the non-Jewish peasant is said to have the ability to understand the Jewish joke.[62] Fuchs's truncated version of this classic joke reinforces a Jewish sense of intellectual superiority when it comes to the world of *Witz* (and in general) given that his generic *goy* (or Olsvanger's three individual types) need to have the joke explained to them. In this particular case, the Jews' sense of self-satisfaction (with the Jewish joke and with their wittiness) coexists with the joke's self-mockery and this coexistence affirms Fuchs's analysis of Jewish self-mockery as bolstering a "justified self-esteem" as discussed earlier. Fuchs's maxim is placed in quotation marks and therefore derived from a Jewish narrator (presumably Moszkowski) who refers to the non-Jew by the Yiddish/Hebrew name of *Goj* (*goy*). One notices that Fuchs maintains this foreign word and its Yiddish usage in offering the direct confrontation between the Jew and the non-Jew. While this term is often controversial in its contemporary English usage, the same pejorative charge in German usage did not exist during Fuchs' time.[63] While the word itself may have had more neutrality in those days, Fuchs's appropriation of the maxim certainly insults the non-Jew who is presumably not smart enough to get the Jewish joke. How might this gesture be explained? Is this a playful "German" self-ironic gesture on Fuchs's part? Or did Fuchs think of himself as somehow more Jewish given the biographical fact that he had married a Jewish woman (Grete Alsberg) the previous year and therefore that he was now in more of a position to understand Jewish jokes or even given the license to use a term such as *goy* because of his recently adopted "insider" position? Even though these joke speculations are difficult to assess, Fuchs's use of this nomenclature in the context of telling a famous Jewish joke only adds to the overall ambiguity of his own subject position in navigating the slippery terrain of Jewish self-irony.

## Comic Unmasking in an "Honorable" Jewish Joke

As he rounds out his chapter on "Jewish Self-Irony," Fuchs praises the genre of the Jewish joke book and he singles out two Berlin editors in particular who are deserving of praise for their rich compilations—Alexander Moszkowski and M. Nuél: "The finest and richest in Jewish self-irony, however, can be found in the countless Jewish jokes of which Alexander Moszkowski has compiled a number of the very best. The book of Jewish jokes edited by M. Nuél contains many more" (309).[64] He then focuses on one more Jewish joke classic to serve as a case study. This selection is found in the popular compilation of the German-Jewish newspaper writer Manuel Schnitzer who published *Das Buch des jüdischen Witze* (*The book of Jewish jokes*) in 1907 under the peculiar pseudonym of M. Nuél.[65] This witticism belongs to the genre of "baptism jokes" that makes fun of converted Jews and whose punch lines generate comic slippage as these newly found Christians lapse into their former (and "hidden") language (Yiddish) or religion (Jewish ritual practices). This practice of comic unmasking is what Fuchs (citing Nuél) refers to as "the abrupt and droll revelation of the Jewish soul" that has been concealed underneath the trappings of Christianity and that offers the return of the (Yiddish) comic repressed in an explosion of laughter. In this particular story, we find two former Jewish families who have assimilated into the upper echelons of German Christian society and who are about to arrange a marriage for their children. From a psychoanalytical perspective, the attraction of this particular joke for Fuchs could have something to do with the already mentioned recent development in his own biography. For the German "with the Jewish-sounding name" married a Jewish woman in 1920 when he turned fifty years old.[66] In light of this recent matrimonial fact, the matter of religious conversion was certainly on his mind. Fuchs relates the joke in the following manner:

> From this collection, I cite one that clearly illuminates that the self-ironic Jewish joke consists not only in puns, in wordplay, but that its potent effects are primarily based on the abrupt and droll revelation of the Jewish soul, as Nuél says very correctly in his preface: "The son of a famous German jurist, who — although a baptized Jew — held the highest judicial positions and who had been raised to the peerage, became engaged to the daughter of a banker, who likewise came from a famous Jewish family albeit in another area of endeavor. He, too, the papa of the young bride, had been born Christian, for his father had already been baptized. The bride's mother is especially happy about the event, and says to the bride-groom: 'You know, I have always wished for a son-in-law exactly like you. . . .'" "And how should that be?' he says with a smile. 'You know . . . just a nice Christian young man from a *bekoweten* [honorable] Jewish family.'" (309)

Fuchs clearly found an ally in Schnitzer who shared his own views about the self-ironic function of Jewish wit and it is assumed that Fuchs also appreciated his Germanic mode of presentation of Jewish jokes in that they are jargon-free (in contrast to the 1830s anti-Semitic books that satirized the Jews). Regarding the first point, the preface includes the following excerpt as Schnitzer frames the Jewish joke in relationship with Jewish self-irony and in terms of a mocking of one's own weaknesses: "[The] Jewish joke reveals the Jewish character, the weaknesses of which are the object of its mockery. But one must not forget that it is always the Jews themselves who chastise their vanities."[67]

Sander Gilman has written on Schnitzer's "folkloric collection" and he also analyzes this particular baptism joke. Gilman understands Schnitzer's manner of telling the above joke as typical of his style to universalize the discourse of the Jewish joke and to present it in fully acceptable German:

> This joke is typical of the entire volume. It presupposes absolutely
> nothing on the part of its audience; indeed, it creates the assumption
> that the audience would perceive Yiddishisms (even terms such as *goy*
> [non-Jew] or *gannef* [thief] which had established themselves in German slang long before the turn of the century) as totally unintelligible.
> Schnitzer rejects any particularism in the discourse of the Jews....
> Schnitzer's ideal reader is one who is an exclusively German-speaking
> Jew, one who speaks German but does not have a Yiddish accent
> [*mauscheln*] and does not use Yiddishisms.[68]

In this case, what subverts this ideal and what makes the joke funny however is the very intrusion and slippage of the Yiddish particularity (the use of the word *bekoweten*) that ruins the purely Germanic and Christian posturing. The proud "Jewish" mother is unmasked when she cannot repress her *nachas* — or joy — that she derives from her daughter's honorable marriage.

Sigmund Freud also relished Jewish jokes utilizing the technique of "comic unmasking" where the assimilated Jew blurts out something in Yiddish at the decisive moment at the point when that person's defenses are down. This is reminiscent of the joke told in his *Witz* book about the pregnant baroness who is only really ready to go into labor when she slips into Yiddish in order to express her pain: "A doctor and the baron are playing cards while waiting for the baroness to go into labor. They hear her say in French, "*Ah, mon Dieu, que je souffre!*" Her husband jumps up, but the doctor says it is not time yet, so they go on playing. Later they hear the woman cry out in German, "*Mein Gott, mein Gott, was fur Schmerzen!*" Again, the husband expects the doctor to check on his patient, but the doctor says that it still is not time. At last they hear the woman cry, "*Ai, waih, waih geshrien!*" The doctor throws down his cards and says, "It is time."[69] Freud comments on the content of this joke in terms of how "pain causes original nature to break through all the layers of education."[70] But one should also focus on form and content in this particular case. In other words, it is the "best medicine" of the Jewish joke that allows the original Yiddish word or expression to break through the acculturation process and thereby transmute Jewish pain and suffering into laughter. This is often the lesson and moral to be learned from self-ironic Jewish jokes. Fuchs also understood and appreciated deeply this capacity to transform suffering into laughter. After all, he also wrote these most empathetic and poignant lines in the introduction to *Die Juden in der Karikatur* that identifies (with) the roots of Jewish wit in terms of pain and suffering. Here, we overhear one of Fuchs's expressions that is distinctly philo-Semitic in sentiment: "One should always listen to the ringing of the fool's bells, but, alongside that, the serious sonorous bass tone; the agony of the other, those who are attacked . . . this sound always must be heard" (3).[71]

## The Specter of Adolf Hitler and National Socialism

There is a specter haunting Fuchs's chapter on "Jewish Self-Irony" and its name is National Socialism. This reworking of the famous Marxist adage of *The Communist Manifesto* alludes to a common theme that adheres to many of the case studies in this book. In this particular case, the haunting of Jewish self-irony by the specter of anti-Semitism is both figurative and literal and it produces a tragic and bitter irony when cast in the light of future history. This is on account of the visual framing of this last chapter of *Die Juden in der Karikatur* with the "Anti-Semitic Campaign Poster for the Reichstag Election" published and circulated in 1920 (fig. 8). But this brand of anti-Semitism is not of the old-fashioned religious kind. Instead, this caricature is a nasty piece of racist propaganda perpetrated by none other than Adolf Hitler in the very same year of the founding of the National Socialist Party. The frustrated painter turned aspiring political actor combined his major interests given the fact that he was the graphic artist of this anti-Semitic political poster as he autographs the picture by signing his name in the abbreviated form of A.H. It is a chilling juxtaposition in historical hindsight that achieves the blackest of humors when the unwitting Fuchs positions it above the inscription: "XI. Die jüdische Selbstironie."[72]

The theme of haunting continues as revealed in the stereotypical substance of Hitler's anti-Semitic caricature in which a grotesque profile of a hook-nosed, thick-lipped, and swarthy Jewish man shadows the profile of a young and attractive Aryan maiden. Both look to our left as they are framed in a red circular orb while the signature of the artist is placed at the lower right side of the circle. Two swastikas (one on each side) adorn the top of the frame and the word *Deutschland* is inscribed across the bottom of the poster. Meanwhile, there is a cryptic object in the shape of a rectangular box that looks to be an open-lidded and empty coffin placed between the caricature and the word *Deutschland* and it sits there as an ominous and symbolic placeholder in its suggestion of where the Jews belong in the National Socialist vision. The obvious fear that Hitler plays upon in this image is miscegenation and the erotic phantasm that it conjures in imagining that the lecherous old Jew will violate and harm this young German maiden in an act of racial defilement (*Rassenschande*).

It is fascinating to examine how our cultural historian situates the Führer's foray into the art of caricature to generate politics by other means. Unknowingly, Fuchs reads Hitler as a gifted political satirist who uses this visual

Figure 8. Adolf Hitler, anti-Semitic campaign poster for the Reichstag election (1920). Reprinted in Fuchs, *Die Juden in der Karikatur*, 303.

medium to make fun of the Jews. In other words, Hitler shows himself here to be someone who knows how to use Jewish self-irony against itself. Fuchs's interpretation occurs earlier in the book in the section on "The Anti-Semitic Poster" (273–276) that is somewhat removed from the placement of the image on page 303. In the face of Hitler's overt racist positing and posturing in this anti-Semitic caricature, Fuchs sidesteps a direct condemnation of Nazi racism.[73] While commenting on how these anti-Semitic posters possess a satirical focus and while acknowledging the extreme effectiveness of such posters,

Fuchs's misdirected analysis focuses instead on the lack of an impression that he believes this type of caricature will make on "sophisticated and discerning minds":

> In the elections for the German National Assembly in 1919 and in the elections in Austria in 1920, the walls were covered in part with these extremely effective anti-Semitic campaign posters in all cities in Germany and Austria in which the satirical character was quite in the foreground. I provide here a few characteristic examples and refer in particular to the swastika poster that bears as its text the sole word "Deutschland." This rather ridiculous-looking maiden with her gaze fixed on the world who is supposed to embody Germanic Deutschland in this poster is no more likely to impress sophisticated and discerning minds [*anspruchsvolleren Gemütern*] than the repulsively ugly and grotesque Jewish caricature [*häßliche Judenfratze*] standing next to her. (274)

By remaining within the bounds of reason, Fuchs gives the public too much credit in terms of its powers of sophistication and discernment when viewing this caricature composed by the future Führer. From this perspective, it did not matter that the German maiden looked "rather ridiculous." What mattered much more was what the juxtaposition of the German maiden and the old Jewish man symbolized (and triggered) in the German psyche. In other words, Fuchs undervalued the affective power and the mass appeal of the Nazi leader's satirically charged propaganda and its scapegoating tactic as it played upon German emotional fears (and nightmares) of the grotesque Jew as a sexual predator and as spectral presence.

In light of Hitler's satirical election poster, it is interesting to take a look at the reception history of *Die Juden in der Karikatur* during the Nazi era. For instance, Siegfried Kadner as the author of *Rasse und Humor* (Race and humor) did not think that there was any trace of anti-Semitism or ambivalence about the Jewish question in Fuchs's text. However, he believed that the pictures told a very different story. According to this simplistic reading, there was a wide gap between Fuchs's verbal philo-Semitism and his visual anti-Semitism. Indeed, Kadner believed that Fuchs's book gave an unintentional boost to the Nazi cause and its propaganda machine because of all the grotesque anti-Semitic illustrations that confirmed what they had been saying all along. For Kadner, the inclusion of the anti-Semitic campaign poster with the two swastikas designed by Hitler would have been an obvious case in point. He writes: "In the book *Jews in Caricature* by Eduard Fuchs . . . the text (and no wonder with this author) comes off as Jew-friendly. But the illustrations work rather involuntarily as an advertisement against Judaism, even if in the end, it is proclaimed that 'The sun is rising in the East, and not only for the Jews.'"[74] Here, Kadner alludes to Fuchs's idyllic ending that envisions a universal Marxist-Leninist utopia (see the next section).

When one reads Fuchs's analysis of the Hitler campaign poster from a post-Holocaust perspective, it is very difficult to reconcile his neo-Marxist rhetoric in light of the dark history of the racial genocide that followed. In order to understand this particular blind spot in Fuchs's analysis of anti-Semitic caricature, we need to return to his Marxist ideological framework and his insistence that economic interests were at the root cause of social and political phenomena. As previously discussed, Fuchs insisted that it was class rather than race that served as the primary rationale for Jewish caricature's being in the world. In this way, Fuchs incorporated the standard model for an economic explanation of anti-Semitism as it was developed by the late nineteenth-century Social Democratic leader, August Bebel.[75] Bebel believed that anti-Semitism was the result of the social upheavals perpetrated by those subgroups who were displaced by the rise of capitalism and who were blaming the Jews as a class or as a social group for these unstable conditions.[76] These conflicts would pass away in the ideal society to come. In times of economic crisis, the Jews became the identifiable scapegoats for the transformations of anonymous capital. Following this logic, Fuchs argued that there was a rise in the number of Jewish caricatures in periods of economic and social transformations and a decline during periods of stability. The following reasoning helps us to better understand the tenor of Fuchs's interpretation of early Nazi anti-Semitic caricature and the Hitler election campaign poster: "If the Jewish question were only a question of race, then one would encounter Jewish caricatures constantly because racial difference is a constant one. However, because it is first and foremost a class question, one encounters them only from time to time, or only when the class question escalates into conflict in line with an intensification of the class struggle" (111). Here, we see the limitations of Fuchs's analysis of Jewish jokes and caricatures and its focus on class issues in the face of the ominous rise of an overt anti-Semitism on the political Right based on an inflammatory racist ideology in Germany at the very moment of his book's publication in 1921.[77]

This neo-Marxist denial of race as a paradigm for understanding the new face of anti-Semitism in the wake of World War I also comes through in the chapter on Jewish self-irony when Fuchs relates another anecdote — one that also has the structure of a Jewish joke — in order to underscore his views regarding the importance of class divisions and his opinion that they have become more important than religious (or racial) divisions in the current political landscape of the Weimar Republic. Fuchs insists that there is no longer any unity among all Jews or all Christians on any particular issue. This passage finds Fuchs spouting doctrinaire Marxist rhetoric as he splits the Jews and Christians into rich and poor in terms of their interests, feelings, and life worlds:

> Therefore, the poor Jew cannot be compared in his feelings with the rich Jew, but on the contrary with the poor Christian. And so it is with the rich Jews whose primary feelings are the same as those of the rich Christians. In other words: the poor and the rich Jew each have their own, or rather, their separate worlds of feelings. Besides that, the extensive declassing of the Jews stamps the poor Jews almost as pariahs while leaving the rich Jews completely untouched. For example, the Social Democratic police president in Berlin sends the poor Jews who are causing trouble in the Grenadierstrasse in a police wagon to a concentration camp in Zossen. Meanwhile, the Social Democratic president [Friedrich Ebert] sends his rich Jewish assistant [Walter] Rathenau from Berlin to Wiesbaden in a coach wagon in order to engage in diplomatic talks [*zur Schachermachen*] with the Christian Jew [Louis] Loucheur. (308)

This contemporary anecdote that seeks to illustrate the paramount importance of class differences refers to the German Minister of Reconstruction (and soon to be Foreign Minister) Walther Rathenau's diplomatic talks in Wiesbaden with the Christian convert Louis Loucheur who was serving as the French minister of the devastated regions that took place in the middle of June 1921.[78] Fuchs's use of the term of *zur Schachermachen* in order to describe the diplomacy and deal-making can be translated as haggling, huckstering, or bargaining and it points in a satirical manner to the repressed Jewish peddler in the constitution of these political leaders. Moreover, it inscribes the same term used by Marx in his essay "Zur Judenfrage" to denounce the secular cult of the Jews as the champions of capitalism. However, the bitter irony and sad truth of Fuchs's class analysis lies in the fact Rathenau would be assassinated on the streets of Berlin on June 24, 1922, one year after the publication of his book in a hate crime committed by members of the ultra-nationalist Organization Consul in collaboration with the violently anti-Semitic and racist German Nationalist Protection and Revenge League (Deutschvölkischer Schutz und Trutzband) considered to be a political precursor of the Nazi party. In this way, the role of race again turns out to be a serious blind spot for Fuchs's analysis given his Marxist (mis)understanding of what was at stake for all German Jews, rich or poor, confronted with racially based anti-Semitic hatred.

## Final Reflections: The Setting Sun

Fuchs discusses the question of the grotesque in his work on Chinese ceramics in the Tang Dynasty: "Decadent times and sick brains also incline toward grotesque representations. In such cases, the grotesque becomes the shocking reflection of the fact that for the times and individuals in question, the problems of existence have taken on an appearance of unsolvable complexity."[79] In the face of the Jewish question and the existence of anti-Semitism in all of its religious, racial, and nationalist (folk) varieties, Jewish jokes and caricatures (substituting here for grotesque representations) offered both profound insights and comic relief into the problems of existence that already had taken on the appearance of unsolvable complexity for Fuchs and for his German and Jewish readers in the aftermath of the German defeat in World War I. However, one wonders why Fuchs was not able to draw any negative connections between Jewish self-irony and anti-Semitism in *Die Juden in der Karikatur*. Was this just a mere oversight on his part? After all, he was not averse to criticizing the convert and Jewish renegade Johannes Pfefferkorn for his satirical anti-Semitic diatribes in the sixteenth century.[80] Was there something callous or insensitive in Fuchs not seeing this as a potential problem for his own time? Or should we rather given him the benefit of the doubt and say that it would have been out of the ordinary to draw a negative connection between Jewish self-irony and anti-Semitism circa 1920 and therefore that Fuchs should not be faulted retrospectively? After all, even the Jewish Centralverein had registered no complaint as of yet in the early years of the Weimar Republic. Or perhaps this lacuna was a symptom of his own latent anti-Semitism as a second-generation Marxist and as a follower of Sombart's ideas making Fuchs someone who, according to Micha Brumlik, was imprisoned in the negative assumptions of his time. On the other hand, there is no doubt that Fuchs thought that he was acting in a strictly philo-Semitic manner by attributing a self-confidence to the Jews (as expressed in Jewish self-irony) that was not to be shaken or toppled even by the denigrations of anti-Semitic jokes. These are difficult questions and perhaps they pose an "unsolvable complexity" for any definitive interpretation of Fuchs's thinking about Jewish jokes and caricatures and their relation to anti-Semitism at the beginning of the Weimar Republic.

Nevertheless, Benjamin's perceptive essay on Fuchs hides an answer that helps explain Fuchs's failure (or his "tragedy of good intentions"), and that answer revolves around Benjamin's striking critique of cultural history and its limits. Fuchs's essay is the site where Benjamin first put into print one of his most famous aphorisms: "There is no document of culture which is not at the same time a document of barbarism. No cultural history has yet done justice to this fundamental state of affairs, and it can hardly hope to do so."[81] Given that Fuchs saw his book, as stated in the subtitle, as a contribution to cultural history, *Die Juden in der Karikatur* would suffer from this same problem: it cannot do justice to the fundamental barbarism of the cultural documents that it presents to its readers. Here it becomes clear how Benjamin's damning dialectical critique comes to bear upon Fuchs and his naive cultural historical assumptions. Writing in the mode of cultural history, Fuchs could not fathom that his book of and on Jewish caricatures—and its chapter on Jewish self-irony in particular—was Janus-faced from the start such that each Jewish caricature and each Jewish joke serves simultaneously as a document of culture *and* a document of barbarism. The excessive and exaggerated displays of the Jews in caricature function as both a source of truth *and* as a source of debasement and distortion. In the dark light of Benjamin's dialectical critique, the flipping of Jewish self-irony into anti-Semitism would be another case study in this cultural/barbaric dialectic—the transformation of the Jewish caricature or the Jewish joke as a cultural good into its service as an evil symptom of anti-Semitic barbarism. Trapped in the accumulative and progressive logic of cultural history, Fuchs was not able to grasp Benjamin's profound (and "destructive") insight whether living at home in his beautiful villa in Berlin-Zehlendorf in 1921 or in exile in Paris in 1937 after having escaped from the Nazis.[82]

Fuchs ends the chapter on the subject of Jewish self-irony and *Die Juden in der Karikatur* in an ideologically charged manner that reveals his Marxist political biases once more as he looks to the East and to the future. Just a few years after the Bolshevik Revolution, Fuchs fantasizes the emergence of the Soviet Republic as the place for Jewish and world redemption in the messianic era of communism that he believes is imminent. There are many accounts of Marxism as a secular version of the Jewish messianic impulse and Fuchs appears to be in line with this tradition. In holding out the promise of an ideal society to be run according to Marxist principles, Fuchs rules out the return to the Zionist homeland and the American dream as promised lands for the Jews. Indeed, Fuchs reduces the United States and Palestine to the past; it is rather the emergence of the Soviet revolution that is on the side of "historical development" and looks to the future of history. Given that Fuchs joined the German Communist Party (KPD) shortly after it was founded in

Figure 9. Rachel Szalit-Marcus, "Die Fahrt nach Amerika, oder Die Amerikafahrer: Die Sonne geht im Westen auf" (ca. 1920; The Journey to America, or the America Travelers: The Sun Rises in the West). Reprinted in Fuchs, Die Juden in der Karikatur, 267.

1919, this political conviction and interest in the Bolshevik Revolution should come as no surprise.

In this context, Fuchs refers to a Jewish self-ironic caricature by the Polish-born Jewish female graphic artist Rachel Szalit-Marcus who illustrated a collection of stories by Sholem Aleichem (fig. 9). This particular illustration shows the character Motl with his family in a carriage on the road to America:[83] "'The sun of the Jews rises in the West,' it says under the sheet Die Amerikafahrer. In America, they hope to find a home and redemption from the oppressive ordeal of life — so it was yesterday. Historical development has set things right — the sun of the Jews does not rise in America, it also does not rise in Palestine. The sun rises in the East. And not only for the Jews" (310). If Jewish self-irony is the defense mechanism of a persecuted minority and a coping mechanism amid "the oppressive ordeal of life," then one wonders about its chances for survival in the utopian society to come. Would there be any need for Jewish jokes and caricatures in this ideal world without anti-Semitism? And why would there be any need for the further production (and protection) of Jewish self-irony in a world without Jews given that the secular Marxist messiah will have performed another conversion process to render them superfluous? This would be the irony to end all self-ironies. One senses that the collector and historian of caricature Fuchs would go out of business in this brave new world. With this utopian vision and Marxist-Leninist fantasy, I take leave of Eduard Fuchs's *Die Juden in der Karikatur* with the sun rising for the Jews — and for all humanity — in the East and with Jewish self-irony setting in the West.

# 3
# Of Watchmen and Comedians
*Jewish Jokes and Free Speech in Weimar Germany*

Hateful and transgressive jokes always raise the possibility of censorship, especially in politically troubled times. While the Weimar Republic is often viewed as a democratic society where free speech reigned supreme, it also enforced a number of laws for hate speech and these were applied to offenders frequently. Not surprisingly, the biggest culprits were Nazi propagandists Joseph Goebbels and Julius Streicher who were both prosecuted for anti-Semitic speech on numerous occasions. In the decade between 1923 and 1933, Streicher's newspaper *Der Stürmer* was either confiscated or tried on thirty-six different occasions and the infamous Jew-baiting editor served two prison sentences. A number of these cases involved the publication of highly offensive anti-Semitic cartoons featuring vicious satirical caricatures. But the laws governing hate speech against communities of faith in Weimar Germany could also target self-deprecating Jewish comedians. This chapter reviews a fascinating case study where self-mocking Jewish jokes told by Jewish comedians were branded as a dangerous and censurable type of speech by the leading Jewish defense organization in Germany.

## Alfred Wiener and the Centralverein at Jewish Wit's End

Alfred Wiener (1885–1964) is remembered today as one of the first and foremost Jewish cultural officials in Germany to sound the alarm regarding the rise of the National Socialist Party and the threat that it posed to Jewish life in particular and to the Weimar Republic in general. Given his high-ranking status in the Central Association of German Citizens of Jewish Faith (Centralverein deutscher Staatsbürger jüdischen Glaubens), Wiener served as the

German Jews' vigilant watchman who warned against Hitler and the Nazis starting as early as 1925. Three years later, he established an office in Berlin within the Centralverein known as Büro Wilhelmstrasse that was devoted to denouncing and documenting anti-Semitic activities and that issued anti-Nazi materials on a regular basis until it was forced to close in 1933. Founded in 1893 in Berlin to oppose the rise of anti-Semitism and to promote the civil rights of Jews as German citizens, the Centralverein was the largest and most influential Jewish community and defense organization in Germany, and it had a membership of about sixty thousand people in 1926. In 1922, it also launched the newspaper *Central-Verein Zeitung* (CVZ), which became the means by which this organization spread the news of the day, propagated its political and cultural agenda, and denounced anti-Semitic activities in print on a weekly basis.

Given this historical background, it is fascinating to turn to the article that Wiener wrote for the *CVZ* on November 13, 1925, that would serve as the opening salvo in the Centralverein's self-declared "cabaret combat campaign" against the excesses of Berlin theaters in an organized effort to censor self-ironic Jewish comedians whose gags had crossed the line into what they deemed to be self-hate speech.[1] In this piece, Wiener condemned a range of recent joking phenomena directed against the Jews including the publication of a joke book that he thought grossly misrepresented Jewish life. The title of the article points to four contemporary comic manifestations in different media where Jewish humor was making its mark in Germany — "Kabaretts, Witzbücher, heitere Wochenblätter, und die 'jüdische Witwe'" ("Cabarets, joke books, humor magazines, and the 'Jewish widow'").[2] The last title refers to the realm of stage theater with a "biblical comedy" that was written by the playwright Georg Kaiser.[3] With its "no joking around" subtitle and its professional by-line ("A serious word from Dr. Alfred Wiener"), this article attempted to set the record straight that such joking matters were not to be taken lightly.

Was it just an accident that Wiener identified the Nazis as the biggest threat to the Jews in 1925 and that he also penned an article in the *CVZ* that investigated the anti-Semitic potential of Jewish wit and the limits of self-deprecating Jewish jokes in that same year? If we regard all of these activities as part of the policing functions of the Centralverein, and if we view its raison d'être as denouncing any perceived threats to German-Jewish civil rights whether coming from inside or outside the community, then this particular conjuncture of denunciations makes perfect sense. An important part of Wiener's role was to act as the arbiter of Jewish taste and public opinion. After all, he was responsible for assessing the accuracy and appropriateness of cultural representations by or about the Jews and whether any of them had crossed the line into the realm of anti-Semitism. In this capacity, Wiener posed that age-old question of whether something was to be considered good or bad for the Jews. This question sounds like it could be part of a Jewish joke, but it signals here Wiener's prescriptive moral valuations demarcating whether a Jewish joke should or should not be censored.[4] In this particular article, Wiener criticized four examples of cultural production in the realm of comedy that he deemed to have a negative impact on Jewish life in Weimar Germany.

Nevertheless, Wiener did not begin this article lashing out against Jewish humor in general nor even attacking Jewish humor that made fun of Jews (regardless of who was the teller of such jokes). Instead, he starts things off with what appears at first glance to be a liberal openness toward Jewish jokes and even those that are critical of Jewish weaknesses: "No one can claim that the Jew in his peculiarities and weaknesses is exempt from the jokes of the day nor from the ridicule and mockery of the poet." At the outset, Wiener's analysis exhibits some permissiveness in its framing of the Jew as a comic "character [*Typ*] of our time comparable to the businessman, the Lieutenant, or the student of the humor magazines." He also suggests that the Jews should be able to take a good joke like anyone else. In this light, only cringing cowards or hypocrites (*Duckmäuser*) would complain, "if Jewish commercial agility, the cunning of the Little Moritz, or the occasional parvenu-like behavior of Herr Neureich [literally, Mr. Newly Rich]" were to serve as the subjects of Jewish jokes. With these opening lines, Wiener recalls Sander Gilman's point that the Jews had entered into German civil society in the early nineteenth century through their ability to make and take a joke about themselves.

Wiener's and the Centralverein's editorial position would change dramatically over the course of time — not only in the ensuing years but even within the space of the next few months. By the end of April 1926, an editorial attributed to the Centralverein's director and secretary general Ludwig Holländer appeared in the CVZ condemning Jewish jokes about the comic figure of Little Moritz as objectionable misrepresentations that should not be tolerated by readers. The editorial insisted: "When 'Little Moritz' turns out to be a loud-mouthed Jewish lad in school who acts unbefitting of a child and who is totally unconstrained and morally deficient; when the essence of this humor resides in having a Jewish smart aleck [*Frechling*] contradict all notions of children's moral constraint, decency, and naiveté — this is no longer humor, wit, or comedy, but rather a crude distortion of Jewish types [*rohe Verzerrung jüdischer Typen*] that exist neither in Eastern Europe nor here with us."[5] This example illustrates the shrinking level of tolerance for one genre of Jewish self-mockery within a time span of only five months.[6] Similar to Wiener's disclaimer, this particular article also begins with a feint toward comic liberality that is then brought back to rigid borders and limiting constraints. One sees how the editorial seeks to deflect the obvious charge of censor from itself given its implicit call for the policing of Jewish humor. For Holländer fears the Centralverein leadership being cast as narrow-minded moralists who constitute a new breed of comic and aesthetic Philistines. Thus, his moral invective seeks to rally the people against those corrupting and transgressing Jewish jokers who produce what he calls "pseudo-comedy" and who disfigure and distort the facts of Jewish social and cultural life. He writes: "Those who fight humor and comedy are rightfully regarded as Philistines. . . . But everything has its limits. There is a pseudo-humor and a pseudo-comedy, which, by disfiguring and distorting existing facts, must lead to the corruption of the people [*Volksverderbnis*]."[7]

But we are getting ahead of the story here and we must return first to what was troubling Dr. Wiener in November 1925 if he had no particular problem with the three types of Jewish jokes that he considered to be appropriate modes of (self-)mockery. Wiener soon leaves this more permissive path and assumes the moral high ground. His first complaint relates to the production of an unnamed cabaret skit that involves the comic representation of a morally corrupt Viennese-Jewish businessman and his family wherein the Jewish daughter is satirized as the slut of the ball who more than mingles with every suitor at the party. In his response, Wiener defends the honor of Jewish women and lashes out against this genre of smutty jokes that demeans them.[8] Wiener is incensed at how "Jewish artists and Jewish cabaret owners degrade themselves in front of a large circle of spectators as such smut and obscenities [*Schweinereien*] in Jewish trappings are passed off as characteristic of a Jewish household."[9] Wiener invokes the nonkosher animal of the pig as part of his moral invective against this particular brand of Jewish cabaret and its transgressions. Moreover, he is saddened by the uproarious response of the Jewish public to such shameless self-mockery: "And the saddest and most revolting thing is this — a public that is Jewish in part, particularly in Berlin, neighs and whinnies to such shamelessness." Demanding uprightness and respectability, Wiener condemns the animalistic response of the audience members who are now figured as donkeys and laughing hyenas. Wiener's analysis also recalls Eduard Fuchs's observation that, in the eyes of their anti-Semitic critics, the self-mocking Jewish joke allies the Jew to the shamelessness of the prostitute.[10] Wiener concludes his review with some stern words noting that this is just one of many cases where the Jewish cabaret has been slandering and corrupting the Jewish community. The watchman then issues a cease-and-desist order in the name of the Centralverein that puts every Jewish cabaret in Germany on notice: "Further examples can be lined up. We are in no way willing to let ourselves approve of such disgusting slander in the long run and we will find the ways and means to address these indignities as they deserve in tone and intensity. If this warning does not suffice, then we will press our standpoint more emphatically."[11]

Then Wiener turns his attention to the publication of a joke book that he finds to be offensive on a number of counts. Wiener's previous openness to Jewish "jokelore" fades as he reviews the recent publication of *Lacht Euch Laune!: 1000 Witze* (Laugh yourself happy!: 1000 jokes) edited by Ernst Warlitz.[12] Now his anti-Semitic antennae are at the ready as he listens for any type of hateful transmission in this immensely popular joke book:

> *Lacht Euch Laune!* is a book of one thousand jokes edited by Ernst Warlitz whose printing is already in the twentieth thousand. Whether Mr. Warlitz is a Jew or a Christian is unknown. Whether he larded his so-called joke book with a number of Jewish jokes (which are none at all) out of base or malicious intent remains a moot point. But which German or Eastern European Jew speaks sentences like: "Press yourself on my heart and tell me what you feel!" [*Drück'n Se mers af mei Herz un sogn Se mer, was Se spüren!*"] Such "cultured types" draw from masters of the caliber of the Nationalists [Artur] Dinter and [Richard] Kunze. . . . Far worse: What common actions and shameful dispositions are foisted upon the Jews in most of these jokes. He betrays his fatherland for a few pieces of money. He deceives his friends. His wife is the mistress of immorality. His religion is for him an object for haggling.[13]

It is interesting to note that Wiener remains indifferent here to the question of authorial intentions. He believes that it is quite irrelevant in this case whether the compiler is a Christian anti-Semite, a self-hating Jew, or neither one. As it turns out, the Leipzig-based comedian Ernst Warlitz was actually a homosexual and therefore he possessed an outsider sensibility of another type and one that soon would be subject to Nazi persecution as well with the demise of the Weimar Republic.[14] Similarly, Wiener also claims that he does not care about whether these "so-called" Jewish jokes came from "base or malicious intentions" or not. Of course, this polite expression functions as a code word for anti-Semitic hatred. But whatever the cause, the negative effects of such a book must be countered by him. Wiener assesses that there is a problem both in terms of its form (the stereotypical use of Jewish jargon) and content (attributing immoral and indecent actions to Jewish characters). It is especially noteworthy that Wiener aligns these Jewish comic characters to the stereotypical misrepresentations of the German nationalist leaders and avowed anti-Semites, Artur Dinter and Richard Kunze. Refusing to lower himself by reciting any specific examples, Wiener lashes out against these joke distortions that cast the Jews as disloyal and deceitful traitors and that reinforce in this way the anti-Semitic and nationalist stereotype of the Jewish "stab in the back" that had been perpetrated against Germany at the conclusion of World War I.[15]

If we examine one particular joke in Warlitz's edited volume that takes up the subject of anti-Semitism, then we can begin to see how and why Wiener did not approve of this volume. "Cohn buys a parrot. The last owner has taught him the word 'Jew.' As Cohn comes home with the parrot, he curses him immediately: 'Jew!' Then Cohn says to it: 'Now, with a nose like yours, is it necessary for you to be an anti-Semite?'"[16] This ambiguous joke cuts a number of ways. For one, it is a self-mocking Jewish joke wherein Cohn makes fun of his own people by invoking and reinforcing the anti-Semitic caricature and distorted image of the big-nosed Jew. But the joke also makes fun of the parroting of the anti-Semites who repeat their hate speech against the Jews without thinking. Then again, it is possible to read this big-nosed parrot as a self-hating Jew in disguise in what would constitute a type of Aesop's fable. However, the ability to pick up on such comic ambivalence and subtlety remained outside of the range of the watchman and his appointed task to defend the Jews against anti-Semitic curses no matter what the source — even if the exclamatory utterance of *"Jude!"* was derived from a jocular parrot. All in all, the subject of anti-Semitism was never to be taken lightly by the Centralverein.

For Wiener, the joke book at hand was part of the politics of Jewish misrepresentation. Wiener's critical assessment cries out distortion and disgrace and it is filled with moral condemnation as well as the fear that Warlitz's book will foment prejudice in the "unprejudiced reader." If not calling for an outright ban, Wiener is adamant that no decent or self-respecting person (Jew or otherwise) should buy this joke book: "We strictly refuse that we are represented in this way by people who do not think even in the slightest about gaining a true picture of Judaism. Certainly, the book contains this or that joke about us, which one can acknowledge with a smile, but what is put before the unprejudiced reader in general is a disgrace, and every Jew and every decent man should never buy such a book." Here the zealous Wiener represses the obvious fact that the Jewish joke constitutes at times an iconoclastic zone of transgressions and indiscretions whose comic effects rely on some degree of indecency and on the loss of (self-)respect. He also never acknowledges that many of the same jokes in this volume are to be found in other Jewish joke compilations edited by Jews.[17] Instead, Wiener stakes out the watchman's position that there are strict limits as to what can be tolerated when it comes to Jewish joking in each of these four case studies. One cannot tolerate the "hate speech" of anti-Semites and Nazis and one cannot tolerate "self-hate speech" if the source turns out to be Jewish cabaret comedians or Jewish joke books. That Wiener made these claims and invoked the ban of censorship at the height of the Weimar Republic in November 1925 rather than at some time after 1931 is quite telling regarding both his views of the fragility of the supposed democratic institutions around him and of the subversive power of a certain type of noxious and distorting Jewish joke that he felt had to be condemned.

However, it appears that Wiener's warnings were not heeded in the months ahead and that is why the Centralverein organized two protest meetings in Berlin against the Jewish cabaret comics the following spring. In an article published in the CVZ, it was reported that seven hundred supporters gathered in the auditorium of the Fürstin Bismarck School in Charlottenburg on April 22, 1926, in order to protest against *"das mauschelnde Kabarett"* (the Jewish-accented and mumbling cabaret). The article also reported that an additional three hundred people were denied entrance to this rally. Later that same day, another assembly of five hundred people met in the eastern part of the metropolis at the Union Hall on the Greifswalder Strasse. At the end of these meetings, both assemblies passed the following stern resolution:

> On April 22, 1926, the many hundreds of assembled members and friends of the Central Association of German Citizens of Jewish Faith lodge a protest against the gross mockery [*grobe Verhöhnung*] and mindless distortion [*geistlose Verzerrung*] of Jewish character and Jewish institutions in a large number of theaters and cabarets of Greater Berlin. No Jew who retains his honor and decency should support such sham art [*Scheinkunst*]. The assembly calls on the Central Association to carry out the fight against these excesses in cabaret and theater by any means at its disposal. The Central Association is assured of the assistance of all right-minded individuals without distinction of class and religion.[18]

Holländer insists upon a moral standard that aligns Jewish self-mockery with indecency and dishonor and that frames its comedic practice as a pseudo-art (*Scheinart*). Although Wiener did not speak at either of these two events, the *CVZ* and the *Vossische Zeitung* reported that a number of the speakers were other important officials of the organization who impressed upon the audience "the manner in which certain comedians actually foster anti-Semitism."[19] While Holländer's editorial published the following week did not put into print the dreaded name of anti-Semitism, he did make the same point using somewhat subtler language. Here again, we see the casting of the discussion into appropriate and censurable modes of Jewish wit and the fear that the distorted self-image will become the norm rather than remaining in the comic realm and viewed as the exaggerations of caricature. In addition, while Holländer attempts to make a distinction between appropriate and censurable Jewish jokes here, it is not that easy to know where to draw this line in actual practice:

> No one will censure those who recognize Jewish types and make them the subject of a humorous, comical, or satiric consideration. For as with every people, so Jewry also has its comic aspects. But if one starts from a distorted image, this must not lead to making the distortion the rule as it were and thus to impose a stigma on an entire people that now must widen and deepen already existing prejudices, especially if confirmed from Jewish lips [*wenn sie aus jüdischem Munde bestätigt*].[20]

Here, the CVZ articulates one of the standing objections made against Jewish self-mockery — that these self-stigmatizing jokes affirm and intensify already existing anti-Semitic prejudices and that this stigma will spread all the more if and when confirmed by Jewish comedians who provide the enemies of the Jews with further ammunition. This particular point was underscored in the CVZ in the reprinted excerpt of Emil Factor's review of the demonstrations originally published in the liberal newspaper *Berliner Börsen-Courier*: "It is even more painful when the speakers belong to the same tribe and when they awaken the impression in the opposing party — 'So they are, and they even boast of it!'"[21] In this specific context, Siegmund Feldmann's scathing review of the KadeKo and the other Jewish cabaret troupes published in *Die Weltbühne* in December 1926 is most relevant. The theater critic positioned this brand of Jewish wit as nothing less than self-hate speech with this provocative and pithy title: "Jeder Jude sein eigner Antisemit! [Every Jew his own anti-Semite!]"[22]

Holländer was particularly sensitive to the anti-Semitic accusation that the Jews wear only a thin "mask of civilization" (*Zivilisationsmaske*) that would be torn away by self-deprecating jokes to reveal the Jew's barbaric underside.[23] Taking up the rhetorical position of the watchman, Holländer asserted that the Jewish public did not realize the dangers and the risks of their laughter in this case. Thus, the Centralverein leader strove to maintain middle-class respectability and sobriety and to get the Jews of Germany out of harm's way by removing these comedic risks. According to Holländer: "But they laugh harmlessly because they believe in the harmlessness of the performers and the representation. They are not aware that ignorant Jewish and non-Jewish circles see these representations as Jewish types, namely types of a large number of Jewish Germans who, according to this view, are refined only by a 'mask of civilization' that falls away at the first touch." Given this assumption, Holländer feared the loss of civilization and civility for *both* Eastern and German Jews and he condemned the comic attacks launched against Eastern Jews not only by German Jews but also by their fellow countrymen. While it was easy for a German-Jewish audience to feel superior and make jokes about cheap and dirty Eastern European Jews (*Ostjuden*), Holländer deplored such acts of defamation that "make the cultural contrast between Eastern and Western Jews the object of bad jokes [*übler Witze*] and thereby appeal to the instincts of their Jewish listeners."[24] Meanwhile, he was outraged by the self-deprecating jokes of mercenary Eastern European Jewish comedians: "We have experienced anger in recent times. We have asked with astonishment how Jewish men who come from Eastern Europe . . . give a distorted picture of their homeland and of the Jewish people of their homeland for mere purchase in order to make fun of themselves and their kind."[25] In this situation, Holländer's call was one of sober restraint in order to affix tightly the mask of civilization to the faces of both Eastern *and* Western Jews and, in this way, to armor them against a type of anti-Semitic attack that utilized laughter and mockery.

## Kurt Robitschek's Defense of Self-Directed Jewish Wit

For the sake of allowing equal time on this controversial issue, the CVZ invited the famous Berlin cabaret director and Jewish comedian Kurt Robitschek (1890–1950; fig. 10) as well as the cabaret singer Kurt Gerron and gave them the opportunity to offer a rebuttal at their demonstration (fig 10). A written version of Robitschek's defense was later published below Holländer's editorial of April 30 as "Der Standpunkt der Künstler" (The artist's viewpoint). The piece constitutes in part Robitschek's rationale for the ongoing deployment of an aggressive brand of Jewish wit in his theater.[26] Founded on December 1, 1924, by Robitschek, the comedian Paul Morgan, and the actor and singer Max Hansen, the Kaberett der Komiker (KadeKo, Cabaret of Comedians) was such a hit that it soon moved to a bigger venue on the Küfurstendamm that seated 450 people in 1925 and then, in September 1928, to Lehniner Platz, an even larger theater of 950 seats designed by the renowned Berlin Jewish architect Erich Mendelsohn. Their satirical performances involved singing and dancing as well as verbal wit in comic monologues and via song lyrics.[27] Morgan and Robitschek achieved early success with their mock operetta *Quo Vadis?* (Whither goes thou?) and performed it at their inception in late 1924.

Figure 10. Felix H. Man, *Kurt Robitschek, Conferencier, Germany*, 1930. (Photo by Felix H. Man / ullstein bild via Getty Images.)

It parodied the silent historical film of the same name set in Rome during the early years of the tyrannical rule of Emperor Nero. KadeKo's version conflated Hitler with Nero (played by Morgan) and thereby mocked the Nazis' early failed attempts to seize power.[28] Thus, the skit is considered to be the first Hitler parody ever on stage. As part of the production, Curt Bois played the

Roman soldier named Gojus who wore an oversized swastika on his breast.[29] One would think that Robitschek would have been very popular among Jewish audiences based on this particular production with its outer-directed mockery that was performed over three hundred times in total. But KadeKo's humor was known for its impudence and irreverence meaning that it cut both ways and that it spared no one. One recalls in this regard that *Die Frechheit* (The audacity) was the name of KadeKo's comic journal that was edited by Robitschek. From this perspective, Robitschek represented the comic outlaw whose impudent, insolent, or irreverent behavior in pursuit of laughter could trigger the defamation of Jewish character at any moment and who therefore had to be subject to close scrutiny and policing by the Centralverein and its watchmen.

Even before the first performance of *Quo Vadis?*, the prescient Robitschek and Morgan also put into print a self-deprecating Jewish joke featuring a character who appears on first glance to be an Aryan type and a Nazi party member in their coedited joke book *Die Einsame Träne* (The lonely teardrop, 1924). The joke, titled "Im Bade" (In the bath), works on a number of different levels and it offers a perfect example of one that cuts both ways as it mocks both "dirty Jews" and "Nazi brutes" (fig. 11). The stereotype of the unclean Jew without regard for personal hygiene certainly starts off this joke but then it moves beyond this figure to confront the emerging threat of Nazi anti-Semitism. The joke offers an outlet for Jewish fear and anxiety related to the rise of this new enemy and the threat of a German — rather than Russian or Polish — pogrom this time around. The *schlemiel* of the story is Barches who takes his twisted name from the German/Yiddish and the designation given to the bread used in Jewish rituals that is known among East European Jews as *challah*.

> The year was up. Barches visited the bathhouse again to take a bath in the communal space. In the tub next door sat a blond giant, the typical appearance of the national male ideal wearing an invisible swastika on his forehead.
>
> Shy and fearful, Barches sat in his tub. He dared not to speak a word lest not to induce any pogrom.
>
> As the blonde man raises himself in all his stately size, Barches's gaze roams along his shape. Suddenly his face brightens, and he asks the other joyfully:
>
> "Tell me, when do we have the Day of Atonement this year?"[30]

When the Aryan-looking blond man with the "invisible swastika on his forehead" turns out to be circumcised and Jewish, it is a major relief for Barches and, by extension, for the Jewish people as a whole. The invisible swastika is

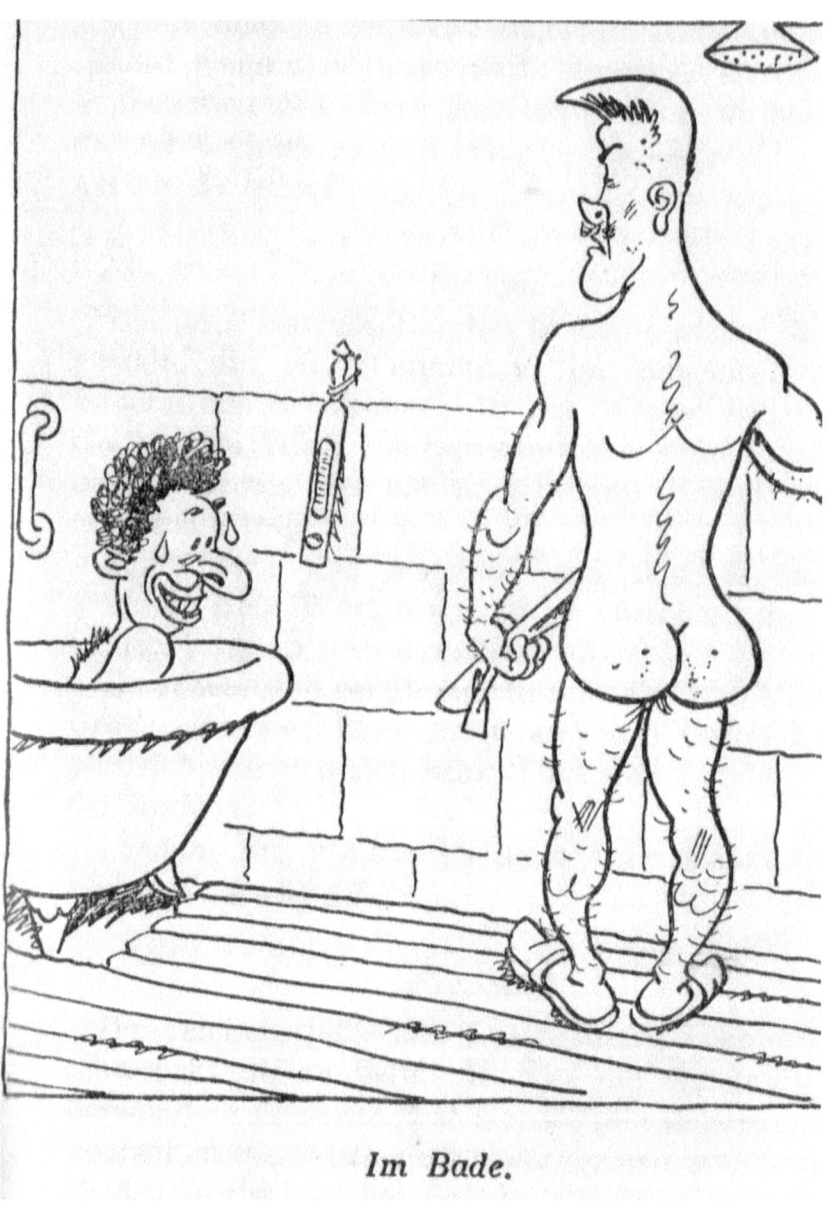

Figure 11. Paul Simmel, *Im Bade* (In the Bath). Caricature. From Robitschek and Morgan, *Die Einsame Träne*, 97.

converted (literally and figuratively) to the visible mark of Jewish difference in the circumcised penis that is not overtly named in this subtle joke. With this corporeal revelation, Barches joyfully pops the communal question regarding the date of Yom Kippur and the fear of the other evaporates in this brilliant example of a joke as wish fulfillment. In this way, the punchline of the joke parallels the famous Eastern European joke in the train compartment where the same question breaks the ice by revealing to the religious Jew that the assimilated looking man who is sitting across from him is Jewish after all and that he now can let his guard down. Such a joke is ambivalent because even while it reinforces negative Jewish stereotypes,[31] it also confronts the emerging risk of Nazi anti-Semitism.[32] The joke mocks indirectly the Nazi racist doctrine that a Jew cannot look like or pass as an Aryan in physical type. However, one also can make the argument from Wiener's and Holländer's perspective that its "happy ending" diverts and makes light of this emergent problem as well.

If we look closely at Robitschek's speech at the rally as summarized in the newspaper, we notice that it contained a number of gestures that must be viewed as appeasement strategies for the censors. Ever the consummate performer, Robitschek knew that this appearance on stage here was not just fooling around as it was at the KadeKo theater. Instead he had to assume the serious pose of the concerned Jewish citizen who cared about Jewish civil and religious rights and who did not want to see them violated in his cabaret. Thus, Robitschek gave his less than smiling audience the assurance that every "tasteful cabaret artist and director will condemn in the most severe way any *faux pas* [*Entgleisung*] on stage that injures the religious feeling of a fellow citizen."[33] This comment appears to be Robitschek's attempt to put himself into the good graces of the Centralverein and its concern that Jewish wit was defaming Jewish religious practices and institutions. After all, Holländer's editorial states: "The mockery of Jewish religious institutions in such performances cannot be condemned enough. For it is rude to ridicule that which any religion holds sacred and to arouse the base instincts of an ignorant lot at the expense of a deeper religious feeling."[34] Responding to this point, Robitschek went on to insist that his own controversial production provocatively titled *Kaddish* did not intend to ridicule that sacred Jewish ritual of the mourner's prayer. Robitschek performs a rhetorical spin (*Dreh*) of his own by insisting that the public should let the comedians confront the "serious" issues of the day including religion: "Just let cabarets perform songs and numbers that deal with serious — even religious — themes concerning Jews. The much-contested song 'Kaddish' belongs there."[35] This concerned statement was very different from the light-hearted and carefree position that he took about the harmlessness of Jewish jokes in his editorial collaboration with Paul Morgan just a few years earlier in *Die Einsame Träne* (The lonely teardrop). In this way, Robitschek fought back against those Centralverein members who were shocked by what they saw as an iconoclastic usage of the sacred mourner's prayer in the profane context of the smutty cabaret. The clever Robitschek does not comment on this impudent reading of the song but rather steers the conversation in this more patriotic direction. Thus, one newspaper account of the proceedings reported that Robitschek was able to convince the Centralverein members at the assembly that this song was not a disgrace (*Schande*) against Jewish religious piety but rather a glorification of German Jews who had fought in the recent world war—as it recounts a widow's grief over the loss of her husband.[36] Rather than remaining in a gray area that would situate KadeKo's *Kaddish* as a performance of comic ambivalence, the Jewish humorist appeases his detractors with this single-minded and uncontroversial interpretation.

In another gesture that sought to accommodate the Centralverein audience, Robitschek insisted that he was on the side of morality or at least that this was his ultimate goal as a cabaret director in response to their accusations: "The name of cabaret is discredited. Professionals will strive to make the cabaret stage into a moral institution. But the road is long and tedious." Robitschek further invokes the word *serious* in three places as he seeks to infuse Jewish cabaret with cultural import and to counteract the implied charges that he and his KadeKo colleagues were engaged in frivolous Jewish self-hate speech. Assuming the role of respectability, Robtischek again insists that his humor was committed to taking on serious issues. His call for cabaret as a "serious art in the midst of gaiety" frames (and contains) its humor as committed to social and political satire. Clearly, Robitschek did not want to let the likes of Wiener have sole possession of the claim to seriousness. (Remember: when Wiener began the Centralverein's campaign against wit that shades into anti-Semitism, he sub-titled his article "A serious word.") Thus, both the Jewish documenter of Nazi atrocities and the Jewish comedian who made fun of Nazis (and Jews) claimed that they were doing what they were doing in all seriousness. The following excerpt continues in its call for a quid pro quo on the part of each party in the debate and the need to take each other seriously: "And if [making cabaret into a moral institution] is once completed, then serious Jewish poetry will have contributed a large share to its cultivation. So, take it seriously if your cabaret finds your protests worthy; but then let it also maintain serious art in the midst of gaiety. Do not bind the cabaret—only unleash it from the bonds of bad taste."[37] Even though Robitschek appears to be cozying up to his Jewish critics in some respects here, he still asserts the need for his cabaret not to be bound to the dictates of its detractors.

Pursuant to this point, Robitschek took a firm stand on the importance of the freedom of comic speech in his address to the Centralverein assembly and in his rejection of "petty censorship." He also acknowledged the ambivalences that are comedy's special and nonnormative province. From this perspective, the previous citation becomes quite ambiguous for it is difficult to know exactly what Robitschek meant by something as subjective as "bad taste" in this context and who was to serve as the proper judge between "permissible satire" and censurable "tastelessness." The cabaret director's call for free speech reads as follows: "But—for God's sake—no petty censorship [*kleinliche Zensur*]! Wit and satire have to be allowed, even if here and there an individual gets hurt badly. There are no norms to determine where permissible satire ends and tastelessness begins. They need to be discussed on a case by-case basis. So: let's discuss [*verhandeln*] first, and then act [*handeln*]!"[38] Robitschek insists here that every joke and skit must be considered on a case-by-case basis without exception. While the intervention and invocation of the Creator ("for God's sake") may be viewed as ironic, Robitschek's remark also reminds readers that perhaps only divine judgment can rule regarding the difference between what is permissible and what is not. All in all, Robitschek makes his plea for the aggressive and tendentious Jewish joke in a space where the individual's exposure to ridicule is part of what it means to live in a democracy, and this view—and the badly hurt feelings that this inevitably brings with it—problematize the comic's defense of the need to protect religious feelings earlier in this same article.

Assuming that Robitschek was on his best behavior at the regulative body that was the Centralverein assembly and that he took a much more restrained stance on the question of joking morality as well as on comic artistic license when confronted by and addressing this somewhat hostile audience of censor-mongers, it is worthwhile to investigate this hypothesis further by reviewing the introduction to Robitschek and Morgan's book of jokes, *Die Einsame Träne: Das Buch der guten Witze* (*The lonely teardrop: the book of good jokes*) published in 1924. While the book does not call itself a book of Jewish jokes, it is pretty close to one given that the editors have this to say: "The predominant type of humor also in this collection is Jewish."[39] The title of the introduction (worthy of the wit of a Tristam Shandy) already lets us know that Robitschek and Morgan are playing on their home turf where the comic outlaw takes artistic license and evades any institutional demand for restraint and censorship—"Some inappropriate words from the editors so that this book can be escorted on its way [Einige unpassende Worte die diesem Buche seitens der Herausgeber zum Geleite auf den Weg mitgegeben werden]."[40] There is no need for appropriate and appeasing words or for a serious tone here.

Instead, the comedians adopt a merry facetiousness that puts their readers in the mood for laughter. Ironically, the text incorporates the theme of censorship in a hilarious self-reflexive account of how the book came into existence that makes fun of the editing process itself. Robitschek and Morgan tell us that they started out with the 45,659,387 jokes that they knew. But "the death penalty had already been fixed by the supreme court [*Reichsgericht*] in the retelling of 38,767,124 jokes so these had to be eliminated from the manuscript at the outset."[41] It is as if the political threat of censorship — whether from the secular courts or from the religious community — were always already hanging over the heads of the KadeKo foreshadowing the trials and tribulations they would face from the Jewish defense league on the one hand and from the Nazis and nationalists on the other hand.

If we look at the jokes that Robitschek and Morgan collected in *Die Einsame Träne* (The lonely teardrop), there are a number of them that are directed against religious Jews and therefore they go against the Centralverein's party line. These jokes certainly run the risk of offending Jewish religious feeling and the KadeKo comics do not shy away from telling them as part of their arsenal. A few of them function as religious demystifications that make fun of the supposed miracles of the "Wonder Rabbis" while a few others challenge rabbinical authority directly.[42] In another example, a man beats his chest so hard during the confession of his sins on the Day of Atonement that he cracks his ribs.[43] There is also a joke that would bear out Wiener's warning that such permissive joke books make fun of their religion and turn it into an "object for haggling." That one features the old religious *schnorrer* Meier who haggles and pleads with the archangel Gabriel for God's charity and who becomes the butt of the joke when the response is measured out in the Lord's time.[44] Finally, there is the ambiguously provocative joke entitled "*Nicht so heftig!*" (Not so hard!) that takes place on the holy fast day of Yom Kippur and that has some fun with both the religious Jews (since the joke is about the transgression of the fast day and the dietary laws) and the freethinkers (since this blasphemous desire is thwarted by what appears to be a supernatural act of God) (fig. 12). Here, Elias Bernstein is tempted by the smell of sausages from the local street vendor and he asks about their price. When this request is met with a clap of thunder from the heavens, he confesses: "One is still allowed to ask!"[45] Incidentally, the same joke (with the same punch line) was told in the Warlitz volume that Wiener found so offensive.[46]

Meanwhile, Robitschek and Morgan include other witticisms in the book that revolve around shady business practices as the reader encounters a procession of cheap, greedy, and deceitful Jewish comic characters who are obsessed with making money even if and when their actions transgress ethical

Figure 12. Paul Simmel, *Nicht so heftig!* (Not so hard!). Caricature. From Robitschek and Morgan, *Die Einsame Träne*, 111.

values and the codes of morality.⁴⁷ They recall Wiener's lament against Warlitz regarding "what common actions and shameful dispositions are foisted upon the Jews in most of these jokes." One doubts whether the Centralverein would have found any of the Jewish jokes narrated by the two Jewish comics palatable after the organized demonstrations of the "cabaret campaign" that began in spring 1926. For example, a greedy nephew acts shamefully when he misinterprets the last will and testament of his rich Uncle Nathan to mean that he is entitled to buy himself a huge diamond for his tie instead of a beautiful gravestone for his generous benefactor.[48] In another example of a common and base action, a man asks for a room in the famous Hotel Esplanade in the Potsdamer Platz in Berlin and learns that the rates get cheaper as one ascends so that the nightly rate is thirty marks at the very top floor. The Jew is still not satisfied: "Thanks! Your hotel is too low [*niedrig*]."[49] Of course, the punch line plays with the double meaning of the word as base and mean and thereby reflects back upon this cheap Jewish joke character. There is also a sprinkling of Rothschild jokes that fit with the profile of the avaricious Jewish commercial subject.[50] Robitschek and Morgan even tell a few little Moritz jokes of the type that Holländer wanted to censor. One of the last jokes in the book shows us how little Moritz moves easily from mathematical universals to Jewish haggling in his school lesson: "'Moritz, how much is 6 x 6?' To which, he answers: '36 — no obligation' [*Freibleibend*]."[51] All of these specific examples show Robitschek telling self-mocking jokes in his collection that distort the Jewish religion as well as the moral character of the Jews and that flout the Centralverein watchmen's agenda.

Immediately after their pronouncement that the jokes in the volume are predominantly Jewish, the editors make a bold statement that seeks to counter their detractors with an assertion that runs counter to the seriousness that Robitschek invoked before the Centralverein assembly two years later. In marking their jokes as harmless, Robitschek and Morgan adopt the opposite rhetorical strategy — that one should not take the Jewish jokes of *Die Einsame Träne* seriously at all. In this way, the unstable Jewish joke vacillates from dangerous threat (harmful) to carefree amusement (harmless):

> The predominant type of humor also in this collection is Jewish. There will always be some who will find a ridiculing of the nation and religion in these harmless jokes [*harmlosen Scherzen*]. The editors know no better defense than to note the "Foreword" to Alexander Moszkowski's *Die Unsterbliche Kiste* [The immortal chest]. If one were to reject this allegation appropriately, then, one would have to become in any case the plagiarist of the person who made this excellent joke collection that is, above all, wittily [*geistreich*] introduced. The editors of this book hereby honor him by gently rising from their seats.[52]

This is a strange intertextual moment in the history of Jewish joke books. Here, Robitschek and Morgan's defense refers in passing to the most popular collection of Jewish jokes at the time and its author — the Berlin Jewish satirist Alexander Moszkowski. The invocation of the "jokologist" Moszkowski and his witty introduction takes us back to its original publication in 1911 to a decidedly different historical moment during the reign of the Kaiser Wilhelm II and before the start of World War I. Rather than spelling out further reasons as to why it is a legitimate practice to include self-mocking Jewish jokes in their collection (beyond their view that the jokes are harmless) and why it should not be considered as self-hate speech that ridicules the Jewish people and religion (and thus akin to anti-Semitic utterances), the authors refer and defer to this earlier defense composed by Moszkowski. While they rise figuratively to honor their satirical elder statesman, these two Jewish wits do not rise to the occasion in providing a rationale of their own. Therefore, it does well to turn to Moszkowski's words of wit and wisdom and to review his sage advice on this particular subject. Here then follows Moszkowski's lengthy citation written in his florid prose regarding how to respond if and when one accuses the Jewish joke (and joker) of self-hate speech and anti-Semitism:

> There are namely — listen! listen! — a great number of dazzling Jewish jokes whose epic representatives are not portrayed as ideal figures exactly. And when such a joke appears in print, then the accusation of the hatred of the Jews with all the attributes of indignation is bound to appear quite quickly. Mind you, one may tell it and be sure that the listener will tell it again with a clear expression of joy, and as long as one disseminates it verbally, these jokes are Jewish. But they become anti-Semitic just by contact with the printing paper. How does one get around this roadblock? Should one simply suppress or keep quiet about them in a collection that makes claims to comprehensiveness? One does not desire this from an editor of a chest [*Kiste*] who would sooner bite off his tongue than that he swallow a joke. One is satisfied with his assurance that he recognizes in the field of the joke only an aim or a purpose [*Tendenz*], specifically the joke's purpose [*Witztendenz*], and that he rejects the generalization of an incidental nasty characteristic of an individual figure in a jest upon the public at large. The Jewish joke jewels are in their totality such good showpieces that they can be exhibited often before the whole world without producing any cause for sequestering particular ones in a secret drawer. But to take away every pretext for painful wincing on the part of those overly sensitive types, I have served up the "Degenerate Sprouts" — so that they are separated from the rest of the community quite blatantly and they are to be found all together in a special compartment bearing their mark of Cain.[53]

Similar to Robitschek's plea for judging the joke on a case-by-case basis, one notes that Moszkowski does not want us to generalize the Jewish joke's staging of "an incidental nasty characteristic of an individual figure." Moszkowski also makes an interesting point about the difference between the oral and written format of jokes as providing the potential ground by which a Jewish joke becomes anti-Semitic in its character. Unlike when it is told privately, the joke acquires a public when it is put into writing. In other words, it now circulates in a public space where it cannot be contained so easily and where one does not know exactly who is appropriating and retelling them (Jews or non-Jews). For Moszkowski, "the accusation of the hatred of the Jews" appears quite quickly in this format as Jewish jokes are converted into anti-Semitic barbs by mere virtue of their inscription. Moszkowski's witty logic illustrates here the thin line and the wavering border between Jewish self-irony and anti-Semitism and how they can appear as two sides of the same coin. Like Robitschek's later appeal to free speech, Moszkowski refuses to disavow or to censor this type of Jewish joke and his first inclination is to exhibit them together with all the other jokes in his treasure chest. However, since Moszkowski does not want to alienate the "overly sensitive types" among his readership, he comes up with a witty compromise but one that is inadvertently prophetic both in its act of segregation and in its nomenclature. With a chapter of his book designated "Degenerate Sprouts," Moszkowski compartmentalizes these volatile and inflammatory Jewish joking utterances and, in saying that they bear the mark of Cain, he adds a Biblical figure that supports the view that these jokes are anti-Semitic in nature. Of course, the Jewish satirist was trying his best to be funny here as he "takes back" the epithets of Jewish degeneracy and cursedness and as his comic performance of Jewish self-mocking wit opens itself up to the charge of anti-Semitism. One can see why Robitschek and Morgan would have been rising from their seats to applaud Moszkowski for these deft comic maneuvers. But we also sense that if someone like Albert Wiener had read this particular passage in Moszkowski's book, he would not have been amused at all. Rather, the German-Jewish community's watchman would have seen the signs of an old religious anti-Semitism (in the mark of Cain) and the portents of the new racialist one (in the form of degeneracy) at play and as part of a misguided attempt at Jewish self-deprecation that was no laughing matter at all.

## Conclusion

At the outset of this chapter, I asked the following question: Was it just a coincidence that Wiener identified the Nazis as the biggest threat to the Jews in the very same year (1925) that he also wrote an article in the *CVZ* that examined the anti-Semitic potential of Jewish wit and the limits of self-deprecating

Jewish jokes? This convergence was no accident if and when we consider that the debate about the Jewish joke and its limits was closely linked to the Jewish question in general and that it functioned as a type of barometer for the status of intercultural relations and dialogue (or lack thereof) between Germans and Jews. At the same time that the Jewish watchmen of the Centralverein spoke out against the Nazis as an external threat, they also began to police the Jewish comedians as an internal threat. What we have here is a contest between a Jewish self-policing organization that wanted to censor free speech about the Jews and a group of playful comedians who wanted to evade such controls. Alfred Wiener, Ludwig Holländer, and the other Centralverein leaders asserted that Jewish self-deprecating jokes and anti-Semitism met at the censurable crossroads of Jewish self-hate speech. Meanwhile, Kurt Robitschek and other Jewish comedians responded to these charges — both seriously and facetiously — by arguing against "petty censorship" and demanding the freedom of comic speech whether it took place on the cabaret stage or in the joke book in a defense of both inner- and outer-directed Jewish humor.

Despite Robitschek's calls for freedom of comic speech, the Centralverein continued to go after him and the KadeKo in the following years. Things came to a head in December 1927 when the Centralverein's legal counsel Arthur Schweriner published an article that criticized the performances in a number of cabarets. He condemned the ongoing use of demeaning jargon in the KadeKo as well as Robitschek's disrespectful reference to his theater as a *"Musensynagoge"* (a synagogue for the Muses — and "amusement") in *Die Frechheit* (The audacity). Schweriner also reprinted a letter from a "friend of the Centralverein" that conflated Jewish self-mockery in the cabarets with organized anti-Semitism. It stated: "Although Jews themselves, cabaret artists who have no feeling for necessary tact and who help to spread the anti-Semitic caricature [*das antisemitische Zerrbild*] of the Jews through their presentations support the anti-Semitic movement against which honorable Jews have been fighting for years. All defense efforts are repeatedly thwarted by this kind of comedy that is not afraid to give a false picture of Jewish nature and values in an undignified mockery of the public."[54] After this denunciation, a furious Robitschek turned "insult comic" himself and wrote a nasty letter to the Centralverein's legal counsel upon which Schweriner fired back with a libel suit. The CVZ reported the incident this way: "However, Mr. Robitschek has let it be known in a letter dated December 18, 1927, that is full of insults against our Lord Counsel Arthur Schweriner that he has learned nothing after all. Perhaps the libel suit now presented by Mr. Schweriner against Mr. Robitschek will have a healing effect."[55] As Peter Jelavich points out, "Since the Centralverein was known for repeatedly taking anti-Semitic agitators to court on grounds of libel and defamation, the move may have made a symbolic equation of Robitschek with the Jews' greatest enemies."[56] The case was settled out of court in January 1928 when Robitschek issued a statement of apology: "I declare that I wrote the letter of December 18, 1927, to the Central Association of the German Citizens of Jewish Faith in great excitement. Insulting the Lord Counsel Schweriner was far from my intention. If Mr. Schweriner has seen a personal libel or slander in my communication, I hereby express my regrets."[57]

This incident took place some months before the KadeKo moved into their new and much larger theater so that alienating a mainstream Jewish clientele would have been something that Robitschek wanted to avoid at all costs. But despite these spacious new digs, the KadeKo's golden days were short-lived as the Nazi street provocations with riotous actions on the Kurfürstendamm in September 1931 made many people afraid to attend their theater. Robitschek quipped off-stage about the aesthetics of Nazi political theater in the following witty and wise commentary: "What Hitler does, what he trumpets and stages, is political [Erik] Charell. An old political comedy is refurbished and equipped with girls, which in this case are called storm troopers."[58] In such a climate, political satire on the stage whether it was against the Nazis or even self-directed against the Jews would become too dangerous and Robitschek advocated for mindless and diversionary entertainment that would give his audience "freedom from thinking serious thoughts [Nichtnachdenkenmüssen]."[59] Given this drastically constrained situation devoid of satire, there was nothing for the Nazis nor for the Centralverein to complain about given that there was no longer any argument to be had between what constituted "permissible satire" and what counted as "tastelessness" in late KadeKo cabaret.

In summary, the KadeKo debate of 1926 affords the opportunity to think about the stakes of Jewish wit when venturing into territory that provided fodder for anti-Semitism during the middle period of the Weimar Republic. For the Centralverein, the stakes were just too great and therefore what they deemed to be comic self-hate speech had to be limited. Indeed, the Centralverein argued that such jokes did not count as comic at all anymore. The Centralverein also took the moral high ground condemning what it viewed as the mercenary reasons that motivated these Jewish comedians. In the following statement, Holländer was clearly at wit's end: "But it is far worse now that Jews present in public the wicked characters of mankind in a jargoning manner and make fun of themselves and their peers for the mere sake of income. Whoever does this, it is no longer a joke. It is not humorous; it is self indulgent and impudent."[60] Meanwhile, Kurt Robitschek and the cabaret comics did not take these attacks lying down. They countered this mercenary accusation with an appeal to a democratic ideal of free speech. Even while tempering himself

Figure 13. Dr. Alfred Wiener at his desk at the Library in Manchester Square, London, 1953. (Courtesy of the Wiener Library, London.)

in deference to the Centralverein assembly, Robitschek's bold defense of Jewish wit was necessarily confrontational and satirical: "Wit and satire have to be allowed, even if an individual gets hurt badly here and there." If particular Jewish jokes exposed themselves to anti-Semitic recuperation, then this was a risk that was worth taking and worth laughing about. For Robitschek, Jewish self-deprecating wit was nonnegotiable, and as the contents of his coedited joke book reveal, it was central to his framing of the modern Jewish (joking) experience at the time of the controversy. Like Moszkowski, Robitschek would rather bite off his tongue than swallow a joke. But we also know that Robitschek was forced to change with the times in order to stay afloat. The glory days of a Berlin cabaret featuring aggressive satire and Jewish jokes full of self-mockery were already over by the middle of 1931.

Both Wiener and Robitschek were pioneers in offending the Nazis but in strikingly different ways—the Jewish watchman through the meticulous documentation of their atrocities and the Jewish comedian through the provocative use of satire and the power of laughter. Therefore, both needed to flee Germany when the Nazis ascended to power in 1933. Soon after the Nazi takeover, Robitschek left Berlin for Vienna and then traveled to London before arriving in New York and changing his name to Ken Robey. He would continue his comic pursuits there even working to revive the KadeKo until his death in 1950 at the age of sixty. Meanwhile, Wiener arrived safely in London with his collection in 1939 and opened the Jewish Central Information Service on the fateful day of September 1. He would continue to expand that collection until his death in 1964. His archive of Nazi propaganda is now known worldwide as the Wiener Library for the Study of the Holocaust and Genocide (fig. 13).[61] While standing on opposite sides of this mid-twenties debate about Jewish wit and its limits in Berlin cabarets and in Jewish joke books, both the watchman and the comedian were able to escape and outwit the Nazis and the Holocaust, and, as a result, both of them died of natural causes in the years after World War II.

# 4
# "Far from where?"
### Erich Kahler and the Jewish Joke of Exile

"Today Judaism is exposed to the most savage attacks in Germany. The movement that has now risen to the heights of power actually sees in the fate of Judaism the fulcrum of the German future and, indeed, the future of humanity."[1] So begins the first version of the foreword to Erich Kahler's *Israel unter den Völkern* (Israel among the nations), which he wrote in Wolfratshausen (near Munich) from July until November of 1932 during the waning months of the Weimar Republic. This untimely meditation was published by Delphin Verlag in Munich in February 1933—just days after the Nazi's takeover of power at the end of January (fig. 14). In a perceptive essay, historians David Kettler and Volker Meja write about Kahler's cultural mission: "Kahler placed problems of German *Bildung* at the center of his diagnosis and therapeutic response to the cultural crisis, but he had no reservations about speaking as a Jew of a kind. In a book that infuriated the Nazis when they came to power and led to Kahler's exile in 1933, *Israel unter den Völkern*, he gave the mission of saving German culture to Jewish men of culture."[2] In other words, Kahler thought that Jewish spiritual and moral purpose (as applied to a secular context) combined with German *Bildung* (with its values of "tolerance, cultured self-cultivation, and the primacy of individual autonomy"[3]) could still manage to save the day and redirect the future. From this vantage point, the story of Erich Kahler provides us with the portrait of a highly refined and idealistic *Bildungsjude* or "Jewish man of culture" at the turn of the twentieth century who would become subject to a life of exile when these hopes were dashed.

Born Erich von Kahler in 1885 to a wealthy and titled Jewish family in Prague and participating in the cultural elite there and later in Vienna where he was raised, his impressive intellectual biography and self-cultivation included

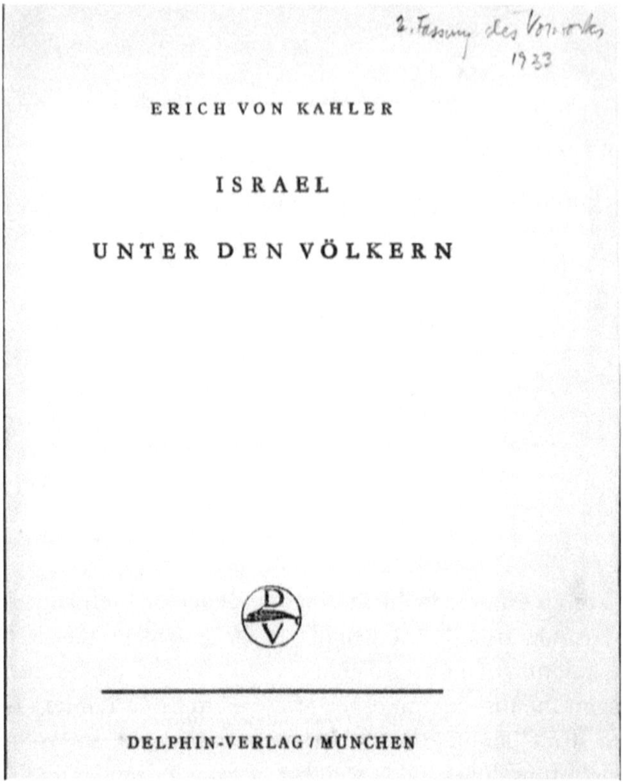

2. Fassung des Vorworts 1933

ERICH VON KAHLER

ISRAEL

UNTER DEN VÖLKERN

DELPHIN-VERLAG / MÜNCHEN

Offizin Haag-Drugulin AG. Delphin-Verlag München

Kahler, Israel

1. Autorkorr, Fahne 1—16 23. 1. 1933

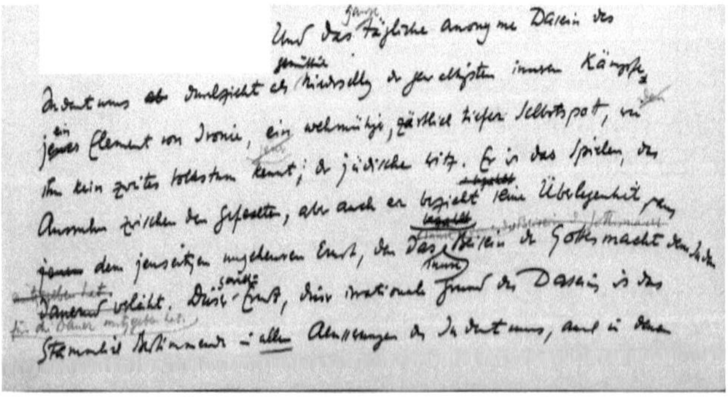

Figure 14. Manuscript materials related to Erich von Kahler's *Israel unter den Völkern* (1933). (*Clockwise*) Title page of the book with handwritten notation, printer's galley information dated January 23, 1933, and excerpt from author's handwritten manuscript. (Courtesy Leo Baeck Institute, Center for Jewish History, New York.)

studies in a wealth of humanistic disciplines at the universities in Munich, Berlin, Heidelberg, and Vienna (where he earned his PhD in 1908). In light of his broad humanist education alone, it is not difficult to frame Kahler as a *Bildungsjude* in a number of aspects that fit into the framework elaborated by the German-Jewish cultural historian George Mosse.[4] According to Mosse, "The word *Bildung* combines the meaning carried by the English word 'education' with notions of character formation and moral education." In addition, the *Bildungsjude* was often a cultural elitist who valued art and literature that was serious, deep, and refined and who believed that these were to be found in the cultural achievements of Germany. In his study of the young Kahler, Gerd Lauer discusses how "*Bildung* retained the aura that had elevated the arts and literature above the quotidian of the bourgeois world.... Kahler wanted not only to share in this aura but also to be himself the new man and poet."[5] The *Bildungsjude* (as a German-speaking Jew) also looked down on Eastern European Jews (*Ostjuden*) as well as on those crass commercial Jews who were only interested in making money and in materialist values.[6] Such a value system predisposed Kahler to affirm Jewish wit only up to a point — if and when it advanced *Bildung* either in the form of an increase in wisdom or in knowledge.

Kahler, however, parted ways with the typical rational and liberal *Bildungsjude* of this period on account of his neo-romanticism.[7] His appreciation of intuition, irrationality, and faith had its roots in the fact that he was educated within the sphere of influence of the poet Stefan George and his circle during his formative years. In *The Renaissance of Jewish Culture in Weimar Germany*, German-Jewish historian Michael Brenner relates how Werner Cahnmann (a leading figure in the Centralverein) was quite taken with Kahler's ideas about the importance of *Bildung* as well as with his idea that the Jews constituted a distinctive tribe (*Stamm*) with a unique religious inheritance based on "dialogue with God" (33). In 1930, Cahnmann wrote the following letter to Kahler that articulates their shared view on the limits of rationality: "I am of the opinion that our friends in the camp of liberalism and Enlightenment are dangerous friends for us ... because rationalism dissolves all kind of distinctive existence.... The maintenance [of a distinctive Jewish existence] is only possible in alliance with the Romantic forces in German *Bildung*."[8]

Nevertheless, Kahler's idealistic message that *Bildungsjuden* such as himself had a mission to save Germany did not stand a chance in the face of the Nazi's brutal censorship; his book was branded as Jewish contraband, and only a few weeks after its publication, it was confiscated and destroyed, thereby falling victim to one of those savage attacks that Kahler had decried at the beginning of his book. By sheer accident, only two known copies of this first edition exist today — one is in the Princeton University Library (Kahler's own copy) and one in the Deutsches Literaturarchiv in Marbach. A second attempt was made to publish the book with the famous Schocken Verlag in Berlin later in 1933, but the Nazis destroyed that edition as well. In the meantime, Kahler himself had taken flight from the Nazis, moving first to Vienna, then to Czechoslovakia, and finally to Switzerland where he succeeded in publishing a slightly edited version of the book with the Humanitas Verlag in Zurich in 1936. Kahler notes in a letter to his friend Thomas Mann on March 21, 1935, that only the last section of the book ("Ausblick," or "Outlook") underwent revisions. The new version reflects the hopelessness of any German-Jewish rapprochement and it speaks of the inevitability of Jewish exile and suffering. In his 1935 letter to Mann, Kahler marks the "immeasurable" difference made by the interval of those three intervening years: "I have become so uncertain about the impression it makes nowadays because except for the recently revised final section, it was written some three years ago, in Germany and for Germany, and at the time was intended to bring about a pause for reflection [*Besinnung*] on both sides. But now it is already too late for that by an immeasurable span of time [*unmessbare Frist*]. I am beyond it; events have gone beyond it."[9] While Kahler concluded the original version of the book with the impossible hopes of a message urging reconciliation, the revised final section concludes with a sorrowful line from Hölderlin's *Hyperion* that cuts to the (broken) heart of German-Jewish estrangement in the Third Reich: "*Und wehe dem Fremdling, der aus Liebe wandert und zu solchem Volke kommt* [And woe to the stranger who wanders out of love and comes to such a people]."[10] But there is also room for bitter irony in the foreword that assumes the structure of a Jewish joke in its defiance of the laws of noncontradiction when Kahler reviews the demonizing illogic of anti-Semitic propaganda in the next sentence: "The Jews had reason to be especially satisfied given the universal authorship that is attributed to them in the world process. They should have been responsible equally for capitalism as well as socialism, war and peace, revolution and restoration . . ."[11]

It is in the context of the Swiss publication of the book that an excerpt was selected for inclusion in the June 1936 issue of the exile magazine *Jüdische Revue*. Published by Manfred George in Mukacevo, Czechoslovakia, from 1936 to 1938, this celebrated journal contained essays and speculations on the grim cultural situation at hand by leading contemporary Jewish writers living in exile. (Other contributors to this issue included Nahum Goldmann, Max Brod, and Arnold Zweig.) Given this background, the excerpt that Kahler selected for this publication was given the fitting title "Der Deutsche und der Galuthwitz" ("The German and the exile joke").[12] Excepting the excision of one line, it consisted of a continuous selection taken from part 3 of the book

("*Judentum und Deutschtum*" or "Jewishness and Germanness," 149–154). Framed in this manner, Kahler's sophisticated analysis of Jewish wit took on an independent existence even as it served as a teaser for readers to promote his book as a whole. This text offers an exemplar of how the Jewish joke became a rhetorical figure in the larger cultural debates between Germans and Jews at this crucial moment of intercultural collapse and therefore provided its readers with a means by which to understand the nature, the meaning, and the extent of this breakdown.[13]

## A Close Reading of the Argument

It is significant that "Judentum und Deutschtum" is the title of that part of the book from which the section related to Kahler's analysis of Jewish wit is derived. A number of Kahler's writings are structured in terms of this binary opposition that characterizes Jewishness and Germanness in an essentialist manner.[14] The lure of essentialism never was a problem for Kahler, and he never wavered from his strong belief in national or tribal characters with distinct natures and dispositions. Thus, Kahler's approach to German-Jewish intercultural breakdown at the time of the collapse of the Weimar Republic and the rise of Nazism was based on a number of binary oppositions regarding the distinctive character traits of these two peoples. For Kahler, it was the responsibility of the cultural historian to analyze and systematize the precise nature of these German and Jewish characters and to highlight their affinities and their differences. Kahler's attempt to define Jewishness and Germanness predisposes his character analysis to perform a bifurcation of Jewish and German senses of humor in line with this overarching dichotomy. Nevertheless, it is important to deconstruct this rigid approach, particularly when dealing with something as mobile and fleeting as wit and humor. The opening pages of Todd Presner's *Mobile Modernity: Germans, Jews, Trains* provides a valuable strategy regarding how contemporary German-Jewish studies needs to confront the problem of essentialism and to challenge the strict separation and the pristine purity of these two terms at hand. This hyphenated — or slashing — practice calls for an acknowledgment of "German/Jewish" contamination and the mutual imbrication of these two unstable terms. As Presner writes: "In the case of German/Jewish we find the two terms consistently 'contaminated' by one another. They overlap; they become blurred; they switch places. One of the terms cannot be adequately articulated without the other."[15] In making this deconstructive move, Presner turns to the radical work of Jacques Derrida to remind us that it is only through such binary oppositions (e.g., *Deutschtum* and *Judentum*) that we are able to invoke something like the truth. Presner recalls: "For Derrida the enactment of a division or separation is always suspect because it is through such divisions that truth claims are grounded."[16] This chapter reviews how this "enactment of a division" operates in the case of Kahler and his categorical thinking as he accepts certain national or tribal stereotypes and as he grounds the "truth of wit" by means of a strict separation between Germans and Jews.

The primary opposition that guides Kahler's book — and that actively forgets the blurring of the borders that are also in play by the German-Jewish "separatrix"[17] — is the unbridgeable gap that exists for Kahler between German *Körperlichkeit* (physicality or corporeality) and Jewish *Intellektualismus* (intellectualism). In putting the Jews on the side of intellectualism, Kahler's analysis takes up a rhetorical figure for defining the modern Jewish subject that had acquired much negative spin in anti-Semitic propaganda from Hans Blüher who spoke of "Jewish-destructive intellectualism" in 1922 to Joseph Goebbels's announcement of the end of Jewish intellectualism at the book burnings in Berlin in 1933.[18] That is why Thomas Sparr remarks: "In Kahler's stereotypes, the distorted anti-Semitic image of the Jew as other [*Fremdbild*] becomes the Jewish self-image on the eve of National Socialism."[19] In contradistinction to the anti-Semites who employed this stereotype, the Jewish diasporic historian however recognized that it was the juxtaposition of Jewish intellectualism with German corporeality that led to their mutual mistrust and aversion. According to Kahler, this stark contrast generates the "existential aversion" that the Germans feel toward "the recognizable traits of the Jewish type" (149).[20] As he begins his analysis, Kahler elaborates upon this point by employing associations that already touch upon the realm of Jewish wit (*Vorwitz, Gewitztheit*) yet without naming it directly. The negative stereotype of the Jew as joker begins to emerge in the following excerpt with its emphasis on a light-hearted and iconoclastic character that does not take things seriously:

> One chides the Jews for "intellectualism," for being too forward [*Vorwitz*] and for their craftiness [*Gewitztheit*], for irony and skepticism, for not taking things seriously [*das Nicht-ernstnehmen*] and not holding things sacred [*Nicht-heilighalten*], for corrosive and subversive [*zersetzende*] criticism and for the undermining of ideals. One accuses the Jews of "rootlessness" ["*Wurzellosen*"], of groundlessness, of an alienation from nature and home that shies away from physical labor — one wants to say from all proper work. (150)

This last point rightly puts the joke (and the joker) on the side of play and leisure, in a space of laziness far removed from the realm of work. Kahler's mention of "corrosive" criticism also echoes the common accusation made against Jewish wit.[21] After this litany of anti-Semitic accusations, Kahler pauses to mark the superficiality of this character analysis that views the Jew out of context. Nevertheless, Kahler also understands the grounds of this German anti-intellectualist perspective because he too believes that an overemphasis on the mental faculties to the exclusion of everything else can "cause damage on both sides" (150).

This was not the first time in the book that Kahler had criticized excessive "Jewish intellectualism" and the simplistic view that Jewish wit was derived from the Enlightenment and its "rationally critical" tendencies. Kahler says exactly the same thing much earlier in the study and at the point when he argues that it would be a mistake to understand Jewish wit as rooted in rationality and hyper-intellectualism. Kahler seeks to dispel this "truism" by framing the source of Jewish wit as irrational and as something that is a direct result of a dialogic encounter between the individual and God or, as Kahler frames it, "the intimate result of the mightiest internal struggles."[22] Kahler would make this same point quite succinctly in the English publication of *The Jews Among the Nations* years later at one of the few points in the book when he raises the subject of Jewish wit: "Jewish dialectics and witticism, which often are misunderstood as extreme intellectualism, stem, in fact, from rather irrational sources: they trace back to a religious stance of generations, to the age-old dialogue with God."[23] This is certainly an important context through which to understand the Eastern European *shtetl* humor inherent in the classic Tevye stories of Sholem Aleichem that feature the milkman's ongoing arguments with God that contain elements of irony, profound self-mockery, and melancholy.[24] However, Kahler does not cite this example given his German-Jewish boundary lines. Interestingly, the accomplished Jewish folklorist Immanuel Olsvanger also shared this viewpoint with Kahler in the aptly titled *Contentions with God*.[25] Kahler introduces the concept of Jewish wit and the Jewish joke for the first time amid a series of paradoxes of which the foremost is the "terrible otherworldly seriousness" out of which its laughter is derived. In this excerpt as well as in others, Kahler zeroes in and affirms the paradoxical gravity of Jewish levity. This also relates to Kahler's sobering view that Jewish wit must not stray into the realm of the "merely frivolous." Kahler's conclusion that the French-Jewish philosopher Henri Bergson's vitalism offers a contemporary example of "fashionable" Jewish irrationalism is also pertinent in this context, especially in light of Bergson's contribution to the modern study of humor with his authorship of a significant philosophical study on *Laughter* published in 1900:[26]

On a daily basis and as the intimate result of its mightiest internal struggles, an element of irony runs through the anonymous being of Judaism, a melancholic and delicately profound self-mockery that is second to no other folk: the Jewish joke. It is a mode of play, the taking of a breather between battles, but, in addition, it draws its superiority from the terrible otherworldly seriousness that the inner presence of the power of God has given permanently to the Jews as a dowry. This mighty seriousness [*gewaltige Ernst*], this irrational foundation of being, is the tribal determinative in *all* the utterances of Judaism, even in those that might appear to be merely frivolous upon a superficial glance. "Jewish intellectualism," which the period of the Enlightenment met halfway all too gladly, clearly did much damage to Germans as well as to Judaism itself. But one should not overlook that the other stream in the Jews is much more original than the rationally critical, that it is the ruling force until they are in contradiction. And that the strongest counterforces against rationality had their source in the Jews themselves long before its fashionable renewal today — i.e., the worldwide movement of irrationalism led by the Jew Bergson. (37–38)

Kahler then focuses specifically on the excessive risks often posed by the Jewish joke in order to frame its proper limits so that it will not become a destructive or corrosive force in the world nor lose its proper (and profound) grounding: "It is undeniable that there is also sometimes with the Jews a terrible hypertrophy of wit [*schlimme Hypertrophie des Witzes*], which is a veritable cauldron of hazards. Wit is beneficial but also really only bearable out of the greatest seriousness, only as the high spiritedness of genuine joy or genuine sorrow. It is frightful as the vapidly permanent state of affairs that eats away at all essences. Jewish wit comes out of a deep space of destiny and it is laden with sorrow in its proper sense" (150). The "hypertrophy of wit" signals for Kahler the excessive and disproportionate growth of one part of modern Jewish subjectivity to the detriment of the Jew as a whole. The modifier "*schlimme*" also connotes here that too much joking and too many witticisms constitute a Jewish sickness that is very different in nature than Scholem Aleichem's "best medicine." With the hypertrophy of the Jewish joke, the image of the Jew now appears in the form of a caricature. Kahler has no sympathy for the less than serious pranksters among his own tribe. In the next paragraph, he lashes out against these empty-headed jokers who deal only in trivialities and superficialities and who give Jewish wit such a bad name. Kahler laments: "To speak freely, in some of these trivial creatures who have been cast out from their inner selves and who have become subject to the floating debris of external events, only the empty mental function of the joke has been left over and ripples through their completely shallow existence" (150–151). Later, he condemns those "compulsive joke jugglers who are deprived of all esteem" (153).[27] With such gestures, Kahler repeats the high cultural censuring of the "determinedly unrespectable" theatrical performances of the infamous Berlin cabaret artists the Herrnfeld Brothers as "frivolous" and as consciously opposed to the self-cultivating ideals of the *Bildungsjude*.[28] Nevertheless, Kahler's serious attempt to police and regulate Jewish wit as a means to cultivate wisdom and to promote the cultural ideal of *Bildung* is bound to fail because it is impossible to banish those Jewish jokes that come from the subject position and the long-standing tradition of self-mockery and self-denigration. Such an abject mode of self-expression beyond the realm of self-cultivation has played a key role in coping with the trials and tribulations of modern Jewish cultural experience and it often served as a direct response to anti-Semitism. This strain does not bind Jewish wit to wisdom but rather to the difficult and often absurd experience of living as a minority and persecuted people. In contrast to the more culturally conservative and elitist Kahler, the German socialist Eduard Fuchs did not have a problem with this lowbrow level of abjection in his text on "Jewish Self-Irony" (1921).[29] However, this difference of opinion also might be connected to the seriousness of the times in which Kahler wrote and revised his treatise in contrast to a more carefree disposition that permeated the early years of the Weimar Republic.

But it is not necessary to enlist such extreme cases as the Herrnfeld Brothers in order to underscore that Germans took issue with the Jewish joke. In other words, Kahler also acknowledges that the "corporeal" Germans even had a problem with that serious and sad type of Jewish wit (partaking "of the bitterest knowledge") that he himself was at pains to champion. It is at this point in the character analysis of "Judentum und Deutschtum" that Kahler offers a more detailed account of his binary opposition between two senses of humor at the limits of mutual understanding—between the scintillating and fleeting Jewish joke that is offered in boisterous expression and the heavy and ponderous German jest that is part of a more tempered sense of humor. The hyphen at the heart of the German-Jewish symbiosis no longer communicates but rather fractures across the cavity and chasm of laughter. Kahler asserts that each side of the dividing line does not get the other side's jokes and that this produces a situation that is "immediately dangerous." The inability of the "physical German" to get the joke of the "witty Jew" leads not only to misunderstandings and coldness between these two peoples; it also pushes the German into a type of Jewish character assassination where the negative stereotyping of anti-Semitism cannot be far behind. In a nutshell, the German remains rather "clueless" (*ratlos*) when it comes to the Jewish joke in Kahler's troubling assessment. With this essentialist gesture, Kahler expounds upon German and Jewish folk joking differences providing another variant on the long-standing opposition between *Humor* and *Witz* that emerged in nineteenth-century debates.

> To the physically inclined German with his heavy consciousness, the fleeting joke [*der flüchtige Witz*] is not important at all. To him, there corresponds the ponderous jest and tempered humor with merriment throughout its subterranean atmosphere and not a specifically marked boisterous expression. Before the Jewish joke itself in its best and deepest type—a joke that shivers and shimmers through a thousand-fold and is of the bitterest knowledge and sweetest human warmth—before this joke, the German is clueless. It does not penetrate him, let alone overwhelm the space of destiny out of which he stirs. And in this state of perplexity and bewilderment, all of the dangers that play between these two essences awaken. The physical German feels that the witty Jew is a treacherous, unreliable, mischievous creation from which one has only to expect embarrassing surprises. (151–152)

The "treacherous" terms that cling to this witty, prankish, and "mischievous" Jewish character will go hand in hand with Kahler's penetrating analysis of the "German Michel" and his sense of being betrayed at the hands of his Jewish enemies to be reviewed in the next section.

Kahler locates another binary opposition in character traits when he contrasts Jewish skepticism with German faith and when he examines the aggressive role that skeptical Jewish wit plays in its opposition to belief systems. For the Jewish joke "dares itself as irony or even with a caring intent as the skeptical criticism of content [*Inhalte*], applying itself precisely to the faithful efforts of the Germans" (152). Kahler then summarizes: "And here unfolds the opposition of skepticism to faith which brings misunderstanding and ill-feelings to a head" (152). For Kahler, the irony and skepticism of the Jews comes from the "clash between idea and world"—between their desire to idealize a transcendent God and their life of suffering in exile on earth. Here, Kahler joins wit and wisdom as he reviews the "long-suffering" history of the Jews thereby giving credence to the "laughter through suffering" hypothesis. This clash "has ground out more than their sense of humor [*Witz*], it has sharpened their wits down to the core [*es hat sie bis tief hinein gewitzigt*]." Furthermore, Kahler argues that the "bitterness" and "impatience" that the Jews experience in this distressing situation drives them "into mockery [*in den Hohn*]" (153). Kahler situates Jewish skepticism as "the long-suffering reversal of their religion" and therefore as a loss of faith and idealism. Jewish skepticism — as expressed in part by Jewish jokes — takes aim at the value system of the Germans and their belief in "partial things, autonomous orders, abstract principles" that the Jews see in a critical light as rather a "fall from humanness [*Abfall vom Menschtum*]" (152). Naturally, the Germans would not take lightly to such criticism of their faith, values, and beliefs. Here again, Kahler invokes the word *Vorwitz* to denote not only that this involves Jewish impertinence, cheekiness, and forwardness but also to connote the corrosive trace of Jewish wit that adheres to the body of this word: "But such criticism works upon the Germans as cold and rational *Vorwitz*, as a disrespectful disturbance of their faith [*Glaubens*] and as an undermining [*Zersetzung*] of their essential values" (153).

With this basic binary opposition and its "essential values" set in place on both sides, there also comes the possibility of contamination or of a blurring of the borders when Kahler argues for (and affirms) a certain type of witty German that helps to explain the concept of a German-Jewish symbiosis. This adds further nuances and qualifications to Kahler's argument as he asks his reader not to take his ideal typology too literally lest his plotting of German and Jewish characters become an exaggerated caricature of itself. Just a few pages before the section of the book tackling "the joke of exile," Kahler proposes a further distinction that differentiates two modes of German character — a pre-Christian (pagan), pre-European, and pre-intellectual *Germanismus* and a more civilized and humane *Deutschtum*. Along these newly reconfigured lines, Kahler argues that the tradition of *Deutschtum* is more akin to and even appreciative of Jewish intellect and spirit (and by extension, Jewish wit). Kahler affirms the work of the *"Geistige"* as an intellectual or spiritual dimension that humanizes this type of German subject (*"Das Geistige humanisiert den Deutschen"*) thereby enabling the heralded symbiosis of *Deutschtum* and *Judentum* (145). These Germans are a perfect match for the Jews in their shared affirmation of *Bildung* stressing the humanist values of tolerance and self-cultivation. On the other hand, Kahler frames *Germanismus* as the return of the repressed corporeal tradition that flaunts its hatred of the Jews and is represented by the Nazis as its latest adherents in his own time. Kahler points out that the increase in "hostility against the Jews" coincides with "the revolt of corporeality" and its rejection of the intellectual as well as in the rise of a racialist ideology.[30] What he does not mention here — but what is also implied — is that this group of anti-Semites seizes upon the frivolous type of self-denigrating Jewish jokes (the type that he himself does not tolerate) in order to use them for their own purposes and against the Jews. For Kahler, this distinction also moves in the opposite direction to the extent that he locates a justifiable "Jewish anti-Germanism" as the natural corollary of this mode of Germanic anti-Semitism:

> The anti-Semitism about which the Jews complain is countered on the other side by a Jewish anti-Germanism and this word has its right and profound meaning. It speaks involuntarily from the fact that the nature that is warring against the Jews is not the German [*das deutsche*] but rather the Germanic [*das germanische*]. This is of course not to be taken literally because neither is everything today of Germanic origin that essentially turns the people against what is Jewish nor are all traits of this primordial Germanic being turned against what is Jewish. Germanic only stands rather for that of the dumb, partial, unredeemed, and corporeal primordial state [*Urstand*] in all *Deutschen*, for the pre-Christian, pre-European, pre-intellectual layer of being that is pre-*Deutsche* at the same time. And, not accidentally, the hostility against the Jews has become so strong with the revolt of corporeality along with the impulse to return to an original racial type [*rassichen Ursprungstypus*]. There is strictly speaking no antagonism between *Deutschtum* und *Judentum*, however there is a Jewish anti-Germanism and, in the sense indicated, a Germanic hostility [*germanische Feindseligkeit*] against the Jews. (145)

This more nuanced dichotomy and the introduction of a hostile "Germanism" as a third term offers a more finely tuned dissection of German-Jewish intercultural breakdown at the time of the collapse of the Weimar Republic and it is allied to the Nazi's construction of the Aryan myth and racial ideal. However, it does not alter the fact that Kahler's grounds his truth claims about the nature of Jewish wit in yet another overarching and stereotypical binary opposition (the witty Jew versus the dumb German). Moreover, Kahler's contention that Jewish wit can be aligned solely to the mental faculties remains open to the contaminating criticism that the joke is always somehow related to the body as well. Such a critique of Kahler's position would summon the writings of the Russian literary theorist Mikhail Bakhtin.[31] Bakhtin's analysis of the carnival and the carnivalesque takes the position that laughter always involves the release of the lower bodily stratum. While Bakhtin's theory of carnivalesque laughter and its history is derived from a Christian context, it is possible to transpose its comic thrust to a Jewish folk context as well and to argue that Jewish wit represents the subversion and transgression of prevailing Jewish religious laws, norms, and institutions that allows a space for blasphemy and for the mocking of the sacred. Even if Jewish wit involves hairsplitting logic and mental calisthenics at times, these jokes release a laughter that erupts from the body (individually and collectively). This perspective and its deconstructive impact problematize Kahler's idealizing attempt to liberate Jewish laughter from the corporeal life.

## The Figure of *the Deutsche Michel*

Shortly before the section of *Israel unter den Völkern* that was excerpted as the essay "Der Deutsche und der Galuthwitz," Kahler invokes an allegorical figure in German national mythology — *Der Deutsche Michel* (Michael the German). In the same way that John Bull represents the national character of Great Britain and Uncle Sam symbolizes the United States, Michel personifies Germany and its conception of itself. This visual symbol has served various purposes and it has been put to use since the early modern period. In the seventeenth century, Michel stood as the defender of the purity of the mother tongue — for a German language not to be corrupted by foreign elements. During the revolution of 1848, he stood for national unity and for defending the rights of the people. Since the first half of the nineteenth century, Michel has often been depicted in the realm of caricature where his most distinguishing marker in physical appearance has been his nightcap. In this regard, he often has appeared as a comic and clownish figure. As such, Michel is cast in the German *Real-Encyclopedia* of 1846 as the satirical personification of the "follies and absurdities" (*"Thorheiten und Verkehrtheiten"*) of the German nation.[32] The Polish historian and his latter-day "biographer" Tomasz Szarota relates how the symbolic uses of Michel shifted considerably in the short period between before the World War I and the Nazi takeover when Kahler's book was published:

> Before the outbreak of World War I, Michel is depicted symbolically in the Social Democratic press as the people enslaved by the government, deciding to condemn the militaristic policies and German imperialism. The same Michel transforms himself in August 1914 for the same Social Democrats into a symbol of national unity and patriotic rebellion. In 1919 Michel is stylized in caricature as the innocent victim of the victorious powers that dictate the unjust Treaty of Versailles by the law of the jungle. Soon after, the Nazis took him up and laid claim to him for themselves, only to banish him from their political propaganda.[33]

The caricature of the Deutsche Michel by Werner Hahmann was published in the July 6, 1919 issue of the German humor magazine *Kladderadatsch*, just a week after the signing of the Treaty of Versailles on June 28 (fig. 15). "Ihr Recht!" (Their Right!) underscores Szarota's analysis of the representation of the German Michel "as the innocent victim of the victorious powers." Dressed in his expected nightcap, the miniscule and disarmed Michel is forced to sign the Peace Treaty with a gargantuan gun held to his head. This forced deal with the Allies is figured as a pact with the devil (who is observing the scene from behind the curtain) and as one that is signed under coercion as the winners dictate the law. It is interpreted as a case where "might makes right" as the overpowering gun appears much mightier than Michel's harmless feather pen.

When tracing Michel's appearance in Kahler's texts, the first thing to note is how Kahler characterizes him in the context of the German defeat after World War I as mapped out by Szarota and illustrated by Hahmann's caricature. Kahler's Michel appears as the one who has been betrayed by his many enemies. The analysis begins with a list of national and folk stereotypes perceived through a German lens and projected from the losing side of the battlefield. These are the "striking counter-images" that are juxtaposed with Michel's "true-hearted" image of himself in the wake of World War I:

> The Jew is in this way a "master of masks," the Italian false, the Englishman a cold hypocrite, and the Frenchman a smooth and empty superficial sort. They are all only the striking counterimages of the self-image of the true-hearted and honest German Michel who is duped and outwitted [übertölpelt] and who is full of suspicion toward any compromise that has no other way out than by a knockdown [Niederschlagen]. In point of fact, the Germans are the most betrayed folk—not only by people, but also betrayed by events again and again—because they are the most believing folk, because they are always in a state of expectation. (148–149)

One can see how the image of Michel described by Kahler contributes to the binary oppositions that I have outlined already in my discussion of the Jewish joke as the honest and believing German is "outwitted" by the ironic and dissembling Jew (who is deemed the "master of masks"). In this way, Kahler frames the Deutsche Michel as a witless figure. Donned in his nightcap, this sleepy-headed somnambulist appears to be just too slow and sluggish to catch the drift of the sharp-witted Jewish joke and joker. Kahler even goes so far as to ground the German's "existential feeling of betrayal" by the Jews on the mere fact that they reject the value the Germans place on physicality and therefore on the sheer matter of their difference ("through the mere existence of the other"). Kahler proposes this prejudicial thesis a few pages prior to the

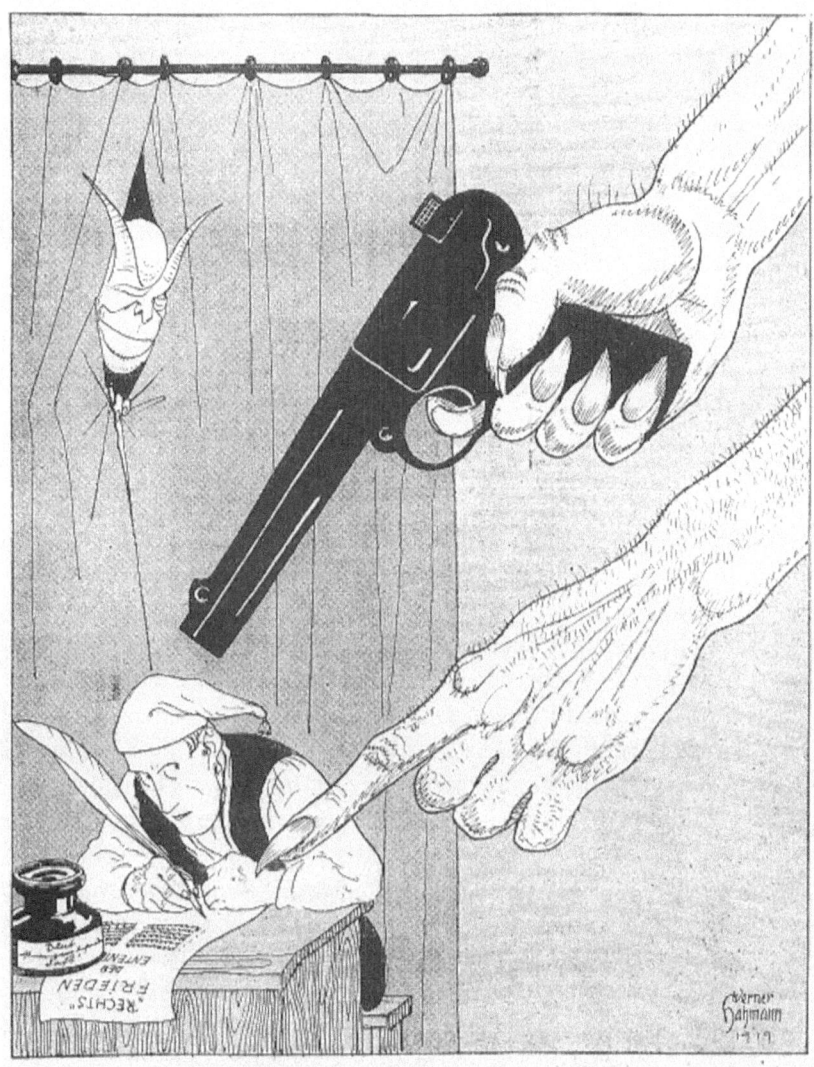

Figure 15. Werner Hahmann. *Ihr Recht!* (Their Right!). Caricature. *Kladderadatch*, no. 27 (July 6, 1919).

previous citation: "Thus everything that the Germans feel against Jews is in the last analysis a protest of corporeality, however much it may be interpreted mentally [geistig]. The root of all the contrary feelings of Germans against Jews—as also against the Roma and the Southerners—is an existential feeling of betrayal, the betrayal *par excellence* and once and for all: through the mere existence of the other, the corporeally conscious German already feels himself betrayed" (147).

The German Michel reappears in two of Kahler's later texts published in English, and both of them flesh out his reading of this folk character and his characteristic attributes. In both cases, Kahler stresses that the naïve and trusting Michel "gets it in the neck." This is the figure of speech deployed by Kahler to signal how Michel is betrayed and punished severely by his enemies. This expression serves as the companion to the other violent image used to illustrate Germany's loss in World War I as being "stabbed in the back" by those civilians (including a large share of Jews) who overthrew the monarchy and declared Germany's surrender. The first instance of this stereotypical usage appears in the 1944 essay "The German Problem: Origins and Development" where Kahler introduces Michel in relationship to a German inferiority complex derived from its delayed nationhood and that consists in the feeling of "always being taken in" on both an individual and collective level. Michel appears in this context as the naïve and gullible country bumpkin who falls prey to the deceptive Jewish city slickers: "Because of this very real inferiority in social intercourse, which is intensified perhaps by a kind of genetic memory of his country's historical shortcomings, the German has developed an almost constitutional feeling that he is always being taken in, individually and collectively. The German's typical picture of himself is as the 'German Michel,' a clumsy young yokel wearing a nightcap, open-hearted, naive, trusting—and always getting it in the neck."[34] When Kahler published the English version of *The Jews Among the Nations* in 1967, he returned again to the figure of the German Michel but using much harsher language positing him as a hostile figure and as the justifiable target of the type of Jewish anti-Germanism discussed earlier. Nevertheless, the passage also begins with a nod to the German-Jewish symbiosis and to those "cultivated" Germans who "were constitutionally close" to the Jews. In this way, Kahler re-inscribes the earlier distinction between *Deutschtum* and *Germanismus*. In marking the points of connection between the Jews and this type, Kahler stresses a shared interest in self-criticism and self-irony. Despite the gap of three decades, Kahler turns again to Jewish wit as the rhetorical figure to mark the ability of the two peoples to get along—the sharing and the mutual understanding of jokes as the marker of German-Jewish intercultural success with one segment of the population in contrast to "that opposite type of German" for whom Michel becomes the unfortunate representative:

> The Jews were constitutionally close to the type of alert, cultivated, open-minded, and open-hearted Germans who are self-critical and self-ironical just as the Jews are. But they were irrepressively [*sic*] hostile to that opposite type of German, in whom German history produced an ineradicable inferiority complex, a persecution complex; who could not overcome bitterness about Germany's having missed her hegemonial day, the glory of predominance that all the Western nations have enjoyed, and who projected the national failure outward, at the expense of other peoples. The mythical impersonators of this self-image are *der reine Tor, Siegfried*, the trustful hero who was stabbed in the back, and most particularly *der deutsche Michel*, the good, honest, naive simpleton wearing a nightcap to indicate his drowsiness, his sluggishness. He is the one who always gets it in the neck, who is constantly cheated and outwitted, by the perfidious British (*das perfide Albion*), the treacherous French and Italians, and especially by the tricky Jews. Unfit to cope with this ubiquitous conspiracy, having no other resource left but his strong arm, he rolls up his sleeves and strikes, blindly, rapturously, with an inordinate joy in the physical performance. It is just such indulgence in violence which the Jews felt was always ready to break loose from the inner insecurity of this German type, and to which they are particularly sensitive.[35]

The mythical figures that delineate the hateful tendencies of "Germanism" in this last version are Richard Wagner's Siegfried as the innocent fool "who gets stabbed in the back," and the German Michel "who gets it in the neck." This covers both German complaints over the betrayal of the Treaty of Versailles. As in the original passage in *Israel unter den Völkern*, Kahler refers to Michel as "constantly cheated and outwitted" by all of his enemies and "especially by the tricky Jews." The brute force and physical violence of Michel as he lashes out against his enemies is also indexed by Kahler in a manner that complements his original thesis regarding German corporeality in contradistinction to Jewish wit and fleeting Jewish jokes.

An examination of an anonymous caricature that addresses the anti-Semitic use of Deutsche Michel in the 1920s (fig. 16) when he was taken up by the Nazis and other ultranationalists (as mentioned by Szarota) further illustrates Kahler's points. In this image, the "tricky Jew" takes the shape of the greedy capitalist while the "good, honest, naïve simpleton" Michel assumes the role of the exploited worker. Following Kahler's points about Germany's "inferiority

Figure 16. Anonymous, *The German Michel is pulled by the Jew with a nose ring*. Caricature. 1920s. (Reprinted by permission of Alamy Stock Photo.)

complex" and "persecution complex," Michel is enslaved by the top-hatted and big-nosed Jewish capitalist who is pulling him around by the nose ring like enchained chattel with the help of his cane. Dressed up in a workman's apron, the physicality of Michel is stressed in line with Kahler's ideas about German corporeality and he carries a heavy sledgehammer over his right shoulder. He also appears in his typical somnambulistic state as he follows the Jew's orders and does his bidding. All in all, this post–World War I anti-Semitic portrayal illustrates the "cheated and outwitted" Michel enslaved to Jewish capital.

About the same time that Kahler's 1936 book with its sharp analysis of the figure of the German Michel as the representative of "the most betrayed folk" was published in exile in Switzerland, the brilliant communist visual satirist John Heartfield published the photomontage *Hitler Tells Fairy Tales II* in the *Arbeiter Illustrierte Zeitung* on March 5, 1936, during its final period of exile in Prague. In it, Heartfield mocked the German national symbol in its new Third Reich guise (fig. 17). In Heartfield's staging, the puppet-like Michel appears in his eponymous sleeping cap but he also wears a Nazi pin on the lapel of his jacket to demonstrate his present ideological bent. His shiny boots also reflect a militaristic posturing that evokes the new standard in SS footwear. Michel stands with his hands held up as if he had been placed under arrest surrounded by a ring of toy soldiers and military weapons. However, if one looks closely at this ring of artillery canons and even a model airplane, they are all facing and pointing in the opposite direction. The same goes for the troops who are all moving away from him. But this departure of the troops does not stop Hitler from making a big scene to get his propagandistic message across that German Michel is under attack. To invoke another fairy tale, Heartfield maps a scenario taken straight out of *The Boy Who Cried Wolf*. Heartfield's caption reads, "and then the poor German Michel screamed so long, that finally the whole world believed him: 'Help, help, I'm surrounded!'"[36] Kahler's suggestion that German Michel is "full of suspicion" — what he would later discuss in terms of a "persecution complex" that marks the Germans as victims of a "ubiquitous conspiracy" — is certainly in evidence in Heartfield's visual satire that is uncannily similar in this respect.

Nevertheless, Kahler's representation and analysis of the German Michel on these three separate occasions represses the fact that this German "autostereotype" (to use Swabota's term) appears as a comic or clownish figure at many points throughout its history. According to Frazer Stephen Clark, this "sleepy-headed dreamer" must be understood as "Germany's famous satirical personification in word and image."[37] However negative or laughable, Michel was the subject of numerous caricatures particularly in the *Vormärz* period as Germany moved toward defining its own national self-image. Kahler appears

Figure 17. John Heartfield, *Hitler erzählt Märchen 2* (Hitler tells fairytales 2) Photomontage. Magazine cover from AIZ, March 5, 1936. (© The Heartfield Community of Heirs / SOCAN [2019])

to ignore the satirical dimensions embodied in "the plump and somnolent figure of Der deutsche Michel" intentionally,[38] and, in this way, Kahler is able to keep him separated from any self-critical or self-ironical dimensions of German cultural expression. Indeed, there is no desire on the author's part to find any parallels between Michel's characterization as a buffoon and the Jewish satirical tradition of jokes and stories that target the fool as *schlemiels* or *schlimazels*. In Kahler's defense, one could say that his focus on this national symbol after World War I occurred at a much less jovial time for Germany and for the betrayed Michel.

In his desire to create a clear dichotomy between fleeting Jewish wit and ponderous German humor, Kahler similarly overlooks the coupling of the mythical German prankster Till Eulenspiegel with the shrewd troublemaker and prankster Hersch Ostropoler derived from Eastern European Jewish folklore. Such a crafty trickster character differs greatly from the corpulent and often lazy Michel. However, Kahler's rhetorical efforts and his selective telling of history are aimed here at keeping his basic dichotomy free from German-Jewish intercultural contamination at the level of folk heroes. By overlooking the figure of Till Eulenspiegel, he is able to secure and maintain his overarching distinction between German physicality and Jewish intellectuality. Composed near Munich in the shadows of the Nazi rise to power, Kahler's analysis parts ways with the writings of Jewish folklorists Chayim Bloch and Heinrich Loewe at the beginning of the Weimar Republic and their comparative approach to folk humor. While the *Bildungsjude* Kahler focused only on the wit of the German Jews in "Judentum und Deutschtum," these folklorists compared the humor of the *Ostjuden* with the Germans. Bloch not only mentions the crafty German comedian, he even compares Till Eulenspiegel to the East European Jewish legend directly in the very title of his study, *Hersch Ostropoler: ein jüdischer Till Eulenspiegel des 18. Jahrhundert: seine Geschichten und Streiche* published in 1921. In the preface, Bloch insists that Hersch "was in his delightful and poignant mockery equal to Till Eulenspiegel."[39] Furthermore, Kahler's systematic repression of the links between a Jewish and a German sense of humor is in sharp contrast to the analysis of the Berlin-based Heinrich Loewe who stressed the intimacy of the German *Schwank* with Jewish *Witz* as comedic forms and who underscored the resemblance between Till Eulenspiegel and any number of the witty Jewish characters that comprised his own edited compilation, *Schelme und Narren mit jüdischen Kappen* (Pranksters and fools with Jewish caps) published in 1920.[40] All in all, Kahler's Michel is set apart from both these German and Jewish pranksters who would make for a more complicated account and that would reveal the mutual imbrication of German and Jewish wit and humor.

## Rabbi Browne and the Limits of "Wise Jewish Self-Irony"

In December 1945, Erich Kahler published a somewhat harsh, even "cruel" (as he himself confessed), book review of Rabbi Lewis Browne's massive anthology *The Wisdom of Israel* in *Commentary* magazine.[41] Kahler was particularly critical of this popular author's mistreatment of the subject of Jewish wit and he saw this fault as linked to the overall incompetence of the anthologist in terms of both his faculty of judgment and his powers of discrimination. In Kahler's assessment, Browne's wrong-headed editorial inclusion of most of the Jewish jokes in his volume simply could not be excused nor explained away. All in all, the author of *The Wisdom of Israel* showed none whatsoever when dealing with the subject of Jewish wit. Kahler writes: "And here we come to the second basic fault of the anthology: the absence of a considered judgment, of a nice discrimination and a feeling for differences of quality. While aphorisms such as those quoted above seem only superfluous, the presence of certain bits of contemporary Jewish humor [*gewisser moderner jüdischer Witze*] in this collection is inexcusable [*unverzeilich*]."[42]

Nevertheless, there was one joke that hit home for Kahler and that tickled his funny bone. It touched him so deeply because it spoke and laughed about the sad truth of homelessness and exile. Even though this joke featured an Eastern European rabbinical protagonist, this German Jewish emigré completely identified with it. The joke spoke directly to his own life in exile given that he had been forced to relocate to the United States in 1938 and that he had become a naturalized citizen in 1944.[43] All in all, this is a joke that struck Erich Kahler because of its being in and about exile. According to Richard Raskin who devoted an academic essay to its variants and meanings, the placement of the so-called "Far from where?" joke in Russia in Browne's anthology is a subterfuge for this is "a classic Jewish refugee joke" that first appeared in public in 1939.[44] If that is the case, then it makes even more sense how and why Kahler was moved by his encounter with Rabbi Browne's version. It is an anecdote that has lost its navigational bearings as well as its sense of being centered or orientated. Fleeing from anti-Semitic persecution in the Russian empire and in pursuit of steady employment, the rabbinical wanderer moves from the pogroms of Russia (whether Kishinev, Kiev, or Bialystok) to the sidewalks of New York, and then on to the far reaches of Argentina. This is how this wandering witticism reads in Rabbi Browne's narration: "The pogroms at the turn of this century caused widespread migration, and a certain rabbi found himself roaming all over Europe, looking for a new post. Finally, he crossed to New York, and there, after months of correspondence, he was informed of an opening in Argentina. When a friend tried to dissuade him from going, saying Argentina was too far away, the wanderer sighed: 'Too far away? From where?'"[45]

Significantly, this was the first time that Kahler included a Jewish joke in his analysis of Jewish humor and this might relate to the changed circumstances of living as an exile in the United States. In the less formal and stuffy air of America and in a place already priding itself about the association of the comic with the Jewish character, Kahler lightens up a little and tells this "joke of exile" which spoke to him directly and concretely. As a German Jewish refugee, Kahler unconsciously projected his own flight from the Nazis onto the pogrom structure of this version of the joke set in Eastern Europe (ca. 1900) when he recites it in his book review. The joke undergoes the slightest of changes but the slips in narration speak volumes about his subject position at Holocaust's end as the self-identifying Kahler inserts one parenthetical word not found in the Browne version in order to denote his own status in exile and to confirm Raskin's research — "(refugee)." Another minor alteration is Kahler's replacement of the friend trying to dissuade the Rabbi to a man trying to dissuade "his (refugee) friend." This second change allows Kahler to step comfortably into the role that was formerly occupied by the wandering Rabbi:

> Certainly, the Jewish humor [*Jüdische Witze*] of our time should not be banished from an anthology of Jewish wisdom [*Weisheit*]. Among these products of sad self-irony [*leidenden Selbstironie*] are some that show flashes of deep insight [*blitzenden Tiefsinn*], a most precise self-recognition and a marvelous knowledge of human conduct; they illuminate the tragedy of Jewish existence in a single word. An example of this sort of humor is given on page 623: "When a man tried to dissuade his (refugee) friend from going to Argentina, saying it was too far away, the wanderer sighed: 'Too far away? from where?'"[46]

Kahler later casts a favorable aesthetic judgment on this joke when he refers to it as "beautiful and serious." In the immediate wake of the Holocaust, Kahler is clearly attracted to the "Far from where?" anecdote because of the way in which it manifests its "laughter through tears" or, as he puts it, how it "illuminate[s] the tragedy of Jewish existence in a single word." This anecdote also resonates with Franz Kafka's stunning parable and "joke of exile" entitled "My Destination" with which Kahler was most certainly familiar.[47] It is fascinating to pursue Raskin's thesis that the joke first appeared in New York on a radio broadcast by the American critic and commentator Alexander Wollcott in 1939. In that very same year when World War II broke out in Europe (which was Kahler's second year in American exile), he published a lengthy essay in English on "Forms and Features of Anti-Judaism" that contains a grim passage about two real-life incidents in contemporary Jewish life that resonate with the Jewish refugee's predicament as narrated in the "Far from where?" witticism (and in similar stories such as the "Haven't you got another globe?" joke). It is exactly this type of situation to which the protagonists respond with their bitter laughter. Here, Kahler takes up the figure of "no man's land" (*Niemandsland*) to articulate the inability of the fleeing Jews of Europe to find a space of sanctuary and refuge. Kahler alludes in this text to two contemporary incidents that were making headlines. The first one refers to those Polish Jews who had fled east to escape the advancing German army in December 1939 and then "found themselves trapped in a no-mans-land about a mile wide on the west bank of the Bug [river]"[48] when they were denied entry to the Soviet Union. The second incident relates to the MS *St. Louis* that left from Hamburg in 1939 but was denied entry to Cuba, the United States, and Canada before it was sent back to Europe. Certain aspects of this passage link up with the suspended state of animation that permeates the Jewish joke of exile that Kahler shared with his friend Thomas Mann in 1951 (see later in this chapter). In both incidents, the Jews find themselves subject to the aporias of "no man's land" and in need of a "joke of exile" (*Galuthwitz*) in order to provide some serious comic relief that will "illuminate the tragedy of Jewish existence in a single word": "Formerly when the Jews were driven from one country, there was always another to take them in. It remained for our times to create an intellectual situation in which Jews must camp out on a river island between two borders, exposed to the rigors of winter in 'No Man's Land,' or range the world for weeks in ships that can land them nowhere but in the arms of inevitable torture and death. These are the earthly milestones of Jewish history—exile, wandering, 'No Man's Land.'"[49]

In his review of *The Wisdom of Israel*, Kahler insists that Jewish wit should not be placed in a state of banishment or exile from Jewish wisdom. On the contrary, he seeks to restore wit and wisdom to their common etymological ground. Nevertheless, there are serious limits to the state of coexistence wherein wit and wisdom can intersect and reside harmoniously side by side. Too often, the case becomes otherwise for Kahler if and when the intent of the joke strays from what he deems as "wise Jewish self-irony." Although his two analyses are bookended by the rise and fall of the Third Reich (1932 and 1945), Kahler's policing of the Jewish joke in his review remains quite consistent with his analysis in *Israel unter den Völkern* and his earlier condemnation of the "terrible hypertrophy of the joke":

> But the bits of "humor" ["*Witze*"] that surround this very beautiful and serious joke are vulgar and shameful—as indeed is most of the humor

in this book. They do not flow from wise Jewish self-irony [*weisen jüdischen Selbstironie*] but from that undignified self-mockery and self-contempt [*würdelosen Selbstverhöhnung und Selbstverachtung*] that unfortunately can also be found among the Jews. Humor of this sort is not something to lay stress upon; it confirms the truth of much for which we are justly reproached. [*Witze dieser Art sind nicht etwas, was man herzeigen sollte; sie bestätigen die Wahrheit von manchem, was man uns mit Recht vorwirft.*] In any event it has nothing to do with wisdom [*Weisheit*] and does not belong in a book like this.[50]

Kahler's Jewish joke dichotomy juxtaposes serious jokes and frivolous jokes, good jokes and bad jokes, beautiful jokes and vulgar jokes. As might be expected, Kahler refrains in his review from reciting any of the "vulgar and shameful" jokes that do not make the grade for him. He will not stoop so low nor let himself be contaminated by any of those unfortunate examples that he sees as "undignified self-mockery and self-contempt." Like many joke analysts before him, he appears to be quite concerned about the potential toxicity of the Jewish joke and its harmful and corrosive effects. And the thing that he appears to be the most concerned about and what he finds to be the most disconcerting of all is the possibility that these self-contemptuous jokes play into the hands of anti-Semitic rhetoric and their hateful smear campaigns. The thin line between the Jewish joke and anti-Semitism becomes blurred again as "wise Jewish self-irony" slips into "undignified self-mockery and self-contempt." But what is most peculiar about Kahler's assessment is that he does not simply say that the reason why people should not tell these jokes is because they confirm negative Jewish stereotypes or because they give a false impression of what it means to be Jewish. Instead, what Kahler appears to be saying is that such bad jokes serve to confirm the truth of much of what anti-Semites rightly, justifiably, and legitimately accuse the Jews. In this regard, a better translation of Kahler's text would be—"These jokes confirm the truth of much that one accuses us legitimately." The attacks of the anti-Semites on Jewish character would appear to have some foundation and justification as Kahler considers how and why such anti-Semitic rhetoric actually could be justified. Has Kahler somehow lost his own sense of good judgment here in taking up the point of view of the anti-Semitic attacker? Or is he simply being overly cautious and sensitive at a moment when six million of his European brethren had so recently perished? After all, he could have spoken of their "prejudicial" or even "mistaken" rather than their "rightful" or "legitimate" accusations. Whatever the rationale, Kahler's negative assessment offers another index of his own cultural conservatism and elitism and the belief that the Jewish joke needs to be placed in the service of education (*Bildung*). Lacking wit in the service of wisdom and without the presence of a pedagogical purpose, the Jewish joke risks confirming "the truth of what one accuses us legitimately." Interestingly, Kahler's prescient viewpoint on the negative risks of Jewish wit was confirmed by the mobilization of the Jewish joke in Siegfried Kadner's *Rasse and Humor* in 1936.[51] The Nazi propagandist made exactly this type of argument—that Jewish jokes confirm the truth of all the negative things that the Nazis were saying about them. In this way, the "vulgar and shameful" Jewish joke becomes a scapegoat as the humor of Jewish self-contempt engenders vitriolic anti-Semitic diatribe as its logical conclusion.[52] One questions though whether Kahler too should have taken such "vulgar and shameful" Jewish jokes as indices of the truth. Indeed, the more absurdly self-deprecating and abject Jewish jokes are, the less their hold on the reality principle and any engagement with the telling of the truth.

But just what are these "bits of 'humor'"—with the scare quotes placed by Kahler around the word *Witze* here in order to signal to readers that the author does not find them amusing at all—that surround the exile joke in Browne's anthology and that Kahler found to be so distasteful? A closer look at the two jokes that precede and follow the praiseworthy exile joke that "shows flashes of deep insight" reveals their levels of toxicity. The first joke offers another version of the famous "skeptical joke" that appeared in Freud's *Witz* book where one trader accuses his friend of lying to him about his destination. Instead of the cities being listed as Lemberg and Cracow, they are now the rhyming pair of Pinsk and Minsk. Freud admired this joke as an absurd and "precious story" that uses the technique of "representation through the opposite" to the extent that "the second one is lying when he speaks the truth, and speaks the truth by means of a lie."[53] However, one surmises that this same joke strikes Kahler as an example of "undignified self-mockery" that implicates these two Jewish traders in a web of deception and lies. In this way, the joke not only speaks badly of their character, it reflects badly on the Jewish character in general. In foregrounding a Jewish propensity for lying, this joke ironically "confirms the truth . . . for which we are justly reproached" (as Kahler puts it). The fact that this joke was taken up by Siegfried Kadner as an example of Jewish mendaciousness indicates that Kahler's fears turned out to be grounded (see chapter 5). Browne's version of the joke reads:

> Two traders who made the rounds of the provincial fairs selling the same sort of merchandise chanced to meet on a train.
> "Where are you going?" asked the first.

"Me?" answered his rival with an air of innocence. "I'm on my way to Pinsk."

"Hh!" snorted the other, "You tell me you are going to Pinsk because you want me to believe you are going to Minsk. But I happen to know you really are going to Pinsk, so why do you have to tell me a lie?"⁵⁴

Meanwhile, the second joke involves the story of two Polish Jews who leave the *shtetl* to seek their fortunes in the European capitals of Berlin and Paris. This "vulgar and shameful" anecdote in Kahler's view casts the Jewish *parvenu* in the role of an ungrateful and dishonest stockbroker who quite consciously forgets to pay back the loan to his fellow countryman and who tries to cover up his immoral behavior on the grounds of a specious argument that he wraps in French patriotism. The joke therefore reveals how two Polish Jews who had grown up in same *shtetl* are later divided along the nationalist lines of France and Germany:

Two Polish Jews left their native village to seek their fortunes in the West. When they reached Berlin, one of them felt he had gone far enough, but the other wanted to push on to Paris. Lacking sufficient funds, however, he begged his friend to lend him an extra hundred marks, promising to return them with interest out of his very first earnings. Needless to add, he did not send them back even without interest. Ten years later, the fellow who had settled in Berlin was sent to Paris by his employer, and while there he was amazed to discover that his old friend was reputed to be a highly successful stockbroker. So he went to him and said, "Look, Itzik, I'm still a poor man, and you're supposed to be very rich. Why haven't you ever paid me back my hundred marks?" "*Quoi?*" cried the other, drawing himself up and suddenly lapsing into French. "Pay you back? First you Germans must give us back Alsace-Lorraine!"⁵⁵

Browne's chapter on "Jewish Humor" goes on to enumerate many jokes about "slow-witted" *schlemiels*, "cunning" *schnorrers*, and, finally, the "moronic" tales that document the fools of Chelem.⁵⁶ To Kahler's way of thinking, most of these jokes have "nothing to do with wisdom" and nothing to do with "wise Jewish self-irony." While these jokes may make people laugh, Kahler sees them as examples of the laughter of shame and self-contempt. As this European *Bildungsjude* clings to his elevated sense of Jewish wit grounded in a "mighty seriousness" that exemplifies the pedagogical pursuit of wisdom as well as in the service of ethical and cultural formation, he appears to be in no mood for the vulgar and inferior cultural productions of this American anthology.

## "Are You Crazy?": Kahler Tells an Exile Joke to Thomas Mann

But this turns out to be not the only joke of exile that captivated Kahler as revealed in a letter that he wrote to his close friend and patron Thomas Mann during the spring of 1951. It was the renowned German novelist who encouraged Kahler to go to Princeton, New Jersey, in 1938. There, Kahler would meet with other famous refugees including Albert Einstein, Herman Broch, and Erwin Panofsky, and he would make his home (One Evelyn Place) the center for the circle of German Jewish refugee intellectuals that would become known as the Kahler-Kreis. After Mann moved to California in 1942, their correspondence picked up again during the next decade until Mann decided to return to Europe settling in Switzerland for the final years of his life (1952–1955). It is in this context that we can understand Kahler's letter to Mann dated April 14, 1951, a letter colored by Cold War anxieties and written against the backdrop of the McCarthy witch hunt of which Mann had become a target. Kahler strikes an apocalyptic tone in this letter in the face of the ominous threat of nuclear war ("for there is simply no escaping from what is going to happen this time"). The letter is devoted primarily to the ongoing question of the subject in exile and not being at home in the world. Given that the return to Germany (East or West) was not an option, the two speculate as to where Mann should live out his final years. Kahler has negative things to say about both the delusions of mighty America and the illusions of a slowly recovering Europe amid the Marshall Plan. He then throws out a third exotic way that would take his old friend to India only to withdraw this idealized suggestion on the grounds of impracticality. Kahler pleads with Mann to stay put in the United States and to "resist where we are." It is then that Kahler recalls a pertinent Jewish witticism that he recounts for Mann. It is another joke about exile that helps to relieve the tension that he is feeling at the potential loss of his comrade in exile. One hears the traces of the popular Yiddish word *meschuggene* lurking in the punch line of this German version of the anecdote:

> In this connection, I must tell you a little anecdote that illustrates our situation incisively [*pregnant*]. Two friends are crossing the Atlantic, one sailing from Europe to America, the other from America to Europe. In the middle of the ocean the ships meet and pass. The friends

standing at the rail recognize one another, and both call across the water simultaneously, "Are you crazy?" ["*Bist du wahnsinnig?*"][57]

The joke leaves the passengers and the reader without resolution and in a perfect state of suspended animation somewhere in the middle of the Atlantic Ocean between the old and the new worlds. The joke plays out the fantasy to inhabit a "no man's land" at sea. That is the joke's elegance and its eloquence. The sentiment that is expressed in this joke is very close to one that Salcia Landmann tells about the experience of a wandering German Jewish refugee named Mr. Kohn who shuttles back and forth between Europe and Israel circa 1933 and who finds it difficult to settle down amid the woes of the world: "At the beginning of the time of the Nazis, Mr. Kohn constantly shuttled back and forth between Europe and Israel. When he lands in Israel for the third time, someone asks him if that makes any sense. 'Here is not good — and over there it is even worse. Everywhere there's *Tsuris* (trouble). One only has peace and quiet on the ship.'"[58]

But neither Kahler nor Mann can tarry with the punch line nor remain poised at the mad crossroads of the two ships that meet and pass each other in the night. We have seen already how Kahler endorses the traveler sailing to America in a point of self-identification with his own situation. Thomas Mann's response also refuses to leave things suspended in a "no man's land." He takes a deep breath of the "idiotic vileness" and apocalyptic doom and gloom of 1951 before he opts for the traveler who is moving in the opposite direction toward Switzerland. As mentioned, Mann decided to follow in the footsteps of the man sailing eastward the following year thereby escaping from "the barbarous infantilism" that constituted American life for him during the 1950s. Mann curiously responds to Kahler's entreaties and "striking" anecdote in a way that takes it at face value:

> Have men ever had to inhale so poisoned an atmosphere, one so utterly saturated with idiotic vileness? We live in a world of doom from which there is no longer any escaping. Your "Are you crazy?" anecdote is striking enough [*schlagend genug*], except that in my opinion the man sailing westward is just a trace crazier, for despite the fact that dear Switzerland may be even more pro-American than some Americans, it seems to me that in general the European mentality does not come up to the barbarous infantilism we have here.[59]

From this exchange of letters, it becomes clear that Kahler felt a great degree of comfort and a sense of intimacy with Mann to the point that he had no reservations in sharing a Jewish joke with him. Mann had served as Kahler's interlocutor since the days of *Israel unter den Völkern* and there even exists an exchange of letters between them that includes Mann's response after he read the manuscript one year before its Swiss publication. At that time, Kahler had confessed to Mann "that in the boundless misery of the present-day world there is indescribable comfort in the intellectual and human closeness to you."⁶⁰ Coincidentally, a few of Mann's comments in the letter that elicited this affirmative response focused specifically on Kahler's views regarding Jewish wit about which Mann expressed a great deal of sympathy. Mann restates Kahler's binary opposition in contrasting Jewish "ironic mother wit" in contradistinction to the crude and lumpish German "psyche bound to the flesh." Given Kahler's knowledge of Mann's predilections, it makes perfect sense why he had no qualms telling him the "Are you crazy?" anecdote sixteen years later. The German-Jewish symbiosis is no longer to be viewed as a success story, but rather as a painful embarrassment as Mann underlines the difference between a credulous German corporeality and an ironic Jewish cosmopolitanism in his epistolary review of *Israel unter den Völkern*.

> I felt closest to you in the passages which arouse a kind of tragic cheerfulness [*tragischer Heiterkeit*], such as the one about "vain knowledge" ["*vergeblichen Wissen*"] of the inevitable disillusionment of a "mighty faith" ["*gewaltigen Glaubens*"]. In a few truly poetic lines, you make us feel the embarrassment and painfulness [*Peinlichkeit*] of such a symbiosis, on the one hand, the ironic mother wit [*ironische Urgewitzheit*] of old cosmopolitan blood [*alten Weltblutes*], and on the other hand, the credulity [*Glaubenskraft*] of a crude psyche bound to the flesh [*plumpen Fleischesseele*].⁶¹

In lauding Kahler as a gifted writer whose passages "arouse a kind of tragic cheerfulness" in his analysis of the "German-Jewish question," Mann also positions his friend in the Nietzschean tradition of the gay scientist and the cheerful and serene attitude that the German philosopher found in his analysis of Greek tragedy.⁶² This allusion also evokes Nietszche's famous dictum and profound statement about our need to laugh to keep from crying in *The Will to Power*: "Perhaps I know best why man alone laughs; he alone suffers so deeply that he *had* to invent laughter. The unhappiest and most melancholy animal is, as is fitting, the most cheerful."⁶³ But, in this case, the prime mover of Kahler's "tragic cheerfulness" is neither Hellenistic nor Nietzschean in its origin. It rather comes from an attitude derived from Jewish wit and its uncanny ability to laugh through suffering.

## Being Chosen for Exile

In the *Festschrift* paying homage to Kahler on his sixty-fifth birthday, Thomas Mann stressed the significance of exile for this split subject: "Not too many people are aware of it; his life was split in two by the German calamity of 1933 that made him an exile cast forth in an alien world."[64] The casting of Erich Kahler as an exile has been the subject of two intriguing essays — Gerhard Lauer's "The Empire's Watermark: Erich Kahler and Exile"[65] and David Kettler's "The Symbolic Uses of Exile: Erich Kahler at Ohio State."[66] Both scholars raise interesting points about Kahler's life in exile and its impact upon his ideas about history. For instance, Lauer argues that "the isolation of exile" in the United States nourished "Kahler's apocalyptical philosophy of history" (71). However, neither of these essays covers the contemporary significance of the Jewish question nor the Hebraic legacy of *Galuth* (exile) and how such factors relate to Kahler's understanding and formulation of being in exile. This final section hopes to fill in this gap in a modest way by unpacking Kahler's somewhat contested views regarding Jewish exile at the time of the publication of *Israel unter den Völkern* and in relationship to the chosen excerpt "Der Deutsche und der Galuthwitz."

It is impossible to determine from the archival records how and for what purpose the title "Der Deutsche und der Galuthwitz" was affixed to the Kahler excerpt published in the *Jüdische Revue* in the summer of 1936. Nevertheless, the title does run parallel to the structure of a number of other Kahler titles that compare and contrast the two peoples (e.g., "*Judentum und Deutschtum*"). Here, the phrase *Galuthwitz* (that can be translated as either the "joke of exile" or the "exile joke") substitutes or serves as a placeholder for the Jews themselves. Other than its inclusion in the title, the excerpt does not mention this keyword that denotes Jewish exile, nor does it address either *Galuth* or *Galuthwitz* as a specific concept that needs to be analyzed. Unlike his later use of case studies in the Lewis Browne book review or in the Thomas Mann letter, there is no close reading of any particular "exile joke" on display that can function in an exemplary manner and thereby help to explicate the choice of this title. But at the same time, there is something metonymic in the way that Kahler's *Galuthwitz* stands in for the Jew and for the Jewish question as a whole. It forces one to consider the possibility that the situation of the Jews in Europe in 1936 (and beyond) was to be likened to a bitter joke about Jewish exile. It was as if a "joke of exile" was being played upon them, one that forced them to ask questions like the punch line of that other famous Jewish refugee joke that showcases a mordant wit and the "bitterest knowledge" — "Haven't you got another globe?"[67]

While Kahler does not use the term *Galuth* anywhere in this excerpt, he does refer to it specifically near the end of the volume and in such a way that addresses the intellectual and spiritual mission of the Jews historically and in the present. Kahler acknowledges that the term has become discredited because of the Zionist movement where it has acquired a purely negative and pejorative meaning in contrast to life in the promised land of Israel. However, this does not deter Kahler from affirming this concept as part of the transnational destiny of the tribe called Israel and its ongoing spiritual, intellectual, and ethical mission in the world as a whole: "*Galuth* will remain as long as our mission [*Sendung*] remains, as long as Israel itself remains. It is discredited today, not only among the Gentiles [*Andern*], even in the Jewish community [*Judenheit*] itself. But that makes no difference" (169). Kahler then spells out the need for Jews to live an exemplary life in Diaspora, especially in such troubled times evoking in an oblique manner the Jewish obligation to perform *Tikkun Olam* (to repair or heal the world): "But furthermore, the Diaspora will have for itself the duty of the assignment [*Pflicht der Uebertragung*] to further remove all suffering and hardship" (169–170).

As expected, such pro-exilic rhetoric did not please the Zionist nationalists of Kahler's day for whom this condition could only be associated with a negative state, with a feeling of being uprooted from one's own native soil and subject to alien rule. In response to Kahler's Diasporism, the Czech émigré Viktor Kellner who had settled in Palestine in 1911 published an extended book review and meditation on *Israel unter den Völkern* in 1936. Kellner derided and disparaged Kahler as a *"europagläubige Jude"* ("Jew who believes in Europe") and remarked "the center is in the Diaspora for Kahler."[68] Kellner cuts to the heart of the ideological matter: "Here stands one principle against the other — denial of exile [*Galuthverneinung*] against affirmation of exile [*Galuthbejahung*]."[69] In contrast to Kahler, Kellner insists that Jewish creativity and productivity can only happen in a land that they can call their own: "The Jewish people as a whole has never been creative in the Diaspora but on the contrary, always on the soil of their own homeland alone.... The building of Palestine is for us the central task of the next generations of Jews — as opposed to Kahler, for whom the emphasis of Jewish being and effort lies in the Diaspora [*Zerstreuung*] and for whom Jewish Palestine, although desirable and something to be encouraged, remains a peripheral matter indeed."[70] It is not known whether Kahler ever read this book review by Kellner but he later would have an exchange of letters with Gershom Scholem in the summer of 1967 that contains echoes of this earlier difference of opinion with Kellner regarding the proper place of Diaspora (affirmation of exile) and Zion (denial of exile) in contemporary Jewish life.[71]

For someone in the mindset of *Galuthbejahung*, Jewish wit was deemed to be one of those cherished cultural goods and especially during a period like the one in which Kahler composed and published *Israel unter den Völkern* (1932–1936). For here the Jews of Germany were confronted with another major moment of exile (*Galuth*) — not an exodus from the land of Israel but rather an exile from within Diaspora when they were forced out of their dwelling place of almost one thousand years (Ashkenaz). In these sorrowful times of displacement and exile, the Jewish joke again provided comfort and solace for these refugees from the Nazis. Thus, the expulsion from Germany would have represented for Kahler another "experience of the clash between idea and world" that served as a breeding ground for Jewish wit and for a general sharpening of their wits. In such a situation, Jewish wit could help to alleviate the homesickness that the German Jews were feeling and on which Kahler commented in these few heavy sentences found in his book after the excerpt published as "Der Deutsche und der Galuthwitz." Kahler even alludes here to the suicides of his comrades in response to the rise of Nazism: "[German Jews] are just like the Jews of other countries who are deeply interwoven and marked by the soul of their home ... the most severe homesickness [*Heimweh*] still plagues some of them even after they have just been expelled from this country by means of the basest form of human persecution of all time. And not a few of them have even preferred to leave the world rather than Germany" (155).

In this dire situation of exile and persecution, the Jewish joke served as the means to "illuminate the tragedy of Jewish existence" yet again. Interestingly, Kahler returned to the subject of *Heimweh* in *The Jews among the Nations* but this time to recite a telling refugee joke with "an ironical truth" dating from the Nazi period and presumably around the time of the publication of *Israel unter den Völkern*. In contrast to the earlier volume, Kahler narrates the following German-Jewish intercultural anecdote with a punch line that makes fun of the very homesickness of the Jews. The story features the famous non-Jewish pacifist writer and author of *All Quiet on the Western Front* who takes up the question of *Heimweh*. The punch line here ("No. I am not Jewish") reverses itself to serve as a point of implication and identification for the Jewish émigré who recites this anecdote and his being chosen for exile: "The German émigré, Erich Maria Remarque, hit an ironical truth with the answer he is said to have given to a Nazi emissary who wooed him with the promise of the highest honors if he would be willing to return to Germany. When he refused, the Nazi asked him: 'Are you not a bit homesick?' 'Homesick?' Remarque said, 'No. I am not Jewish.'"[72]

In its shrewd combination of wit and wisdom, the Remarque anecdote functions like the other "serious" and profound refugee jokes that Kahler savored. However, Kahler never embraced the Jewish joke carte blanche. Instead, he took a much more tempered approach to Jewish wit for he remained wary of its potential toxicity and corrosiveness ("that eats away at all essences") as well as the ways in which some of these jokes played into the hands of anti-Semites. That is why Kahler warned against the "terrible hypertrophy of the joke" and why he spoke of the "Germans' disparaging image of the Jews" as that "prejudiced view that is halfway stuck to a truth" (154).

But even if we take issue with Kahler's joking conservatism and his regulatory attempts to bring Jewish wit within acceptable confines in support of the values of wisdom and *Bildung*, this Jewish historian and cultural critic whose life moved further into exile and diaspora deserves a great deal of credit for his sharp and prescient analysis on the eve of Germany's collapse. Taking Jewish wit as a serious object of study, Kahler understood the status of the Jewish joke in Germany to be a cultural symptom of German-Jewish intercultural relations in general. This meant that if most Germans were no longer getting or enjoying Jewish jokes anymore, if these witticisms had become somehow "misunderstood and unreasonable," then this was a sign of disharmonious and disagreeable relations between them and a sign that there were even more serious troubles and dangers lying ahead. The misfiring of the Jewish joke could only lead to coldness and the opening up of a hollow space or chasm between these two peoples. And if the Jews and the Germans were finding themselves at wit's end and in a position of unequal power relations, then this impasse could only mean that the two peoples had reached a dangerous and hopeless place of abandonment and loss. In the waning days of the Weimar Republic, Kahler reviews this humorless and unbridgeable gap that was the total opposite of anything such as the sharing of superiority that he found necessary for the staging and mutual appreciation of Jewish jokes:

> Wit is a sharpened utterance, the utterance of exuberance, of superiority. It has to rely on a like-minded and receptive company, on an agreement based on the same superiority. A misunderstood and unreasonable joke is not only senseless; it immediately becomes dangerous. It creates coldness, a hollow space between people, a subsidence [*Absacken*] in the one against the other and an abrupt feeling of being abandoned and being lost [*Verlassen- und Verlorensein*]. (151)

# 5
# Of Jokes and Propaganda
## The Mobilization of the Jewish Joke in the Nazi Era

Describing "The Characteristics of Propaganda," the French philosopher and sociologist Jacques Ellul reviews how total propaganda demands the integration of the enemy into one's own frame of reference. Ellul refers to this extreme totalitarian model as the "propaganda of self-criticism." To quote Ellul: "That the enemy of a regime . . . can be made to declare, *while he is still the enemy,* that this regime was right, that his opposition criminal, and that his condemnation is just—that is the ultimate result of totalitarian propaganda. The enemy (while still remaining the enemy and because he is the enemy) is converted into a supporter of the regime."[1] My argument in this chapter is not that the Jews were somehow brainwashed and converted into supporters of the Nazi regime as the result of any successful propaganda campaign. It is rather to demonstrate how the Nazi's appropriation of self-deprecating Jewish jokes as anti-Semitic propaganda during the Third Reich served as a crucial means by which to demonstrate that the Nazi's condemnation of the Jews was completely justified and that they were only reiterating the negative things that the Jews were saying about themselves already. In this manner, the Jewish joke was reinscribed by the Nazis as a model for the propaganda of self-criticism.[2]

This peculiar paradox of the "enemy supporter" is reminiscent of the absurd logic that is contained in many classic Jewish jokes and their radical reversals. For instance, two Jews are dining together in a restaurant and both decide to order trout. When the food arrives, one friend serves himself the bigger piece and gives his companion the smaller portion. Upon hearing the complaint that this is a most impolite thing to do and that, if his companion were serving, he would have taken the smaller portion, the server points out that this is exactly what the other has on his plate, and then asks him why he is complaining. In this way, a rude or even unjust act gets twisted (and enlisted) as something that the victimized diner desired in the first place.[3] This example suggests that there might be a structural affinity in the cunning and conniving logic upon which both jokes and propaganda rely. But the Jewish joke in particular lends itself to the propaganda of self-criticism for an even more important reason. This is derived from the fact that both "self-criticism" and "self-irony" lie at the heart of the Jewish joke and these elements are part of the prevailing understanding about how it functions from the time of Sigmund Freud to the Holocaust.[4] To reiterate Freud's analysis in *Jokes and Their Relationship to the Unconscious*: "The occurrence of self-criticism as a determinant may explain how it is that a number of the best jokes have grown up on the soil of Jewish popular life. I do not know whether there are many other instances of a people making fun of its own character to such a degree."[5] Interestingly, this same truism is expressed in the treatise on race and humor published by Siegfried Kadner in 1936. The Nazi propagandist comments: "It is known and should by no means be denied that the Jew applies much self-irony, and that the most effective jokes about Jews come from Jews."[6]

In light of this specific characteristic, it should not be surprising to learn that there are numerous instances of the mobilization of Jewish jokes in the service of the propaganda of self-criticism during the Nazi era. Both jokes and propaganda have always been understood using the strategic language of warfare as weapons to be mobilized and both share a type of mobility in regard to how they operate and fluctuate.[7] The mobilization of the Jewish joke as a totalitarian propaganda weapon involves a double-edged strategy that satirizes and mocks the Jewish enemy while taking the joke all too seriously at the same time. In this way, Nazi propaganda claims that its character assassination against the Jews finds its factual basis in the negative stereotypes found in Jewish jokes that support the anti-Semitic position. This study concentrates on the Nazi's twisted appropriation of the Jewish joke by focusing on a case history that sheds light on the dynamics whereby the Jewish joke was mobilized to serve the "propaganda of self-criticism" in the Nazi era, thereby turning self-critical and self-mocking Jewish jokes against themselves. In this manner, the Nazi's "joke propaganda" took the form of a cruel laughter of superiority that targeted the Jews as an inferior race. But before proceeding with a detailed analysis of Kadner's *Rasse und Humor* and its devious manipulations of the Jewish joke in the service of Nazi propaganda, I would like to provide some general observations about the Nazi theory and practice of jokes *in* propaganda and to counteract the claim that humor did not play a significant role in the arsenal of Nazi propaganda weapons.

## Humor in Propaganda: Nazi Theory and Practice

In *Ethnic Humor Around the World: A Comparative Analysis*, the late sociologist of humor Christie Davies subjects a genre of ethnic jokes about a group that he calls "excluded enterprisers" to a cross-cultural analysis. The negative stereotype of the Jewish businessman as an alien economic body and his clever (what Davies calls "canny") but ethically suspect and dishonest practices become a central figure in this joking genre. Davies begins with a statement that compares these Jewish swindler jokes with the themes of anti-Semitic propaganda and he locates their point of intersection in the following manner: "There is a notable congruence between the content of these jokes and that of anti-Semitic prejudice, ideology, and propaganda."[8] Even though he acknowledges the coincidence in content, Davies refuses to believe that these jokes play an important role in the expression of anti-Semitic sentiments. As he states: "I am also skeptical of the view that jokes based on the canniness script are an important vehicle for expressing anti-Semitic sentiments."[9] Later, he enumerates the horrific imagery of Nazi propaganda that compares Jews to vermin, lice, maggots, and spiders among other vile creatures and he asks rhetorically: "With rhetoric and images like these, who needs jokes?"[10] My intent in this chapter is to revise Davies's reservations through a consideration of the theory and practice involved in the Nazi mobilization of humor in general and the Jewish joke in particular as a means by which to propagate and reinforce anti-Semitic stereotypes of race and culture. I want to demonstrate how Kadner's *Rasse and Humor*—a book that served an analogous function to Davies's compendium of *Ethnic Humor around the World* in the Nazi Weltanschauung—needed Jewish jokes based not only on the canniness model and but also on other much less sympathetic scripts as an important vehicle by which to express and mobilize anti-Semitic sentiments during the Third Reich.

Davies's underestimation of the role of jokes and joke theory in Nazi rhetoric and imagery might be contrasted with the views expressed by the emigrant sociologist Hans Speier in *Witz und Politik: Essay über die Macht und das Lachen*. In the section on "The Laughter of the Powerful," Speier insists on the joke as a propaganda weapon and even proposes a new category to signify this practice of war by other more humorous means—the "ideological joke." In contrast to Davies, Speier discusses the necessity of these ideological jokes: "Indeed, the merest reference to the powerful laughing at the oppressed would be incomplete without a reference to the joke which is used by totalitarian regimes as a weapon of propaganda. Its victims are political, religious, and ethnic minorities (or the foreign enemy). These are the jokes and caricatures in the comic papers and cabarets of national socialist Germany which not only may have been presented, but had to be presented. [One] might describe this modern product of the mind as 'ideological jokes.'"[11] In order to redress Davies's account, it is necessary to review the primary texts of the major Nazi tacticians and strategists of the "ideological joke" to understand how the inducement of a hostile and aggressive laughter against the Jewish enemy could function as an indispensable weapon in their theory and practice of propaganda.

In his instructive handbook on *Propaganda and National Power*, the Nazi party's leading propaganda theorist and radio chief Eugen Hadamovsky reviews the principles of his craft. In the section on "Psychological Foundations," there is a specific place allocated to derisive laughter in general and for caricature in particular in the arsenal of propagandistic weapons directed against the enemies of national (socialist) power. Hadamovsky compares and contrasts mockery and fear as two crucial activating ingredients in the Nazi propaganda mix. Both are to be understood as catalysts or stimulants for inducing that agitated state of psychological readiness in the masses conducive for the best reception of the party's positive suggestions — what the Allies later would call indoctrination or Nazification.

> Caricature, misrepresentation, and one-sidedness appear to belong in propaganda. Laughing at the enemy is as necessary as to fear his strength. The doctrine of suggestion — while contestable in many ways — has discovered a law that is most probably the case when it claims that suggestion first takes effect in a state of agitation and excitement. Mockery and fear are sensitive reactions — agitations — that encourage the introduction of suggestion. Mockery gives the feeling of superiority because wherever there is laughter, there is also trust in victory. Meanwhile, fear immediately presses into action an active attitude because it believes in the recognition of dangers. Thus, mockery and fear are two components of propaganda indispensable for its success.[12]

With his totalizing if not totalitarian comments about laughter ("Mockery gives the feeling of superiority because wherever there is laughter, there is also trust in victory"), Hadamovsky adapts a Hobbesian view of laughter where humor arises from the "sudden glory" that comes in the recognition of one's superiority over others.[13] According to Hadamovsky, the subject position of the Nazi laugher is the dominating voice of an authority that trusts in victory and that feels superior when it laughs out loud. Structured like propaganda itself, the Nazi subject is only capable of investing in a mocking and derisive laughter aimed at ridiculing the enemy. There is no opening that allows for a shred of self-doubt—for that undercurrent of ambivalent feeling that would generate laughter (in the Jewish self-ironic tradition) as the mark and release of tension or as self-doubt. In this way, Hadamovsky's propagandistic views on Nazi laughter and the necessity of other-directed tendentiousness exclude the possibility of Jewish self-directed wit by its very definition. All in all, Hadamovsky's systematic exclusion of the possibility of a minor voice capable of another type of (self-ironic) laughter confirms Nazi comic rhetoric as cruel and authoritarian.

Meanwhile, the young propagandist Joseph Goebbels (to whom Hadamovsky's book is dedicated) began his rabble-rousing career in the mid-1920s through a systematic campaign of Jewish name-baiting, caricature, and jokes in his newspaper, *Der Angriff* (The attack). These attacks were targeted specifically at the Berlin police chief constable, Bernhard Weiss. In giving Weiss the negatively charged and pejorative nickname (*Spottname*) of "Isidore," Goebbels uses a classic strategy of tendentious jokes. As Freud remarked and as Goebbels practiced: "A tendentious joke need be nothing other than a verbal joke as regards its technique. For instance, jokes that 'play about' with proper names often have an insulting and wounding purpose."[14] The Nazi propagandist as political prankster picked up successfully on the social stigma attached to bearing this stereotypical Jewish name in Germany and applied it tauntingly to Weiss. Goebbels and his Nazi caricaturist colleague Hans Schweitzer compiled their best efforts in a book demonstrating the effectiveness of their combined strategy of jokes and propaganda — an abrasive mixture and mix-up of laughter and hatred — *Das Buch Isidor: Ein Zeitbild von Lachen und Hass*.[15]

Goebbels also proved himself to be an avid instigator of tendentious jokes aimed at deflating the power and authority of Weimar political personalities as well. In commenting upon the change of a proper name by a Jew from Sternberg to Stebens in *Der Angriff* on March 12, 1928, Goebbels reported the news in a manner that is modeled upon a classic Jewish joke. "Mr. Kanalgeruch [Sewerstench] has prospects. If he likes and he has friends in the Ministry, he will soon be called Count Hohenheim [Highhome], and will still remain Kanalgeruch."[16] Goebbels's commentary where the high-sounding and aristocratic title (that feels at home) conceals an outcast, debased, and stinky Jewish name is similar in structure to the transposition of names found in the classic scatological joke about the wandering Jew named Moshe Pischachs (or Pinkeles) in the Galician shtetl. He changes his piss-laden name to Moritz Wasserstrahl (Waterjet) in Berlin and then to Maurice La Fontaine when he reaches his peak in Paris. In fact, the satirical journal of the Nazi party, *Die Brennessel*, included an updated anti-Semitic version of this very joke entitled

"Mimicry" where this Jewish émigré arrives in Paris in January 1933 in flight from the Nazis.[17] The joke plays upon the popular anti-Semitic stereotype of the trickster Jew who is a master of mimicry and who blends into his environment in order to assimilate and to pass as a Christian, but who nevertheless undergoes a comic unmasking that reveals his "degenerate" character.

In *Struggle for Berlin*, Goebbels reviews the first two years of his life in the propaganda business and he devotes an extended commentary on the role of political caricature and tendentious jokes as making a significant contribution to that effort. Interestingly, Goebbels acknowledges cynicism as one possible effect in the arsenal of weapons by which to smear the enemy. This last point confirms Adorno, Löwenthal, and Massing's attempt to demystify Nazi propaganda in their essay "Anti-Semitism and Fascist Propaganda" in which they argue that "cynical soberness is probably more characteristic of the fascist mentality than psychological intoxication."[18] (Cynicism plays a key role in my analysis of Kadner.) Goebbels also insists that laughter can replace thinking to good propagandistic effect. "With that there arose a completely new style of political caricature. Caricature goes after its essence with grotesque, ironic, and sometimes also cynical effects. It excites the capacity for laughter more than the capacity for thinking. And, as it is known, he who has the laugher on his side is always right."[19] Ironically, Goebbels's psychological observation about "getting the laugher on his side" is in perfect harmony with Freud's analysis of the tendentious joke and this point of convergence supports Ellul's view that "Hitlerian propaganda was in great measure founded on Freud's theory of repression and libido."[20] In other words, Nazi propaganda was designed for people to find ways to release their repressed aggressive and libidinal impulses upon the Jewish scapegoat as their justified object of hatred.[21] Rather than the Nazi's outright refusal to draw upon this so-called "Jewish science," Freud's concept of cathartic release could serve as the unconscious basis of Nazi propaganda theory and of the part played in it "by jokes in hostile aggressiveness." If one compares Freud's and Goebbels's comments about "getting the laugher on one's side," the only minor difference is that whereas Goebbels stresses the rightness (or even political correctness) of the one who has the laugher on his side, Freud focuses on the "bribe" involved in this type of communication exchange. As Freud writes:

> We are now prepared to realize the part played by jokes in hostile aggressiveness. A joke will allow us to exploit something ridiculous in our enemy that we could not, on account of obstacles in the way, bring forward openly or consciously. . . . It will further bribe the hearer with its yield of pleasure into taking sides with us without any close inves-

tigation. . . . This is brought out with perfect aptitude in the common expression "to bring the laugher over to one's side."[22]

One finds a similar theory and practice regarding the role of mocking humor in propaganda in the writings and actions of Adolf Hitler. The frustrated artist turned Nazi dictator was not averse to composing his own anti-Semitic caricatures for political purposes, as demonstrated by the infamous 1920 election poster when Hitler was serving as party propaganda chief for the fledgling Nazi Party. The illustration juxtaposes the profiles of an ideal German maiden set against a grotesque Jewish bogeyman in the shadowy background. In its foreshadowing of the future, this satirical image (inscribed with the initials A. H.) haunts the final chapter of Marxist cultural historian Eduard Fuchs's monumental book, *Jews in Caricature* (1921).[23]

Keeping such biographical details in mind, it is difficult to accept Davies's comments regarding Hitler's actual thoughts about the place of humor in propaganda in *Mein Kampf*. Davies's reading concludes that Hitler saw "Jewish humor as humanizing those whom they (i.e., the Nazis) wish to demonize and as making a people whom they seek to represent as a malign threat appear comically harmless."[24] But this paraphrase is a misreading of what Hitler actually says in this passage. Hitler does not condemn caricature and jokes as a weapon in any kind of blanket statement. He only complains that Jewish comic papers (i.e., those not serving Nazi propagandistic ends) make Jews appear more "insignificant" than dangerous. To quote Hitler, "His comic papers especially strive to represent the Jews as a harmless little people, with their own peculiarities, of course — like other people as well. And the constant effort is to make him seem almost more 'insignificant' than *dangerous*."[25] But if Hitler were opposed to anti-Semitic jokes and caricatures in principle, then it is difficult to understand why he and the party leadership would support the publication by the Munich-based publisher Franz Eher of the weekly *Die Brennessel* (*The stinging nettle*) beginning in 1931 which aspired to become the Nazi *Simplicissimus* and whose issues were filled with scores of anti-Semitic jokes and caricatures. The framing of such venomous satire as a Nazi weapon of propaganda and as an antidote to Jewish journalistic poison is quite overt in an advertisement for *Die Brennessel* which appeared in the pages of the official party newspaper, *Illustrierte Beobachter* (Illustrated observer): "We set our new weekly journal *Die Brennessel* against this poison of Jewish incitement and of making things contemptuous. It will be an excellent propaganda weapon for our supporters."[26] Published from 1931 to 1938 with a weekly circulation of 80,000 copies, this stinging satirical journal with its witty barbs might be viewed in metaphorical terms as issuing the preparatory strikes that set the stage for the barbed wire that was to follow in the Nazi's escalating scale of aggressions against the Jews as their despised and despicable enemy.[27]

At its most disturbing, the Nazi's crossing of laughter and propaganda raises the specter of death and even the possibility of something approximating a lethal joke. This deadly discourse relies in a figurative sense upon the German expression *sich totlachen* or "laughing oneself to death." But, in Nazi propagandistic rhetoric, this action is by no means a self-reflexive one. There had to be a direct object for this aggressive or even sadistic type of laughter. This is why the sloganeering title of Nazi caricaturist Walter Hofmann's (aka Waldl) 1937 book reads *Lacht ihn tot!* (Laugh him to death!) with a preface by Gunter d'Alquen, the editor of the SS newspaper *Das Schwarze Korps*, titled, "*Wir lachen sie tot*" ("We laugh them dead"; see fig. 18).[28] Theodor Adorno and his colleagues wrote of fascist anti-Semitic propaganda as nothing but the projection of a desire for the ritual murder of the Jews.[29] Nazi joke propaganda expresses this murderous wish by means of a cruel and tendentious laughter. The conflation of the language of jokes and warfare reaches its heights in D'Alquen's final exclamation and its wishful thinking. Like propaganda, the

Figure 18. Cover for Walter Hofmann, *Lacht ihn tot!: Ein tendenziöses Bilderbuch von Waldl* (Laugh him dead! A tendentious book of images by Waldl, 1937).

joke is a barbed weapon that is fired at the Jewish enemy and that is desirous of his death. These joking projections take the symbolic form of murderous projectiles. "Cannonier Waldl has loaded his batteries. The volleys [*Salven*, also used for bursts of laughter] are fired, and whoever gets hit, we laugh them dead!" If there are any remaining doubts as to the ethnic identity of this enemy, the cover illustration is most explicit in its vilifying caricature. Squeezed between the title (*Laugh him dead!*) and the subtitle (A *Tendentious Picture Book*), we see a ghastly, ghostly globule-like creature on stage as if at some freak show. The bald, grimacing figure wears sunglasses that deny the possibility of any humanizing gaze into his eyes. The figure is nothing but a Jewish bogeyman — a stereotypical Nazi fantasy and monstrous construction. This recalls another component of the Frankfurt school analysis: "Fascist propaganda attacks bogies rather than real opponents, that is to say, it builds up an *imagery* of the Jews . . . and tears it to pieces, without caring much how this imagery is related to reality."[30] Four identical members of the audience who stand for the undifferentiated collective will of the psychology of the masses — i.e., the avid consumers of Nazi joke propaganda — are depicted open-mouthed as they fire salvos of aggressive and hostile laughter at this Jewish other. This image illustrates how joke warfare (i.e., laughing the Jewish other to death) could act as a means of collective bonding and agitation in the Nazi arsenal of weapons. Like other propagandistic weapons, it served to reinforce the cult's doxological stereotypes and it assisted in uniting and mobilizing the German masses into the mindset that later would support actions with deadly consequences.[31]

As a key Nazi joke propagandist, Kadner also joined the ranks of these authors who were appreciative of the value and profundity of the expression *totlachen* or "laughing to death." For instance, he reminds his readers at the beginning of *Rasse and Humor* that "phrases such as 'the story is a scream' or 'die laughing' ['*zum Totlachen*'] show how closely tragedy touches upon comedy in the consciousness of artistic speech."[32] Then, he goes even further to relate a sadistic and tortuous story taken from the Thirty Years' War that is full of ambivalent laughter and with ominous overtones for the death cult of the Thousand Year Reich: "One of the most heinous tortures devised by bestial soldiers during the Thirty Years' War consisted of binding the victim, rubbing salt into the naked soles of his feet, and then letting goats lick this off. These unfortunates have literally 'laughed themselves to death [*zu Tode gelacht*].'"[33]

## Reviewing Kadner's Deadly Discourse on the Jewish Joke

With its application of Nazi eugenics and racial doctrines to the study of humor, Kadner takes up the Jewish joke with the heavy and cruel burden of anti-Semitic ideology. Kadner's major thesis in *Rasse und Humor* is that "the manifold varieties of humor and comicalness are only to be understood from the bottom up if they are considered not only in a national but also in a racial context."[34] Consequently, the book devotes chapters to unpacking the essence and evaluating the humor and comedy of races on a pyramid that descends from the noble Nordics to the base and degenerate Jews. Kadner therefore has little patience with the philosophical treatise of "the French Jew" Henri Bergson because of its attempt to grasp laughter beyond racial differences as a universal human phenomenon. As Marcus Patka summarizes: "Even eugenics grappled with the phenomenon of humor, whereby it classified humor generally according to races and peoples. Thus, the nationalist author Siegfried Kadner in his book *Rasse und Humor* mocked the 'Jew' Henri Bergson for that reason alone — because he examined humor as a universally human phenomenon, which already constituted the opposite of the racial doctrine."[35] Remember that there were two editions of *Rasse and Humor* — the first one was published in 1936 by J. F. Lehmanns Verlag in Munich while the second, slightly expanded edition was published in 1939. Although *Rasse und Humor* has a few negative comments about the Jews and their relations to humor here and there, only the chapter "*Spitzfindigkeit und Zynismus*" ("Sophistry and cynicism") reveals Kadner's full racialist exegesis of the Jewish joke and its connection to the Jewish question. For the second edition, changes to this chapter were minimal, with the exception of its title, which Kadner altered to the even more racially taunting "*Jüdischer Zynismus*" ("Jewish cynicism").[36] In this chapter, the reader witnesses how Kadner's analysis of the Jewish joke gives way to readymade formulas derived from Nazi propaganda. Having shifted away from its original source and recipient, the Jewish joke now fuels the fires of racist diatribe and becomes a means to an ideological end as Kadner gives each joke an anti-Semitic twist that explodes with mockery, hostility, and aggression against the Jewish fiend. Operating by means of Ellul's propaganda of self-criticism, it is as if these Jewish jokes themselves — offering what the Jews say critically about themselves — serve as testimony and evidence to prove and justify all the horrible things that the Nazis have been saying about the Jews. In this way, the propaganda of self-criticism converts Jewish jests into Nazi proofs.

Throughout his analysis, Kadner argues that these Jewish jokes are masking something deadly serious. Reiterating the first lines of the last chapter in Eduard Fuchs's *Die Juden in der Karikatur*, the Nazi ideologue refers to that well-known characteristic of "Jewish self-irony": "It is known and should by no means be denied that the Jew applies much self-irony, and that the most effective Jewish jokes [*Judenwitze*] derive from Jews." However, the Nazi propagandist then parts ways with the Marxist cultural thinker and his class analysis when he interprets Jewish self-irony as "striving to remove racially conditioned seriousness into the harmless light of drollery."[37] This analysis involves a most cynical gesture on the Nazi propagandist's part. While Kadner accuses the Jewish joke of cynicism and sophistry, these qualities adhere to his own text, and the attribution of such characteristics to Jewish wit might be understood as a form of projection. This gesture locates another typical strategy of the propagandist. As Ellul writes: "The propagandist will not accuse the enemy of just any misdeed. The accusation aimed at the other's intentions clearly reveals the intention of the accuser."[38] In this case, the playful possibilities of Jewish joking discourse—that is, that these jokes are posing, that they have been made in jest—are countered with Nazism's cynical posturing that these comic utterances are true statements about the Jewish character as revealed by the Jews themselves. By interpreting these Jewish anecdotes as nothing more than mini documentaries that depict the character flaws and the vices of a condemned race, the Nazis seek to eradicate their status as jokes in the same way that they seek to eradicate the very tellers of these tales. In his infamous diary entry from March 1942 that is most pertinent to the Jews being at wit's end, Goebbels writes, "Judaism has nothing to laugh about."[39] Restaging this declaration, Kadner's deadly discourse on the Jewish joke transforms levity to the utmost gravity so that, in the end, the Jewish joke itself will have nothing to laugh about. From this sobering perspective and its return to "racially conditioned seriousness," Kadner's rhetorical strategy recasts the self-ironic Jewish joke and its "drollery" in a harmful light or as hard-core anti-Semitic doctrine that bolsters Nazi racist ideology.

Beginning with its title, *Rasse und Humor* sets in place the central opposition common to both propagandistic activity and tendentious jokes where it becomes a matter of friend against foe, of us against them. Indeed, the title *Rasse und Humor* would expel the Jew from both terms of entitlement. In other words, Kadner argues that the Jew has neither race nor humor. In this way, Kadner repeats the stereotypical terms already set in place a century earlier with the rise of the discourse on the *Judenwitz* in Germany as documented by Jefferson Chase in his rigorous examination of the careers of the satirical *Judenwitzler* (Jewish jokers) Heinrich Heine, Ludwig Börne, and Mortiz Saphir as already discussed.[40] Kadner privileges the German as "racial humorist" and devalues the Jewish other as an "anti-racial joker."[41] In this way, the book makes a sharp distinction between wit and humor along racial lines. Kadner argues that while Jews have learned the aggressive art of joking, they are incapable of those life-affirming and milder forms of humor that seek merriment rather than punch lines. At the beginning of the chapter, Kadner provides an assessment of the undue and "intrusive" influence of the Jews on German intellectual and cultural life and on mass media. Whether the medium is film, the theater, the press, or the world of entertainment, he finds that Jewish comedy has stamped its contaminating imprint. But while the Jew has had an important influence upon forms of expression involving comedy and jokes, Kadner insists "true humor lies outside the Jewish essence."[42] The opening paragraph already sets up the binary opposition and the ethically tinged hierarchy between true German humor and false (and sophistic) Jewish jokes: "Since the 'Emancipation' [*Loslassung*], Jewry played an ever more intrusive and active role in the intellectual life of Europe, and particularly in Germany, imprinting its stamp so unmistakably at the start of the twentieth century on the press, the theater, places of entertainment, and later, film such that it also set the tone in the forms of expression of comedy and wit—true humor lies outside the Jewish essence."[43]

If this dichotomizing tactic were not simplistic enough, the combination book review and promotional advertisement for *Rasse und Humor* (which appeared in the SS tabloid *Das Schwarze Korps*) paints matters even more black and white, or rather Nordic and Jewish: "Humor is something specifically Nordic. Unlike the joke, humor cannot be an acquired skill; it is inborn. This is not true of *Witz*. Joking wit and satire are artificial constructions."[44] The reviewer then goes on to propagate a demonic image of the Jewish joke and joker as both foreign and parasitic: "Jewish *Witz* has nothing in common with the other European peoples. It is essentially foreign and alien as are the Jews themselves and, therefore, it makes only a guest appearance in each land. And it is characteristic of precisely the Jewish race that it cannot bring forth any humorists, but rather only subversive and corrosive cynics [*zersetzender Zyniker*] who intrude upon the affairs of people to whom they don't belong."[45] In labeling and libeling the Jews in this destructive manner, the Nazi tabloid adds to the long-standing anti-Semitic accusation that the alien body of Jewish wit is corrosive and corrupting to German culture. Furthermore, the condemnation of the comedic Jew as a cynic underscores the second part of the chapter title in the 1936 edition of Kadner's book and its revised title in the 1939 edition.

In its second exclusion, the book argues paradoxically that the Jews constitute a race that is not really a race. On this point, Kadner incorporates the ideas of the leading Nazi racial theorist of the time, Hans F. K. Günther.[46] In setting up this binary opposition, Günther argued that while the Nordic race constitutes an ideal type, the Jews constitute only a mixture of races. Günther's rhetorically driven anthropological inquiry ("How could anyone speak of a "Jewish race"?[47]) feeds the Nazi imaginary and its popular negative stereotyping of the Jew as a mongrel and bastard breed. Keeping this racial theory in mind, one comes to a better understanding of the conclusion of *Rasse und Humor* whose rhetoric parallels that of the book review. In contrast to Davies's assessment of Hitler, both statements demonstrate that Nazi ideology propagated a view that the subversive cynicism of the Jewish joke constituted a dangerous menace to the German body politic as a whole. Kadner writes: "The impulses derived from him in the comic realm are anti-racial and racially generic. They are not supplementary, but of a corrosive [*zersetzender*] and caustic [*ätzender*] nature, sustained in their consequences, but, for that very reason, even more dangerous to the German body politic [*Volkskörper*] in its entirety."[48] Kadner also acknowledges the influence of Günther and his brand of Nazi eugenics at the climax of the book when he invokes Goethe (whom Kadner reads as an arch anti-Semitic thinker[49]) and his *Faust* as a means to demonize the Jews (with another dig at their "ambiguous pseudo-logic") as well as other "counter-bred races." This essentialist passage functions as a call to arms while making stark and extreme binary oppositions between the Nordic race and the Jewish devil (among other "others").

> That a racial duel [*rassischer Zweikampf*] is being fought in the conflict between Faust and Mephisto, a struggle between the Nordic man with his insatiable hunger for experience, knowledge, and action, and the counter-bred races [*Gegenrassigen*] who want to choke him in indulgence, inertia, stupidity, and remorse, between bold sincerity of thought and ambiguous pseudo-logic [*zweideutiger Scheinlogik*] has already been expressed by Hans F. R. Günther in his book, *Knight, Death, and the Devil*.[50]

With the invocation of *Spitzfindigkeit* as the first word of the title of this chapter on the Jewish joke, Kadner draws upon a family of meanings that includes sophistry, nitpicking, hairsplitting, quibbling, casuistry, and subtlety. It is easy to understand the connection of the term *sophistry* to the rhetorical strategies deployed by Jewish jokes.[51] After all, sophistry relates to that ancient Greek tradition of pre-Socratic philosophers often accused of making fallacious and specious arguments with the intent of deceiving the public. Sophists (not unlike propagandists and jokesters) are often viewed as those who use rhetorical argument and persuasion to replace (or trump) the search for authentic truth. There is a pejorative connotation to the use of such terms as sophistry and casuistry and how they apply clever yet fundamentally unsound reasoning especially in resolving ethical questions. But Kadner has a specifically Jewish model in mind when it comes to tracking down the sophistical and casuistic tendencies of the Jewish joke and this occurs in his commentary on the Talmud. He proposes the Talmud as the master school for both the Jewish legal arts as well as the Jewish joke. Although the deplorable racist slurs do not stop in this section, the proposition leads to one of Kadner's more insightful passages as he explores the institutional basis that would account for the frame of mind that produces the dexterous, hair-splitting logic that accompanies the Jewish joke:

> Of course, the Jewish joke is not yet dismissed. It is of an intellectual nature, plays opposites against each other in an overstated sharpness of thought or chases a thought up to its summit and then shows it in its real or apparent absurdity. The Talmud provides the systematic and species-appropriate schooling of these faculties. For the Jews, the Talmud means not just a collection of religious regulations and statutes, but a unique and excellent training ground to justify and give reasons for doctrines as well as to defend or refute them; to turn them into their opposite with the appearance of legality, and finally to turn them into black and white. Apart from the sordidness and moral indecency of many points, the Talmud is not empty flights of thought, but the master school of the Jewish legal arts and of the Jewish joke.[52]

Kadner cannot resist pointing to the "sordidness and moral indecency" of Talmud thereby aligning it to the Greek tradition of sophistry and its deployment of argumentative acrobatics in the service of deception. Kadner then goes on to comment on the interrogative mode that pervades these Talmudic stories and that again offers a striking parallel to the structure of the Jewish joke: "It is significant that the question again answers a question, which by no means provides a conclusion: then follows the view of a respected scribe. Not infrequently, there arises half a dozen questions, and the adversarial playing off of their casuistic explanations provides precisely the training field of Jewish sophistry [*Spitzfindigkeit*]."[53]

What is striking about these two passages in *Rasse und Humor* on the Talmudic basis and roots of the Jewish joke is that the Nazi propagandist offers some of the same insights found in contemporary Jewish scholarly sources. The young Gershom Scholem in one of his late 1918 *Diary* entries noticed that there were some startling connections to be drawn between interminable Talmudic analysis and Jewish self-ironic wit as high-minded rabbinical disputation descended into lowbrow comic bickering. Scholem's analysis also contains the pointed reflection that Jewish wit may be viewed as a "capricious method" of Talmudic study that proceeds by mathematical progression in order to offer a Jewish version of the Latin *reductio ad absurdum*. In the following startling *Midrash* (interpretation), Scholem reaches the Kabbalisticinclined conclusion that "every Talmudic analysis contains an infinite number of jokes":

> What does "Talmudic" mean? In the perverted modern usage, it means the splicing of words in a judgment to bring out the contradictory elements. Practiced as a capricious method, it's a mechanical way to produce an infinite number of jokes by means of a mathematical progression of analysis. And in every mathematical progression there is an endless series of prime numbers; similarly, every Talmudic analysis contains an infinite number of jokes. Systematic disputation is the rule governing the series. The Jewish joke, when it is turned ironically against itself, also uses this form of Talmudic process, admittedly in a very different fashion than is commonly applied.[54]

Furthermore, the Zionist philosopher of education Ernst Simon and his illuminating essay "Zum Problem des Jüdischen Witzes" (1928) emphasizes the Talmudic strategy of *Pilpul* (literally, peppering) as a source for the sharpened thinking and logical acrobatics often deployed in Jewish wit. As Simon elaborates: "A further characteristic of Talmudic thought has been designated as 'Pilpul,' [i.e. mental acuteness in harmonizing different or even contradictory Talmudic sayings] or in later times as 'Chilluk' [i.e, discriminating thinking]. In such cases, one finds sometimes an exercise in logic that has become nearly or entirely an end in itself and overshoots its own target [*Denkziel*] in its revolutions. It was also conducted quite intentionally — 'to sharpen the pupil's wits.'"[55]

Kadner draws upon two case studies from the Talmud in order to illustrate his points. The first is the case of Rabbi Hisda that addresses whether one should say a forgotten blessing over food even after having eaten. Hisda answers this question with another question making a witty analogy to stinking breath and the abject body (which is always a good source for laughter). According to Hisda's analogy, "If one has eaten garlic such that he spreads an odor, should he eat more garlic so that his odor should be spread even more?"[56] The stinky choice of this anecdote allows Kadner to slip in a negative stereotype about the unhygienic Jewish body. The second case study refers to Talmudic debates about whether it is permissible for a Jew to extinguish a fire on the Sabbath and the use of a "Shabbos Goy" as the way out of this dilemma. Kadner obviously appreciates this Talmudic tractate because it illustrates how the Jews set up double standards and do not have any ethical qualms about the instrumental use of Christians to do their bidding when it comes to their holy Sabbath. It also is reminiscent of and structured like a Jewish joke in light of the Jew's "noncommittal manner of speaking" where he ambiguously sidesteps having to make a definite imperative statement whether to "extinguish it!" or "don't extinguish it!" According to Kadner, this indirection allows the Jew to keep himself from harm "through the aid of the *Goyim* without even [committing] an offense against the letter of the law."[57] There are definite parallels between the noncommittal manner of speaking in this Talmudic passage and the Jewish defendant's repetition of the ambiguous phrase "most probably" in one of the jokes that Kadner relates about a conniving Jew's inability to swear in a court of law as to whether or not he paid his accuser a certain sum of money (see later in this chapter).

Despite the previously discussed alignment of Nazi propaganda with Freudian ideas about the release of repressed aggression against the enemy, Kadner, in *Rasse und Humor*, has little sympathy for Freud himself. Before he can reshape and mold Jewish joke theory in line with Nazi tenets, Kadner must take on Freud and the psychoanalytic theory that dominated the discourse on the Jewish joke. Kadner's reading of Freud has all the trademarks of a smear campaign, and it begins with a completely conscious racial slur. It is ironic that Kadner's attack on Freud avoids attributing the element of tendentiousness in any way to Freud's theory of the joke. But Freud's ideas about the aims of the tendentious joke are most applicable to the way in which he is set up as the scapegoat and enemy in Kadner's aggressive analysis. This turns out to be another example of the Nazi propaganda machine learning the tricks of their trade from Freud and then using them against the psychoanalytic master. According to Freud, "By making our enemy small, inferior, despicable or comic, we achieve in a roundabout way the enjoyment of overcoming him."[58] Kadner's aggressive attack focuses on the psycho in Freudian joke analysis and reads the unconscious discipline as a Jewish science dependent upon diseased minds—of guilty consciences and "pathological emotional processes." The Nazi slogan "The Jew is Guilty!" appears to be lurking in the background of these comments. Kadner's critique of the Viennese "sexual magician" again embodies the distinction between healthy Nordic humor ("uninhibited and natural merriment") and diseased Jewish jokes at the theoretical basis of *Rasse und Humor*. All in all, Kadner's analysis pathologizes both Freudian psychoanalysis and Jewish *Witz*.

> It could only occur to a Jew, Sigmund Freud, to represent the joke as a result of pathological emotional processes [*krankhafter Gemütsvorgänge*], as something that is at first unconscious and then a reasonably controlled and playfully expressed "slip" [*Fehlleistung*] of the mental functions. The outer harmony or the similarity of the sound of words will be used to generate a playful permutation with

concepts, a game in which the psychoanalyst, i.e., Sigmund Freud himself, is able to recognize a guilty or bad conscience as the primary cause. We are not in a position to follow the peculiar sexual magician on this path since we believe in an uninhibited and natural merriment, but we are willing to admit that Freud's research applies to the full extent for his fellow Jews.[59]

The analysis concludes with the backhanded compliment that Freud's understanding of the derivation of Jewish jokes in "pathological emotional processes" is quite appropriate for his sick and degenerate Jewish compatriots.

There seems to be an inverted moral to many of the Jewish jokes that Kadner extracts and manipulates from the classic compilations of the genre. The moral is quite simple and quite simplistic. The Nazis are justified in excluding this group from German society and treating them in an immoral and unjust manner because the Jews (as witnessed by their jokes) have proven themselves to be both an immoral and unjust people. The invocation of negative stereotyping—constituting a common feature of both anti-Semitic jokes and propaganda—lines up a composite picture of the Jew as liar and cheat, as lacking in honor and respect, and as unable to keep his oaths. It is interesting to point out that Kadner always frames his Jewish character types as a motley assortment of *Schnorrers*, vagrants, and good-for-nothings in contrast to other versions of the same jokes. For instance, Kadner characterizes and contextualizes the so-called *Minjam* who makes his living by filling in as the necessary tenth man for communal prayers in the synagogue as a "Galician pickpocket from the Moabit section of Berlin."[60]

Both Kadner and Freud interpret a classic Jewish joke that foregrounds the question of truth. However, their drastically different interpretations have us wonder whether it is in truth the same joke. Kadner mobilizes the joke as a proof of the insincerity and shiftiness of the Jewish mind. Pure and simple, this is a tendentious story that reveals the Jew as a compulsive liar and, thus, the moral links up with a central theme of Nazi propaganda. In the rush to mount evidence for his racial character assassination, Kadner takes the Jewish joke as a serious statement about an alien and inauthentic way of life in which a primary deceitfulness forecloses the possibility of honest and perfect communication. The political charge of framing this joke about Polish Jews as compulsive liars in Nazi Germany in the period between 1936 and 1939 or a few years before the Jewish question would enter its Final Solution must be emphasized.

> That the conversation between one Jew and another presupposes the same mental gymnastics in which all sincerity [*Aufrichtigkeit*]

and "being on the level" [*Gradheit*] are furthest from their minds is demonstrated in the following.

Chaim meets his friend Herschel in the train.
"*Nu*, Herschel, where are you going?"
"To Lemberg."
"*Nebbich*, you say to me you are going to Lemberg, so that I should believe that you are going to Warsaw. But, indeed, you are going to Lemberg. So — for what are you lying!"[61]

In contrast, Freud argues that this sophisticated Jewish joke that "works by the technique of absurdity" is not about lying or about moral failure, but rather about how the truth is not just the description of the way things are. His version of the joke (traveling from Lemberg to Cracow) illustrates that one has to take into consideration how "our hearer will understand what we say" when one speaks "the truth." Freud questions the so-called correspondence theory of truth and argues that this Jewish joke belongs to a unique set of tendentious jokes that he classifies as *skeptical*. Freud's analysis impersonalizes the joke as he seeks to remove the possibility of Jewish scapegoating. It is not Herschel the lying Jew who is under attack here but the certainty of knowledge itself. "What they are attacking is not a person or an institution but the certainty of our knowledge itself, one of our speculative possessions."[62] It is also significant to point out that Freud's way of telling the joke incorporates this dimension of epistemological doubt left out in Kadner's version. Kadner focuses only on the issue of belief ("so that I should believe"). In Freud, the line of lying reasoning set forth by the unnamed Jewish skeptic happens in a joke space that doubts both the desire for belief ("you want me to believe . . .") *and* the certainty of knowledge ("but I know in fact that . . .").[63] Finally, the sophisticated logic of the hearer of the Lemberg-Cracow joke (who listens in the space of a "double take") suggests to us the more radical and deconstructive view that the lie (in its double negation) is somehow a necessary precondition for the constitution of the truth in the first place.

Kadner returns to Freud one more time in the chapter in order to make some further disparaging remarks that are set off from any specific joke analysis per se. Here, Kadner mobilizes the Nazi's propaganda of self-criticism in a new way not only to reinforce the racist epithet of the "dirty Jew" but also to foreground the anti-Semitic stereotype of the Jews' obsession with and corruption by "filthy lucre," and he does so in a way that makes Freud the very source of this debased viewpoint. Toning down and partially sanitizing Freud's more abject diction (i.e, *Kot*, or "feces," *Dreck*, or "dirt"), Kadner recalls the psychoanalyst's scatological association of money (*Geld*) and dirt (*Schmutz*) to turn him into an object of mockery and derision. Here, Kadner alludes to Freud's infamous paper on "Character and Anal Erotism" (1908) where he wrote in part: "It is possible that the contrast between the most precious substance known to men and the most worthless which they reject as waste matter ('refuse') has led to the specific identification of gold with feces."[64] Kadner neatly ignores the fact that Freud argues that the anal character functions as a universal category of human personality and that the identification of money and feces is not limited to just one culture (or, as he would have it, to one "race"). Instead, the Nazi propagandist works to police the borders of the Jewish race and nation identifying it as a "money and feces" ghetto. In this way, Freud's representative status as the founder of the "Jewish science" of psychoanalysis takes with him the entire Jewish people with this particularized portrait of degeneracy. Kadner's satirical gesture — one that possesses some measure of scatological humor in itself — not only grounds this negative stereotype as a racial characteristic but also seeks to frame Freud as typical representative of an avaricious and mongrel race who will never be able to achieve scientific objectivity. Again, Kadner gives Freud another backhanded compliment at the conclusion of the following commentary: "And we think of Sigmund Freud again who wanted to demonstrate that money and dirt were intimately related to each other and occasionally stood for each other in the primal words and in the symbols of the language of dreams. Thus, researchers too cannot get beyond the borders of their race and nationality. In terms of the depth psychology of his own 'hybrid race' [*Mischrasse*], Sigmund Freud was undoubtedly right about this case as well."[65]

The reference to Freud as trafficking in dirt also sheds some light on the incorporation of another anti-Semitic caricature by Kadner. He reproduces Eduard Thöny's "Galizien" caricature published in the fall of 1907 in the leading German satirical magazine *Simplicissimus* (fig. 19). This cartoon depicts two capped and bearded Eastern European Jews in black shtetl garb — one bearing an exaggerated toothy smile and the other with a contorted facial expression holding up his left hand to fit with the so-called *mauscheln* stereotype. (In other words, he has been caught in the act of talking with his hands.) But the stereotype of the dirty Jew really hits home only when we read the caption beneath the image: "Why are you scratching yourself? Do you have fleas? — "What do you mean fleas? Am I a dog? I have lice."[66] While Thöny's framing of the joke reads as an anti-Semitic one at first glance, it is quite possible that the original version was directed against the "bad" hygienic habits of Eastern European Jews by their more acculturated Western Jewish brethren. However, this type of distinction is not something that mattered to Kadner in the least given his blanket downgrading of the entire "Jewish race." As Marcus

Figure 19. Eduard Thöny, *Galizien* (Galician Jews). Caricature. From *Simplizissimus*, 1907. Reprinted in Kadner, *Rasse und Humor*, 205.

Patka comments, "Consequently, a differentiation between the Eastern and Western Jewish world cannot be found in Kadner."[67]

Another stereotypical anti-Semitic accusation against the Jews throughout the ages has been that they do not keep their oaths. On the level of religious difference alone, this accusation becomes complicated when one considers that a Jew by definition could not swear on the Christian Bible and therefore was excluded from this cultural practice. (Thus, another way to frame the problem would be to say that the Jew could not make oaths to keep in the first place.) This situation led to the creation of special forms of oaths in courts of law throughout the Middle Ages designed especially for Jews (*Oath More Judaico*). Many of them were filled with anti-Semitic taunts such as forcing Jews to stand on a sow's hide or bare-footed. Given this history of ridicule in relation to oaths, the Nazis took up the accusation of Jewish duplicity by secularizing the rhymed folk wisdom attributed to Martin Luther — "Trau keinem Fuchs auf seiner Heid und keinem Jud bei seinem Eid [Trust no fox on his heath and no Jew on his oath]." In fact, Julius Streicher's *Stürmer* Verlag published a children's book of the same title in the form of vicious and mocking caricatures the same year as the initial publication of Kadner's *Rasse und Humor*.[68]

Kadner takes up the deceitful accusation against the enemy without even seeing the need for much of an argument. Steeped in anti-Semitic discourse, the point would appear so obvious to the reader as an accepted stereotype of "Nazithink" that all Kadner had to do was allude to it followed by an apt self-critical Jewish joke in order to confirm the doxological opinion and to draw out a proper reading of the joke in line with the "propaganda of self-criticism." Kadner's exclamation of outrage here operates like a method of "telegraphing" that has been written in some Nazi Morse code to be understood only by those sharing the same ideological discourse and persuasion:

> As about honor, so too about oaths! The attitude is aptly reflected in the following dialogue:
> Chairman: "So how do you swear? Have you paid the accuser the sum of money?"
> Defendant: "Most probably."
> Chairman: "There is no 'most probably' when it comes to an oath. You must swear, I have paid or I have not paid."
> Defendant: "Yes. This is how I would like to swear."[69]

The structure of this joke also would serve a Nazi well because it puts the enemy speaker on the defensive as the one who stands accused in a court of law. But the undecidability and vacillation exhibited by the joke in general and by the Jewish joke in particular which foregrounds an interrogative mode of being will not be heard in this Nazi court of law and its quest for sworn certainty. Instead, the defendant's ambivalence will be twisted as a sign of dubiousness and deception. Indeed, this joke propaganda strategy helped to prop up and justify the Nazi's political objective of putting the Jew outside the protection of the law.

The "propaganda of self-criticism" extends to the (high) cultural domain as well. The goal here is to make the Jew confess illiteracy — or even degeneracy — when it comes to matters of German high culture. The following one-liner including Kadner's tendentious intervention serves such a purpose. "Mrs. Isaacson — she is not among the cleverest — is asked: How did you like the performance of Tristan? Nu, she says, I laughed."[70] For the Nazi culture vulture, the response of Mrs. Isaacson partakes of the greatest blasphemy because she has taken Richard Wagner's mid-nineteenth century opera *Tristan and Isolde* — one of the most serious achievements of German high culture — as a joke. In framing this joke, Kadner cannot allow it to stand by itself without a snide and mocking comment. This Wagnerian must underscore how the degenerate Jew cannot appreciate true art and is incapable of high culture. Yet, in informing the reader about the IQ of the speaker, Kadner also implies that the reader does not have the intelligence to judge her intelligence. Kadner's intervention is an attempt to contain the subversive possibilities of this joke and to influence the reader to accept the cultural status quo, or a world where *Tristan and Isolde* is a tragic drama that assumes mythic proportions and that demands profound contemplation. With the slightest of denigrating remarks, Kadner becomes a control freak and delivers a Jewish joke with a biased plotline in line with Nazi cultural propaganda.

In contrast, the Jewish satirist Alexander Moszkowski also recounted a version of this same joke in his lecture on the philosophy of the Jewish joke in 1921. Rather than Kadner's one-liner that is a monologue of a stupid Jewish woman, Moszkowski frames it as a dialogue between two Jewish businessmen. This version brings another socio-historical context to the joke that compares the cultural capital of the unenlightened *Ostjude* from Poland with his more assimilated and enlightened German-Jewish colleague. This contrast helps to explain why the visitor would not have had any prior knowledge of Wagnerian opera. The stranger from the East asks his Berlin counterpart for some advice about how to get around in the big city.

> "I am indeed a stranger in Berlin. Where should I go in the evenings?"
> "So. Go to the opera house."
> "What's playing at the opera?"
> "*Tristan and Isolde.*"

"What's *Tristan and Isolde*?"
"That's a laugh!"[71]

In contrast to Kadner's cynical reading designed to obliterate Jewish comedy by striking a serious pose, Moszkowski seizes upon the irony implicit in a joke about transforming tragedy into comedy. "One may properly doubt whether this tragic work of art in its total depth has taken to the stage in such a form for this spectator."[72] Unlike Kadner, this German-Jewish cultural assimilator seeks to frame the Jewish joke as a part of the humanist tradition of Western philosophy. Thus, he invokes Seneca ("a serious thing is a true joy") and Nietzsche (who referred to "the Wagnerian *Parsifal* as the stuff of operettas") as two philosophical parallels to this Jewish joke that moves us from the sublime to the ridiculous. In this way, Jewish wit deploys an ironic distancing that is designed to deflate the pretensions of the tragic sensibility and to push Wagner into the realm of the comically hysterical.

It is not surprising that Kadner also tells a version of a joke that plays between the valuations of German and Yiddish. A boy named Sigismund is reading a book in German and he repeats each phrase with Yiddish intonation and word choice informing his father at the end that he is in the process of translating Schiller into German and therefore into the normative linguistic idiom (*"ich verdaitsch mer den Schiller"*).[73] For a Germanist like Kadner who wrote a book on proper usage of the German language,[74] this "Germanizing" joke (that prefers *verdaitschen* to *verdeutschen*) would represent a degenerate perversion of linguistic and cultural norms.

This joke also needs to be understood in relation to the history of the debates about the German language (touched upon earlier in this chapter) and the nationalist fear that the purity and integrity of German was in the process of being corrupted by the invasion of these foreign elements. Kadner's comment before the introduction of this joke—"about the mixed form [*Mischform*] of the Jewish jargon language [*Mauschelsprache*]"[75]—is ideologically loaded not only because it condemns Yiddish as a mongrel language corrupting the purity of German but also because the term *Mauschelsprache* (as the language literally derived from Moses) devaluates Yiddish as jabbering and deceitful.[76] It also resonates with his earlier negative and mocking remarks in chapter 3 of *Rasse und Humor* about *"das Mauscheln"* (26) that show a high level of distrust of the Jewish tendency to talk "with their hands" (*"Reden 'mit de Händ'"*) when they revert to their secret language amongst themselves as well as their Janus-faced ability to conceal such "comic" (*komisch*) gestures when in the company of their host nations, including the Nordic race. As Kadner relates: "In a repulsive-strange sense, he knows how to disguise himself cleverly and eloquently, but he falls back inevitably to what is naturally given to him, to his own proper rhythm when among his own kind."⁷⁷ Marcus Patka elaborates upon this passage: "For the anti-Semites, the flawless use of the German language was only a mask that would serve the Jews to camouflage their own true interests. For [Kadner's] investigation, it remains crucial that the anti-Semites already had declared the Jew to be a 'joke figure' per se long before the NS-hate sheet, *Der Stürmer*."⁷⁸

Sander Gilman reminds us that the German nationalist's attack on the use of *mauscheln* also targeted the Jew in the role of the writer "who both perceived the world differently and articulated this difference through their language" and that "it is in the rise of journalism at the beginning of the nineteenth century that the image of the Jew and the image of the journalist began to be intermingled."⁷⁹ Speaking in an ironic language of jokes and mockery, these Jewish journalists were not to be trusted especially, as in the case of Moritz Saphir, because of their Jewish tone that was defined by mid-nineteenth-century contemporaries as "nihilistic satire."⁸⁰ Later in the same chapter, Kadner pursues this very line of attack on Jewish joker journalism and its abuses of German language and culture by condemning the witty writings of Moritz Saphir, Ludwig Börne, and Heinrich Heine: "In conscious hostility [*Feindseligkeit*] against state and society, church and economy, against the traditional bonds of human communal being, Jewish wit confronts us in its cynical form with corrosive sharpness and irony in such figures as Ludwig Börne (Baruch) and Heinrich Heine (Chaim Bückeburg)."⁸¹ The stigma attached to Jewish/Hebraic names finds its way into Kadner's analysis in parenthetical form. In this way, Kadner uncovers the Jewish origins of these Christian literary converts who had bought their entrance tickets into high European culture. What begins as a seemingly harmless joke playing between German and Yiddish gives Kadner great offense and it yields to a full-fledged ideological attack against the entire witty tradition of Jewish cultural production (i.e., the *Judenwitz*) and its proponents (the so-called *Judenwitzler*).

Another propagandistic use of a classic Jewish joke in Kadner's text occurs in the visual medium. This involves his reprinting of a mocking caricature drawn by the Nazi artist Hans Schweitzer (1901–1980) under the pen name Mjölnir. Schweitzer styled himself as the hammer of the Norse mythological God Thor and was well known for his propaganda posters commissioned by Goebbels. This caricature was originally published in *Das Schwarze Korps* on October 31, 1935.⁸² Here is an example wherein the mere transposition of the joke's original context and setting makes all the difference as it reveals the prevailing Nazi sentiment on the question of Jewish resettlement. This is the joke about two Jews who find themselves on a sinking ship — an apt metaphor

OF JOKES AND PROPAGANDA 177

(„Das Schwarze Korps" 31. Okt. 1935).

Zeichnung: Mjölnir

„Hilfe Sigi, das Schiff geht unter!"  „Was schreiste Isi, is es dein Schiff?"

Figure 20. Mjölnir, "Hilfe Sigi, das Schiff geht unter!" ("Help Sigi, the ship is going down!"), *Das Schwarze Korps*, October 31, 1935. Reprinted in Kadner, *Rasse und Humor*, 210.

for the situation of German Jews in this period (fig. 20). It reads: "'Help, Ziggy. The ship is sinking!' 'What are you screaming for, Izzy? Is it your ship?'" Meanwhile, Paul Nikolaus's Jewish joke book *Jüdische Miniaturen* presented a strikingly different version of this joke eleven years earlier during the heyday of the Weimar Republic. This version finds Baruch and Finkelstein in the starring roles on a boat traveling to America thereby riding a different wave of emigration but with the same basic content.[83] The title of Nikolaus's version of the joke, "Egoism," illustrates the thrust of Jewish self-irony at play here. In comparison, Mjölnir's version puts his comic characters Ziggy and Izzy on a ship christened the "Monte Zion" and bound for Palestine, and Kadner adds this pointed caption: "(Satirical allusion to the establishment of special shipping to Palestine.)" In this context, the Nazi's version of the joke takes on new dimensions beyond merely mocking the Jewish stereotype of fixating upon personal wealth and property in the face of imminent disaster. Using "satirical allusion," this caricature puts every emigrating Jew in the position of Izzy and Ziggy given the fact that any Jewish refugees lucky enough to flee Nazi Germany were not allowed to take their personal property with them. Moreover, it is obvious that this caricature also expresses in the form of a joke the deadly serious and other-directed death wish inherent in the Nazi's desire to see their Jewish enemies (like the ancient Egyptians) drowned at sea rather than allowing them to leave Germany and to arrive safely in their ancient homeland of Palestine in order to start a new Zionist-oriented life.

The Nazi propagandistic program that informs Kadner's Jewish joke analysis becomes most overt in its concluding paragraphs. A chapter that is supposed to focus on the analysis of the Jewish joke ends with a vicious attack and condemnation of *Rassenschande* (racial defilement) — the Nazi racialist terminology for sexual relations between Aryans and Jews. To make this point in line with Nazi eugenics, Kadner turns to the early nineteenth-century German author Wilhelm Hauff whom he describes as one of the "first soldiers of racial satire."[84] Hauff would receive posthumous acclaim in the Nazi era in light of his authorship of the anti-Semitic novella *Jud Süss* (1827) which was adapted at the behest of Joseph Goebbels and which became the most notorious Nazi propaganda film when released in 1940. In *Rasse und Humor*, Kadner mobilizes Hauff's short story "Fantasies in the Bremen Ratskeller" (1827) that mocks the other-directed sexual desires of its German character Herr Zwerner for the Jewess, Rebecca Simon. Kadner's reading and interpretation of the Jewish joke vanishes completely as it foregrounds a proto-Nazi diatribe warning against the dangers of miscegenation. By means of this distinctly antiromantic narrative, the Nazi reader is brought back to the present and to the passage of the "Law for the Protection of German Blood and German Honor" (promulgated in Nuremberg in September 1933), which made German-Jewish sexual intercourse punishable by means of imprisonment, and at its extreme, by the death penalty. In the end, Kadner's joke analysis shows its true racist colors by means of a tendentious invective directed against all forms of mixing with "the alien-blooded creature" (*"das fremdblütige Geschöpf"*).[85] Losing track of his original object of study, Kadner's conclusion departs from the analysis of the Jewish joke by mobilizing an anti-Semitic satire that foregrounds the Nazi propaganda agenda explicitly.

The possibility for German-Jewish intercultural dialogue or even an attitude of "live and let live" has passed away in such a passage. For Kadner, the Jewish joke testifies instead to the unbridgeable gap between cultures that have been reified into races. The Jewish joke — which had long provided a means for intercultural intimacy and exchange — now becomes the means by which to confirm and further propagate the Nazi doctrine of radical racial difference. Kadner describes a case of communication breakdown: "Two racially, spiritually, and culturally separate worlds! There is no bridge that crosses from the one to the other. At no time is there any linguistic understanding [*sprachichen Verständigung*]."[86] Here, Kadner's Nazi joke propaganda wants to have it both ways. On the one hand, the Nazi ideologue understands perfectly well that the Jewish joke testifies to everything negative that the Nazis have been saying about the Jews in their propaganda. Thus, the Jewish joke confirms that they can treat the Jews as second-class citizens or even as subhumans. On the other hand, the Nazi will never understand the enemy Jew and his cultural productions (i.e., Jewish jokes) because these are the products of completely alien bodies. In other words, the Germans (now called Aryans or the Nordic race) do not and will never get the Jewish joke as it now begins to resemble the condition of radical alterity. Here we have reached the Nazi's logical impasse when it comes to the Jewish joke. This double bind might resemble the Talmudic logic of a Jewish joke, but, alas, it bears the cynical mark of Nazi propaganda and of a strategy that sets up the Jewish joke as its enemy and as its other while miming its comedic and sophistic moves for its own tendentious purposes.

## Conclusion: Counterpropaganda

This chapter has offered a historical account and critical assessment in response to Christie Davies's underestimation of the important role of jokes and the theorization of jokes in Nazi propaganda and in the expression of anti-Semitic sentiments. Davies states provocatively and asks rhetorically: "Religious and racial anti-Semitic propaganda . . . depicts the Jews as a disease, as bacilli, parasites, lice, maggots, vampires, as a spider or an octopus strangling and consuming the world. With rhetoric and images like these, who needs jokes? Why should those whom we know to have been and who in some countries continue to be overtly aggressive bother to mask their hatred with humor?"[87] First, I demonstrated that tendentious humor was not conceived in Nazi propaganda theory as a covert mask for hatred but rather as a channel for aggression and as a weapon to mobilize public opinion against the Jewish enemy. Indeed, the lurid imagery of Nazi propaganda enumerated by Davies was often cast via the media of hostile jokes and caricatures. The richly illustrated issues of *Der Stürmer* and other Nazi tabloids registered the hallucinatory phantasmagoria of anti-Semitism in exactly these ways.[88] The Nazi imaginary unfolded in a comic book world of panels populated by Jewish monstrosities designed to induce fear and provoke laughter.[89] Moreover, the casting of the

Jews in these exaggerated and comedic terms would lead to no guilty pangs of conscience regarding their mistreatment. It is not a question of jokes versus propaganda (i.e., "With rhetoric and images like these, who needs jokes?"). Rather it is to understand how the Nazis cast the Jewish "disease" via the comic arts of exaggeration and vilification — via the satirical imagery of visual caricature and the barbed rhetoric of verbal jokes. Much of this chapter has offered a close reading of how a book like Kadner's *Rasse und Humor* affords a racist and tendentious reading of the Jewish joke that interprets them as true statements about Jewish character and that mobilizes them as anti-Semitic testimonies. Kadner's treatise designed to make the Jews appear inferior, despicable, and immoral provides us with an example of someone who needed Jewish jokes to further the ends of Nazi racist propaganda and to bolster the campaign to make Jews appear less than human. In this way, Kadner constructed a deadly discourse on the Jewish joke that helped to pave the way to the Nazi's Final Solution of the Jewish question. In sum, the cruel laughter of Kadner's Jewish joke appropriations and manipulations managed to achieve a Nazi version of Ellul's "propaganda of self-criticism."

But the mobility factor implicit in both the Jewish joke and propaganda allows for another turn or spin. If the Nazis mobilized self-critical Jewish jokes to make propaganda against the Jews, then the oppressed Jews countered by making Jewish jokes about propaganda — mobilizing jokes designed to expose Nazi propaganda as a discourse of lies. As might be expected, one of the major targets of the Jewish joke as counterpropaganda in this era was the Nazi propaganda machine itself. In this manner, the Jewish "propaganda joke" challenged the Nazi's "joke propaganda." These were a part of the well-known genre of political jokes known as the *Flüsterwitze* (whisper jokes) passed around as a living oral tradition that served as a weapon of psychological and spiritual resistance against the Nazi regime during the Third Reich.[90]

Given the difficulties of publishing such subversive jokes in the German Reich, the last joke quoted here has been taken from an American compilation by the Chicago Rabbi S. Felix Mendelsohn in his volume *Let Laughter Ring* (1941).[91] The book devotes forty pages to anti-Nazi jokes in the chapter on the "Third Reich." Published earlier in the same year when the United States entered World War II, the book marks the alliance of the Jewish joke with the rising American tide of anti-Nazi sentiment. Working on the side of the Allies, these tendentious jokes promote an American idea of freedom — the linguistic substitute for laughter in the title — as they are hurled against the Nazi enemy and its dictatorship.

Many of these jokes propagate a most critical and distrustful attitude toward the Nazi propaganda machine led by Joseph Goebbels that it interprets as nothing but a lie-producing factory. This chapter also demonstrated how Goebbels and Freud were not that far apart on the psychological function of jokes in propaganda and the need to bring the laugher over to one's side. In a final Jewish joke, the propaganda minister visits a psychoanalyst for advice about a personal problem. For further context, other jokes in the Nazi era mocked Goebbels for both his physical deformity (clubfoot) and his similarity in appearance to many Polish Jews. Indeed, one barbed joke even managed to combine a critique of propaganda along with ridicule aimed directly at Goebbels's physical handicap. In this way, the proverbial German folk wisdom about the inability of lies to get very far was rewritten to match Goebbels's physical deformity in the form of a *Flüsterwitz:* "One no longer has to say: Lies have short legs. Now one says: The lie has a short leg."[92] Naturally, this background information helps to explain the identity crisis that torments the Goebbels character in this joke (and that makes him closer to a self-critical and self-conscious Jewish joking character). Rather than focusing only on aspects of enemy inferiority like a typical tendentious joke engaged in character assassination, the punch line of this final Jewish joke turns toward the larger question of truth in the face of propaganda. It puts Goebbels in the bind of the classic paradox demarcated by the Cretan's statement, "All Cretans are liars." The following tendentious joke puts an ironic spin on Goebbels's diarist epigraph and the authoritarian attempt to nullify "Jewish laughter." It leaves him and us standing (or limping) before the distorted mirror of Nazi propaganda and wondering what to believe — not to believe.

> Paul Joseph Goebbels, Nazi minister of propaganda, confided in a close friend that he is suffering from chronic self-consciousness. "Even after a successful oration I am tormented by a painful feeling of inadequacy," said Goebbels.
> "The best thing to do is to consult a psychoanalyst," suggested the friend. "I know how you feel about Jews, but if you go to Dr. Gottfried Meyers he is sure to help you." Secretly Goebbels went to the psychiatrist and told his story.
> "You are suffering from a pronounced inferiority complex," said Dr. Meyers. "The antidote is auto-suggestion. Stand before a mirror for fifteen minutes daily and repeat. 'I am important — I am significant — I am indispensable.' This will cure your self-consciousness."
> "Your remedy is useless," said Goebbels. "I never believe a word I say."[93]

# 6
# Jewish Joke Reparations and Mourning in Post-Holocaust Germany

In the face of the dead seriousness of the virtual destruction of European Jewry during the Holocaust, it might be deemed frivolous to look at the publication of a few dozen Jewish joke books in Germany in the wake of this tragedy and expect to find something of culturally historical significance. At its worst, both joke books and joke investigations might appear to be disrespectful to the memory of the dead, even constituting a laughing at their expense.[1] Nevertheless, as Goethe said of the satirist Lichtenberg—there was a problem hidden wherever he made a joke.[2] While acknowledging the risks of frivolity and disrespect, this chapter assumes that the discourse related to post-Holocaust Jewish joke books conceals an important set of social, cultural, psychological, political, and economic problems that demand our considered attention and analysis. Therefore, it seeks to demonstrate how post-Shoah Jewish joke books and the debates surrounding them became an exemplary site for both Germans and Jews to address—and not to address—the recent trauma that was haunting them, if only under the guise of what might be dubbed in its double-dealing fashion as a process of "joke reparations" or even one of "joke mourning." Amid the tendency toward intellectual and spiritual reparations in the cultural sphere, the Jewish joke was seized upon as a cultural asset or good (*Kulturgut*) to perform what might be called *geistreiche Wiedergutmachung* (witty, joking, and ingenious reparations). In an irony of history, it was the joke—always a site for the lifting of inhibitions and repressions—that allowed for a partial lifting of the rigorous taboos related to anti-Semitism, the Jews, and the Holocaust in the Federal Republic of Germany that had blocked a confrontation with the horrors of recent memory and, for better or worse, provided an occasion to deal with (or to divert) these devastating matters on the level of a collectively cathartic laughter.[3]

This chapter focuses on the critical reception of one Jewish joke compilation in particular—Salcia Landmann's *Der jüdische Witz*.[4] While trained as a philosopher in Basel and Zurich, where she published a dissertation in the study of phenomenology and ontology in 1939, Salcia Landmann (1911–2002) would turn her attention to Yiddish folklore and language as her major area of research and writing after the Holocaust (fig. 21).[5] Her book on Jewish humor became a pop cultural phenomenon in Germany where it reached the top of the charts and stayed on the bestseller list for months. All in all, it generated about one hundred reviews in the popular press. Over the course of the next decade, *Der jüdische Witz* in its various hardback and paperback editions sold over 500,000 copies. The phenomenal success of this book should raise suspicions that something funny—in the sense of extraordinary—was going on over and beyond the realm of the merely frivolous. The overwhelming attention devoted to *Der jüdische Witz* in the early 1960s (and the fierce negative reaction that it spawned in the Jewish intellectual community) demonstrates that it touched a nerve—or, more to the point, an open wound—in German and Jewish cultural consciousness only fifteen years after at the end of World War II and in the period of official restitutions to the State of Israel and to individual Jews who were victimized by the Nazis during the Holocaust. These reparations paid by the German government to Jewish victims became known as *Wiedergutmachung* (literally "making good again"), and they were approved in the Bundestag in March 1953 with the passage of the Federal Compensation Law, which was revised later in 1956.

What exactly was happening in this idealization and valorization of Jewish joke production around 1960? What was its possible connection to the attempt of both Germans and Jews to come (or not come) to terms with each other and with the suffering of the recent past? Even if there were no longer a "Jewish question" in need of solution and few Jews living in Germany after the Holocaust, Jewish jokes and joke books could become a staging ground and a lightning rod in order to play out larger issues related to German-Jewish cultural memory and intercultural dynamics, and the complexities of philo-Semitism and anti-Semitism—of the stereotypes of good Jews and bad Jews—in the era of *Wiedergutmachung*. Ironically, even if some of them tended to portray Jews in terms of ancient anti-Semitic stereotypes, joke reparations claimed and proclaimed Jewish jokes as a cultural good in need of restitution and part of the (over)compensation process of making Jewish things good again in post-Holocaust Germany. While Freudian psychoanalysis delineated a psychic

Figure 21. Brigitte Friedrich, *Salcia Landmann*, 1988. (Reprinted by permission of Süddeutsche Zeitung Photo / Alamy Stock Photo.)

economy of the joke based on saving (*Ersparnis*) and expenditure (*Aufwand*), this joke analysis attempts to inscribe a psychological and political economy of the Jewish joke in the post-Holocaust era relying on the interconnections of indebtedness, reparations, and making good again.

Packed between the sentimentally theatrical staging of the life of Anne Frank which gave the Holocaust a human child's face in the late 1950s and the televised trial and eventual execution of Adolf Eichmann in Jerusalem from 1961 to 1963 which gave the Holocaust its most inhuman face,[6] the publication of *Der jüdische Witz* (1960) offered the mass media and the public some "comic relief" from the high drama of the Holocaust. Miming the Jewish joke transmutation process itself, the public could work off some repressed suffering and guilt through the enjoyment of a regurgitated dose of entertaining, accessible, anonymous, and exterminated Jewish folk cultural production. Here was a magic laugh remedy that could offer something to anti-Semites, philo-Semites, and neutral or undecided parties alike. For while, as Landmann suggests, this was a book that made it possible to laugh again in relation to the Jews after the Holocaust,[7] such a consideration leaves open for interpretation whether this process involved a laughing *at* or a laughing *with* the Jews.[8]

Almost a generation before the cultural debate in West Germany about the Holocaust and its mourning sparked by film director Hans-Jürgen Syberberg's *Our Hitler* (1977) and the screening of the Hollywood television production *Holocaust* (1979),[9] the amazing success of and controversy surrounding *Der jüdische Witz* provided a way for Germans and Jews to deal with the gaping problem of cultural memory (loss) whether this encounter (i.e., joke reparations) was considered to be a true work of mourning, a therapeutic remedy, a laughing abreaction, a diversionary tactic, a sign of an inability or unwillingness to mourn, or as nothing but a big — or even offensive — joke.

## Unpacking Joke Mourning

By referring to the problematic of joke mourning, this analysis juxtaposes two key terms from Freud's *Der Witz und seine Beziehung zum Unbewussten* (*Jokes and their Relation to the Unconscious*, 1905) and "Trauer and Melancholie" ("Mourning and Melancholy," 1917). It suggests that it is necessary to negotiate the border between *Witzarbeit* and *Trauerarbeit*, between the work of joking and the work of mourning, between laughing and grieving in order to understand the reception of the post-Holocaust Jewish joke book. While Freud's disciple Theodore Reik once wrote an essay on the psychoanalytic relationship between Jewish jokes and melancholy as overly self-abasing and self-critical modalities, he never dealt specifically with the problem of jokes and mourning (or of jokes in the service of mourning). Furthermore, he did not pursue this line of thinking at all in his later book on *Jewish Wit* (1962) written after the Holocaust and published in the United States (in English) about the same time as Landmann's book.[10]

The deployment of the term joke mourning marks an unstable linguistic shifter whose meaning reverses itself depending on whether the emphasis is placed on the first (i.e., joke mourning makes a joke of mourning) or the second term (i.e., the joke as a type of mourning). This complex expression allows one to consider the double role of the Jewish joke in the postwar era as something assisting the work of mourning and as something threatening to turn the work of mourning into a joke. The coining of this Janus-faced term takes its cue from two parallel investigations that employ one of the operative terms in the same shifty manner: Freud's concept of "'joking' brevity" and his ambivalence regarding the kind of economy achieved in the joke work if and when it requires the expenditure of so much effort to construct its word condensations—"*Die Kürze des Witzes ist eine besonderen, eben die 'witzige' Kürze*" ("A joke's brevity is of a peculiar kind—'joking' brevity");[11] and Eric Santner's description of the shift in emphasis in the postmodernist appropriation of Walter Benjamin's "analysis of *mourning* play as one of mourning *play*." There is a distinct parallel between the post-Holocaust "*joke* mourner" articulated in this text and Santner's postmodern mourner who "while insisting on this condition of loss and dispersion, tries to move beyond mourning."[12]

The problematic of joke mourning also leads to a discussion of the most painfully and joyously read of all twentieth century novels, James Joyce's *Finnegans Wake* (1939). The title of Joyce's work is based on an Irish vaudeville song describing the adventures of Tim Finnegan, a hod carrier and a "dacent gaylabouring" man, who apparently dies in a work-related accident while in a drunken stupor. The book opens at his wake or the festive deathwatch of his friends over his coffin. This is an all-night vigil that includes singing, dancing, drinking and, overall partaking in the "shoutmost shoviality."[13] In a section reversibly entitled "Gay Anguish, Anguished Gaiety," the French intellectual Georges Bataille takes up this old Irish folk custom in *Finnegans Wake* as the affirmation of "a paradoxical example of a gay reaction in the presence of the work of death." Bataille elaborates: "The Irish and Gallic custom of the 'wake' is little known, but it was still observed at the end of the last century. It is the subject of the last work of Joyce, *Finnegan's Wake*. It is the mourning vigil for Finnegan. . . . His family invited all his friends, who honored him all the more in abandoning themselves to dancing for a long time and to hard drinking to his health."[14] Mixing tears and laughter and in a parallel to the *jüdische* Witz, Finnegan's wake is a complicated procedure that mourns and celebrates the dead (and death in general) simultaneously—that laughs while grieving and that grieves while laughing.

It would be possible to transpose the scenography of this Irish wake to the practice of Jewish joke mourning in the era of *Wiedergutmachung* with the publication of Landmann's book. While the mourning vigil for Finnegan relies on dancing, singing, and drinking, joke mourning in memory of the Jewish victims of the Holocaust would consist of the recitation of the humorous tales and jokelore that this exterminated folk culture generated, circulated, and laughed about. Jewish joke mourning demarcates a complex practice on the road to a "recovery" mixing retrieval, restoration, and covering over again. The joke mourner of the Holocaust grieves a condition of irrevocable loss, restitutes as part of "making things good again," and attempts to move beyond mourning via the transmutation of suffering into liberating laughter. But the reversible strategy of joke mourning is tricky because just as one could say that those laughing with *Der jüdische Witz* are mourning through joking, one also might claim that such joking *risks* the work of mourning, or even acts as if nothing serious had happened at all.[15]

If one turns to the reflections of the Jewish joke collector, Salcia Landmann, about her bestselling book, it becomes clear how joke mourning and its reversibility creep into her seemingly straightforward account of the book's contribution to the postwar normalization of relations between Germans and Jews: "When my book *Jewish Wit: Sociology and Collection* was published by Walter Press in 1960, it was received with enthusiasm by the press almost unanimously. It was considered as a step toward the normalization of relations between Jews and Germans. One was *lightened* after the terrible events of the Nazi era finally to be able to think again about European Jewry other than only with horror and grief [*Schreck und Gram*]."[16] In this passage, joke mourning makes the turn toward German-Jewish normalization into a stutter step. For the final sentence of this citation does nothing other than to articulate joke mourning as a procedure that—like the German-Jewish past—resists mastery (*Vergangenheitsbewältigung*). Landmann's Jewish joke book is said to offer the chance to reintroduce comic relief and to divert horror and grieving. But if the lightening brought by the Jewish joke owes its derivation—as well as its chance for reparations—to the horror and grief of the recent Jewish experience, then the Jewish joke book and its success would testify to a paradigmatic work of joke mourning—that laughs itself out of but also *away from* grieving—whether Landmann admits this or not.

This chapter reviews the divergent responses to Landmann's book as a means to articulate the problematic of joke mourning and joke reparations in the post-Holocaust context. Rather than seeking a set definition of this phenomenon, my inquiry is concerned with the entry of joke mourning into German-Jewish cultural discourse in any number of guises. In other words, the joke mourning complex engenders a wide range of possibilities for its reception—the joke as work of mourning, the joke as substitute for mourning, the joke as a diversion for mourning, the joke as a shortcut for mourning, the joke as the incapacity for mourning, and even the joke as the other of mourning. This inquiry offers the chance to explore how Landmann's Jewish joke book opened a space wherein a constellation of reversible desires and affective responses were crystallized in the interweaving of laughing and grieving. This inquiry will attempt to understand the connection of this crystallization process to the related problems of indebtedness and reparations in order to grasp the overall political economy of the Jewish joke in response and in reaction to the problematic of *Wiedergutmachung*.

## Of Mourning Rituals and Salvage Operations

For over four decades until her death in May 2002, Salcia Landmann was provided with numerous occasions to speculate about the authorial and editorial intentions at the origins of her bestseller. Even when asked to write a foreword to advance the German publication of an American compendium of contemporary Jewish humor in 1982, Landmann began her remarks with a backward glance at her own pillar of laughs and how things stood twenty-two years earlier. This revelation of intent exposes mourning at the origin of *Der jüdische Witz*: "With my book *Jewish Wit: Sociology and Collection* that was first published in 1960, I thought I had created a kind of requiem for the Jewish joke. Indeed, its optimal conditions for existence were extinguished after the Jewish Holocaust of the Hitler years."[17] It is clear from the above passage that Landmann frames her joke collection as a work of mourning that responds to the physical and cultural devastation unleashed by the Nazis against the Jews in the Holocaust. In an unpublished letter to the author, Landmann underscores her intention through the use of further funereal phraseology: "*Das stimmt sogar — es ist ein Nekrolog* [This is true even — it is an obituary]."[18]

But if Landmann's monumental task is to bind Jewish joke collection to a discourse of mourning and nostalgia in a post-Holocaust scenography, then the choice of an imported Latin word that frames this service for the dead in the terms of a specific Christian religious ritual (the requiem mass) appears to be most peculiar. This is especially unusual for someone who prided herself on her authoritative knowledge of Yiddish and Jewish intellectual and religious traditions. One wonders why Landmann never referred to her achievement either in Yiddish or Hebrew with reference to the Jewish mourner's prayer, the *Kaddisch*. Indeed, she could have resorted to one of her favorite tactics in *Der jüdische Witz* whereby she uses a Yiddish/Hebrew phrase and then either puts its German equivalent in brackets or explains it in the glossary. In this manner, the reader learns about the "*Kadisch*, a., j. *Kádisch*" as the "*Gebet männlicher Nachkommen für verstorbene nahe Verwandte* [Prayer by male offspring for deceased close relatives]."[19] Another section titled "Mame-Loshen" includes a joke entry for this mourning ritual that becomes doubly ironic when juxtaposed with Friedrich Torberg's biting polemic against the book a year earlier (fig. 22). It reads: "*Kaddisch (Totengebet) = Zeitungskritik*

[*Kaddisch* (Prayer for the Dead) = Newspaper Critique]."[20] Nonetheless, by selecting "Requiem" rather than *"Kaddisch"* or *"Totengebet"* to explain her achievement, Landmann reveals her own scripted subject position as a Jewish mourner who services primarily a non-Jewish or Christian mass audience in the wake of the destruction of European Jewry.[21]

The choice of the word *requiem* (or obituary) when applied to the Jewish joke brings further incongruities and contradictions. For this book of Jewish jokes designed for laughs has been cast in terms of the utmost solemnity. Taking a look at the encyclopedic menu offered by a requiem, one wonders what there is to laugh about amid a "solemn chant (as a dirge) for the repose of the dead" or a "musical composition in honor of the dead." What would a requiem of the Jewish joke sound like, and where would it provide a space for laughter? One wonders what there is to laugh about in this post-Holocaust staging of the Jewish joke steeped as it is in figures of mourning and loss. It seems that by binding the Jewish joke to a discourse of mourning in this way, the joke collector hopes to protect herself from any charges of taking matters too lightly or laughing at the dead. But this pious strategy cannot master the complexity of joke mourning. For Landmann in this instance not only represses the risk that joke mourning dishonors the dead, but also the other possibility that joke mourning provides a *proper* means to honor the dead by means of laughter (e.g., the Joycean option of Bataille's anguished gaiety).

The post-Holocaust figuration of the Jewish joke collector as mourner is already inscribed in a postwar reissue of one of the three Jewish joke books that serves as a major source for Landmann's own collection. In *Röyte Pomerantsen or How to Laugh in Yiddish* (1947), the Jewish folklorist Immanuel Olsvanger mourns the passing of the Jewish joke in a discourse that is full of nostalgia and loss. Again, one notices the use of grave expressions such as "sad duty" and "grim monument" to describe a joke book designed to teach readers how to laugh in Yiddish and that articulates this problematic space of Jewish joke mourning: "The horrible events of the last years make this book stand out as a grim monument over the mass grave of a world that is no more. It is therefore a sad duty to rescue from oblivion the popular treasures of that folk. . . . We shall never forget them."[22] These remarks can be read in tandem with Landmann's comments regarding her own role as joke mourner and salvage operator. She recollects: "I wanted to do two things with my book: to show the tragic background of the Jewish joke and to collect this type of joke once again especially today for German readers after the demise of European Jewry and thus to keep it from oblivion."[23] Both statements reveal a shared intention on the part of these post-Holocaust collectors to work through their mourning via salvage and rescue operations that would construct the Jewish joke and joke book as a monument, as a kind of legible and laughable tombstone rather than a buried treasure.[24] In this way, the process of collection and recollection transforms the Jewish joke book from folkloric record of everyday life into the guardian of eternal memory. This is articulated in Olsvanger's "we shall never forget them" or Landmann's "to be kept from being forgotten" (*vor dem Vergessenwerden bewahren*). In this manner, the Jewish joke book becomes a metonymic token or keepsake standing in for the mourning of the loss of European Jewry during the Holocaust and replacing the injunction to never forget the victims.

As a concomitant to Landmann's position as joke mourner and obituary columnist, she has to argue that the Jewish joke perished in the Holocaust. For, if the Jewish joke did not really die, this would cast doubts on her entire project of joke mourning. Landmann's discourse on the death of the Jewish joke leads her to taking up strange if not unfounded positions in the original edition. For instance, she contends that there are no Jewish jokes in the new State of Israel because the Israelis have no need for them when they have military weapons at their disposal. Or the Jewish joke in America has been displaced by the talking cure of psychoanalysis. Landmann adamantly returns to the scene of the crime and her equation that the death of the Jews means the death of the Jewish joke: "Only after the extermination of the Jews there [in Poland] has [the Jewish joke] come to an end. And together with Judaism, the Jewish joke has also died . . ."[25] However, Landmann's use of the three dots in her text after what should have put a full stop to signal an end to Jewish joke production betrays that the story goes on and that this dramatic pause might be just a sentimentally driven and overblown rhetorical device. A bit later, in the final section that equates the present with death, titled "*Der jüdische Witz in der Gegenwart und sein Tod*" (The Jewish joke in the present and its death), Landmann continues her elegy of Jewish wit via another comparison with the Holocaust wherein the joke appears to have fared even worse than the Jews. Playing the part of salvage operator and antique collector, Landmann pushes the Jewish joke into the past where it assumes the scattered status of cultural remnant. Even though this joke mourner acknowledges the fragmenting invasion of alterity into the scene of collection, the sense of estrangement is somehow mastered (at least for the time being), and the emphasis remains focused on understanding and recollection ("*noch sammeln*"): "A part of the Jewish people has managed to survive the Nazi terror—but not its humor. It belongs today to the Jewish past, just as the German folk tale belongs to the German past. We can only collect it and understand it so long as it has not yet become too alien to us in its presuppositions."[26]

Even though she was later forced to alter this hardline stance slightly with the rise of Jewish humor in the United States, Landmann remained pretty consistent in her assertion regarding the death of the Jewish joke.[27] Again, one gets the feeling that Landmann's extended joke mourning (whether the joke *really* died or not) functions as a substitute for her mourning of the victims of the Holocaust. Indeed, Landmann stages a rather comical discourse that mourns and heralds the death of the Jewish joke simultaneously for over forty years. ("The Jewish joke is dead; long live the Jewish joke!") One would have thought that one eulogy would have been enough. While readers are told over and over again by Landmann that the Jewish joke is dead, one witnesses the proliferation of more and more editions of her book, with more and more contributions (including new jokes) from readers and revivers. Miraculously, this process of Jewish joke mourning constitutes a living off of death, a laughing off of death. It delineates the operations of a psychical and political economy wherein every fresh obituary on the death of the Jewish joke spreads sad feelings of sorrow, guilt, and indebtedness (joke mourning) that work to promote yet another round of laughing expenditure and investment in the book (joke reparations).[28]

Jürg Ramspeck's remarks in an early review of the book unravel how the Jewish joke feeds off its own "death" under the heading *"Ein historischer Schatten"* (A historical shadow). At the origin of the book's publication and before its multiple resurrections, Ramspeck already deciphers and foreshadows the spectral and speculative logic that guarantees its many happy returns by pointing to the *revenant* or the ghost-like status of the Jewish joke in the wake of the Holocaust: "At the time when Salcia Landmann makes these statements on a December afternoon in the year 1960, the Jewish joke is dead, beaten to death, a ghostly historical shadow [*ein gespenstischer historischer Schatten*] henceforth—what lies between it in its prime and our days is the most horrible mass murder of all times."[29] The very flow of Ramspeck's dramatic phrasing wherein the Jewish joke moves from dead corpse, to murder victim, to ghostly historical shadow enacts the resurrecting process of its restitution as a cultural good in the era of *Wiedergutmachung*. As in the narrative of *Finnegans Wake*, the process of mourning which would lay the joke to rest revives it in its recollection and retelling so that one is left wondering whether the Jewish joke ever really died in the first place. But if that were to be the case, then Landmann's extended practice of joke mourning would take on the blackest of humors, and it may even constitute a most ingenious Jewish joke.

## The Jewish Joke After the Holocaust: Transmuting Suffering into Laughter

In *"Jüdischer Witz aus Jüdischer Trauer?,"* Elizabeth Petuchowski reviews and takes issue with the thesis that the Jewish joke springs from sorrow, grief, and mourning. Viewing Judaism as an active and affirmative religious practice,

Petuchowski attempts to shift the terms of the discussion and the source of Jewish humor from mourning (and death) to survival (and life). Nevertheless, Petuchowski realizes that in historical terms the *"Witz aus Trauer"* (joking out of suffering) hypothesis became a virtual truism in regard to defining the Jewish joke in the period after 1933.[30] Curiously, Petuchowski does not focus on the catastrophic events that contributed to the wide dissemination of this theory. Instead, she prefers to speak in general terms about a malaise called Judaism: "In 'Psychology of the Jewish Joke,' it is alleged that mourning and sorrow initiates the joke — that it is 'a kind of defense against the manifest circumstances and conditions of life, a rebellion against the overwhelming superiority of Destiny' (Kreppel V). The joke, as it was shown here, serves at the same time as a cure for an ailment that is called Judaism. This theory is so well known that it hardly counts — in the 1980s — as a great discovery."[31]

The reference here to the "Psychologie des jüdischen Witzes" alludes to an essay written by Jonas Kreppel that begins his Jewish joke compendium, *Wie der Jude Lacht* (How the Jew laughs) published in Vienna in the year of the Nazi's rise to power in Berlin. In this text, Kreppel also introduces the concept of laughter mixed with heartache and he registers it in both Yiddish *Mameloshen* and German *Muttersprache* as *"Lachen mit Jaschtescherkes (Lachen mit Herzweh)"* to convey the joke mourning (*"Witz aus Trauer"*) thesis with an expression aimed straight at the heart.[32] Petuchowski fails to discuss how Kreppel's popular psychology of the Jewish joke as "laughter with heartache" posed a direct challenge to the popular definition of Freud and his psychoanalysis of the Jewish joke that relies on a model of Jewish self-criticism in order to understand the wit and laughter of the Jews.[33]

Nevertheless, Landmann's *Der jüdische Witz* continues to rely on the Freudian self-critical model of the Jewish joke and to stress over and over how the Jewish joke functions as the weapon and defense of the defenseless. Oddly enough, while Landmann has no problem defining her activities as a post-Holocaust joke collector as a work of mourning, she herself does not (for the most part) adopt the theory of the Jewish joke as the transformation of suffering into laughter. But this does not mean that this theory is absent from her publication. Instead, it finds a surrogate advocate. For the introduction of mourning as the basis of the theory of the Jewish joke finds favor in the speculations of Carlo Schmid who was asked by Landmann to write the foreword to her book. In this way, while the theory may be missing from her essay on *"Der Jüdische Witz und Seine Soziologie"* (The Jewish joke and its sociology), the book is set up by a foreword that responds directly and emphatically to the political culture and sociology of this post-Holocaust period by stressing the theory of the Jewish joke as the transformation of suffering, mourning, and grief (*Trauer*) into laughter.

It might appear odd that a leading Social Democrat and the vice-president of the West German Bundestag would be writing the foreword to a book on Jewish jokes and acting as an authority. This promotional gesture seems to raise suspicions regarding Landmann's rather ethnocentric contention that one should focus on the quality of the Jewish joke itself and not only on the psychological and political factors of the day in assessing the phenomenal success of her book.[34] But there is no denying that this specific framing gesture underscores the political economy of the Jewish joke in the era of *Wiedergutmachung* wherein a leading German political authority and exponent of German-Jewish reconciliation would lend his voice to and support for the reinscription of Jewish jokes (as well as Jewish survivors) into the German cultural and social landscape approximately fifteen years after the end of World War II.[35]

As Schmid formulates his understanding of the Jewish joke, the joke mourner's keyword (*Trauer*) appears twice in this short text. In the first instance, the Jewish joke itself is defined as mourning the gap that exists between what is right and what is real. As incongruent as it appears, when it comes to the Jewish joke, mourning and melancholia surpass the situation comedy that shows on the surface. Schmid writes: "And yet I felt something that touched me about the comedy of the situation: a melancholy of a different character, with something like mourning about it wherein the right [*Anspruch*] and the real [*Realität*] obviously never meet."[36] Assuming the form of a philosophical maxim, the second instance occurs toward the end when Schmid concludes, "The Jewish joke is sorrow or mourning about the antinomies and aporias of Being taken cheerfully."[37] In this somewhat defensive manner, Schmid's philosophical gesture diverts and displaces joke mourning from the particular and the personal (i.e., mourning or sorrow over the victims of the Holocaust in the year of our Lord 1960) to a consideration of more global, impersonal, and universal matters (i.e., mourning or sorrow over the aporias and antinomies of Being with a capital B).

Within the context of defining the Jewish joke in terms of mourning at this historical moment of *Wiedergutmachung*, one might refer to a later statement that "ghostwrites" Schmid in Fritz Muliar's "Nachwort" to *Das grosse Buch des jüdischen Humors*. While it props up the theory of the "great humanist" that transmutes teary-eyed sorrow and suffering into laughter, his exact phrasing is not found in Schmid's text. Muliar falsely attributes: "The Jewish joke — 'these are tears that have become a laugh.' Thus, the great humanist Carlo Schmid characterizes the wit of the Jews."[38] This should be compared as well with the opening statement of another book of Jewish anecdotes published in 1961 containing an even more stereotypical positing of the "*Witz aus Trauer*" thesis. Seemingly aware of the paradoxes of joke mourning, this rather pathetic version stops short of laughter leaving only the trace of a smile mixed with a trail of tears: "[The Jewish joke] flows from the suffering of life, from the pain of the times. It has its origins in tragedy.... It rarely triggers laughter, much more often that smile in which glistens a tear."[39]

But Schmid's text does not only hold to a *definition* of the Jewish joke based on Holocaust mourning. It also recites a Jewish joke that is derived from an earlier era and that appears to be overdetermined given the fact that post-Holocaust joke mourning and reparations are lurking just beneath the surface. Schmid's joke displacement entertains a paradoxical situation of financial and moral debts and reparations that generates a radical reversal in the terms of indebtedness. To add another bitter irony, the anecdote is recounted in reference to the very treaty that scapegoated the Jews after Germany's defeat in World War I:

> With the knowledge of such a paradox, another one arises: that a situation of a certain magnitude turns into its opposite, understood not metaphysically, but rather concretely: that if one owes a banker a million dollars, then he has his borrower [*Schuldner*] in his hands: that, however, if the debt [*Schuld*] is twenty million, then the borrower has the banker in his hands ... Regarding this, a big banker in Berlin during the twenties had explained to me quite clearly the essential political core of the reparations problem that the Treaty of Versailles had created.[40]

Here, Schmid's elliptical inscription of the three dots between the recitation of this ironic anecdote from the 1920s and its recollection in 1960 hints that something (unspeakable) has been left out of this account—something that may not be subject to any possible accounting. The punchline of the Versailles reparations joke reverberates in the age of *Wiedergutmachung* in making a joke out of a state of indebtedness that may never be repaid—even going so far as to pose a radical reversal in the relations between the debtor and the creditor. This reversibility resonates with the problematic of joke mourning in general. Transferred to the era of *Wiedergutmachung*, Schmid's Jewish joke parable informs us of a paradoxically irreparable situation where the post-Holocaust Jews have the German bankers in their hands because the guilty Germans owe the Jews far too much. However, whether the purchase of this Jewish joke book would aid and abet the paying back of this debt (as Schmid presumably believes) or rather only serve to increase the debt has been left an open question. This sets up a situation that is similar to the comic God portrayed in a Jewish joke about Abraham and Isaac that functions as a parable for *Wiedergutmachung*: "Both Joel and Moishe have received reparations owing to their persecution during the Third Reich. On the way home, Joel says: 'Was it not well advised that the Lord in heaven did not allow the killing of Isaac by Abraham?' To which Moishe asks: 'What do you mean, Joel?' 'If he had, then he would never have been freed from reparations [niemals von der Wiedergutmachung losgekommen].'"[41] As the joke concludes, one will never be able to free oneself from reparations. To better consider the two sides of this Janus-faced situation, I will next compare and contrast philo-Semitic versus anti-Semitic investments in Landmann's joke book and explore the ambivalent character of such joke reparations further.

## Treating Landmann's Book as A Philo-Semitic Success Story

The Hamburg politician and advocate of Wiedergutmachung Eric Lüth issued a statement in 1952 that demonstrated how the restitution of the Jewish contribution to modern German culture functioned as a necessary by-product of his personal quest to achieve peace and understanding with the new State of Israel. Lüth urges, "Therefore the task of our generation and the next one will be to reawaken the great Jewish contribution to the development of Germany in the consciousness of our people."[42] There is little doubt that the success of Landmann's Jewish joke book rests in part on this genuine philo-Semitic desire to revive a sense of the great Jewish contribution to the development of Germany on the level of (folk) culture in the postwar era. Indeed, it might have been both its ability to break taboos and the ironic and satirical stance of *"der jüdische Witz"* in relation to Jewish and German "development" that made it a good cultural asset during such a difficult and strained time in German-Jewish relations.

Meanwhile, Landmann advanced the theory of the Jewish joke in the service of German-Jewish understanding by telling an anecdote of her own for a change in her 1972 introductory essay "Zum jüdischen Witz." In it, she unwittingly assumes the role of the Jewish matchmaker, the *Shadchenit*. According to Landmann, with the success of her book, enthusiastic readers began to send her their favorites by the hundreds. Landmann added many of these contributions to later expanded editions so that her book began to resemble a collective effort. In appreciation, Landmann published the names of the contributors in the back of her book. It was the publication of this list of donors (*Spenderliste*) that led to the following anecdote that illustrates how joke expenditures led to conjugal payoffs. It affords an idealistic take on the contribution of the Jewish joke toward German-Jewish reconciliation in the post-Holocaust era: "Some lost sight of each other during the Hitler years. In my 'donor list,' they found each other again. In one case, it even led to the marriage between a Jewish emigrant overseas and his 'Aryan' school sweetheart after whom he had sought in vain in the current eastern part of Germany after the war. The woman had fled to West Germany. May the list of donors continue to fulfill its purpose not only as an expression of my gratitude but also as a meeting place for lovers of Jewish humor!"[43] This anecdote puts us in the middle of a joke parable that evokes and confirms both Jean Paul's witty definition of *Witz* and Theodor Vischer's addendum. Jean Paul: "Joking is the disguised priest who weds every couple"; Vischer: "He likes best to wed couples whose union their relatives frown upon."[44] Transported into this anecdote, Salcia Landmann becomes the disguised priestess (i.e., Jewish matchmaker) whose jokes (for which she serves as the metonymic substitute) reunite this postwar couple — even if their parents (hinted at in the marked racist pejorative "Aryan") may not have approved of this match. This reunification saga becomes both the perfect *Wiedergutmachung* love story and joke parable. The Jewish joke as mediator and meeting place brings them together under a comedic canopy that acts as a bridge between East and West and between German and Jew for a generation desperately seeking reconnection and reconciliation. From this perspective, the Jewish joke would be viewed as a more effective tool in comparison with the contemporaneous establishment of Jewish-Christian encounter and dialogue groups in Germany.[45] As a mode of interpersonal communication seeking communal and therapeutic laughter, the joke, according to this view, helped to restore intimacy and intercultural understanding between Germans and Jews.

It was exactly this argument that resonated with the German press. Landmann's Jewish joke book could serve "as a potential basis for a new understanding between Germans and Jews" in terms of a direct encounter between Germans and Jewish survivors and in terms of a process of mourning by which the victims were recalled to life through their humor.[46] Josef Müller-Marein's book review in the German weekly *Die Zeit* therefore hailed the Jewish joke as therapeutic remedy.[47] It expressed the sincere hope that a cathartic laughter induced by a shot of Jewish humor could somehow relax or ease the tensions, blocks, and cramps in the German body politic in the wake of the Holocaust. If the Jews had used their wits to cope with the sufferings and sorrows meted out to them as a persecuted and victimized people, then the postwar Germans — suffering from Jewish genocidal guilt and seeking reconciliation — could borrow some of their Jewish victim's own medicine — something akin to laughing gas — in the palliative joke preparation packaged by Landmann to help heal the wounds with laughter.

In the same way that he felt that anti-Semitic support of the book only made the debt worse (see the next section), Friedrich Torberg argued that these philo-Semitic joke reparations were also counterproductive and constituted an unhealthy solution. Torberg insisted that they would induce even more tensions if they inverted values to the point where every book, no matter what its quality, became automatically good if written by a Jew. While Torberg understood the genuine motives behind *geistige Wiedergutmachung*, he feared the underside of philo-Semitism and *geistreiche Wiedergutmachung*. Torberg's satirical critique of the glorious reception of *Der Jüdische Witz* leads him to the following formula: Making good again means making bad again if and when it makes the bad good again. Torberg explains his position:

> God save the Germans from their tension and their cramp [*Verkrampfung*], and anyway they will resolve it with the help of this book! But it would be a most unhealthy and tense solution [*verkrampfte Lösung*] on their part. The spasm [*Krampf*] comes in a completely misunderstood need (even if sprung from the noblest of motives) to make "spiritual and intellectual reparations" ["*geistige Wiedergutmachung*"] that apparently do not allow one to find a book to be bad if it was written by a Jew, an emigrant, or anti-Nazi resister or if it (naturally, in a "positive" way) belongs to one of these three relevant topics. In full awareness of my avant-garde risk, I would venture to say that the book of a Jew . . . may be bad too and that the doubtless desirable relaxing [*Entkrampfung*] of the relations between Jews and Germans is not promoted but rather hampered if one remains silent about the case in point.[48]

Even though he was a friend and an admirer of Torberg's polemic,[49] Robert Neumann did not see any unhealthy underside in his own philo-Semitic reading of the book and its success. While this Austrian-Jewish parodist believed that *Der jüdische Witz* is a "*hanebüchene Sammlung*" ("outrageous collection") for formal reasons, Neumann saw respect rather than disdain on the part of German enthusiasts of the book in their newly won ability to treat the Jew as an object of a "sunny humor" in contrast to the Nazi's beastly rhetoric of a few years earlier. Neumann writes therefore of a philo-Semitic success story based on a theory of laughing abreaction as a form of joke mourning. This psychoanalytic treatment offers its German adapters a method that purges and discharges the repressed traumatic events of the Holocaust with the telling of these old Jewish jokes:

> Nevertheless, this Landmann collection is amazingly successful in Germany. [This is] not because one wants to laugh about the Jews in an anti-Semitic manner yet again. On the contrary, it is something of a benefit to have brought the Jews to such a high degree of impar-

tiality that one cannot see them as sub-humans, but rather as objects of a sunny humor, on par with the forgetful professor and the other German comic strip characters. Laughing at the jokes of Salcia Landmann, the German abreacts [*abreagiert*] his Auschwitz.[50]

Whether consciously or not, Neumann's analysis contains a word play that is loaded with significance that foregrounds how the German releases and works off the guilt and repressions associated with the Holocaust by means of a redemptive laughter. To recite the moral of the story, "Laughing at the jokes [*Witze*] of Salcia Landmann, the German abreacts [works off, gets rid of] his Auschwitz." In this complicated process of joke mourning — of laughing as or instead of mourning and thereby releasing repressed emotions — the joke appears to be engaged in an alchemical purification process of the spirit that gets rid of all negative impurities (i.e., the image of the "bad Jew" as sub-human dregs). In this cathartic manner, *Der jüdische Witz* helps the German mourner to get rid of his Auschwitz and to leave only an ashen laughter behind.[51]

This is not very different from another aspect of Torberg's assessment of the philo-Semitic reaction to Landmann's book that he describes as inducing something like a tingling feeling rather than as a laughing release of tension. For Torberg, the subliminal and sublimating process of joke mourning provides an easy and attractive way to achieve mastery of the past, and, at the same time, to experience good entertainment value at no extra charge: "Unconsciously (or, as it's better said in New German: subliminally), the readers who like this book get the same pleasant tingling feeling as the critics who praise it: they have overcome and mastered the past and they have been well entertained in the process too. One cannot ask for more."[52] Here, Torberg touches upon his doubts regarding joke mourning and his fear that it shortcuts and short-circuits the mourning process. In short, he finds it to be wanting. The sarcasm embedded in his concluding sentence ("one cannot ask for more") inscribes his criticism of joke mourning as both an abbreviating and accelerating process that does not ask for the "more" that is required in order to mourn the Holocaust as an unmastered (if not unmasterable) past both for his and for future generations.

Related to this point, Torberg also fears that the practice of joke mourning advocated by Landmann can become a diversionary tactic that uses the pretense of German-Jewish understanding to mask the massacre at the basis of such cultural production and to set it beyond repair. In other words, philo-Semitic joke mourning might well cover over what has produced the need for Jewish joke reparations in the first place. According to Torberg, joke mourning as diversionary tactic and as comic relief gives those well-meaning individuals who have gathered together to give the Jewish joke a proper burial the illusory impression that it died of natural causes rather than on account of an irreducible violence. These individuals use the Jewish joke as a healing salve to forget about the gaping rupture that separates the glory days of Weimar Republic from the Federal Republic of Germany. In promoting this deluded mindset, Landmann operates, according to Torberg, "with such carefree pleasure, as if the deceptive concept of that horribly short period of German-Jewish agreement would be confirmed in the meantime as glorious and not arising from among the bloodiest of all the back-spinning wheels of history." He continues, "All this makes it easy for well-meaning individuals to indulge themselves out of the friendliest intentions to achieve the desired impression that the Jewish joke died, so to speak, a natural death."[53] The natural death of the Jewish joke in the philo-Semitic scenario of joke mourning buries another story that cries out bloody murder. But what if this story of bloody murder were not considered to be a back-spinning incident in twentieth-century history? Although this is an extreme and politically reactionary formulation, it forces us to look at the anti-Semitic reading of Landmann's Jewish joke book and its deadly discourse that, at its worst, treats the mourning process itself as nothing more than a joke. In other words, what if the post-Holocaust joke book re-empowered anti-Semites and their hateful mockery of the Jews?

## Deciphering an Anti-Semitic Success Story

At the time when Salcia Landmann was in St. Gallen, Switzerland writing and editing *Der Jüdische Witz* for publication, another kind of writerly activity was underway on the other side of the border that registered a resurgence of anti-Semitism in Germany: the so-called *Schmierwelle* (or graffiti wave) that took place in December 1959 and January 1960 and that numbered approximately five hundred incidents. The most serious of them involved the desecration of the Cologne synagogue with swastikas and anti-Semitic slogans (e.g., "*Juden raus*") on Christmas evening.[54] Coincidentally, Landmann includes a timely joke in her collection that alludes to the Cologne synagogue desecration directly:

> What is courage?
> If one is prowling around at night with a paintbrush near a synagogue, and there is a policeman at a distance of five meters away.
> And what is arrogance?
> If the person in question goes towards the policeman and asks: "Is Jew (*Jude*) written with or without an 'h'?"[55]

Many of these incidents took place at Jewish cemeteries involving the desecration of gravestones and monuments.[56] Thus, the return of the (anti-Semitic) repressed in postwar Germany was staged on the burial grounds wherein the sites of Jewish mourning became the targets of so-called "prankish" attacks.

Naturally, the West German government tried to downplay the incidents via two rhetorical strategies. On the one hand, they made light of the anti-Semitic wave as the work of vandals, rude boys, and pranksters who were out to raise hell without any political intentions. On January 16, 1960, Chancellor Konrad Adenauer delivered a radio broadcast where he described the wave as "almost exclusively loutish behavior without political foundations" and where he referred to the perpetrators as louts (*Lümmel*). Coincidentally, one of the findings of the opinion polls conducted under the auspices of the Institute for Social Research (Institut für Sozialforschung) in Frankfurt investigating public reactions to the incidents was that those classified as adult anti-Semites employed the same rhetoric as Adenauer with a strategy of disowning and disavowal. As Peter Schönbach concluded in his English summary: "Many ... tried to ward off their disquieting associations and guilt feelings by magnifying the psychological distance between the incidents and themselves. They achieved this by representing the incidents to themselves and others as unpolitical pranks of hoodlums and foolish boys."[57] In addition, the German government used a Cold War strategy that put the blame on sinister outside elements — the East German government — who, they claimed, put the vandals up to anti-Semitic acts as a means of destabilizing Western democracy. In either case, the scapegoating mechanism that had haunted the Jews in Germany before World War II had new targets in this attempt to displace a resurgence of anti-Semitism to the margins or to the "other" Germany.

Yet, assuming that this was just the work of foolish boys, one finds a fascinating parallel between the playful pranks carried out in an anti-Semitic graffiti campaign and the appeal of Jewish jokes containing a latent or manifest anti-Semitic content (even if as the unintended consequence of Jewish self-criticism and self-irony). From this perspective, both tendentious jokes and graffiti smears might be seen as two parallel actions that use doxological slogans and comic stereotypes to express prejudice and hostility against the Jew as social other. Thus, whatever the best intentions of its author,[58] it is against this sociocultural background that one has to admit the plausibility of the hypothesis that Landmann's book could provide another way of going against the grain in the *Wiedergutmachung* era by offering an outlet to express anti-Semitic stereotypes and to laugh at the Jews. From this perspective, reading (and laughing at) *Der jüdische Witz* or condoning the graffiti wave might be interpreted as two ways of breaking the rigid taboos against anti-Semitism.

And, in its most extreme version, these acts would mark not an inability to mourn but rather an unwillingness to mourn.

In this sociopolitical context, Torberg argues that it is an anti-Semitic consciousness that explains in part the phenomenal success of *Der Jüdische Witz*. In other words, the making good again of the Jew and of Jewish cultural production in postwar Germany relies on the reintroduction of negative stereotypes that depict the Jew as being far from good. Yet, after reading Torberg's critique of anti-Semitic stereotypes in Landmann, one has to wonder: How could any Jewish joke book eliminate the following list of stereotypes and still be classified as such? In other words, the articulation and mocking of group stereotypes is at the heart of Jewish and of ethnic humor in general. Also, Torberg's polemic intentionally represses the self-irony and self-mockery that often accompanies the staging of the anti-Semitic stereotypes in Landmann's book (not to mention overlooking the irony and satire that informs his own polemical thrust).

> It serves rather the "once more collected" evidence that Jews are deceitful and greedy, dishonest and devious, dirty and disgusting, stupid, brash and uneducated, brutish in feeling and whining, disrespectful and insensitive, cowardly and afraid of water, physically inferior and inferior in character. . . . That they are, in short, exactly the same, that they talk the same, act the same way and probably look exactly the same as the worst vulgar anti-Semitism has always wanted to admit starting from the aforementioned *Kikeriki* through the penetrating penny joke booklets with titles à la 100 *pikfeine Lozelach vün ünsere Lajt* to *Der Stürmer*.[59]

According to Torberg, it appears as if Landmann's joke book itself has played a practical joke on its readership in this paradoxical act of *Wiedergutmachung*—restoring Jewish wit as a positive cultural good while reifying negative distortions of the Jew and even reviving the deadly discourse on the Jewish joke at the same time. Torberg's critique does not focus on any "militant hatred of Jews" or, in sociological terms, the group in Schönbach's study who displayed "mild to strong anti-Semitic reactions" (16 percent). Instead, it focuses on the resurrection of old habits in the average person on the street that accounts for the broad appeal of Landmann's book in his opinion.

> The book has become a success precisely *because* it is anti-Semitic, *because* it suits the ideas that an average German citizen has of the Jews (not always out of militant hatred of the Jews, but often only out of precious habit) or he lets himself take lessons from Hitler (not

necessarily out of political party activist conviction, but simply out of obedience). And, in any case, nothing better can happen to the average German citizen today than to have it confirmed — moreover by the Jews themselves — that the Führer was right about this point as well. He had it right in any case when it came to the Bolsheviks and the highways. . . .[60]

This flashpoint restages a popular defense mechanism of postwar thinking that attributed political foresight and accuracy to the Führer (in hindsight) as a means of rationalizing anti-Semitic sentiments. Theodor Adorno also refers to this same Cold War–era reversionary tactic: "Or the beloved argument: 'Hitler was right about so much. For example, he realized the danger of Bolshevism in time; well, he would have been not entirely wrong about the Jews either.'"[61] Adorno then blasts this doxology by raising the counterargument that it was Hitler himself who created the situation that led to the postwar Russian menace. While Adorno reviews the logical sequence of the invocation of the Hitlerian retrospective fallacy from Bolshevism to anti-Semitism, Torberg goes from Bolshevism and "Autobahnism" (the myth that the German highways were Hitler's original idea) to anti-Semitism by recalling the negative stereotypes disseminated by the Jewish joke.

But Torberg was not the only Jewish critic offended by the anti-Semitic elements in Landmann's book. Jan Meyerowitz would confirm and expand upon Torberg's anti-Semitic argument a decade later in *Der Echte Jüdische Witz* by focusing on the negative impact of the book in terms of a language indebted to and informed by what might be called *Wiederschlechtmachung* ("making bad again"). Published in 1971, Meyerowitz pursues the authentic (*echt* instead of *schlecht*) and non-anti-Semitic Jewish joke as a way of combatting the overinflation of its value and even its counterfeiting in the speculative joke economy of *Wiedergutmachung* during the previous decades. Paradoxically, he begins with an argument that points to an increase of what is owed to the Jewish joke on account of Landmann's venture. Like Friedrich Nietzsche's argument from *On the Genealogy of Morals*, Meyerowitz is able to link the linguistic registers of moral and financial joke indebtedness on the part of Landmann in his use of the word *schuldig* as he focuses on the irreparable guilt and debt that remains after (or on account of) the era of *Wiedergutmachung*:[62] "This attempt has remained the task of pretty much all who are guilty, and the wide distribution of the book is a major, maybe irreparable mishap. We would not talk about it if it were not such a *historical* derailment. The press has generally praised the book — probably with the intention of *Wiedergutmachung*. Certainly, [Landmann's] *Sociology and Collection* has been for many Jews almost as repulsive and painful as much that was written in the Nazi period."[63] Ironically, the book that represents the drive toward Jewish joke reparations has caused an incredible amount of damage and it turns out to be a misfortune that may never be repaired. For Meyerowitz, the work of mourning and atonement as well as the cause of moral dignity and cultural restitution for Jews will never be advanced in Germany with this bankrupting and abject book that perpetuates anti-Semitic stereotypes as well as a Jewish "self-besmirching tendency" ("*selbstbesudelnde Tendenz*").

Meyerowitz raises the stakes of his critique in his last statement where he goes so far as to suggest a flashback to the Nazi era in the time warp that is opened up by Landmann's Jewish joke book. While this might appear to be overblown rhetoric on Meyerowitz's part, it must be confirmed that there are specific jokes in *Der Jüdische Witz* that did appear, for instance, in the Nazi satirical journal *Die Brennessel* in the mid-1930s in exactly the same form — albeit in a different historical context and for different purposes. These were jokes that had been part of the Nazi propaganda campaign to use self-critical Jewish humor against the Jews as a means to confirm all the negative things the Nazis had been saying about the enemy.[64] This might explain what Meyerowitz means by the "*historical* derailment" and slippage that he experiences. Instead of being a work of mourning or reparations, Landmann's offensive joke book raises evil demons and haunting memories of the Jewish experience in the Nazi era. Inversely and perversely, it reenacts and repeats for both Germans and Jews the pain and suffering that would make the work of mourning that more difficult to complete and overcome.

In the light of these anti-Semitic readings, it is productive to turn to Alexander and Margarete Mitscherlich's *Die Unfähigkeit zu trauern* (*The Inability to Mourn*, 1967) for psychoanalytical support of the anti-Semitic thesis that the success of Landmann's Jewish joke book rests on an inability and unwillingness to mourn in postwar German society. From this perspective, Jewish jokes do not allow for any authentic identification with the victim and therefore they defer the work of mourning (which is exactly Torberg's critique of Landmann). There is the further distinct possibility that laughing at Jewish jokes and negative stereotypes allows for the venting of repressed aggression against the Jews.[65] According to this theory, joking tendentiousness would bolster German defense mechanisms against the guilty recognition of past wrongs committed against the Jews. Given such an anti-Semitic twist, the incredible "lightness" of Jewish jokes becomes one of the "reaction-formations through which the realization of the overwhelming burden of guilt is kept far away."[66] Laughing at Jewish jokes and at negative Jewish stereotypes staves off the collective melancholy that would ensue in a work of total mourning. In this way, it is part and parcel of what the Mitschlerlichs see as the "successful defense against the melancholy of the masses."⁶⁷

## Torberg versus Landmann on Jewish Joke Mourning and Reparations

Friedrich Torberg launches his satirical polemic against both Salcia Landmann and *Der jüdische Witz* with the following pointed witticism that is a veritable mourning joke (*Trauerwitz*):

> In a Moravian Jewish community, there was a well-known eulogy orator who was used for all funerals — if the survivors were able to afford this because he was not cheap.
>
> Once again, a respected member of the community had passed away, and the family — who did not exactly have the reputation of generosity — inquired about the cost of a worthy obituary [*Nekrolog*].
>
> "It all depends," said the much-coveted orator. "The big and really astounding grave speech, which I do only in exceptional occasions, is appropriately quite expensive but it is worth the money. Everyone cries — the mourners, the rabbi, even the pallbearers. What can I tell you? The whole cemetery is bathed in tears. It costs two hundred guilders."
>
> "Two hundred guilders! We cannot spend so much."
>
> "Well, then, take the one for one hundred. It is still very poignant. I guarantee you that all the mourners weep and perhaps even the Rabbi will blow his nose a few times."
>
> "We don't place any value on this. Did you have nothing cheaper?"
>
> "I've got it. For fifty guilders. However, only the immediate family members cry."
>
> "Even fifty guilders is too expensive for us for a eulogy. Is there any other?"
>
> "There is," said the orator not allowing himself to show his impatience, "still one for twenty guilders. *But it already has a slightly humorous impact!*"⁶⁸

Torberg contrasts this elegant version of the joke about the professional funeral orator with the rather clipped version narrated by Landmann in order to criticize the shortcomings of her book in terms of plot, character, punchline, and delivery. However, there is more than meets the eye in Torberg's joke selection. For it is possible to consider this mourning joke (in either version) as a parable for Torberg's critique of Landmann and her questionable "Shoah business" practices that have capitalized undeservedly on the political economy of Jewish joke reparations. In other words, this calculating mourning orator (*Trauerredner*) with such a keen sense for the business of death might be none other than Salcia Landmann herself who has produced an overvalued product and who has profited from the steady stream of investment and interest in Jewish joke reparations and mourning in the post-Holocaust era. The punchline of Torberg's version of this anecdote is also applicable to our speculations on joke mourning because it poses how even a solemn eulogy can reverse itself into something humorous if and when the price is right (or, in this case, wrong). In this way, the punchline exhibits how laughter always remains an implicit possibility and risk to any practice of mourning.

A reading of this joke as a parable for Landmann's own practice of Jewish joke mourning also provides insights into her version as compared with Torberg's narration. She presents the same joke in the following manner: "In a small community that could remunerate its Rabbi only very modestly, it was common for members of the community to pay extra for each individual rabbinical service. A citizen now ordered a eulogy from the Rabbi for his late father. The Rabbi offered him the following: I have a very beautiful sermon, but that also costs eighty guilders. I have a second one for you, also a quite beautiful sermon in stock that you can have for fifty guilders . . . And then I've got a sermon for twenty guilders — but I must confess openly: I myself cannot recommend this one to you!"[69] Whether conscious or not, the incorporation of certain elements might have hit too close to home for Landmann. Thus, the character of the *Trauerredner* in Torberg's version has been transformed into the more neutral officiating rabbi. In addition, the reference to *Nekrolog* — the very term that Landmann uses to describe the eulogistic function of *Der jüdische Witz* — has been reduced to a simple sermon (*Predigt*). Finally, this comparison also points to another fascinating displacement that occurs in the punchline. Unlike Torberg's punchline, Landmann's version is bereft of all references to humor and focuses instead on the rabbi's negative recommendation against the purchase of the discounted eulogy. For the offer of a cheap obituary with a guaranteed humorous effect encapsulates Torberg's critique of Landmann's diversionary project of joke mourning to the letter.

In *Jewish Self-Hatred*, Sander Gilman discusses the controversy around the staging of *The Diary of Anne Frank* in the United States during the 1950s. By comparing the statements of the original scriptwriter Meyer Levin with those of the final scriptwriting team of Goodrich/Hackett, Gilman ingeniously shows how the stereotypical images of "good" versus "bad" Jew and the projections of philo- vs. anti-Semite dominate and structure the post-Holocaust debate over the legacy of Anne Frank.[70] During the same period and in much the

Figure 22. Friedrich Torberg signs his book *Die zweite Begegnung* (The second encounter) at the US Information Center in Vienna, April 19, 1951. (Courtesy of Image Archive of the United States Information Service in Austria [US 23.157], Österreichische National Bibliothek.)

same fashion, the virulent debate between Torberg and Landmann over the legacy of the Jewish joke (whose rhetoric threatens to go beyond the bounds of propriety) is staged around images of good Jew versus bad Jew and the proprieties of Jewish joke mourning and reparations. The accusations that they hurl at each other rest upon the basic opposition of the good versus bad mourner of the Jewish joke in particular and of the Holocaust in general. With this in mind, this section is not so much interested in reviewing the content of the debate, but rather how its staging is structured around the figures of good versus bad practices of mourning.[71]

In light of this dichotomy, the original mourner's joke enables us to obtain some fresh insights. Torberg tells this mourning joke in its two versions with the intention of demonstrating to the reader that there is a good way and a bad way to tell this joke, and in turn, to mourn the dead and their folk cultural production (Jewish jokes). With his elaborate staging of this mourning joke, Torberg wants to show that he knows how to be a good joke mourner and to respect the dead in contrast to Landmann who has proven that she does not know how to be a good joke mourner nor how to respect the dead. However, Torberg does not dispute the good intentions of Landmann and her salvage operations: "Salcia Landmann certainly has had a pro-Jewish purpose in mind, namely, the rescue and salvation of the Jewish joke."[72] Nevertheless, he challenges the suitability of the means that she has selected to accomplish this noble end. This failure transmutes a philo-Semitic intention into an anti-Semitic effect and makes Landmann a bad mourner in spite of herself. In this manner, her attempt to save the Jewish joke turns out to be both damning and damaging. Through a close reading of the jokes in her collection, Torberg exposes this bad mourning practice on a variety of counts.[73] After this exposé, the rhetorically twisting conclusion turns Landmann's supposed innocence regarding the anti-Semitic effects of the book into the very grounds for an admission of her guilt. In this way, the moral of the story illustrates a radical reversal and an unintended consequence in demonstrating how Landmann's Jewish joke reparations generate even more indebtedness: "This book is anti-Semitic from the ground up, and so, whether or not she wanted to or knew that, Salcia Landmann delivers only the latest decisive proof of the murderous irrelevance and unrelatedness [*mörderische Beziehungslosigkeit*] with which her subject matter is attacked."[74]

The pejorative use of the adjective *murderous* in this context (and elsewhere in the text) also points to another central theme in Torberg's critique of Landmann. Torberg insists that Landmann is not just a bad mourner of the Jewish joke but, moreover, its murderer. Or perhaps, the act of murder has led to her bad mourning. With biting sarcasm, his polemic charges that it is not the Nazis who have exterminated this Jewish cultural asset but rather Salcia Landmann's butchering of the Jewish joke in this collection. Unwittingly, she too becomes a party to the deadly discourse on the Jewish joke. Of course, this criticism is already present in the article's subtitle, "*oder Salcia Landmann ermordet den jüdischen Witz*" (that Salcia Landmann murdered the Jewish joke). It also helps to explains why the title begins with the stereotypical exclamatory cry of pain and suffering often articulated in the Jewish joke (i.e., "*Wai geschrien!*") that is raised by Torberg against her book from the outset. In another satirical-polemical essay loaded with hyperbole, Edwin Hartl adds to this murderous conflation of deadly accusations. In its turn (for the worst), Landmann's *geistreiche Wiedergutmachung* has staged no less than a mock Holocaust directed at the Jewish joke. As Hartl comments, "This sad and mournful bestseller: a mental [*geistige*] Holocaust on Jewish irony and self-mockery."[75]

While Torberg never explicitly refers to himself as the "good mourner" in this debate, a biographical text written by Harry Zohn suggests this image.

In reviewing the controversy with Landmann, Zohn refers to Torberg as "the vigilant one" ("*der Wachsame*"). Interestingly, this term evokes the same role of the watchman played by the Centralverein leaders against the Jewish cabaret comedians during the Weimar Republic. According to Zohn, Torberg becomes the good mourner in the role of the watchman who keeps vigil over the Jewish joke and its good name in order to protect it against Landmann's dubious distortions. In contrast to Landmann's reification of anti-Semitic stereotypes, Torberg's critique undertakes the mourning vigil that the Jewish joke deserves: "Several years ago, the vigilant one exercised sharp criticism of *The Jewish Joke*, a book by Salcia Landmann that was ominously a bestseller in Germany, even though (or perhaps because) it contains many stereotypical distortions of Jewish humor and Jewish character."[76]

Meanwhile, Landmann depicts Torberg as the villain who seeks to ruin her worthy work aimed at the proper mourning of the Jewish joke. As she introduces him in a letter to the author, Landmann recalls Torberg as someone with a dubious alias who conceals his proper Jewish name. Here, Landmann constructs the scene like the invasion of the "big bad wolf" into her fairy tale narrative. The recounting begins with a character description that reads more like an assassination: "But there lived in Vienna a Jewish hack [*jüdischer Schmock*] — I cannot find another word to describe him — named Fritz Kantor, who wrote under the name Torberg. . . . Now he was sitting in Vienna with some reparations money [*Wiedergutmachungsgeldern*], with which he edited a monthly magazine."[77]

There are two pejorative terms in this description that an analysis of the staging of joke mourning and reparations cannot overlook. The first — which she would prefer not to use because it threatens to step over the bounds of propriety, yet she uses it nevertheless — involves the loaded depiction of Torberg as a "*jüdischer Schmock*" which brings not only obscene connotations of the male genitalia, but also anti-Semitic overtones in that it refers to the professional journalist as a hack, and more particularly, the Jewish journalist as hack and, by extension, as a satirical joker. Indeed, the adjective "*jüdischer*" is redundant when looked at in the context of the cultural history of this negative Jewish stereotype in German society and its derivation in the character of that same name in Gustav Freytag's play *Die Journalisten* (1852). Freud's *Witz* book also refers to the satirical character of *Schmock* and his negative attributes (with anti-Semitic overtones) as "one of those uneducated people who misuse and trade away the nation's store of culture."[78] This characterization would seem to sum up rather nicely the mutual character assassination at work wherein both Landmann and Torberg brand each other as uncultured poseurs whose business it is to abuse and devalue this cultural treasure of the

Jewish nation (i.e., "*der jüdische Witz*"). Furthermore, Landmann inadvertently exposes in her second offensive remark the political economy of the joke that serves as the condition of possibility for the debate and its high yield of interest. For Landmann supplements the accusation of *Schmock* with the information that it is only on account of reparations money (*Wiedergutmachungsgeldern*) that this Jewish joker journalist has gone back into business in the first place.

In this same letter, Landmann moves the discussion from the branding of Torberg as bad mourner to the establishing of herself as good mourner. She responds directly to Torberg's specific accusation that she has murdered the Jewish joke with the stylistic inadequacies of her joke delivery. Landmann defends herself by arguing that she was not presenting a "cabaret" version of the Jewish joke but rather a historical document. As salvage operator, she has done a public service by rescuing and (re)collecting this cultural good (*Witzgut*) before it was too late. The pathos of this self-exonerating dramaturgy mounts as Landmann props up her status as the good joke mourner. Far from being the Jewish joke's murderer, only she has shown the proper respect and piety for the murdered Holocaust victims with the exact transcription of these last joking communications. In contrast to Torberg's use of adjectives attributing active perpetration to Landmann (e.g., "*mörderischem Zugriff*," or murderous attack), the fortunate Swiss survivor Landmann shifts the focus of murderous modification to the murdered victims of the Holocaust with whom she identifies and whose folk stories she salvages and tells through her joke compilation: "The latter can agree in so far as I published not a cabaret presentation, but a *collection*, namely the joke property [*Witzgut*] of a murdered community [*gemordeten Gemeinschaft*], which I appropriated verbatim where possible out of respect for the murdered writers [*gemordeten Verfassern*] and what each of them thought."[79]

Yet Landmann realizes that Torberg is not the only Jewish writer who criticizes her joke book. Unlike the non-Jewish critics who unanimously praise her book as a work of proper mourning (as a joke requiem) and as an act toward intercultural normalization,[80] there are a few other "Jewish colleagues" who do not appear to be so thrilled or even so collegial when discussing her book. Landmann defends herself against these critics with a response that makes a "traditional" and authoritative claim to a greater degree of Jewish authenticity:[81] "With the growing success of the book . . . there naturally came attacks as well. Several from the former Jewish 'joke centers'—i.e., Vienna, Berlin, etc.—and from the pens of Jewish colleagues. Among other things, they overlooked that a fairly solid knowledge of the Jewish intellectual tradition [*Geistestradition*] is required for this purpose."[82]

However, there is also a way of interpreting this narrative wherein the Jewish joke itself and its folk wisdom yields an answer regarding what is really going on in this debate over what is to be deemed good and bad mourning, good and bad reparations. Ironically, the situation described by Landmann reduplicates the structure of a Jewish joke that assumes an important place in the history of Jewish jokelore itself. It is a comic ditty (attributed to the Weimar satirist and joke collector Alexander Moszkowski) that focuses on the question of the Jewish joke's reception and makes a sharp distinction between "us" and "them," between Jew and non-Jew, between insider and outsider. This joke serves as the grand finale by which Landmann concludes her book in the metasection, *"Der Jude und Sein Witz."* It is the exact same joke (in the same abbreviated version) quoted by Eduard Fuchs in his analysis of Jewish self-irony discussed earlier:

> Alexander Moszkowski has put together the Jewish and non-Jewish joke reaction in verse form:
> A Jewish joke with a Jewish accent.
> What a Goy does not understand
> And what a Jew always already knows.[83]

But if one were to take the punchline of this ethnocentric joke seriously and apply it to Landmann's assessment of the reactions to her book, then it would undermine the high praise that the book has received from the non-Jewish critical community as a work of good mourning and convert such reviews into either mis- or non-understandings. On the other hand, this piece of folk wisdom would help to explain the know-it-all (*Besserwisser*) views of those Jewish critics who claim expertise when it comes to the Jewish joke and who thus condemn her book as spreading anti-Semitic tendencies and a work of bad mourning.

This amusing situation whereby a Jewish joke classic boomerangs on its editor/narrator relates to another punchline having to do with Jewish joke reception that offers the full version of Moszkowski's one-liner. This is the one about four different reactions (farmer, squire, officer, and Jew) to the Jewish joke and how it is only the Jew who does not laugh after being told a joke. It serves as the penultimate joke in Landmann's collection where the punchline reads: "But if one tells a joke to a Jew, he says: "I know that one already! And he tells an even better one."[84] Transposed into the critical terms of the debate at hand, it might read, "But if one tells a Jewish critic a joke, he says thus: 'That one is not authentically Jewish' and he proceeds to tell you one that is." Or things might go another way. For it should not come as a surprise to learn that the analysis of Landmann's version of this joke constitutes one of Torberg's most vicious attacks because he argues that her narration ruins the punchline. For the Jew does not tell a better one in the classic Olsvanger version. Instead, he interrupts the teller to tell the same joke in a better way: "But if you tell a joke to a Jew, he interrupts you: 'Ach! An old joke!' — and he can tell it to you better."[85] If this joke were to be transposed to the terms of the critical debate at hand, it might read, "But if one tells a Jewish critic a joke, he interrupts you and tells you that you are not telling it the right way, and he proceeds to tell it to you the better way." There may be no better way to see the exact point of Torberg's critique of Landmann's *Der jüdische Witz* in formal terms as a work of irreparable reparations and as a case of bad mourning than via the repurposed punchline of this classic Jewish joke.

## The Wit of *Wiederjudmachung*: Jewish Jokes with a Pay Back

Several "reparations jokes" comment on the processes of *Wiedergutmachung* itself. In formal terms, these jokes make their point through the comic techniques of reversal and inversion, techniques that are suited perfectly for taking on the reversal and inversion of official values in Germany in the wake of the defeat of the Nazis and the shift that transformed the Jewish referent from a negative to a positive attribute — from anti- to philo-Semitism.[86] These jokes employ word play and inverted logic (taking logic for a spin) to make fun of the sudden turn of events and abrupt "about-face" in the German political and cultural scene that "made" all things Jewish "good again." In addition, the wit of *Wiedergutmachung* also points out how there were some negative traits of the sordid past still clinging to this new chapter in German-Jewish relations.[87]

The first reparations joke could be read as a metacommentary on the popular success of Landmann's book and its ability to appeal to both philo- and anti-Semitic sensibilities. This joke was not included in the first publication of her book in 1960, but it was added later. Most appropriately, it is featured in the DTV paperback edition spawned by the initial wave of the joke book's success. It is a rather compact joke, even something approaching the form of a riddle:

> Wiedergutmachung.
> Was ist das Gegenteil von Arisierung? [What is the opposite of Aryanization?]
> Wiederjudmachung [Making Jewish again].[88]

Following Freud's technique of condensation, this joke puts the same verbal material to multiple uses. It relies upon a punning equation that concatenates the good (*gut*) and the Jew (*Jud*) and, in that way, offers a perfect definition for the process of postwar reparations through the official lens of philo-Semitism — i.e., making good again = making Jew again. In this perfect combination of sound and sense, the wordplay that shuttles between "good" and "Jew" conforms to Sigmund Freud's definition of what constitutes a "good joke": "A 'good joke' comes about when . . . the similarity between the words is shown to be really accompanied by another, important similarity in their sense."[89] In linguistic terms, it is both apocope and dialect that enables this substitution. On the one side, the final *e* of the word *Jude* is cut off to form the monosyllabic *Jud*. On the other side, the word *gut* is pronounced in some German dialects in the move from the hard *g* to the soft *j* as *Jut*.[90] Finally, the substitutive play is completed by the closeness in pronunciation between the letters *t* and *d* at the end of these German words.

But there is another twist in this joke of reparations wherein things take a turn for the worse. This comes from the fact that the word *Jud* has a history of usage as a pejorative whether used by Jews or anti-Semites. Now it has been the ambivalent function of the Jewish joke in the era of post-Enlightenment assimilation to articulate and to make fun of the stereotypical images of the Jew in European society — particularly those negative anti-Semitic stereotypes of the "bad Jew" (whether greedy, duplicitous, or dirty). Adorno once referred to anti-Semitism as the rumor spread about the Jews.[91] Perhaps, one can say that self-critical Jewish humor reprocesses the rumors of anti-Semitism into jokes that the Jews spread (and laugh about) among themselves and their hosts. Knowing this history of Jewish jokelore as self-ironic, self-critical, and even self-abasing, the joke of "*Wiederjudmachung*" might be understood as both the internalization and the mocking of the return of the bad Jew in the era of making good again. This ambivalent joke both articulates and makes fun of latent anti-Semitism (and, its underside, Jewish self-hatred) by showing how the pejorative *Jud* (as in *Jud Süss*) lies just beneath the noblest sentiments of *Wiedergutmachung*.

In his critical essay on the use of language in Paul Celan's "*Gespräch im Gebirg*" (written in August 1959), Stéphane Moses has focused on the obsessive reiteration of the pejorative *Jud* in this text.[92] His analysis offers another twist that can be applied to the logic of reversals embedded in the joke of *Wiederjudmachung* and the twin processes of *geistige* and *geistreiche Wiedergutmachung*.

> For Celan, however, language in its innermost capacity can now emerge, but only under the condition that it takes its guilt upon itself until the end: one could speak of a catharsis that Celan's text per-

forms forcefully here (so to speak) on a reluctant language (thus the obsessive recurrence of the word *Jude*, especially in its pejorative and apocopated *Jud*). This display of the language of the oppressed, which becomes satirical mockery of their oppressor at the same time (*"the Jud and son of Juden"*) demonstrates his deep suffering, even a tendency towards self-debasement, but also the desire *to break the taboo*.[93]

For Moses, the post-Holocaust usage of the language of the oppressed (which had been subject to indebtedness and guilt) can undergo a cathartic reversal. But unlike the economy inscribed in Landmann's joke reparations, this happens in Celan only if and when language takes the blame upon itself. Like the self-ironic Jewish joke, this reading of Celan reviews how such a process is often achieved when language is deployed in a parodic and mocking fashion. In its obsessive repetition and mocking cadences, the pejorative *Jud* in Celan (and in *Wiederjudmachung*) undergoes an alchemical transmutation process that makes it good again as the Jewish poet "takes back" the pejorative in a radical reversal of values. Born out of suffering, self-abasement, and mourning, both Celanian language and Jewish jokelore lead us toward post-Holocaust restitutions whether aimed at liberating laughter or poetic transcendence. From this perspective, the word condensations of both Jewish jokes and Celan's poetry provide means of confrontation by which to break through post-Holocaust taboos in the service of the *Jud*'s restitution.

In this way, the philo- and anti-Semitic readings of Landmann's book in the macrocosm of German-Jewish cultural relations are recapitulated in microcosm in the polyvalence of the word *Wiederjudmachung* whether one takes it as an affirmation (*Jud* = good again), a pejorative (*Jud* = bad again) or as a reaffirmation (*Jud* = bad made good again) of the Jew in postwar Germany. To the point and to the punchline, the term *Wiederjudmachung* articulates the entire complex of Jewish joke reparations and joke mourning.

Moreover, there are other peculiarities about this metajoke that deserve mention. First, there is its odd placement in Landmann's compendium. In contrast to conventional historical bookkeeping, Landmann places a joke pointedly titled "Wiedergutmachung" in a chapter titled "Hitlerzeit." A time warp ensues so that a joke about the post-1945 period and the reconstitution of democratic forms in West Germany that included an official policy regarding the indemnification of Jewish survivors is to be found in a chapter that covers the historical period between 1933 and 1945 amid the rule of totalitarian principles and the Nazi's mass genocide of some six million Jews. Naturally, one interpretation might be to say that there is so much continuity between Jewish jokes about the Nazis and Jewish jokes stemming from the horrible legacy left by the Nazis that there was no need to make a division here. Furthermore, it might be argued that such an editorial decision demonstrates one interpretation of the joke itself—that while *Wiederjudmachung* stages the apparent reversal of the policies of the age of Hitler, it also conceals the continuation of anti-Semitic sentiments below the surface in the pejorative rehashing of the negative *Jud*. However, a much more important reason why a joke about *Wiedergutmachung* would be placed in the chapter on the Nazi era points to the problematic of joke mourning and its (belated) timing with which I opened this chapter. As the chronicler of the Jewish joke in mourning, Landmann cannot contradict her assertion that the Jewish joke perished in the Holocaust. A joke such as "*Wiederjudmachung*" and its expression of a revival of the Jewish joke in the postwar era would cast doubt about the joke requiem to which she has invited her readers. Therefore, it is much better to bury this joke alongside the Nazis (and their victims).

This interpretation also would explain the historical inaccuracies in this joke. This returns to the terminological politics that have always been at the forefront of German-Jewish intercultural relations and confrontations. Here, it makes no sense to say that the opposite of Aryanization is *Wiedergutmachung*. The opposite is *Verjudung* (Judaization)—the dreaded process condemned by all anti-Semitic rhetoric in Germany from Fritsch to Hitler to be combatted with the Aryan antidote of *Entjudung* (de-Judaization). In this way, a joke with a punchline about the postwar era has been told in such a way that its question matches the anti-Semitic rhetoric of the days of Hitler rather than the philo-Semitic rhetoric of the days of Adenauer. In the postwar era, the opposite of Aryanization would necessarily be *Entnazifizierung* (denazification).[94] (Naturally, one can always attribute the flashbacked phrasing of *Arisierung* as another inversion instituted by the reparations joke itself.)

The transvaluations of the Jewish referent that demarcate the cultural politics of "*Wiederjudmachung*" are played out in another joke that relies on a playful inversion that brings with it a radical shift in meaning. In the flip of two words, the returned Jewish exile delivers the following witticism and thereby offers a thorough diagnosis of the abrupt shift in German-Jewish relations in the postwar era that exposes something rather unpleasant in the extreme. It is as if the flip of two words could bring everything back to normal and make everything good again in the following witticism: "A Jewish refugee said after his return to Germany: 'The transition from *Jud Süss* to sweet Jew [*süssen Jud*] is not very pleasant for both parties.'"[95] The *Jud Süss* of this joke refers to Veit Harlan's infamous anti-Semitic 1940 film that staged the life and times of Jud Süss Oppenheimer in line with the goals of Nazi propaganda. In *Im Anfang war Auschwitz*, Frank Stern reviews the shift from "bad" to "good" Jew in the pop cultural imagination in Germany before and after World War II. Unsurprisingly, the role of the "bad" Jew is played by Jud Süss. Meanwhile, the "good" postwar Jew—or the "sweet Jew" in line with this reparations joke—turns out to be none other than Nathan the Wise. In this way, the process of restitutions prompts the return to an old stereotypical model of (Jewish) Enlightenment to fill the role of the "good" Jew: "The Nazi's propagandistic image of the Jews was set up against the good Jew—the Jew who was tolerant, enlightened, and ultimately emancipated-assimilated. . . . It was the logic of such a well-intentioned rearrangement of prejudices by which *Jud Süss* was updated in 1945 and replaced by 'Nathan.'"[96] However, this simple philo-Semitic stereotype immediately after the war contrasts sharply with the complexities of Landmann's book and the difficulty of taking the stock characters of Jewish jokelore—schlemiels, schadchens, and *Luftmenschen*, not to mention conniving businessmen—and having them fill the role of the "sweet" Jew. Yet, one can argue that the very ambivalence of these characters explains their appeal to the mixture of manifest philo-Semitic sentiment and latent anti-Semitic resentments that defined the book's success in the era of "Wiederjudmachung."

As a final comical twist, the structure of the *Jud Süss* joke applies to Veit Harlan's own postwar experiences wherein life came to imitate a Jewish joke, that is, his own denazification proceedings in the late 1940s and the many attempts to resurrect his good name and his films in the era of *Wiedergutmachung*.[97] When Harlan was finally cleared of all charges in 1950, he had succeeded in "convincing" the Hamburg jury that he was actually a "philo-Semite" who had made an anti-Semitic film under duress. Harlan blamed Goebbels and the Nazi propaganda machine and therefore he claimed to be a martyr of the postwar denazification process. In this way, Harlan succeeded in incorporating the "sweet Jew" scenario of the joke (which was not very pleasant for both parties) into his own revamped biography and into public consciousness.[98]

A final joke in the era of reparations also foregrounds the dynamics of reversal from the German perspective. In the topsy-turvy world of *Wiedergutmachung*, it is now the guilt-ridden German who assumes the role of the victim formerly taken by the Jews in appropriating and restaging a classic Jewish scapegoat joke. In a 1962 essay, Salcia Landmann presents this early *Wiedergutmachung* joke for American consumption:

> Now for . . . a story that reappeared in the Federal Republic shortly after the downfall of Nazi Germany. The following conversation takes place between an Allied officer and a German.

Allied officer: "The Germans are responsible for all the evil in the world."
German: "No, not the Germans, the cyclists."
Allied officer: "Why the cyclists?"
German: "Why the Germans?"[99]

In this post-Auschwitz substitution of roles, it is the Allied officer who replaces the anti-Semite and the German who replaces the Jew in this well-rehearsed anti-Semitic joke (the bicyclists remain the same). By taking over the role of the Jewish scapegoat, this punchline reconfirms the hypothesis advanced in the Mitscherlichs' *Die Unfähigkeit zu trauern* about the need of postwar Germans to identify with the victim in order to throw off the burden of guilt and responsibility for the crimes committed against the Jews for which the German people stand accused.[100] Thus, in the flip of *Wiedergutmachung*, a prewar joke about the "bad Jew" defending himself against anti-Semitism becomes a postwar joke about the "bad German" defending himself against anti-Germanism and covering up the Nazi past. For the Mitscherlichs, this process of identification provides another screen by which to defer the task of collective mourning. As applied to Landmann's book, such a defensive strategy underscores another psychological reason for the success of the book. Laughing at these Jewish jokes, the German reader can evade his feelings of guilt as former aggressor by identifying with the falsely accused victim that he now believes himself to be in the brave new world of "*Wiederjudmachung.*"

However, there is a bizarre convergence that adds another twist to this comic tale. For at the same time that Landmann was telling an American audience about the German repackaging in the postwar era of this old anti-Semitic scapegoat joke about Jews and cyclists, the Frankfurt School philosopher Theodor Adorno was delivering an address in Germany with the goal of combatting anti-Semitism in which he mobilized the cyclist and his nature (*Radfahrernatur*) as a key metaphor. Adorno uses this image and this idiom ("*auf gut deutsch*") to analyze the anti-Semitic bent in German character, or what constitutes the authoritarian tendency in the German personality:

> The one who is bound to authority, the specifically anti-Semitic character, is really the *underling* [*Untertan*], such as Heinrich Mann presented him, or, how to say it simply in good German, "*die Radfahrernatur*" [the cyclist nature] — which is characterized by a certain type of pseudo-rebelliousness ("There-something-has to-happen-finally, there-order-must-be-created-finally"); but then he is always ready to

cower before the holders of real power, economic or otherwise, and to let them keep it.[101]

Ironically, the cyclist joke backfires if and when one applies Adorno's analysis of anti-Semitism to the German version of the joke. For the very attempt to lift the burden of guilt through the seemingly innocuous comparison with the cyclists is exactly what proves the German to be guilty as charged in a return of the idiomatically repressed "cyclist nature" that frames him as a compliant figure willing to bend to the demands of power in times of crisis. In this striking image, Adorno figures the cyclist with his back bent toward those above and kicking down at those below ("*Oben buckeln, unten treten*") as the authoritarian personality type. Through Adorno's analysis of the anti-Semitic character and its unintentional use of the figure of the cyclist, we arrive at this final paradox. The "pay back" for Landmann's *Wiedergutmachungswitz* and for her Jewish joke book in general (with its exposure of diversionary mourning) would mark yet another increase in post-Auschwitz indebtedness on the part of the Germans if one takes Adorno's conception of their "cyclist nature" seriously. In this way, the mobility of the classic Jewish joke about the cyclists — appropriated as a German joke to comment (self-)ironically upon their own victimhood in the era of *Wiedergutmachung* — is taken for yet another anti-Semitic spin.

Nevertheless, there is yet another perspective from which to understand this recycled joke in its prewar anti-Semitic variety and it can be applied to the postwar anti-Germanic version of this joke as well. As the witty Slovenian philosopher Slavoj Žižek reminds us, the real point of the original Jewish scapegoat joke was to affirm radical contingency in order to refute the "very trap of anti-Semitism" that looks for an inherent characteristic or evil essence in the Jews and that wants to make the fatal assumption of predestination as if there were some valid justification to be found at the root of anti-Semitic hatred. It is on this chance note that the Jewish joke ends with a self-reflexive question that responds to the scapegoat's accusation by only asking why. The stand-up philosopher Žižek addresses the Jewish question in this classic Jewish joke about anti-Semitism and he leaves the questions hanging:

> One of the conclusions to be drawn from this is that, in endeavoring to provide an answer to the question "Why are Jews specifically picked out to play the scapegoat role in anti-Semitic ideology?," we might easily succumb to the very trap of anti-Semitism, looking for some mysterious feature in them that, as it were, predestined them for that role: the fact that Jews who were chosen for the role of the

"Jew" ultimately is contingent—as it is pointed out by the joke about anti-Semitism: "Jews and cyclists are responsible for all our troubles.— Why cyclists?—WHY JEWS?"[102]

By applying Žižek's affirmation of contingency, deconstruction of essences, and contestation of predestination to Adorno's analysis of an authoritarian *Radfahrernatur* as well as to the post-Holocaust joke recounted by Landmann, one avoids falling into the trap of anti-Germanism and its essentialist scapegoating when asking, "Why Germans?"

# Conclusion
## Final Thoughts and Last Laughs

*At Wit's End*, by giving thought to the meaning and significance of the Jewish joke and its laughter, provides insights into a troubling and deadly serious period in twentieth-century Jewish and European history. Reviewing key writers, both Jewish and non-Jewish, in Germany and the German-speaking lands that represent a variety of ideological perspectives (from the Marxist Eduard Fuchs to the Nazi Siegfried Kadner) and cultural positions (from the German-Jewish comedian and impresario Kurt Robitschek to the German-Jewish defense organization official Alfred Wiener), I have explored their views on the complex relationship between Jewish wit and jokes and anti-Semitism. Miming their object of study, it was as if these Jewish joke analysts were seeking a way to release tensions and find some comic relief in their reflections upon Jewish wit amid those difficult and turbulent times. Many of them believed that the ticklish subject of Jewish wit and Jewish jokes raised critical issues and had important things to say about the Jewish question and the cultural crisis surrounding them, whether in the form of Arthur Trebitsch's anti-Semitic diatribe at the end of World War I about the "secondary moves" that denigrated the Jewish joke as the mobile maneuverings of an inferior Jewish spirit or Eric Kahler's pointed reflections on a strand of Germanic corporeal revolt against Jewish intellectualism as exemplified in the nimbleness of Jewish wit that he saw as symptomatic of German-Jewish intercultural breakdown in the early 1930s.

Beyond these earnest claims to joking significance, it is also important to remember the polysemy, ambivalence, and ambiguity endemic to Jewish wit and its slippery resistance to becoming a subject for serious reflection. Related to this point, I have argued that the collapse of a clear-cut distinction between Jewish self-irony and anti-Semitism troubles the work of any analyst who hopes to interpret these jokes in a straightforward or nonambivalent way. Chapter 6, for instance, reviews how even as Salcia Landmann attempted to read these Jewish jokes in a philo-Semitic manner, Friedrich Torberg could just as easily claim that they reinforced anti-Semitic stereotypes, and he even went so far as to accuse her of reformulating the Nazi legacy in the era of reparation (*Wiedergutmachung*). I began this book with Edmund Edel's point that the comic spin (or *Dreh*) was crucial to Jewish wit and that this has something to do with the joke's instability. This tendency for comic inversion (and subversion) keeps the Jewish self-ironic reading and the anti-Semitic reading spinning around each other without any chance for either of them to settle down or to stabilize into a unitary meaning. As such, the ambivalent mimicry and mutual imbrication of Jewish self-irony and vitriolic anti-Semitic jokes directed against the Jews contaminates and mocks any essentialist attempt to distinguish between Jewish and German modes of cultural production along such lines.

Each chapter provides examples of how paradoxes, ironies, absurdities, and comic inversions were unleashed upon these joke analysts often getting the better of them. For example, Arthur Trebitsch condemns the "secondary" thinking and mobile spirit of the Jews as exemplified in their jokes, but he too cannot resist from telling some of his own in his intricate (even convoluted) analysis. Moreover, he cannot help taking up the subject position that recalls the Jewish *schlemiel* character to some extent with paranoid delusions that make him appear as a ridiculous man. In the case of Eduard Fuchs, we encounter the ironic situation of someone who thinks that he is "Jew-friendly" in his analysis of Jewish jokes and caricatures but who cannot escape from reproducing some of the negative stereotypes embedded in his intellectual models (Werner Sombart and Karl Marx) and the Communist Party line to which he adhered in ideological terms. Not to forget the final irony, that even though Fuchs appears to appreciate the Jewish joke, his utopian vision of communism looks to a future world where it is hard to imagine its need to exist anymore. In chapter 3, the serious slippage of the Jewish joke makes an impresario and a stand-up comedian such as Kurt Robitschek (who should be busy writing comedy skits and fooling around on the Berlin stage) take up the subject position of the serious defender of free speech when Alfred Wiener and the Centralverein attacked him and his Cabaret of Comics in the mid-1920s by insisting on the limits of Jewish comedic expression.

The case of the Jewish historian Erich Kahler exemplifies the failure of this dignified *Bildungsjude*'s attempt to somehow limit Jewish self-irony to the realm of wit and wisdom and his inability to prevent its abject exposure

CONCLUSION

to what he termed "undignified self-mockery and self-contempt." In other words, Kahler was not successful in containing the potential toxicity of the Jewish joke and its harmful and corrosive effects. But when Kahler plays devil's advocate and further comments that these self-contemptuous jokes confirm "the truth of what one rightfully accuses us," the space of a "flipped out" comic inversion and an unintended consequence arises in the possibility of reading him in tandem with the anti-Semitic critics of his day and their insistence that Jewish jokes confirmed the truth of all the negative things that they were saying about the Jews. From this perspective, Siegfried Kadner's Nazi propaganda exploits the overarching slippage and instability that exists between these two terms. In other words, Kadner possessed the shrewd ability to appropriate Jewish self-irony and self-criticism and to use it as fodder for a virulent brand of anti-Semitism. This cynical Nazi rhetoric was designed to obliterate Jewish wit by striking an impossibly serious pose. In seeking to occupy the position where we would be at wit's end, Kadner sought to collapse Jewish self-irony into Nazi anti-Semitism. But this gesture did not stop Kadner from formulating his own brand of tendentious mockery of the Jewish enemy, and it did not stop him from falling into a comic *aporia* of his own. For Kadner argued simultaneously that the Jewish joke confirms all the negative things that the Nazis have been saying about the Jews while contending that there was no possibility for any type of verbal understanding between the Jews and the Germans (now called Aryans) on the ground of the racial differences that put them in a position of radical alterity in relationship to one other. This leads to a logical absurdity and a self-contradiction affirming both the possibility and impossibility of German and Jewish communication with each other. All in all, this laughable paradox finds a Nazi propagandist reveling in and capitalizing on the contamination that exists between Jewish self-irony and anti-Semitism while preaching the rhetoric of racial purity with the utmost vehemence.

This leads me to a final anecdote (or last laugh) sparked by the Jewish joke and its comic instability in a German-Jewish context. Just a few years after the controversy surrounding the publication of Salcia Landmann's book and the Jewish joke reparations that were the subject of chapter 6, the staging of laughter in the service of reconciliation and the strains of Jewish joke mourning in the post-Holocaust era shifted from the Federal Republic of Germany to the fledgling State of Israel. At the start of official diplomatic relations between West Germany and Israel in 1965 and during the first intercultural encounter on a more intimate social level between the new German ambassador and his Israeli hosts, one learns how laughter played a crucial role as an ambassador of good will among the parties involved. The Jewish joke as shared cultural memory and as a mediator — crossing the German *Vermittler* with the Jewish *schadchen* — serves here as an intercultural bridge for these former enemies at a Tel Aviv dinner party. This scene enacts a modern variant of the ritual exchange of words and food transacted between guests and hosts around a festive banquet table. At the time of *Wiedergutmachung*, the Jewish joke has been given a difficult assignment — a task of close-range shuttle diplomacy that is fraught with the danger of having such small talk explode in the faces of the German and Israeli participants with a single faux pas that would offend the chance for healing and reconciliation irreparably. But, as the tale is told, the Jewish joke, with the help of a little prompting on the part of its joke narrator, proves itself to be equal to the task. While it is a pity that the reader is not provided with details of the Jewish jokes told by the young and charming Israeli industrialist, there is a good chance that they had been included in Landmann's collection if not actually culled from it.

The emigré sociologist and Nazi propaganda expert Hans Speier describes and analyses this dinner party anecdote at the intersection of jokes and politics. Interestingly, Speier mistakenly describes the opening of diplomatic relations between West Germany and Israel using the terms of history repeating itself — in terms of a restoration of relations in the fever pitch of *Wiedergutmachung* and its law of returns.

> Certain political jokes can bring atonement between disputants. . . . Add to that a further example. The diplomatic relations between the Federal Republic and Israel were restored [*wiederhergestellt*] only twenty years after the end of World War II under Chancellor Erhard. Understandably, there was initially resistance to the presence of the German Ambassador in Israel. It even led to demonstrations against Ambassador Rolf Pauls who was wise enough not to protest. Fourteen days after his arrival in Tel Aviv, he was invited for the first time to a private dinner party. A young Israeli industrialist entertained the guests with Jewish jokes. Pauls wanted to join in the laughter, but he kept his distance out of tact or reticence. He later reported that the ice was only broken when the charming narrator turned to him with the words: "Laugh, Mr. Ambassador. Give us the pleasure and laugh please."[1]

Yes, a sort of German-Jewish, or more precisely, German-Israeli understanding has been achieved here — but the awkward hesitation of the German ambassador and the double-edged prompting of the Israeli industrialist make it seem as if this was not the most natural of social exercises or exchanges. For the icebreaker is uttered between the imperative command and the impassioned plea, between the poses of the master and the servant, and by extension, between the executioner and the victim that somehow recalls the haunting remnants of an extremely unbalanced Holocaust relationship clinging to this simple postwar German-Jewish joke exchange and encounter. Laugh, damn you, laugh. Please, my dear sir, I beg of you to laugh.[2] Therefore, there may be doubts at the end of the meal as to whether the Jewish joke reparations extracted from Pauls constitute a forced or a natural laughter. Following the lines of Speier's reconciliatory interpretation, they are laughing together as a sign of communion and atonement, as a way of working through the sorrow and the suffering of their shared history — mourning German misdeeds and Jewish victims. But, there is also the possibility confirming Pauls's initial respectful reticence and sense of tact that they are laughing in a space that would divert, disrespect, or even destroy the possibility of proper mourning and atonement. In other words, what is staged here in this joke exchange is both the possibility and the impossibility of forgiveness in one and the same breath, in one and the same laugh.[3]

Only one thing is clear when it comes to reading something as complex and ambivalent as the reversible practices of joke reparations and joke mourning or when it comes to locating whether philo-Semitic or anti-Semitic motives are at work (or at play) in the risible response to these Jewish jokes whether cast as self-ironic or otherwise. They are laughing, and there, in laughter, no one can tell.

# Afterword
## The Jewish Joke in Trump's America

How has the status of the self-mocking and subversive Jewish joke changed since the election of Donald Trump in November 2016? Has the ascendency of right-wing populism in the United States and its concomitant anti-Semitism altered the discourse on Jewish humor appreciably? Has the current toxic political environment brimming with racism and xenophobia moved the threshold of appropriateness in a way comparable to the rise of Hitler and the Nazis at the end of Weimar Germany? Has the anti-Semitic violence of the Pittsburgh Tree of Life synagogue massacre and the Charlottesville Unite the Right race riot somehow silenced the Jewish joke? Has the current political situation become too volatile and pernicious for the telling of certain jokes (deemed by the censors as "politically incorrect") because they can be taken as fuel and fodder for the anti-Semitism of the newly empowered alt-right movement? Or has it made Jewish wits even bolder and more provocative in defending their freedom of comic speech? Are they continuing to appropriate anti-Semitic images in the same shameless and self-conscious manner? And what has been the impact of the hateful anti-Semitic jokes of neo-Nazis communicated via the Internet that often invoke Holocaust humor as their means of provocation and that often attempt to mask themselves in an ironic fashion?

These important and complex questions deserve close inspection and perhaps even a full-length study. In this abbreviated context, I will review three widely publicized incidents that have put the Jewish joke back into the spotlight, marking its renewed relevance to this fraught political and cultural moment. In examining these case studies, the deadly discourse on the Jewish joke in twentieth-century German-Jewish history can function as a key precedent that provides some valuable insights on these current deployments (whether viewed as uses or abuses) in the United States and elsewhere.

## Not Curbing Larry David

In his opening monologue on *Saturday Night Live* on November 4, 2017, Larry David (the veteran Jewish comedian and writer of *Seinfeld* and *Curb Your Enthusiasm* fame) did not get the uproarious response that he might have expected. His routine began with topical Jewish jokes about the recent Hollywood mogul Harvey Weinstein's sexual harassment scandal as something "pretty pretty" bad for the Jews. ("I don't like it when Jews are in the news for notorious reasons. What I want: Einstein discovers the theory of relativity, Salk discovers a cure for polio. What I don't want: Weinstein took it out.") The jokes about Weinstein's transgressions segued into transgressive Holocaust jokes where David mused about picking up fellow female inmates if he had been imprisoned in a Nazi concentration camp. ("I've often wondered that if I grew up in Poland when Hitler came to power and I was sent to a concentration camp, would I still be checking out women? I think I would — 'Hey, Shlomo, did you see that one by Barracks Eight? I've had my eye on her for weeks. I'd like to go up and say something to her.' Of course, the problem is there are no good opening lines in a concentration camp.")

The online commentary in response to this monologue with its cringing denouncers and staunch defenders of David's offensive and self-deprecating jokes reads like a redux of the KadeKo controversy that took place in Berlin during the Weimar Republic that pitted the inflammatory jokes of Jewish comedians against Jewish censors who denounced their self-mockery as anti-Semitic. While the anti-Semitic watchdog of yesteryear Alfred Wiener responded to KadeKo indecencies by writing op-ed pieces in the *Central-Verein Zeitung* newspaper, Jonathan Greenblatt of the Anti-Defamation League chose Twitter to post the following response the next morning: "Watched #LarryDavid #SNL monologue this AM. He managed to be offensive, insensitive & unfunny all at same time. Quite a feat."[1] We may have a new (and abbreviated) communications medium but it is the same old message that seeks to control and suppress the freedom of comic speech. After watching David's monologue, today's conservative institutional watchdog jumps on it as an improper display of "political incorrectness" raising the same old fears of the corrosive and destructive Jewish joke. He goes after the comedian with the criticism that his "offensive" and "insensitive" Jewish humor is unacceptable. Moreover, Greenblatt insults the comedian further by saying that he is "unfunny" — that he finds himself at the end of (his) Jewish wit with these Holocaust pick-up lines.

In reviewing the *SNL* debacle, Jewish humor scholar Jeremy Dauber names the elephant in the room that is missing from most online responses and that makes David's Holocaust jokes appear so inappropriate and uncomfortable in the Trump era. In 2004, David could joke about the meeting of "The Survivors" at a dinner party on *Curb Your Enthusiasm* where a Holocaust survivor and a game show contestant (Colby Donaldson) exchange their hardships. It was a brilliant comedy routine based on miscommunication and incongruity where reality TV got its comeuppance in the face of Auschwitz: "But that thought-provoking *Curb* episode aired in 2004, and this is 2017, after Charlottesville. David's invocation of the concentration camp on Saturday as a kind of peekaboo provocation ... might ring particularly hollow in an America where neo-Nazis march openly on the streets and white-nationalist memes proliferate online."[2] The terrifying events in Charlottesville took place on August 11 and 12, less than three months before David's monologue. For his detractors, this means that David deserves condemnation for bad and insensitive (comic) timing.

Nevertheless, an unrepentant David returned to the show the following week in the character of Senator Bernie Sanders to make fun of any comic censorship guided by cultural taboos, and he did so with some old-fashioned self-deprecating Jewish humor. ("These comics out there who think it's okay to make jokes about concentration camps. That guy should rot in hell.") While he may not know it, David follows in the footsteps of Kurt Robitschek and his spirited defense of subversive Jewish jokes against Alfred Wiener: "But — for God's sake — no petty censorship! Wit and satire have to be allowed, even if here and there an individual gets badly hurt."[3] David also invokes Jewish self-mockery when he frames himself as an inheritor of this self-ironic comic tradition and sense of (scatological) humor at a key point in his stand-up routine. The comedian differentiates himself from Weinstein who represents not only the negative stereotype of the lecherous Jew as sexual predator but also calls attention to conspiracy theories that Jews control Hollywood. In contrast, David jokes that it would be hard to distinguish himself as Jewish except for two things — "if it weren't for the self-deprecation and the irritable bowel syndrome, you'd never know in a million years."

## From Borat to Morad

Meanwhile, the British Jewish prankster Sacha Baron Cohen has stated repeatedly that his Showtime series of extreme political satire, "Who is America?" (2018), was produced in direct response to Donald Trump's assumption of political power. The latest series features Baron Cohen disguised as new offbeat characters in order to stage his pranks and to trick his interviewees; but the most interesting thing to note about the program in comparison with his previous work is its relative lack of anti-Semitic humor directed at Jewish stereotypes. Specifically, the type of humor associated with the idiot savant figure of the Kazakh journalist Borat Sagdiyev who consistently parodied and provoked anti-Semitism with his racist antics during the Bush era (see chapter 1) has split the scene of "Who is America?" In this manner, the traditional dialectic at the heart of the Jewish joke (between self-mockery and anti-Semitic attack) has moved to the margins. In Borat's place, Baron Cohen has created the ex-Mossad Israeli tough guy Colonel Erran Morad who plays a brash and cocky terrorism expert who provokes his guests into outlandish racist and xenophobic behavior. The Morad character provides Baron Cohen with the satirical opportunity to offer a profound critique of extreme right-wing Israeli Zionism — in both its racist proclivities and its strong-arm tactics — as the comic provocateur in the guise of Morad repeatedly prods or dupes his marks to engage in anti-Islamic acts.

The shift in Baron Cohen's comedic targeting to Zionist extremism also offers a direct response to Trump and a changed American political climate that has become more tolerant of populist scapegoating and the alt-right's anti-Semitic discourse. (See Trump's infamous response to Charlottesville as "You also had some very fine people on both sides.") Unfortunately, there is no longer any need for a shock comic to display the hidden anti-Semitism in American life after Charlottesville and Pittsburgh. To recall Sander Gilman, Baron Cohen's days of "self-consciously Jewish appropriation of anti-Semitic images" are mostly over,[4] and he has shifted his self-deprecating Jewish comedy and political satire to the axis of Israel and Zionism. The shift in targets further allows him to mock the American religious right's unqualified admiration and support for the military machine of the State of Israel as well as Trump's unholy alliance with right-wing Zionists. This is at the core of this stinging prankster's most successful and brilliant skit in the first episode with its critique of the Second Amendment as Colonel Morad enlists his American right-wing confederates into the "Kinderguardian" program designed to arm young schoolchildren with guns disguised as stuffed animals. But even if there is an absence of Jewish character defamation in the diasporic sense in the scathing comedy of "Who is America?," this does not change the fact that Baron Cohen remains open to the charges of vulgarity and grossness that have accompanied his abject comedy career and that this is a hallmark of the long tradition of *Judenwitzlor* and of the anti-Semitic attacks upon this unseemly character. It is in this sense that the discourse on the Jewish joke as the corrupt and nihilistic product of vulgar, uncivilized, and dirty Jews continues to inform

Baron Cohen's characters such as his reformed convict and scatological artist, Rick Sherman. While more oblique than Borat's overt ethnic defamation, the potential for anti-Semitic raillery remains, and, in this manner, the comedy of "Who is America?" continues the historical precedent that featured the moral condemnation of Jewish wit in twentieth-century Germany.

## Ironic Nazism and Other Anti-Semitic Antics

The most disturbing feature of the post-2016 landscape though has to be the well-publicized incidents involving anti-Semitic jokes and memes circulated by neo-Nazis and white nationalists on websites and social networks such as *The Daily Stormer, 4chan,* and *Gab.* These alt-right tactics hearken back to the Nazi playbook on jokes and propaganda and the Jew-baiting efforts of Siegfried Kadner and Joseph Goebbels. Whether they exploit self-mocking Jewish humor to racist ends, assume the provocative position of an "ironic Nazism" that seeks to get a charge out of liberal opponents, or invent their own cruel and tendentious barbs aimed at Jews, these anti-Semitic joking strategies often invoke the Holocaust as their inflammatory content as they seek to resurrect Goebbels's haunting words that Jewry has nothing to laugh about.

When the British alt-right provocateur and former Breitbart News editor Milo Yiannopoulos states that "behind every racist joke is a scientific fact"[5] (even if that particular statement was made in the context of bashing women and Asians) or when the *Daily Stormer* style guide recommends "when using racial slurs, it should come across as half-joking—like a racist joke that everyone laughs at because it's true,"[6] we hear the direct echoes of Siegfried Kadner's *Rasse and Humor* loud and clear. Yiannopoulos's championing of "ironic Nazism" on the Internet is a new postmodernist twist in the anti-Semitic plot—something unforeseen in the historical narrative reviewed in this book. This is the perverse claim that many young people who make these cruel and hateful anti-Semitic jokes are not really Nazis but just want to be outrageous and to push the buttons of liberals and their politico-cultural taboos and therefore not dissimilar from Larry David when he tells Holocaust jokes from the opposite side of the fence. According to Yiannopoulos, the boys just want to have (transgressive) fun. Related to this viewpoint, the ongoing defense of the Swedish gaming video blogger PewDiePie (Felix Kjellberg) for his repeated exploitation of tendentious anti-Semitic humor on his enormously popular YouTube channel has been that of irony and satire. Yet his recommendation of a notorious neo-Nazi channel to his followers in December 2018 and his history of links to other alt-right sites make it hard to believe that he is not also in the same camp. As many commentators have pointed out, the unfortunate impact of this type of "ironic Nazism" is still anti-Semitic. As Aja Romano summarizes in an exposé of the YouTube celebrity, "Regardless of PewDiePie's intent, any anti-Semitic commentary — no matter how 'joking' — could have a dangerous effect."[7]

But what is hypocritical about Yiannopoulos's logic is the fact that it denies that many of these ironic jokers *are* practicing neo-Nazis. In the words of *Guardian* columnist Jason Wilson, what we find in many cases is "non-ironic Nazism masquerading as ironic Nazism."[8] Thus, the use of irony not only triggers liberals, but also defuses opponents into not taking neo-Nazis seriously (and not being able to prosecute them for hate crimes). Moreover, Nazi irony serves another purpose — to lure potential followers to the cause using humor as bait rather than old school vitriolic hatred. As the *Daily Stormer* style guide explains: "The reader is at first drawn in by curiosity or the naughty humor, and is slowly awakened to reality by repeatedly reading the same points."[9] According to historian Gavriel Rosenfeld, this is the insidious process and propagandistic effect of digital anti-Semitism as it transforms "from irony to ideology." Rosenfeld also points out how the alt-right's "ironic Nazism" follows the "law of ironic Hitlerization" as applied to internet memes — the more popular the web image, the greater its likelihood of containing ironic Hitler content ranging "from memes of Teletubbies with Hitler mustaches to jokey depictions of the Führer himself."[10] Rosenfeld's conclusions are also linked to Poe's law that is crucial to understanding the neo-Nazi desire to exploit anti-Semitic humor. This states that it is impossible to create a parody of extreme views in the age of the internet that cannot be mistaken as a sincere expression of those views.

Even the American alt-right and white supremacist leader Richard Spencer appropriated this ironic stance when he defended the Nazi salutes in response to his exclamatory utterances ("Hail Trump! Hail Our People! Hail Victory!") at his infamous speech in Washington just a few weeks after the 2016 election. Spencer told PBS NewsHour producer P. J. Tobia, "[this was] clearly done in a spirit of irony and exuberance."[11] In "Ironic Nazis are Still Nazis," Jeet Heer analyzes Spencer's specious joke defense as follows: "Spencer's defense of his followers making a Nazi gesture as being little more than a joke is a familiar protective gesture. . . . The intent seems to be to create a kind of plausible deniability, so if the racism is challenged, there is a prepared rejoinder: *Can't you take a joke?*"[12] To his critics, Spencer is clearly posing here and this is the case of a real neo-Nazi, who wants to dupe you into thinking that this was only a joke salute. That is why Tabatha Southey's article is titled "Neo-Nazis Are No Joke — They Just Want You to Think They Are" and her caption proclaims, "Darkness lurks behind their self-parodying 'humor.'"[13] The quotation marks suggest that Southey does not think that this is at all funny and, indeed, that Nazi self-parody is something located at wit's end. Nevertheless, Southey's article substantiates that we are living in a brave new world asserting neo-Nazi self-parody or even self-irony.

    To inhabit the subject position of the Nazi ironically—this pose and this posturing should sound very familiar to readers of this book—except that it was always something attributed to the comic and masquerading Jews. We have come a long way from Edmund Edel's quotation in *Der Witz der Juden* (1909) that began this journey exploring the discourse on the Jewish joke in German history. Imagine a new book entitled *The Wit of the Neo-Nazis* published in 2020 that would provide another spin. If we substitute the "neo-Nazi" for the "Jew" (whom he has replaced), then this new book would begin in the following ironic fashion: "The neo-Nazi not only loves to make fun of others, but also does not shy away from ironizing his own personality at every opportunity."

# Acknowledgments

This project spans more than twenty-five years from conception to completion, and many people and institutions have helped me along my picaresque journey in pursuit of the discourse on the Jewish joke in twentieth-century German Jewish history.

I am deeply indebted to two academic institutions for their crucial support of this book. From 1993 to 1995, I was a fellow at the Franz Rosenzweig Research Center for German-Jewish Cultural History and Literature at the Hebrew University of Jerusalem working on a project entitled "The Joke and the Question." This was the most stimulating academic environment that I have ever encountered, and I still cherish the memories of our intense seminar meetings with a group of extraordinary mentors and fellows. I am most grateful for the kind and helpful feedback that I received from the center's amazing faculty members and associates including Steven Aschheim, Jacob Hessing, Paul Mendes-Flohr, Hanni Mittelmann, the late Stephane Moses (the center's founder), Gabriel Motzkin, Christoph Schmidt, Itta Shedletzky, and the late Robert Wistrich. I benefited greatly from an amazing cohort of international fellows and from others studying in Jerusalem at that time. Many of them have gone on to distinguished academic careers in German Jewish studies, including Inke Bertz, Jacques Ehrenfreund, Joel Golb, Jeffrey Grossman, Raphael Gross, Carola Hilfrich, Ashraf Noor, Michal Schwarz, Céline Trautmann-Waller, and Martina Urban. Gratitude also goes to my dear friend Martin Bauer who suggested that I apply to the center while I was still based in Berlin in the early 1990s. I also recall wonderful intellectual exchanges and warm hospitality from Linda Renée Bloch, the late Ambassador Walter Eytan and his wife, Beatrice, Sidra Dekoven Ezrahi, Galit Hasan-Rokem, and the late Dov Noy (who graciously invited me into his Jewish folkloric circle).

I presented the Trebitsch chapter at the Center for European Studies at Harvard University where I appreciated helpful feedback from Daniel Goldhagen, Alex Sagan, and Ruth Wisse. I recall the kind assistance and invaluable exchange with the late Jewish humor scholar Rabbi Yitzhak Kertesz who served as librarian at the Leo Baeck Institute in New York until his untimely death in 1995. I thank Judith Wechsler at Tufts University for her generous support and wise counsel especially on the Fuchs chapter and its relationship to the history of caricature. Similarly, I express my gratitude to Ziva Amishai-Maisels at the Hebrew University of Jerusalem for her art historical interest in my research on Fuchs. I also benefitted from intellectual exchanges with Israeli scholars Uzi Elyada, Mark Gelber, and the late Claude Gandelman when I presented the Kadner chapter at the University of Haifa and at Ben-Gurion University of the Negev.

During my sabbatical year (2013–2014), while a visiting scholar at the Center for Jewish History in New York, I was able to write the second half of the manuscript in another stimulating academic environment and with access to the Leo Baeck Institute Archives and the YIVO Archives and Library. I thank Judy Siegel and Christopher Barthel for facilitating this most productive research opportunity. I enjoyed my intellectual exchanges with Elissa Bemporad, Alec Burko, Glenn Dynner, Ofer Dynes, Donna-Lee Frieze, Patrick Benjamin Koch, Anna Manchin, Eddie Portnoy, Sarah Yarrow, and Ori Yehudai, among others. It was also a great pleasure to interact with Michael Kaminer, Norman Kleeblatt, and Jeffrey Shandler while based in Manhattan as well as to have the support of my immediate family (especially my brother Arnol Kaplan) on the other side of the river.

I thank the Anne Tannenbaum Centre for Jewish Studies at the University of Toronto under the leadership of its renowned director Anna Shternshis for a subsidy in support of the publication of this book. I am also grateful for a small research grant in support of image licenses from SIG funds of the Social Sciences and Humanities Research Council of Canada administered by the Department of Visual Studies under the leadership of my colleague Jill Caskey at the University of Toronto Mississauga. Another SIG Enhancement Fund award helped me with the costs for indexing the book. I also want to acknowledge the support and encouragement of my University of Toronto and York University colleagues: Jordan Bear, Ritu Birla, Marcus Boon, Mark Cheetham, Adam Cohen, Natalie Zemon Davis, Robert Gibbs, Shelley Hornstein, Elizabeth Legge, Evonne Levy, Derek Penslar, Nic Sammond, Alison Syme, Holger Schott Syme, and Carol Zemel.

## ACKNOWLEDGMENTS

I recall the valuable conversations and support for this project over the years from dear friends and colleagues Patrick Clancy, Heather Diack, Ed Dimendberg, and Scott Michaelsen. Given his work as an extraordinary editor in his own right and keen interest in Weimar culture, Ed was always there with advice about the manuscript and helped me to envision its place in the publishing world. I also acknowledge my long friendship with Tom Conley whose extraordinary scholarship exemplifies for me the wonderful capacity to combine wit and theory in the study of culture. While teaching at Tufts University (1995–2000), I benefited from my exchanges about Jewish wit and humor among other subjects with Diane O'Donoghue, Linda Olstein, Joel Rosenberg, Reb Moshe Waldoks (of *The Big Book of Jewish Humor* fame), and Jeffu Warmouth.

In terms of intellectual indebtedness, I express my utmost gratitude to Steve Aschheim for his ongoing and unwavering support and championing of this project. The fact that we were both based in New York City during the 2013–2014 academic year was beyond fortuitous as Steve picked up his role again as interlocutor and trusted advisor. In addition to his marvelous feedback on chapter drafts, he never stopped encouraging me to get back to the *Witz* book and to my scholarly roots in European intellectual and cultural history when other academic demands (especially my academic career as a photography historian) pulled me away from this project. In addition to Steve, I am very grateful to Jeremy Dauber for his generous words and strong endorsement of the book. Finally, I extend my gratitude to both Elliott Oring and Jarrod Tanny as the two readers of the manuscript for their excellent feedback and helpful suggestions. Their constructive criticisms have strengthened the book in numerous ways.

This is the third time over the past twenty-five years that it has been my distinct privilege to work with and to benefit from the brilliant editorial engagement of Richard Morrison. Our longstanding association has created a special relationship of absolute trust and mutual respect. He immediately embraced this project with his typical gusto (and chutzpah) and he offered me sage counsel and superb guidance throughout the process. I also want to thank John Garza and Eric Newman at Fordham University Press for their able assistance. Michael Koch has been a rigorous and meticulous copy editor and I have benefited greatly from his feedback and judgment especially regarding the appropriate points for German inclusions in the book.

I am appreciative of the many libraries and archives in four different countries where I conducted research for this project, including the Robarts Library at the University of Toronto, the Widener Library at Harvard University, the National Library of Israel at the Givat Ram campus of the Hebrew University of Jerusalem, the Wiener Library at Tel Aviv University, the Staatsbibliothek Preußischer Kulturbesitz in Berlin, and the YIVO and the Leo Baeck Institute library collections at the Center for Jewish History in New York. I also want to thank the Austrian National Library, the Wiener Library (London), Getty Images, Alamy Stock Photos, and SOCAN (Montreal) for their permission to reproduce key images.

I am grateful for the ongoing love and support of my life partner Melissa Shiff with whom I have shared a wonderful creative partnership full of many successes and challenges over the past two decades. I am always inspired by her artistic brilliance and her courageous spirit, and the more so since she has been dealing with complex health problems in the past few years. Melissa and I are both incredibly grateful for our intelligent and charming son Sacha Kaplan-Shiff whose sparkling sense of humor never fails to bring us much joy and laughter — even when served up with the occasional mischievous prank. I also want to acknowledge the familial hospitality that I have experienced in a warm secular Jewish cultural context since moving to Toronto thanks to my father-in-law Allan and my late mother-in-law Helaine. Additional shout-outs go to Stephanie Breslow, Michael Dickstein, Jessica Eylon, Simon Glass, Rafael Goldchain, Alan and Naomi Kriss, Won Kyu Pak, Christie Pearson, Meredith Reddy, Jeanhy Shim, and Steve Zelinger.

The transformation of suffering into laughter constitutes a Jewish cultural tradition and it has served as a personal ethos for a large part of my life. I owe this unwavering attitude to my father, Leon Kaplan, who has served as a role model for my brother and myself in many ways. While my mother, Sarah, is no longer with us, it gives me great satisfaction to dedicate this book to him in his hundredth year of living, loving, and laughing.

Toronto, Canada
May 2019-February 2020

# Notes

## Introduction: The Joke and Its Questions

Unless otherwise noted, all translations from the German are mine.

1. For an online essay on Edmund Edel and a thorough review of the Jewish joke sources that he draws upon for his analysis, see Jürgen Gottschalk, "Eine doppelt versteckte 'versteckte' Bibliographie in Edmund Edels *Der Witz der Juden*" ["A doubly hidden 'hidden' bibliography in Edmund Edel's *Jewish Wit*"], *Documenta Humoristica Judaica*, http://humoristica-judaica.pirckheimer.org/texte_1.htm. Gottschalk's website provides an excellent bibliographical resource for the study of Jewish humor and it covers Jewish joke books in the German language.

2. For the original German publication, see Sigmund Freud, *Der Witz und seine Beziehung zum Unbewussten* (Leipzig: Franz Deuticke, 1905).

3. Edmund Edel, *Der Witz der Juden* (Berlin: Louis Lamm, 1909), 1.

4. Sigmund Freud, *Jokes and their Relation to the Unconscious*, trans. James Strachey, in collaboration with Anna Freud (New York: W. W. Norton, 1960), 111–112. The full citation reads: "The occurrence of self-criticism as a determinant may explain how it is that a number of the most apt jokes (of which we have plenty of instances) have grown up on the soil of Jewish popular life. They are stories created by Jews and directed against Jewish characteristics." For a fascinating analysis that views Freud's *Jokes* as "an act of identity-based expression," see Elliott Oring, "Sigmund Freud's Jewish Joke Book," in *Engaging Humor* (Urbana: University of Illinois Press, 2003), 116–128. See also Oring's insightful account on the relations of Freud's Jewish jokes to his own personal biography, *The Jokes of Sigmund Freud: A Study in Humor and Jewish Identity* (Philadelphia: University of Pennsylvania Press, 1984).

5. As Markus Patka writes, "Self-irony is mentioned in almost all of the works as the main characteristic of typical Jewish humor." See Markus G. Patka, *Wege des*

*Lachens: Judischer Witz und Humor aus Wien* (Vienna: Bibliothek der Provinz, 2011), 23.

6. Ruth R. Wisse, *No Joke: Making Jewish Humor* (Princeton, NJ: Princeton University Press, 2013), 10. Jefferson S. Chase frames this as a "vicious circle" and states: "'Jewish humor' was incited by anti-Jewish bias, further anti-Jewish bias, in turn, by satiric Jewish humor." See Chase, *Inciting Laughter: The Development of "Jewish Humour" in 19th Century German Culture* (Berlin: Walter de Gruyter, 1999), 3.

7. Sander L. Gilman, "'Jewish Humour' and the Terms by Which Jews and Muslims Join Western Civilization," *Leo Baeck Institute Year Book* 57 (2012): 61.

8. Jeremy Dauber, *Jewish Comedy: A Serious History* (New York: W. W. Norton and Company, 2017), 20. Dauber's use of quotation marks around "self-hating" shows that this pejorative term is often disputed especially by Jewish comedians.

9. Edel, *Der Witz der Juden*, 11–12.

10. Treitschke pronounced this negative judgment (*"Die Juden sind unser Unglück!"*) on November 15, 1879, and it was published as part of a pamphlet dealing with the Jewish question entitled *Ein Wort über unser Judenthum* (A word about our Jews) published by G. Reimer in Berlin the next year. See chapter 2 for details on what Treitschke had to say about Jewish *Witz* in the context of Eduard Fuchs's work.

11. Henry Wassermann, "Anti-Jewish (Modern) Caricature," in *Antisemitism: A Historical Encyclopedia of Prejudice and Persecution*, vol. 1, ed. Richard S. Levy (Santa Barbara, CA: ABC-CLIO, 2005), 105.

12. One can find a number of such examples in Eduard Fuchs, *Die Juden in der Karikatur: Ein Beitrag zur Kulturgeschichte* [Jews in caricature: A contribution to cultural history] (Munich: Albert Langen Verlag, 1921). Gilman refers to one that was originally published in *Kikeriki* that mocks the Eastern Jews on matters of hygiene and that is very closely related to the joke told by Freud in his book.

13. Mary Gluck, *The Invisible Jewish Budapest: Metropolitan Culture at the Fin de Siècle* (Madison: University of Wisconsin Press, 2016), 107. She concludes by insisting on the political instability of this joking tradition: "The tradition relied on irony and comic doubling in order to repudiate the dogmatic political traditions of ultranationalism and anti-Semitism but also the universal ethical claims of Jewish culture and identity."

14. This plays itself out in a number of comparative examples throughout the book as anti-Semites such as Arthur Trebitsch (in chapter 1) and Siegfried Kadner (in chapter 5) reframe Freud's interpretations of Jewish jokes.

15. Patka, *Wege des Lachens*, 23.

16. But Salcia Landman's statement over half a century ago regarding the reaction of nonreligious Jews applies here as well: "This harsh self-criticism in the Jewish joke always leads to the situation where Jews who are alienated from tradition reject them and decry them as anti-Semitic and self-demeaning." Salcia Landmann, *Der Jüdische Witz* (Olten: Walter-Verlag, 1960), 35.

17. Gershom Scholem, *Lamentations of Youth: The Diaries of Gershom Scholem,*

*1913–1919*, trans. Anthony David Skinner (Cambridge, MA: Harvard University Press, 2005), 286–287. I thank Steven Aschheim for alerting me to these profound speculations.

18. In the context of Scholem, Stéphane Moses sees a fascinating connection between the Jewish joke and Kabbalah framing it as a "secular substitute for religion's secret teaching [*Geheimlehre*]" and "therefore essentially a product of Jewish emancipation." See "Zur Poetik des Witzes," in *Signaturen der Gegenwartsliteratur. Festschrift Mr. Walter Hinderer*, ed. Dieter Borchmeyer (Würzburg: Königshausen und Neumann, 1999), 299.

19. According to Landmann, "Freud hatte den Witz als die letzte und einzige Waffe der Wehrlosen bezeichnet [Freud had described the joke as the last and only weapon of the defenseless]." See Salcia Landmann, "Zum Jüdischen Witz," in *Neues von Salcia Landmann: Jüdischer Witz* (Munich and Berlin: Herbig, 1972), 9. While this formula has been attributed to Freud numerous times, I have not been able to locate this citation anywhere in his work. Eike Christian Hirsch also suggests that this is a misattribution in *Der Witzableiter oder die Schule des Lachens* (Munich: C. H. Beck: 2001), 264.

20. Gilman, "Jewish Humour," 61.

21. Chayim Bloch, *Das jüdischer Volk in seiner Anekdote: Ernstes und Heiteres von Gottsuchern, Gelehrten, Künstlern, Narren, Schelmen, Aufschneidern, Schnorrern, Reichen, Frommen, Freidenkern, Täuflingen, Antisemiten* (Berlin: Verlag für Kulturpolitik, 1931), 17. From a deconstructive perspective, Bloch's inclusion of "anti-Semites" as the last type on the list of the cast of characters encountered in these anecdotes illustrates how the anti-Semitic other comes back to haunt the constitution of the Jewish joke in general.

22. Lutz Röhrich, *Der Witz: Figuren, Formen, Funktionen* (Stuttgart: J. B. Meltzler, 1977), 284. In contrast to Bloch and to further problematize matters, Röhrich refers to *Judenwitz* as the contaminated type of joke in this context—"der jüdische Witz zum Judenwitz umgeprägt wurde."

23. For example, the classification of the jokes into two fixed categories does not allow for changing historical circumstances that can alter the social perceptions of whether or not a particular Jewish joke should still be told because it may fan the fires of anti-Semitism even though it seemed harmless in a more tolerant period of history. The insistence upon this binary opposition serves as the ground for the exclusion of the folklorists from this volume beyond the occasional contrasting of their views.

24. In tandem with the Weimar period and the KadeKo's defense of self-ironic Jewish jokes, Daniel Wickberg discusses a parallel situation in the United States where self-directed laughter became a sign of mental health in the same period. He writes: "From the 1890s forward, then, the personality attribute of the sense of humor was defined in terms of self-objectification, the ability to 'take' or see a joke on oneself, the capacity to laugh at oneself. These terms of understanding, and the value attached to them, resonated throughout American culture—particularly from

the 1920's through the 1950's, when they received frequent expression in both the academic and the popular psychology of the day and in the newly powerful mass media." See Wickberg, *The Senses of Humor: Self and Laughter in Modern America* (Ithaca, NY: Cornell University Press, 1998), 107.

25. Flaneur, "Die antisemitische Gebrüder Herrnfeld," *Die Standarte* 2, no. 44 (August 13, 1908): 1391–1393; translated by anonymous as "The Anti-Semitic Brothers Herrnfeld" at https://www.filmportal.de/material/die-juedische-rundschau-on-the-herrnfeld-theatre.

26. Flaneur refers to M. Nuél [Manuel Schnitzer], *Das Buch der jüdischen Witze* (Berlin: Hesperus, 1907) as a positive example in contrast to the Herrnfeld Theater. For more information on the impact of Schnitzer's popular collection in conjunction with Eduard Fuchs's analysis of Jewish self-irony, see chapter 2.

27. See Alexander Moszkowski, *Die jüdische Kiste* [The Jewish box] (Berlin: Dr. Eysler, 1911) and *Der jüdische Witz und seine Philosophie* [The Jewish joke and its philosophy] (Berlin: Dr. Eysler, 1922). The earlier version serves as the basis for the book cover of the present volume.

28. Landmann, *Der Jüdische Witz*, 35. Landmann follows Freud here. His famous distinction between Jewish self-criticism and anti-Semitic brutalization states: "The jokes made about Jews by foreigners are for the most part brutal comic stories [*brutale Schwänke*] in which a joke is made unnecessary by the fact that Jews are regarded by foreigners as comic figures. The Jewish jokes which originate from Jews admit this too; but they know their real faults as well as the connection between them and their good qualities" (Freud, *Jokes*, 111–112). Elliott Oring insists that Freud too had a problem in maintaining his distinction and that his "positive" defense of the Jewish joke seems "self-defeating." He writes: "Despite his claim of a positive foundation for the Jewish joke, Freud's use of these jokes to exemplify displacement, duplicity, sophistry, and faulty logic, as well as assaults on social values, the notion of truth, and the possibility of knowledge, serves to reaffirm the traditional anti-Semitic image of a corrupt Jewish discourse" ("Sigmund Freud's Jewish Joke Book," 123).

29. Freud's version reads: "A Galician Jew was traveling in a train. He had made himself really comfortable, had unbuttoned his coat and put his feet up on the seat. Just then a gentleman in modern dress entered the compartment. The Jew promptly pulled himself together and took up a proper pose. The stranger fingered through the pages of a notebook, made some calculations, reflected for a moment and then suddenly asked the Jew: 'Excuse me, when is Yom Kippur (the Day of Atonement)?' 'Oho!' said the Jew, and put his feet up on the seat again before answering" (*Jokes*, 80). Ruth R. Wisse compares Freud's and Arthur Schnitzler's interpretations of this joke in her "Introduction: The Best Medicine," in *No Joke*, 7–10. For my comparison of Freud's interpretation with Arthur Trebitsch's anti-Semitic reading of the joke, see chapter 1.

30. See John Murray Cuddihy, *The Ordeal of Civility: Freud, Marx, Levi-Strauss and the Jewish Struggle with Modernity* (New York: Dell Publishing, 1974).

31. Arthur Schnitzler, *The Way into the Open*, trans. Roger Byers (Berkeley:

University of California Press, 1992), 113. Theodor Reik's essay "Die Intimität im Judenwitz" ("Intimacy in the Jewish Joke") owes much to this particular passage in Schnitzler and the psychoanalyst acknowledges this point specifically: "We have heard from Schnitzler that the particular kind of intimacy that is the social intercourse peculiar among Jews does not allow this specific feeling of respect to emerge especially." See Theodor Reik, *Nachdenkliche Heiterkeit* (Vienna: Internationaler Psychoanalytischer Verlag, 1933), 74.

32. Schnitzler, *Way into the Open*, 113.

33. Gluck, *Invisible Jewish Budapest*, 106–107. Gluck goes on to discuss the ambivalence raised by the Jewish joke as an object of study and its contested status among scholars. Her account brings new dimensions to the joke dialectic between Jewish self-irony and Jewish self-hatred/anti-Semitism: "The difficulty of integrating *Judenwitz* into serious scholarly discussion can be explained in part by its compromised status as a cultural practice. Associated with negative Jewish stereotypes and crude and deprecating humor, *Judenwitz* has proven to be deeply controversial and has given rise to divergent interpretations among historians of modern Jewry. Was *Judenwitz* a gesture of Jewish self-hatred and masochism or an act of self-assertion and cultural emancipation? Was it a reflection of the degradation of Jewish life in the Diaspora or, on the contrary, a sophisticated alternative to its established cultural codes?" (107).

34. For a published review of the symposium, see Fabian Wolff, "Treffen sich zwei Juden . . . ," *Jüdische Allgemeine Zeitung*, May 23, 2013, http://www.juedische -allgemeine.de/article/view/id/15973.

35. See the press release for the symposium at http://www.fu-berlin.de/presse /informationen/fup/2013/fup_13_100/. Sander Gilman's keynote lecture at the conference was entitled "When Did the Jews Become Funny? A New Debate about the Limits of Representation after 9/11 or an Older Problem." The expanded proceedings were published as Burkhard Meyer-Sickendiek and Gunnar Och, eds., *Der jüdische Witz: Zur unabgegoltenen Problematik einer alten Kategorie* (Paderborn: Wilhelm Fink, 2015).

36. My translation of the online flyer for the symposium reads: "One knows the keyword 'Jewish wit' mainly by the immensely popular collection of anonymous narrative jokes, which Landmann published in the 1960s in many editions. However, is the phenomenon in fact adequately characterized through this book? Already Friedrich Torberg doubted this by imputing to Landmann an unrestrained reproduction of anti-Semitic stereotypes. Our meeting would like to build on this controversy and reopen the debate about 'Jewish wit.'" See "Der jüdische Witz," flyer, http://www.geisteswissenschaften.fu-berlin.de/fachbereich/chronik/2013 /forschung/tagungen/_ressourcen/der_juedische_witz_flyer.pdf?1367. Meyer-Sickendiek's excellent survey "Jüdischer Witz und deutsch-jüdische Moderne" also begins with the Landmann-Torberg controversy. See Hans Otto Horch, ed., *Handbuch der deutsch-jüdischen Literatur* (Berlin: De Gruyter, 2016), 440–462.

37. Brumlik's lecture was ambivalently entitled "'Menschenfeindliches Zerrbild

oder Satire': Eduard Fuchs und *Die Juden in der Karikatur*" ("Misanthropic caricatures or satire: Eduard Fuchs and *Jews in caricature*").

38. Markus G. Patka and Albert Stalzer, eds., *Alle Meschugge?: Jüdischer Witz und Humor* (Vienna: Amalthea, 2013).

39. Gilman, "Jewish Humour," 65.

40. The Anti-Defamation League's letter to Sacha Baron-Cohen is dated August 9, 2004. It reads in part: "While we understand this scene was an attempt to show how easily a group of ordinary people can be encouraged to join in an anti-Semitic chorus, we are concerned that the irony may have been lost on some of your audience — or worse, that some of your viewers may have simply accepted Borat's statements about Jews at face value" (http://archive.adl.org/media_watch/tv/20040809-hbo.html#.UzxKlRZpGfQ). See also Shaun De Waal's review of *Borat* at the time of the film's release and his prediction that Cohen was going to be accused of being a "self-hating Jew" instead of creating "a vicious parody of unthinkingly vicious anti-Semitism." Shaun De Waal, "In Jew Course," *Mail and Guardian* (South Africa), November 17, 2006, https://mg.co.za/article/2006-11-17-in-jew-course. I will return to Baron Cohen's Trump-inspired program "Who is America?" in the afterword.

41. Dauber, *Jewish Comedy*, 48.

42. See Eli Valley, *Diaspora Boy: Comics on Crisis in America and Israel* (New York and London: OR Books, 2017).

43. In the case of Eli Valley, Cathryn J. Prince writes: "As a satirist Valley has received his share of criticism. Actually, criticism might be putting it mildly. He's been called a self-hating Jew, an Israel hater, a Ghetto Jew, and a Kapo. Name the insult or slur, he's heard it before." See "How satire got a cartoonist fired from a Jewish newspaper," *Times of Israel*, September 22, 2017, https://www.timesofisrael.com/how-satire-got-a-cartoonist-fired-from-a-jewish-newspaper/.

44. Another excellent example is found in the provocative Israeli Anti-Semitic Cartoon Contest launched by Amitai Sandy and Eyal Zusman as a direct response to the Iranian Holocaust cartoon contest sponsored by Hamshahri Daily in 2006: "'We'll show the world we can do the best, sharpest, most offensive Jew hating cartoons ever published!' said Sandy. 'No Iranian will beat us on our home turf!'" Sandy is quoted in Jonathan Leggett, "Anti-Semitism, the Jewish way," *Guardian*, March 3, 2006, https://www.theguardian.com/theguardian/2006/mar/03/features11.g2.

45. See Judas Ascher, *Der Judenfreund, oder auserlesene Anekdoten, Schwänke und Einfalle von den Kindern Israels* (Leipzig: Baumgärtnerschen Buchhandlung, 1810). Using this book as a touchstone, the journalist Fabian Wolff reviews the wavering border of the Jewish joke: "The collection is aligned to anti-Semitism but is derived in part from the same sources. Here you can see the perceived 'danger' of the Jewish joke. Some see in it self-irony and the deconstruction of clichés or a Jewish *commedia dell'arte*, as Christina Pareigis (Center for Literary and Cultural Research) aptly put it. For others, it is only the confirmation of these prejudices, if not anti-Semitism" ("Treffen sich zwei Juden . . .").

46. Lippman Moses Büschenthal, *Sammlung witziger Einfälle von Juden, als Beyträge zur Charakteristik der Jüdischen Nation* [Collection of Witty Notions from Jews as a Contribution to the Characterization of the Jewish Nation] (Elberfeld: Bey H. Büschler in Kommission, 1812), translated by Michaela Lang and edited by Elliott Oring as *The First Book of Jewish Jokes: The Collection of L. M. Büschenthal* (Bloomington: University of Indiana Press, 2018).

47. Gilman, "Jewish Humour," 58.

48. Büschenthal, *Sammlung witziger Einfälle von Juden*, iv.

49. Jefferson S. Chase, *Inciting Laughter*, 1. Hereafter cited in text by page number in parentheses.

50. Mary Gluck amplifies Chase's ideas in her discussion of *Judenwitz* in her excellent chapter on "The Jewish Humor Magazine and Collective Self-Parody" in *The Invisible Jewish Budapest*: "*Judenwitz* implied more than simply jokes by or about Jews. It was identified with the nihilism of the Jewish spirit itself that found characteristic expression in irony and malicious laughter. *Judenwitz* was thought to be the creation of rootless outsiders who could never fully master the native idiom" (105–106). Gluck also enlists Mary Douglas's ideas about humor as akin to the *Judenwitz*'s social functions: "The anthropologist Mary Douglas, for instance, has incorporated many aspects of *Judenwitz* into her own conceptions of humor. The joke, she has suggested, was by definition subversive, challenging social control, objectivity, and established conventions. Echoing classic definitions of *Judenwitz*, she saw the essence of humor in terms of 'the leveling of hierarchy, the triumph of intimacy over formality, of unofficial values over official ones'" (106).

51. Moving to the end of the twentieth century, the *Witz* versus *Humor* opposition structures the work of the German literary historian Otto F. Best in *Volk ohne Witz: Über ein deutsches Defizit* (Frankfurt am Main: Fischer, 1993).

52. Many of the important writings of Max Weber on the rise of rationalization and the disenchantment with religion in Western societies were written in this same period. Weber composed most of his essays on the methodology of the social sciences between 1903 and 1917, including "Critical Studies in the Logic of the Cultural Sciences: A Critique of Eduard Meyer's Methodological Views." See Edward A. Shils and Henry A. Finch, eds., *Max Weber on the Methodology of the Social Sciences* (Glencoe, IL: Free Press, 1949), 113–163. In addition, Weber wrote his controversial essay "Science as a Vocation" in 1918–1919. Its central thesis states: "The fate of our times is characterized by rationalization and intellectualization and, above all, by the 'disenchantment of the world.'" See H. H. Gerth and C. Wright Mills, *From Max Weber: Essays in Sociology* (New York: Oxford University Press, 1946), 155. Interestingly, the young Eric von Kahler would begin his illustrious intellectual career with a neo-Romantic rebuttal of Weber's essay. See Eric von Kahler, *Der Beruf der Wissenschaft* (Berlin: Bondi, 1920).

53. To this list, we must add the desire for excremental knowledge too. Freud also played a part in the German reception history of the soldier-scientist John Gregory Bourke, *Scatalogic Rites of All Nations* (Washington, DC: Lowdermilk, 1891). Its publication in Germany featured an introduction by Freud in 1913. See

my contribution to this abject subject ("John Bourkes Scatalog") in John Gregory Bourke, *Das Buch des Unrats* (Frankfurt am Main: Eichborn, 1992).

54. Schnitzler, *Way into the Open*, 113. Bermann's full citation reads: "Deep. Deep like so many Jewish anecdotes. They offer an insight into the tragicomedy of contemporary Judaism."

55. Sigmund Freud, *The Complete Letters of Sigmund Freud to Wilhelm Fliess, 1887–1904*, trans. and ed. Jeffrey Moussaieff Masson (Cambridge, MA: Belknap Press of Harvard University Press, 1985), 254. This comment is taken from a letter that Freud wrote to his friend and colleague on June 22, 1897.

56. To provide further context for this citation, Freud is describing one of his dreams to Fliess: "The material out of which the dream was woven included at this point two of those facetious Jewish anecdotes which contain so much profound and often bitter worldly wisdom and which we so greatly enjoy quoting in our talk and letters." See Sigmund Freud, *The Standard Edition of the Complete Psychological Works of Sigmund Freud*, vol. 4 (1900), *The Interpretation of Dreams* (First Part), 194–195.

57. Gluck, *Invisible Jewish Budapest*, 107.

58. See Max Präger and Siegfried Schmitz, *Jüdische Schwänke* [Jewish droll stories] (Vienna: R. Löwit, 1928). This folkloristic collection puts the Jewish joke in conjunction with this literary form and is a German selection and translation of Immanuel Olsvanger's transliterated Yiddish classic *Rosinkes mit Mandlen: Volksliteratur der Ostjuden* [Raisins with almonds: Folk literature of Eastern European Jews] (Basel: Verlag der Schweizerischen Gesellschaft für Volkskunde, 1920).

59. Edel, *Der Witz der Juden*, 9.

60. Götz Aly, *Why the Germans? Why the Jews? Envy, Race Hatred, and the Prehistory of the Holocaust*, trans. Jefferson Chase (New York: Henry Holt, 2014), 196. The questions in the title reference a famous Jewish joke about anti-Semitism discussed in chapters 3 and 6. To recall Hitler's German idiomatic expression for describing the Jew as being at wit's end and therefore at the end of his mental resources, "Dann ist er mit seinem Latein zu Ende." This ironic phrasing (especially in reference to the Jew) literally means "to be at the end of one's Latin." The German expression implies that even a knowledgeable person speaking the learned language of science (*Wissenschaft*) would be at a loss for a solution. See Christian Hartmann, ed., *Hitler: Reden, Schriften, Anordnungen Februar 1925 bis Januar 1933* (Munich: Saur, 1995), 3.3:289.

61. Louis P. Lochner, ed., *The Goebbels Diaries, 1942–1943* (Garden City, NY: Doubleday, 1948), 148.

62. Edel, *Der Witz der Juden*, 9–10.

63. This strategy also plays a vital role in the legacy of Jacques Derrida and deconstruction. In an interview with Elizabeth Weber dated September 13, 1991, Derrida speaks of a philosophical style in his autobiographical text *Circumfession* that mixes laughter and tears: "I'm not sure you have to choose between laughter

and tears. Good tears are not necessarily free of all smiles. It is possible, as one says, to smile through your tears, to laugh while crying. The tears this text is about ought to rule out mockery, but not necessarily a kind of laughing. On the contrary." Jacques Derrida in Elizabeth Weber, ed., *Questioning Judaism* (Stanford, CA: Stanford University Press, 1993), 58. As such, the discourse of "joke mourning" or of "laughter while grieving" that is delineated in the use of the Jewish joke after the Holocaust and that is the subject of chapter 6 resonates with the strategy of deconstruction.

64. Edited by Calman Levi, this joke book collection with its generic title of *Jüdische Witze* was published in Dresden by M. Fischer sometime between 1910 and 1919.

65. Slavoj Žižek takes up "the fact that Jews who were chosen for the role of the 'Jew' ultimately is contingent" in *Tarrying with the Negative* (Durham, NC: Duke University Press, 1993), 117.

66. The joke's punchline reads with its Yiddish inflections: *"Nu, ah waih hab' ich geschrien!"* See Levi, *Jüdische Witze*, 70.

67. A number of variants were published containing a similar punchline but none of them possess the same title. These versions include "Ausführlichen Bescheid" [Detailed communication] in Avrom Reitzer, *Gut Jontev: Rituelle Scherze und koschere Schmonzes für unsere Leut* (Vienna: J. Deubler's Verlag, 1899), 71–72, and in the anonymously edited and much older collection *Gewaltsachen: Eine Auswahl der besten jüdischen Anekdoten* (Berlin: Hofmann, 1866), 33. Landmann also tries her hand at recounting this joke in her chapter on "Bildung" (education) in *Der Jüdische Witz*, 420.

## 1. Secondary Moves: Arthur Trebitsch and the Jewish Joke

Unless otherwise noted, all translations from the German are mine.

1. Joseph Roth, *Das Spinnennetz* (Amsterdam: Verlag Allert de Lange, 1923), translated by John Hoare as *The Spider's Web and Zipper and his Father* (London: Chatto and Windus, 1988).

2. Arthur Trebitsch, *Geist und Judentum: Une Grundlegende Untersuchung* (Vienna: Ed. Strache, 1919), 174. Hereafter cited in text by page number in parentheses.

3. Michael Brenner, *The Renaissance of Jewish Culture in Weimar Germany* (New Haven, CT: Yale University Press, 1996), 133. Brenner also states that Trebitsch was an "Austrian Jew who considered himself a follower of Otto Weininger."

4. Brigitte Hamann, *Hitler's Vienna: A Dictator's Apprenticeship*, trans. Thomas Thornton (New York: Oxford University Press, 1999), 233.

5. Theodor Lessing states that "no group takes him quite seriously." See *Jüdischer Selbsthaß* [Jewish self-hatred] (Berlin: Zionistischer Bücher-Bund, 1930), 120. This inability to take Trebitsch quite seriously constitutes the (Jewish) humorous subtext of his pro-Aryan lecture tour.

6. Sander L. Gilman, *Jewish Self-Hatred: Anti-Semitism and the Hidden Language of the Jews* (Baltimore, MD: Johns Hopkins University Press, 1986), 249.

7. *Geist und Judentum* was published in Vienna and Leipzig by Verlag Edition Strache. While the cover puts the book into the year 1919, the inside copyright states 1918. Meanwhile, Trebitsch informs the reader below the triple epigraph that the book was written between July 9 and November 30, 1917.

8. Lessing, *Jüdischer Selbsthaß*, 121.

9. Although the adjective *beweglich* has been translated in this instance as mobile, its noun form, *Beweglichkeit*, can be translated as movability, mobility, agility, maneuverability, agility or nimbleness of mind, and nimbleness. All of these words enter as negative traits in the ideal typology that Trebitsch sets up as part of the Jewish mind or spirit (*jüdische Geist*).

10. Later, Trebitsch explains how secondary spirits have a mobile mode of fixation called *Fixationsbeweglichkeit* (43).

11. For a general discussion of the dynamics of self-hatred, see Gilman, *Jewish Self-Hatred*, chap. 1. Gilman sketches Trebitsch's psychology of language as part of his analysis of the rise of anti-Semitic racial science later in the book (248–250).

12. Jacques Lacan, *The Seminar of Jacques Lacan, Book 2: The Ego in Freud's Theory and in the Technique of Psychoanalysis* (1954–1955), ed. Jacques-Alain Miller (Cambridge: Cambridge University Press, 1988), 234. The date of Lacan's lecture ("Desire, Life, and Death") was May 18, 1955. Lacan makes this telling point just before analyzing one of the same vacillating jokes that amused Trebitsch (and that concludes this chapter).

13. Lessing, *Jüdischer Selbsthaß*, 103.

14. Lessing, 103.

15. Lessing, 130. The émigré sociologist Isacque Graeber also framed Trebitsch as a self-hating Jew in the American Jewish press two years after Lessing. Graeber refers to Trebitsch as a paranoid and suicidal "Jewish renegade" and cites his guilt-ridden and self-flagellating confessions: "Thus wrote Trebitsch in his diary. 'The Jew must be destroyed, together with the Jewishness of my own soul.' And he continued in a brief notation dated April, 1920: 'The mere knowledge of my Jewish descent, makes me think as though I carry a contagious disease under my very clothes, that attracts conspicuous looks, from passers-by. And thus I carry the shame, the metaphysical guilt of my Jewish being. Ah, what an accursed one I am . . . at times I even think to commit suicide and end with it my eternal disgrace!'" See Dr. Isacque Graeber, "Hitler's Jewish Teacher," *Jewish Criterion* 80, no. 21 (September 30, 1932): 51.

16. For a reading in opposition to Lessing's reading of Weininger, see Allan Janik, "Viennese Culture and the Jewish Self-Hatred Hypothesis: A Critique," in *Jews, Antisemitism and Culture in Vienna*, ed. Ivar Oxaal, Michael Pollak, and Gerhard Botz (London and New York: Routledge and Kegan Paul, 1987), 75–88.

17. This same sensationalist detail enters into the short entry on the life of Trebitsch in *Das Jüdische Lexikon*, 4.2:104, translation mine. The Lessing text acquires an authoritative value here. Exclusive of the bibliographical details, it reads:

"Trebitsch, 1. Arthur, writer, born in 1880 in Vienna, died there in 1928, published a series of poetic and philosophical works, baptized early, T. was a passionate opponent of Judaism and follower of the German folk movement. He believed that he was pursued by a secret j. world conspiracy which would eliminate him through electro-magnetic rays. T.'s mind was a strange mixture of near genius and pathological features, as Theodor Lessing has demonstrated in his biography of T." Incidentally, it is a bitter irony of history that the exiled Lessing rather than Trebitsch was murdered in Marienbad in the summer of 1933 by Sudeten German Nazi sympathizers.

18. For instance, Lessing points out that "His monomaniac fear of being regarded as a Jew pushed him into absurd and silly (*alberne*) disputes" (*Jüdischer Selbsthaß*, 118).

19. Arthur Trebitsch, *Die Geschichte meines "Verfolgungswahns"* (Vienna: Antaios-Verlag, 1923). This book was published by Trebitsch's own vanity press.

20. See Daniel Paul Schreber, *Denkwürdigkeiten eines Nervenkranken* [*Memoirs of my Nervous Illness*] (Leipzig: Oswald Mutze, 1903). While Schreber associates these rays with emanations from the divine, Trebitsch sees this "electrical influence and suggestibility [*elektrische Beeinflussung und Beeinflussbarkeit*]" as emanating from a band of Jewish scientist conspirators who are out to get him (*Die Geschichte*, 125).

21. Lessing, *Jüdischer Selbsthaß*, 120.

22. Sven Brömsel also focuses on Trebitsch's relationship to Chamberlain. See his "Arthur Trebitsch, der neue Schlemihl," *Weimarer Beiträge* 57, no. 3 (2011): 345–369.

23. Trebitsch, *Die Geschichte*, 155.

24. This is reminiscent of the phrenological anecdote about Trebitsch's cranium that finds him desperate to prove his Aryan status. As Jacques Le Rider relates the story: "[Trebitsch] felt himself persecuted by a 'Jewish Alliance' calling for physicians to come take measurements of his skull in order to confirm that he indeed possessed all the anatomical characteristics of the Aryan." *Modernité viennoise et crises de l' identité* (Paris: P.U.F., 1990), 236.

25. Trebitsch, *Die Geschichte*, 154.

26. The tradition of the mirror as the literary device with which to hold up the Jewish question is a long one in European cultural history. The first anti-Semitic treatise of the convert Johannes Pfefferkorn (with whom Lessing compares Trebitsch) was entitled *The Mirror of the Jews* (1507). It holds up the errors of the Jews to the mirror for all the world to see.

27. This interrogative exchange between the witty man and the Jewish scholar enacts the mirror image of one of the most famous Jewish jokes in which a non-Jew asks a Jew why Jews always answer a question with another question and the Jew replies with the enactment of the question.

28. Gilman writes that a figure like Trebitsch "used the structure of scientific discourse as a means of distancing his identification from the idea of the Jew." See *Jewish Self Hatred*, 248. In this particular case, Trebitsch employs an anti-intellectual

and anti-scientific discourse as a means of distancing his identification with the Jewish scholar.

29. For a fascinating account of the social significance of illustrated humor directed against Jews in the second half of the nineteenth century, see Henry Wassermann, "The *Fliegende Blätter* as a Source for the Social History of German Jewry," in *Leo Baeck Institute Year Book* 28 (London: Secker and Warburg, 1983), 93–138.

30. This caricature is reproduced in Eduard Fuchs, *Die Juden in der Karikatur: Ein Beitrag zur Kulturgeschichte* (Munich: Albert Langen, 1921),195.

31. For a tentative discussion of these figures, see Alex Bein, *The Jewish Question: Biography of a World Problem*, trans. Harry Zohn (Toronto: Associated University Presses, 1990). The ghost is discussed in relation to Heine on page 654; the image of the vampire is discussed in relation to parasitism, 711–712. Trebitsch was no stranger to this second trope. The opening remarks of *Die Geschichte meines* "*Verfolgungswahns*" and its search for the antidote ("*Antitoxin*") confirms this point.

32. Alexander Moszkowski, "*Auserwählte Volk*"s *Witze: 399 Juwelen aus dem jüdischen Kronschatz* (Berlin: Dr. Eysler, 1911), 51.

33. This messianic point of overidentification is emphasized in the foreword to R. Guttenbrunn's hagiographical study, *Der brennende Mensch: Das geistige Vermächtnis von Arthur Trebitsch* [The burning man: The intellectual legacy of Arthur Trebitsch] (Leipzig: n.p., 1930), 3. Guttenbrunn asserts "that a new Messiah has arisen with him for the hard-pressed, mentally contaminated German people because the Saviour was also a Jew by birth, but his teachings represented [only] the first world-historical protest against Judaism!"

34. Weininger understood this paradox in terms of the thin and moving line between love and hate: "One does not hate something with which one has no resemblance. Often only the other person makes us first aware of what unattractive and vulgar traits we have in us. This explains the fact that the bitterest anti-Semites are to be found among the Jews themselves." See *Geschlecht und Charakter: eine prinzipelle Untersuchung* (Vienna: Wilhelm Braumüller, 1910), 413.

35. Walter Laqueur, *The Changing Face of Anti-Semitism: From Ancient Times to the Present Day* (New York: Oxford University Press, 2006), 166. Rather than focusing on Jewish self-hatred, Freud's analysis of the "badly baptized" (*schlecht getauft*) relates to those who have converted to Christendom but who remain "barbarically polytheistic under the surface" (146). See Sigmund Freud, *Moses and Monotheism*, trans. Katherine Jones (London: Hogarth Press and Institute of Psycho-Analysis, 1939). Freud concludes this analysis with a look at the Nazis and their hateful conflation of Jews and Christians: "The hatred for Judaism is at bottom hatred for Christianity, and it is not surprising that in the German National-Socialist revolution this connection of the two monotheistic religions finds such clear expression in the hostile treatment of both" (147–148).

36. Chaim Bloch, *Das Jüdische Volk in der Anekdote* (Berlin: Verlag für Kulturpolitik, 1930), 17.

37. Siegfried Schmitz, "Nachwort vom Jüdischen Witz," in Präger and Schmitz, *Jüdische Schwänke* (Vienna: Löwit Verlag, 1928), 253. In large part, this book is a German transcription of the Latinized Yiddish found in the folkloristic classic, Immanuel Olsvanger, *Rosinkes mit Mandlen* (Basel: Schweizerischen Gesellschaft für Volkskunde, 1920).

38. Schmitz, 257.

39. As opposed to such "us" and "them" dichotomies, it is more to the point to consider the vacillations of the joke context on a case-by-case basis. One must analyze the specific performative and speech communication situation of the jest and consider who is telling the joke and why (narrator), who is hearing the joke and how (audience), etc. Thus, the same joke may be considered "Jewish self-criticism" at the one time, and "Jewish anti-Semitism" the next time, or even an ambivalent combination of the two at one and the same time depending on the circumstances.

40. Schmitz, 257. For a discussion on the relation between *"Witz und Schwank"* and the historical replacement of the second genre by the first one, see Lutz Röhrich, *Der Witz: Figuren, Formen, Funktionen* (Stuttgart: Metzler, 1977), 8–10.

41. This is the title of the account written by the composer and Holocaust survivor Jan Meyerowitz who follows the tradition and the jargon of authenticity. See Meyerowitz, *Der Echte Jüdische Witz* [The real Jewish joke] (Berlin: Colloquium Verlag, 1971).

42. George Steiner, "Our Homeland, the Text," *Salmagundi*, no. 66 (Winter–Spring 1985): 5. My thanks to Sidra DeKoven Ezrahi for turning my attention to Steiner's diasporic call regarding the primacy of the text.

43. For other contemporary examples, see Manuel Schnitzer, *Rabbi Lach: Eine Kulturdokument in Anekdoten* (Hamburg: Verlag W. Gente, 1921), 82; Moszkowski, "Auserwählte Volk"s Witze, 16, and M. Nuél [Manuel Schnitzer], *Das Buch der Jüdischen Witze* (Berlin: Gustav Riecke, 1907), 31.

44. For a portrayal of this particular phenomenon on the silver screen, see Samuel Fuller's film, *White Dog* (1982).

45. William Novak und Moshe Waldoks, "Antisemitismus," *Das grosse Buch des jüdischen Humors* (Königstein: Athenenaum, 1982), 121. Jews did not usually keep dogs in rural Eastern Europe whereas landowners kept them to scare away Jews and others. This led to the idea that Jews were afraid of dogs. As my colleague Anna Shternshis writes, "Fear of dogs was frequently considered to be a Jewish characteristic by gentile neighbors. Memoirs of shtetl residents of Poland in the mid-1800s suggest that some landowners used dogs to threaten Jews who visited them." See the "Dogs" entry in *YIVO Encyclopedia*, http://www.yivoencyclopedia.org/printarticle.aspx?id=2164.

46. While this interpretation reflects a post-Shoah reading of the joke, the attack of the anti-Semitic dog can be traced back in time to early rural *Schwänke* in Germany such as the one about the Jewish peddler named Wertheimer who is attacked by the dogs of the village children pranksters. See Wassermann, "*Fliegende Blätter*," 101.

47. Some Jewish joke commentators did not share Trebitsch's views regarding the overall significance of the *Kalauer* in the Jewish joke repertoire. For a different point of view without the heavy baggage of the secondary spirit lurking in the background, see Edmund Edel, *Der Witz der Juden* (Berlin: Louis Lamm, 1909), 31–32. Edel points to the use of the *Kalauer* by isolated satirists such as Moritz Saphir and Siegmund Haber, but he denies any overall achievement of its prominence in Jewish jokes: "Verbal wit, the so-called *Kalauer* or pun, has of course been utilized as well. Saphir was the true representative of this art of joking which always has some whimsy and whose intellectual legacy was taken up later by Siegmund Haber. But Jewish verbal wit never became prominent in its appearance." The Yiddish folklorist and Jewish joke scholar Alter Druyanov also shared this view. As Itzik Nakhmen Gottesman writes, "Jewish humor, unlike the humor of other nations, was not based on wordplay, but was more profound and based upon a conceptual twist that Druyanov expounded upon in his work, 'The Jewish Folk Joke.'" See Gottesman, *Defining the Jewish Nation: The Jewish Folklorists of Poland* (Detroit, MI: Wayne State University Press, 2003), 70.

48. For a variety of depreciations of the *Kalauer* and the attempt to expel it to the realm of the witless, see Lutz Röhrich, *Der Witz*, 60–61. As Röhrich explains: "But not every wordplay is really funny. If it is too cumbersome or too contrived, then one likes to speak about a *Kalauer* (bad pun or corny joke)" (60).

49. Gilman, *Jewish Self-Hatred*, 250.

50. Or as Trebitsch comments earlier, "That type of joke which so especially likes to use words and their coincidences had to become the appropriate play area for this secondary spirit" (74).

51. Amid the death rattles of the Weimar Republic, the brilliant Jewish diasporic historian Erich Kahler posits a similar theory of intercultural breakdown and the inability for either side to get the joke in terms of another binary opposition between "*Jüdischer Intellektualismus*" and "*Deutscher Körperlichkeit.*" The Jewish anti-Semite and the Jewish historian are linked here in making this connection between the telling of the joke and the impossibility of intercultural dialogue. To simplify matters for this excerpted and cursory glance (to be taken up in greater detail in chapter 4), Kahler posits the following: "To the physically inclined German with his heavy consciousness, the fleeting joke does not matter at all. . . . Before the Jewish joke itself in its best and deepest type . . . before this joke, the German is at a loss." See Kahler, *Israel Unter den Völkern* (Zürich: Humanitas Verlag, 1936), 151. Note that Kahler also associates the Jewish joke with the fleeting, volatile, and fugitive (*flüchtig*).

52. The reader is referred to the outrageous statistical chart in Arthur Trebitsch, *Deutscher Geist—oder Judentum!: Der Weg der Befreiung* (Berlin: Antaios Verlag, 1921), 313. Here, Trebitsch reviews his pitiful book sales during the fiscal year 1920–1921. This chart offers no sales figures on *Geist und Judentum*. Playing both sides of the political fence, Trebitsch blames the Zionist conspiracy ("*Zions allmächtigem Vernichtungswillen*," or "Zion's omnipotent will to destruction") and the obtuse

German public ("*Oberflächlichkeit und die nachlassende Erkenntnisfreude und Erkenntniskraft im deutschen Volke*," or "superficiality and the diminishing joy and power in knowledge in the German folk").

53. For a description of some of these comic interactions in Vienna and Berlin, see Paul Landau's article on "*Der jüdische Witz und Humor*," in *Juden im deutschen Kulturbereich*, ed. Siegmund Kaznelson (Berlin: Jüdischer Verlag, 1959), 895–901. On the history of the Viennese cabaret in the interwar period, see Marcus G. Patka and Alfred Stalzer, "Lachen in der Krise: Kabarett in Wien der Zwischenkriegszeit," in *Alle Meschugge? Jüdischer Witz und Humor* (Vienna: Amalthea, 2013), 67–72. See also Patka's full-length study of Jewish wit and humor in Vienna, *Wege zum Lachens: Jüdischer Witz und Humor aus Wien* (Vienna: Enzyklopädie des Wiener Wissens, 2010).

54. In this context, it does well to recall Trebitsch's primary source testimony from the essay "*Primäres Denken im Lichte sekundären Geistes: Eine Entgegnung*" ["Primary thought in the light of the secondary spirit: A reply"]. Trebitsch asserts: "That, with my thinking, I make and *must* make all the 'secondary' minds into my enemies has long been evident to me!" Trebitsch, *Drei Vorträge mit Zwischenstücken* (Berlin: Borngräber Verlag, 1917), 110.

55. Freud, *Jokes and their Relation to the Unconscious*, trans. James Strachey, in collaboration with Anna Freud (New York: W. W. Norton, 1960), 47.

56. Trebitsch expresses his doubts regarding the healing powers of psychoanalysis as follows: "In this sphere of diseased city dwellers, there enters now that new psychoanalytical science of a decidedly Jewish provenance which thinks that it can hunt down the 'trauma' of eroticism in the most secret hideouts to treat even the diseased mind to a recovery with the same operation" (*Geist und Judentum*, 151). Trebitsch recalls here the venomous Viennese satirist Karl Kraus (also accused of being a Jewish anti-Semite) who mocked psychoanalysis mercilessly. To wit: "Psychoanalysis is the disease of emancipated Jews; the religious ones are satisfied with diabetes." See Thomas Szasz, *Anti-Freud: Karl Kraus's Criticism of Psychoanalysis and Psychiatry* (Syracuse, NY: Syracuse University Press, 1990), 103.

57. *Geist und Judentum*, 73–74. He writes: "The various studies of the joke have never promoted a substantial exploration of the specifically Jewish joke until this day. However, this seems in no way surprising when one considers that all the transmissions and results of a basic mental system could hardly be grasped if this basic system had not been captured precisely as of yet!"

58. See Jeffrey Mehlman, "How to Read Freud on Jokes: The Critic as Schadchen," *New Literary History* 6, no. 2 (1975): 439–461.

59. The punch line of "*Fertige Sach*'" can be translated in a number of idioms: closed case, accomplished fact, finished product, or done deal.

60. Freud, *Jokes*, 62–63. While the punchlines and closure are identical, the devilish details are a little different in Freud's shorter version: "The would-be bridegroom complained that the bride had one leg shorter than the other and limped. The Schadchen contradicted him: 'You're wrong. Suppose you marry a

woman with healthy, straight limbs! What do you gain from it? You never have a day's security that she won't fall down, break a leg and afterwards be lame all her life. And think of the suffering then, the agitation, and the doctor's bill! But if you take *this* one, that can't happen to you. Here you have a *fait accompli.*'"

61. Freud, 63.

62. Freud, 62.

63. This "as if" universe also guides the comedy of the world of Isaac Bashevis Singer's *Gimpel the Fool*. See Ruth Wisse, *The Schlemiel as Modern Hero* (Chicago: University of Chicago, 1971), 60–65.

64. For a literary-critical discussion of the "proper" place of comic discourse in and to the second degree, see Gérard Genette, *Palimpsestes: La Littératur au Second Degre* (Paris: Editions du Seuil, 1982).

65. J. G. Burg provides an explanation of this internationalizing phenomenon of the Jewish joke in the "Beginnwort" to his *Jüdische Anekdotiade* (Munich: Ederer, 1977), 16. Burg writes: "He actually exists as the particular species of Jewish commercial traveler who not only carries his goods but also the intellectual and spiritual heritage of his people from place to place, from country to country, and from continent to continent, whereby the Jewish joke became international like the joke of no other people—equally understood in all countries and of equal validity. . . . On tiring rail journeys and in the long evenings in small hotels where the travelers met, they shortened the time with jokes, and whereby there already followed from this situation almost inevitably the famous opening: 'Two Jews meet' . . ."

66. This is also the gist of the jest in the early Berliner version that appeared under the ironic title of *"Der feine Pole"* in the anonymous compilation *Für Schnorrer und Kitzinim: Sammlung gediegener jüdischer Witze und Anekdoten* (Berlin: Verlag von Cassirer und Danziger, 1887), 57–58. For a discussion of the place of Eastern Jews in the Western mind, see Steven E. Aschheim, *Brothers and Strangers: The East European Jew in German and German Jewish Consciousness, 1880–1923* (Madison: University of Wisconsin Press, 1982). Aschheim discusses Trebitsch's "racist ideas" and his framing of the Eastern European Jews as "poisonous creatures" infecting the German spirit on page 226.

67. This is close to the interpretation of the joke by the psychoanalyst Theodor Reik in *Jewish Wit* (New York: Gamut Press, 1962), 58–59, 188–190. Reik comments: "Eastern European Jewish intimacy, stemming from the high moral density of 'life-is-with-people' in the shtetl, excludes 'respect.'" For a sociological analysis, see Mark Zborowski and Elizabeth Herzog, *Life Is with People: The Jewish Shtetl of Eastern Europe* (New York: International Universities Press, 1952).

68. Freud, *Jokes*, 112.

69. See also the excellent analysis of John Murray Cuddihy, *The Ordeal of Civility: Freud, Marx, Levi-Strauss and the Jewish Struggle with Modernity* (New York: Dell Publishing, 1974). Cuddihy takes this joke to be a sociological parable for the problematic process of Jewish assimilation and their passage into European

civil society in the wake of ghetto life. For Cuddihy, this joke serves both as a model for the assimilation process (i.e., the attempt of the Jew to look respectable in the presence of the gentleman) and its breakdown in the triumph of the old intimate behavior patterns of shtetl life (the sigh of relief that is breathed and the removal of the mask of civility in the recognition of a shared identification). Cuddihy offers this heavily symbolic reading: "All the elements are here: the public, social place (a train); the identification of the Jew as an *Ostjude* (Galician); the relaxed, 'regressive' behavior (misbehavior) in a public place; the advent of the 'gentleman' stranger as the modernizing West ('in modern dress'); the 'pose' of good manners struck, and, finally, the polite intrusion: 'Excuse me . . .' The sudden disclosure of a shared ethnicity reconstitutes the premodern 'Gemeinschaft' which knew no 'public places' with their 'situational proprieties,' which encountered no strangers, which made no private-public cleavage" (22).

70. Anonymous, "*Der jüdische Selbsthass und Weiberverachtung: Otto Weininger und Arthur Trebitsch*" ["Jewish self-hatred and the contempt of women: Otto Weininger and Arthur Trebitsch"], in *Otto Weininger: Werk und Wirkung*, ed Jacques Le Rider und Norbert Leser (Vienna: Österreichischer Bundesverlag, 1984), 123–134. For another study about the diffusion of Weininger in the work of Trebitsch and Lanz von Liebenfels, see András Gerö, *Neither Woman Nor Jew: The Confluence of Prejudices in the Austro-Hungarian Monarchy at the Turn of the Century* (Boulder, CO: East European Monographs, 2010), chap. 5. Hamann, *Hitler's Vienna*, also refers to Trebitsch's *Geist und Judentum* as "longwinded variations on Weininger's argument but hardly anything new" (231).

71. Weininger, *Geschlecht und Charakter*, 436.

72. Weininger, 435. For the English translation, see *Sex and Character*, trans. from the 6th German ed. (London: William Heinemann, 1906), 319.

73. Weininger, *Sex and Character*, 318.

74. Elliott Oring, "Sigmund Freud's Jewish Joke Book," in *Engaging Humor* (Urbana: University of Illinois Press, 2003). Interestingly, Oring argues that Freud (whether unconsciously or not) also adopted part of Weininger's discourse: "Weininger's anti-Semitic claims about Jews find some echo in *Jokes and their Relation to the Unconscious*" (121) and "Freud's presentation of Jewish jokes in *Jokes and their Relation to the Unconscious* recapitulates the charges brought against the Jews by Otto Weininger and others" (126).

75. Anonymous, "*Der jüdische Selbsthass*," 125.

76. Weininger, *Geschlecht und Charakter*, 442–443.

77. This is also the assessment of one of Trebitsch's proponents who is sensitive to his plight to escape the clutches of *Morbus judaicus* (the Jewish disease): "Trebitsch demonstrates it in his fellow Jew Otto Weininger, but it seems that he himself is afflicted with it—because the book is a single cry of pain, it is the harrowing flight of a primary spirit that seeks to wrest himself from the forced torments of a secondary inheritance." See Bernhard Funck, *Morbus judaicus. Primärer und sekundärer Geist nach Arthur Trebitsch's "Geist und Judentum"* (Munich: Birckingen Verlag, 1921), 16.

78. For a discussion of this point, see R. M. Stephenson, "Conflict and Control Function of Humor," *American Journal of Sociology* 56, no. 6 (1951): 569–574.

79. Weininger, *Geschlecht und Charakter*, 438.

80. At another point in the text, Trebitsch restates the dichotomy and shows how the spirit of the Jewish joke accompanies the evil spirit of skepticism: "But this doubting, sneering, and joking [*Bewitzeln*] about all 'questions' never leads to true despair (for which he is much too — 'clever'), but of course the profound happiness of faith in something particular can never arise seeing how secondary mobile persons sit on the fence before everything in the world that is exposed to them" (*Geist und Judentum*, 120).

81. For a wide variety of excellent *Apikorsim* jokes, see one of the swan songs of Jewish joke books in Central Europe — Jonas Kreppel, *Wie der Jude Lacht: Anthologie jüdischer Witze, Satiren, Anekdoten, Humoresken, Aphorismen. Ein Beitrag zur Psychologie des jüdischen Witzes und zur jüdischen Volkskunde* (Vienna: Verlag "Das Buch," 1933), 4, 40, and 62–63.

82. Manuel Schnitzer, *Rabbi Lach*, 151–152.

83. For a fuller exposition of this joking genre, see the chapter on the wit of the "Am Ha-Aretz" in Pinchas Jacob Kohn, *Rabbinischer Humor aus alter und neuer Zeit: eine Sammlung von Anekdoten und "guten Wörtchen"* (Frankfurt am Main: J. Kaufmann, 1930).

84. Henry Wassermann has much to say on this point in his essay on illustrated humor: "The *Fliegende* interpreted the common opinion that Mammon was the deity worshiped by Jews by granting them a virtual monopoly in humorous items concerned with banking and the stock exchange, with buying and selling in all forms. . . . Not all cartoons dealing with the making of money contained Jewish protagonists, but an overwhelming majority of those in which making money was equated with dishonesty did contain them" ("*Fliegende Blätter*," 125).

85. The same joke occurs in practically the same format in Moszkowski, "*Auserwählte Volk*"*s Witze*, in the chapter "*Schlagfertig und Spitzfindig*" (Quick-witted and hair-splitting), 82–83. Agent: "I urge you — buy the house — an inexpensive, nice house, very close to the Dniester." — "Well, what have I heard about the Dniester?" Agent: "That it is indeed a huge river. Do you want to have a nice view — the Dniester flows right in front of the balcony. Do you want to wash your linen — you have the Dniester right there. Do you want to swim or skate in the winter — You have the Dniester in the same way." — "And if ice comes and inundates me? Then the Dniester tears my whole house away!" Agent (in eagerness): "Have you any idea of the distance — where is the house, and where is the Dniester?"

86. See Richard Raskin, *Life Is Like a Glass of Tea: Studies of Classic Jewish Jokes* (Philadelphia: Jewish Publication Society, 1992), 190–193.

87. Stéphane Moses, "*Zur Frage des Gesetzes: Gershom Scholems Kafka-Bild*" ["On the Question of the Law: Gershom Scholem's Image of Kafka"], in *Kafka und das Judentum*, ed. Karl Erich Grözinger and H. D. Zimmerman (Frankfurt am Main: Athenänum Jüdischer Verlag, 1987), 14–15.

88. For a discussion of the links between Jewish wit and the relativization of value, see Alexander Moszkowski, "Die Philosophie des jüdischen Witzes," in *Der Jüdische Witz und seine Philosophie* (Berlin: Dr. Eysler, 1922), 13–15. Note also Moszkowski's personal relationship with Albert Einstein and the fact that he would publish his conversations with the Jewish genius of relativity theory. See *Einstein: Einblicke in seine Gedankenwelt — Gemeinverständliche Betrachtungen über die Relativitätstheorie und ein neues Weltsystem* (Hamburg: Hoffmann und Campe, 1921), translated by Henry L. Brose as *Einstein the Searcher* (New York: E. P. Dutton, 1922).

89. Lacan, *Ego in Freud's Theory*, 234. Freud also examined this joke as "a piece of faulty reasoning" but substituted cake and liquor for the Viennese apple strudel and ice cream. In contrast to Trebitsch's anti-Semitic ideological agenda, Freud does not refer to this joke as Jewish in character. See Freud, *Jokes*, 60.

90. But one cannot assume that this joke is always anti-Semitic in intent. It is narrated appreciatively in praise of the wise guy tactics of Simon Citron in roughly the same version in the chapter entitled "*Koppchen*" (Brains) in Moszkowski, "*Auserwählte Volk*"*s Witze*, 134: "Simon Citron gets himself an apple pie in the pastry shop, but sends it back and chooses a liqueur instead. After he savored it, he rises to go without the recommended farewell. The pastry chef calls after him. 'You, sir, you have not yet paid for the liqueur!' 'I have indeed returned the apple pie to you.' 'Which you had not paid for!' 'Well, have I eaten that?'"

91. Trebitsch poses this analogy as follows: "*Religion oder Rasse, Gefrorenes oder Apfelstrudel!*" [Religion or race, ice cream or apple strudel!"] (211).

92. In Trebitsch's own life, religion and race form a dueling dualism and constitute a double bind. On the one hand, the scientist believes that one's psyche is a necessary expression of racial character. Yet somehow, like in some miraculous immaculate conception narrative, he has managed to escape this racial burden through a religious conversion process. This double bind (and personal loophole) helps to illuminate Trebitsch's contradictory views about the malleability or permanence of racial characteristics. Therefore, a study focusing on the shifts and vacillations in Trebitsch's own conflicted views about race and racial biology would afford a number of parallels with my discussion here.

## 2. Of Caricatures, Jokes, and Anti-Semitism: The Case of Eduard Fuchs

Unless otherwise noted, all translations from the German are mine.

1. Werner Hofmann, "Comic Art and Caricature," in *Encyclopedia of World Art* (New York: McGraw-Hill, 1958), 3:763. The full sentence reads: "E. Fuchs examined the cultural role of caricature which he regarded as a form of illustrated social history."

2. Walter Benjamin, "Eduard Fuchs: Collector and Historian," trans. Knut Tarnowski, in *New German Critique*, no. 5 (Spring 1975): 36. It was originally edited by Max Horkheimer and published as "Eduard Fuchs, der Sammler und

der Historiker," *Zeitschrift fur Sozialforschung*, no. 6 (1937): 346–381. Benjamin also credits Fuchs with the publication of the "first historical works illustrated with documentary pictures" (31).

3. Eduard Fuchs, *Die Karikatur der europäischen Völker vom Altertum zur Neuzeit* [Caricatures of European peoples from antiquity to modern times] (Berlin: A. Hofmann and Company, 1902). Fuchs quickly followed up this successful publication with a second volume in the following year that looked at the caricatures of European peoples from 1848 to the present.

4. Benjamin, "Collector and Historian," 31.

5. Benjamin, 27.

6. Benjamin, 38.

7. Benjamin, 30, 31.

8. Benjamin, 47. The reference to Balzac recalls specifically the figure of the art collector in his novella *Le Cousin Pons* (1847).

9. Eduard Fuchs, *Die Juden in der Karikatur: Ein Beitrag zur Kulturgeschichte* (Munich: Albert Langen Verlag, 1921). Hereafter cited in text by page number in parentheses. The first printing of the book was 12,000 copies and it was reprinted in 1928 with a run of 3,000 copies. Fuchs's connection to this particular publishing house was no accident; caricature was central to Albert Langen who was founder and editor of the most important German journal for illustrated humor and critical caricature at the turn of the century — *Simplicissimus* — until his unexpected death in 1908.

10. See Liliane Weissberg, "Eduard Fuchs und die Ökonomie der Karikatur," in *Babylon* 20 (2002): 113–128. Weissberg refers to the text only once when she asks rhetorically at the end of this provocative essay about the "Jewish" origins of caricature: "Is caricature — creative and abstract — therefore a Jewish art, the final product of a 'Jewish self-irony'?" (126). See also Micha Brumlik, *Innerlich beschnittene Juden: Zu Eduard Fuchs' Die Juden in der Karikatur* [Inwardly circumcised Jews] (Hamburg: KVV konkret, 2012). The title is derived from Karl Marx's pejorative description of capitalists in *Das Kapital*. A review of Brumlik's footnotes demonstrates that he cites the last chapter of Fuchs's book only once but not in the context of the subject of Jewish self-irony.

11. Karl Marx, "On the Jewish Question" ("Zur Judenfrage") was written in the fall of 1843 and published in Paris in February 1844 in the *Deutsch-Französische Jahrbücher*. Werner Sombart, *Die Juden in das Wirtschaftsleben* (Leipzig: Verlag von Duncker and Humblot, 1911), translated in abbreviated form by M. Epstein as *The Jews and Modern Capitalism* (New York: E. P. Dutton, 1913).

12. Weissberg, "Eduard Fuchs," 122.

13. Sombart, *Jews and Modern Capitalism*, 149; translation modified. The chapter is entitled "The Significance of the Jewish Religion in Economic Life."

14. Weissberg, "Eduard Fuchs," 124. Fuchs invokes Sombart's book and stresses its crucial importance quite early: "For the solution of this fundamental problem, there is to my knowledge only one major and significant contribution until now, namely the book by Werner Sombart" (7–8).

15. This reading goes against the grain of Thomas Huonker's biography of Fuchs, *Revolution Moral und Kunst, Eduard Fuchs: Leben und Werk* (Zurich: Limmat Verlag Genossenschaft, 1985). Huonker entitles the section of the book that reviews *Jews in Caricature*—"Gegen den Judenhass" ("Against the hatred of the Jews") (491). This title could lead the reader to the erroneous belief that Fuchs was always on the philo-Semitic side of the fence when dealing with the Jews in caricature.

16. Brumlik, *Innerlich beschnittene Juden*, 65. He continues: "Eduard Fuchs's work is pervaded by a contradiction almost too tragic to be named that is typical in some ways of a 'classic leftist' opinion regarding anti-Semitism. Tied to the period of the young Karl Marx's incorrect and furthermore historically uninformed reduction of Jews and Judaism to the monetary economy, he seeks not only to fight against reactionary and nationalist anti-Semitic agitation in Germany but also to adhere to the folk-psychological, even racist presuppositions of his informants, Marx and Sombart."

17. Sander L. Gilman, "'Jewish Humour' and the Terms by Which Jews and Muslims Join Western Civilization," in *Leo Baeck Institute Year Book* 57 (2012): 63.

18. Freud wrote that he did "not know whether there are many other instances of a people making fun to such a degree of its own character." See Freud *Jokes and their Relation to the Unconscious*, trans. James Strachey, in collaboration with Anna Freud (New York: W. W. Norton, 1960), 111–112.

19. Benjamin also makes this point at the beginning of section 5 of his "Eduard Fuchs" essay: "Fuchs never tires of stressing the value of caricature as a source, as authority. 'Truth lies in the extreme,' he occasionally remarks" (40).

20. Fuchs already speaks about caricature as a source for the truth of the past in the book's foreword where he aligns his study of the Jews in caricature to the study of woman in caricature and thereby pairs these two discriminated minorities as subjects of visual satire: "I happened into this book along my way, just like in my earlier work, *Die Frau in der Karikatur*. Besides the women's question, the Jewish question is one of the most striking areas of specialization in the caricature of all times and peoples. Therefore, I had to write this book one day after I had recognized and proclaimed caricature as an important source of truth for the historical exploration of the past" (iii).

21. Fuchs, *Karikatur der europäischen Völker* (1902), 484.

22. The invocation of Heine at the end of this excerpt recalls something to which Benjamin alluded in his essay that puts Fuchs on the side of (Jewish/French) *Witz* over and against German *Humor*. In this way, Benjamin also takes up the rhetoric of the *Judenwitz* indirectly: "He compares the spirited mockery of the French with the clumsy ridicule of the Germans. He compares Heine with those who remained at home" ("Collector and Historian," 45).

23. Heinrich von Treitschke, *Deutsche Geschichte im Neunzehnten Jahrhundert: Bis zur Julirevolution* (Leipzig: Verlag von S. Hirzel, 1885), 704.

24. Gilman, *Jewish Self-Hatred*, 214.

25. Von Treitschke, *Deutsche Geschichte*, 704.

26. Von Treitschke, 704.

27. On the topic of the "chosen people," Alexander Moszkowski did not follow Fuchs and wrote respectfully of the German nationalist historian in the introduction ("Zum Geleit") of his Jewish joke compilation whose punning and self-mocking title pokes fun at the state of divine election. See Moszkowski, *"Auserwählte Volk"s Witze: 399 Juwelen aus dem jüdischen Kronschatz* (Berlin: Verlag der Lustigen Blätter, 1911), 5. Moszkowski writes: "Heinrich von Treitschke, who spoke out sharply against Israel (but never disrespectfully) was obliged to say: There are no dumb Jews! To be more precise, these words should read: There are none who are witless."

28. Eduard Engel, *Deutsche Stilkunst* (Vienna: F. Tempsky, 1911), 370–377.

29. Curiously, Fuchs refers to him as Fritz in a peculiar Freudian slip as he confuses Engel's first name with that other German-Jewish language philosopher Fritz Mauthner who took up some of these same complex issues.

30. Engel, *Deutsche Stilkunst*, 372.

31. Moszkowski's important lecture on the philosophy of the Jewish joke at the Association for Jewish History and Literature in Berlin was reported in the *Jüdisch-liberale Zeitung* in Breslau (January 14, 1921). The journalist J. P. K. summarized the author's humanist strategy: "Alexander Moszkowski praises the thoughtful shrewdness of Jewish humor and provides examples that all the philosophical problems of humanity have experienced some lightning-like illumination in Jewish wit" (4). It was later published as the introduction to *Der jüdische Witz und seine Philosophie* (Berlin: Dr. Eysler, 1922).

32. Eduard Engel, *Sprich Deutsch! Ein Buch zur Entwelschung* (Leipzig: Hesse and Becker, 1917).

33. See Gilman, *Jewish Self-Hatred*, 226. As Gilman states, "*Speak German!* Also contained an attack on other forms of bad German, including Yiddish and *mauscheln*."

34. Gilman, 226.

35. Fuchs reproduces the covers of a few of these books that mocked the Jews mercilessly for the reader's amusement. However, the case of Itzig Feitel Stern demonstrates the instability of the borders dividing anti-Semitism and Jewish self-irony. On the surface, it appeared that these texts were derived from the pen of a Jewish self-ironist, or even, in the extreme, a Jewish self-hater. Fuchs is uncertain about the authenticity of Stern the author, but he also thinks he might have been Jewish too: "By the way, a Jewish man of letters really could have been lurking behind this pseudonym" (220). From other sources, we learn this was the pseudonym for a German lawyer from Nuremberg by the name of Friedrich Freiherr von Holzschuher, who simulated the role of Jewish author so well that he was able to disseminate his perfectly disguised anti-Semitic propaganda with great success. See, for example, Edmund Edel, *Der Witz der Juden* (Berlin: Louis Lamm, 1909), 14.

36. One sees the readymade response of political Zionism and the demand for the exercise of Jewish national sovereignty when confronted with Fuchs's positing of self-derisive Jewish humor as the response of a minority culture to their ongoing oppression and social humiliation.

37. The Berlin-born psychoanalyst Martin Grotjahn described Jewish self-ridicule as an inward-turned weapon that constitutes a "victory by defeat" (32). "One can almost see how a Jewish man carefully and cautiously takes a sharp dagger out of his enemies' hands, sharpens it so it can split a hair in mid-air, polishes it so it can shine brightly, stabs himself with it, then returns it gallantly to the anti-Semite with the silent reproach: Now see whether you can do half so well. . . . It is as the Jew tells his enemies: You do not need to attack us. We can do that ourselves — even better." Grotjahn, *Beyond Laughter* (New York: Blakiston Division, 1957), 22–23. Incidentally, Grotjahn emigrated to the United States with his Jewish spouse Etelka Grosz in 1937.

38. Following Sombart, Fuchs's language partakes of the search for essences on the subject of Jewish abstract thought and intellectualism: "[T]he Jews are predestined by nature to the abstract activity of the monetary economy. That is really the only reasonable conclusion to draw. In contrast to us Northerners, the Jews are in fact of a purely abstract nature. Therein is the specific essence of their psyche — they are pronounced intellectuals. The ultimate cause of this specific intellectual disposition lies in their origin and in their descent, meaning that it is in the blood of the Jews" (41–42). Even if expressed in a more colloquial way, Fuchs's introduction of the language of essentialist attributes that ends in blood lines demonstrates a rhetoric quite at odds with classic Marxist class analysis and economic anti-Semitism. This excerpt offers a return of the racially repressed in *Die Juden in der Karikatur*. This is why Weissberg also sees a racist strand of anti-Semitism already operative in Fuchs's project to the extent that the book reads "the Jews as (a) caricature" and this assumption leads to "the confirmation of the 'Nordic essence'" as its unconscious norm and ideal (Weissberg, "Eduard Fuchs," 126).

39. When Sombart discusses the characteristic of "Jewish intellectuality" and juxtaposes it with Gentile "brute force," he does so with the help of old Polish Jewish witticisms: "The Jews were quite alive to their predominant quality and always recognized that there was a great gulf between their intellectuality and the brute force of their neighbors. One or two sayings popular among Polish Jews express the contrast with striking humour [*mit schlagendem Witz*] when they say: 'God help a man against a Gentile hand [*gojische Hand*] and a Jewish head [*judisch Kopp*]' and 'Heaven protect us against Jewish *mo'och* [brains] and Gentile *koach* [physical force].' *Mooch v. Koach* — that is the Jewish problem in a nutshell [*diese Worte enthalten im Grunde die ganze Judenfrage*]. It ought to be the motto of this book" (Sombart, *Die Juden in das Wirtschaftsleben*, 315). Similar contrasts can be seen in Erich Kahler (see chapter 5).

40. Jay Geller, *The Other Jewish Question: Identifying the Jew and Making Sense of Modernity* (New York: Fordham University Press, 2011), 271. Geller then reviews Hans Blüher's *Secessio Judaica* (1922) as a good example of an anti-Semitic conflation of Jews and mimicry. See Blüher's racialist framing of the question: "The Jews are the only people who practices mimicry. . . . Jewish mimicry is anchored in the destiny of the race, in the idea of Judea." Steven E. Aschheim also calls attention

to the views of this "radical anti-Semite" and his "theatrical ontology"; see Aschheim, "Reflections on Theatricality, Identity and the Modern Jewish Experience," in *Jews and the Making of the Modern German Theatre*, ed. Jeanette R. Malkin and Freddie Rokem (Des Moines: University of Iowa Press, 2010), 27.

41. A celebrated comedy dealing with the Jewish-American performance of identity is set in the same era of the roaring twenties. Woody Allen's classic film mockumentary *Zelig* (1983) tells the story of the life of the "human chameleon" Leonard Zelig (played by Allen) who excels in both the Jewish art of mimicry as well as self-ironic humor. It is also a relevant point for this project that Zelig goes to work for the Nazis before World War II. Thanks to Steven Aschheim for reminding me of this extremely relevant Jewish-American film comedy reference.

42. Aschheim, "Reflections," 22. He later recalls, "The Jew was portrayed in varying degrees of severity, as a poseur, a mime, a dissimulator par excellence" in the rhetoric of "anti-Jewish resistance" (23).

43. Sombart, *Jews in Modern Capitalism*, 327.

44. This naïve line of thinking inhabits Fuchs's reading of a comic strip by Caran d'Ache entitled *Die Judenfrage* (1898) that enforces the negative Jewish stereotypes of money-grubbing and greed. Fuchs comments, "In quiet times, the witty chauvinist Caran d'Ache glosses the Jewish Question in such an ingenious manner that even the most sensitive Jew can get enjoyment out of it." While reproduced in *Die Juden in der Karikatur* (221), Fuchs also discusses this same comic strip in *Die Karikatur der europaischen Völker vom Jahre 1848 bis zur Gegenwart* (Berlin: Hofmann, 1903), 2:380.

45. Fuchs's text echoes Sigmund Freud's assessment that the Jews recognized their virtues as well as their faults: "Jewish jokes which originate from Jews [. . .] know their real faults as well as the connection between them and their good qualities" (*Jokes*, 111).

46. For instance, one thinks of the pseudonymous Jewish author Flaneur who severely criticized "The Anti-Semitic Herrnfeld Brothers" in an article published in *Die Standarte* 2, no. 44 (August 13, 1908) and reprinted in *Die Jüdische Rundschau* on August 28. The reviewer concludes that the chairman of the Jewish community "should be assured that no anti-Semitic hooligans [*Radauantisemitismus*] have ever hurt the Jewish cause more than Mssrs. Armin and Donat Herrnfeld have in their fragrant Temple of the Muses." The article has been translated into English at the Film Portal website, http://www.filmportal.de/material/die-juedische-rundschau-on-the-herrnfeld-theatre. The Filmportal.de website includes an entire section devoted to the theme of Jewish Humor and anti-Semitism at http://www.filmportal.de/thema/juedischer-humor-und-antisemitismus. Fuchs explicitly referred to and singled out the Herrnfeld Theater as an example of Jewish self-irony: "The most well-known examples of literary self-irony are the Jewish farces [*Possen*], which one encountered for decades in various Jewish theaters in New York. Vienna, Budapest, Berlin (Herrnfeld Theater), and other places. But these are all very coarse examples. They mostly pursued the purpose of money making alone with crude methods" (308–

309). While Fuchs does not illuminate further why these theatrical pieces are coarse and crude, one of them at the very least was the blurring of the boundaries between Jewish self-irony and anti-Semitic rhetoric as confirmed by the article condemning the Brothers Herrnfeld. Steven E. Aschheim also comments on this point within the context of the Brothers Herrnfeld Theater: "Some argued that, for both creators and consumers, such German Jewish self-satire disclosed a pathological internalization of the worst anti-Semitic stereotypes" ("Reflections," 33).

47. Adolf Jellinek, *Der jüdische Stamm in nichtjüdischen Sprichwoertern* (Vienna: Bermann and Altmann, 1881). Chapter 24 is devoted to the subject of Jewish jokes (87–90). Werner Sombart also quotes from Jellinek in chapter 12 on the topic of Jewish characteristics.

48. Jellinek, 87–88. Jellinek's commentary also provides Fuchs with other ideas about the Jews that he does not reference properly. When Fuchs frames the Jew as actor who is striving for applause and approval in a popular stereotype, he borrows from Rabbi Jellinek's language directly: "In this way, the Jew wants to bring to light his intellectual superiority. The Jew is in fact the born actor as well. The actor is hungry for applause. How the audience judges him and his wit (*Esprit*), that is the main thing. It is this way for the Jew too. The applause is for many the indispensable elixir of life" (306).

49. One example from Jellinek is directed against women and deals with aesthetic judgment. It plays on the close relationship between two German words divided only by an umlaut: "This is a beautiful [*schönes*] maiden and, for so long already [*so lange schon*], that she is therefore 'ugly' [*mies*]" (88).

50. Franz Mehring was Marx's biographer, Socialist party historian, and literary critic. Fuchs served as the executor of Mehring's literary estate, the co-editor of his collected works, and as the author of the introduction to Mehring's biography of Marx. Robert S. Wistrich discusses Mehring as an exemplar of "the Socialist ambiguity towards Jews." According to Wistrich, "[This ambiguity] derived from the long-standing anti-Liberalism in the Party and expressed itself in a bizarre campaign against philosemitism in the 1890's. The leading exponent of this line of thought was Franz Mehring, a highly regarded journalist and historian on the Left wing of the *Sozialdemokratische Partei Deutschlands* (SPD) whose views on the 'Jewish Question' were strongly influenced by Marx. Mehring denounced liberal philosemitism as a defense of capitalist privileges, as a hypocritical whitewash of rich Jews." See "Socialism and Judeophobia—Antisemitism in Europe before 1914," in *Leo Baeck Institute Yearbook* (1992) 37, no. 1: 139. Wistrich traces the ambivalent position of the Social Democratic Party in relation to anti-Semitism in general in his comprehensive study, *Socialism and the Jews: The Dilemmas of Assimilation in Germany and Austria-Hungary* (Rutherford, NJ: Farleigh Dickinson University Press, 1982).

51. The original German text reads: "Welches ist der weltliche Kultus des Juden? Der Schacher. Welches ist sein weltlicher Gott? Das Geld." See Karl Marx, *Zur Judenfrage*, ed. Stefan Grossmann (Berlin: Ernst Rowohlt Verlag, 1919), 42.

52. Marx, 49. The original German text reads: "Die gesellschaftliche Emanzipation des Juden ist die Emanzipation der Gessellschaft von Judentum."

53. Sombart, "The Jewish Aptitude for Capitalism," in *Die Juden in das Wirtschaftsleben*, 223. For the English version, see *The Jews and Modern Capitalism*, 133.

54. The image is given prominence in the book with a large color fold-out spread between pages 120 and 121.

55. Fuchs, *Die Karikatur der europaischen Völker*, 398.

56. Czech artist Karel Relink's anti-Semitic illustration and direct quotation in *Der Jude nach der Talmud* (1926) deploys the same motifs — a grotesque top-hatted capitalist with his claws wrapped around the world whose financial power has toppled the crown that is falling off the globe.

57. Sergei Nilus, *Le Peril Juif: Les Protocols des Sages de Sion* (Paris: Société d'edition de propaganda françaises, 1937).

58. See Sander L. Gilman, *Difference and Pathology: Stereotypes of Sexuality, Race and Madness* (Ithaca, NY: Cornell University Press, 1985), 29–35.

59. Immanuel Olsvanger, *Rosinkess mit Mandlen: Aus der Volksliteratur der Ostjuden* (Basel: Verlag der Schweizerischen Gesellschaft für Volkskunde, 1920). For the German translation, see Präger and Schmitz, eds., *Jüdische Schwänke* (Vienna: R. Löwit, 1928).

60. Ruth Wisse, *No Joke: Making Jewish Humor* (Princeton, NJ: Princeton University Press, 2013), 4. Note that the title of Wisse's book performs this same gesture.

61. "E jüdischer Witz Mit e jüddisch Akzent: Was e Goi nicht versteht Und e Jüd immer schon kennt." The attribution to Moszkowski is found in Salcia Landmann, *Der jüdische Witz* (Olten: Walter Verlag, 1962), 645. I will return to her retelling of both the abbreviated and full-length versions of this joke after the Holocaust in chapter 6.

62. In reciting this one-liner regarding German incomprehension of the Jewish joke, Fuchs recalls a similar statement made by Treitschke about the rise of the Jewish satirical style (e.g., Heine, Saphir, and Börne) and the discourse of the *Judenwitz* in German literature in the nineteenth century that was "considered witty, shameless, without any reverence for the Fatherland." According to Treitschke, "The Germans understood but little of the joke [*Scherz*], or at least of the Oriental wisecrack [*orientalische Witzelei*]; they took some insult that was not meant as nasty in all seriousness." In contrast to later Nazi rhetoric, this last point tones down Treitschke's anti-Semitic analysis to some degree. See Treitschke, *Deutsche Geschichte im Neunzehnten Jahrhundert*, 704. The German lack of understanding of Jewish wit also plays an important part in Erich Kahler's interpretation of German-Jewish intercultural breakdown reviewed in chapter 4.

63. See also the infamous article by the German-Jewish journalist Cheskel Zwi Klötzel, "Das grosse Hassen," *Janus* 2, no. 2 (1912/1913): 57–60. Anti-Semites mobilized this article because of its avowal of a Jewish hatred of all things non-

Jewish. Nevertheless, Klötzel insists "the word 'Goy' for a Jew, which is no way an insult, represents a definite and unmistakable line of demarcation."

64. Fuchs refers here to Alexander Moszkowski, *Die jüdische Kiste: 399 Juwelen echt gefaßt; Die Unsterbliche Kiste*, Zweiter Teil (Berlin: Verlag der lustigen Blätter, 1911).

65. M. Nuél [Manuel Schnitzer], *Das Buch des jüdischen Witze* (Berlin: Hesperus, 1907). The baptism joke recounted and interpreted by Fuchs is on pages 59 and 60.

66. Fuchs was listed in the appendix of Siegfried Katznelson, *Juden im Deutschen Kulturbereich* (Berlin: Juedischer Verlag, 1934/1959) under the category of "Nichtjuden, die für Juden gehalten [non-Jews, who were taken for Jews]" with a caption explaining that he had a "jüdisch klingender Name [Jewish-sounding name]." See Weissberg, "Eduard Fuchs und die Ökonomie der Karikatur," 123. As she relates: "Fuchs, who married a Jewish woman from an established Berlin family in 1920 — thus, one year before the publication of his book, draws a direct line between the description of a definite Jewish essence and an anti-Semitic prejudice." To correct the record slightly, Fuchs married Grete Alsberg who hailed from a wealthy Jewish family who owned the Gebr. Alsberg AG department store in Munich (369). She joined her husband in exile in Paris upon the Nazi's assumption of power in 1933. Most of her relatives, however, died in the Holocaust. I have gleaned this information from the informative biography of Ulrich Weitz, *Der Mann in Schatten: Edward Fuchs* (Berlin: Karl Dietz Verlag, 2014).

67. Nuél, *Das Buch des jüdischen Witze*, 9. Schnitzer's book was also featured in the anonymous critical review of the Herrnfeld Theater where it serves as a positive example of Jewish self-irony in contrast to the Brothers' "hateful" anti-Semitism: "Even a spoof on Jewry can be harmless, self-irony and persiflage being deep-seated features of the Jewish character; and all the delightfully corny jokes (which the excellent Manuel Schnitzer has now collected in two superb volumes) generally involve harmless ribbing of our own character and our own mistakes. But what is so disturbing over on the Kommandantenstrasse is the hateful one-sidedness with which Jews as a whole are presented as wretches and cretins" (Flaneur, "Anti-Semitic Herrnfeld Brothers").

68. Gilman, *Jewish Self-Hatred*, 254.

69. See Freud, *Jokes*, 81 and *Der Witz*, 87. The translation of this joke is mine. For a more recent discussion of this joke, see Ken Frieden, "Freud, Women, and Jews: Viennese Jokes and Judaic Dream Interpretation," Solomon Goldman Lectures 8 (January 2003), http://works.bepress.com/ken_frieden/36.

70. Freud, *Jokes*, 81. I take issue with James Strachey's insensitive translation of Freud's *"ursprüngliche"* as "primitive" and I have altered it accordingly.

71. Fuchs was well aware of the incestuous relations between tragedy and comedy and between suffering and laughter when it comes to jokes and caricatures. After all, *Die Juden in der Karikatur* begins with "Laughing and crying are equally inseparable from human life" (1). Meanwhile, the second volume of the *Die Karikatur der*

*europäischen Völker* concludes with these poignant philosophical reflections that are aligned to the tradition of thinking about Jewish wit as the transmutation of tears into laughter: "The great tragedy of laugh-making [*Lachenmachens*] has not disappeared from the world. Despairing pessimism and heart-breaking pain about one's own and about the suffering of others will remain the major source of satirical laughter. This is the great tragedy of laughter. Making jokes is a very, very serious thing. Perhaps the most serious . . ." (475).

72. Thomas Huonker confirms Adolf Hitler as the source of the poster in his biography of Fuchs, *Revolution, Moral und Kunst*, 18. Hitler's anti-Semitic poster is reproduced and discussed further in Ulrich Weitz's more recent biography of Fuchs, *Der Mann im Schatten*, 246.

73. With the benefit of hindsight, the fact that there is not one overt mention of race in Fuchs's analysis of the Hitler campaign poster is astounding in its oversight.

74. Kadner, *Rasse und Humor*, 209–210.

75. Bebel is best remembered for his incisive and insightful epigram — "Anti-Semitism is the socialism of fools" (*"Der Antisemitismus ist der Sozialismus der dummen Kerle"*). It is odd that Fuchs mistakenly attributes Bebel's maxim to Wilhelm Liebknecht (80).

76. Bebel shared his views on anti-Semitism at the Social Democratic Party convention of 1893: "Anti-Semitism stems from the resentment of certain middle-class groups which find themselves oppressed by the development of capitalism and which are destined to perish economically as a result of these trends. These groups, however, misinterpret their own situation and therefore do not fight against the capitalist system but against surface phenomena which seem to hurt them most in the competitive struggle: namely Jewish exploiters." *Protokoll uber die Verhandlungen des Parteitages der Sozialdemokratischen Partei Deutschlands*, Köln, 22–28 Oktober 1893, 224.

77. As shown in the Rothschild case study and elsewhere, the disavowal of race as the primary explanatory mechanism for the existence of caricature did not stop Fuchs from asserting his own racial prejudices following Sombart's conceptual lead.

78. See the *New York Times*, June 15, 1921 for two interesting reports on these negotiations — Edwin L. James, "Germany Makes Offer to France," and Cyril Brown, "Rathenau Lionized in Berlin."

79. Eduard Fuchs, *Tang-Plastik: Chinesische Grabkeramik des VII. bis X. Jahrhunderts* (Munich: Albert Langen, 1924), 44. This passage is also cited in Benjamin, "Collector and Historian," 41.

80. As Fuchs recalls, "In the sixteenth century, as is well known, no Christian reviled the Jews more than the baptized Jew Pfefferkorn" (220).

81. Benjamin, "Collector and Historian," 35.

82. Benjamin elaborates on the flaws of cultural history as follows: "For cultural history lacks the destructive element that authenticates both dialectical thought and the experience of the dialectical thinker. Cultural history, to be sure, enlarges the weight of the treasure which accumulates on the back of humanity. Yet cultural

history does not provide the strength to shake off this burden in order to be able to take control of it" (36). Benjamin's comment about the "weight of the treasure" recalls the heavy burden of Fuchs the collector whose valuable and massive art and print collection foreclosed any dialectically "destructive" impulse.

83. For a Yiddish study that focuses on her illustrations of Sholem Aleichem, see Sabine Koller, "Mentshelekh un stsenes: Rachel Szalit-Marcus illustriet Sholem Aleichem," in *Leket: Jewish Studies Today*, ed. Marion Aptroot, Efrat Gal-Ed, Roland Grushka and Simon Neuberg (Düsseldorf: Düsseldorf University Press, 2012): 207–231. Koller reproduces the image in question on page 221. The Motl works were collected in Rachel Szalit-Marcus, *Mentshelekh un stsenes: zekhtsn tseykhenungen tsu Sholem Aleykhems verk Motl Peyse dem khazns yingl* (Berlin: Klal-farlag, 1922). Kerry Wallach also reproduces this image in *Passing Illusions: Jewish Visibility in Weimar Germany* (Ann Arbor: University of Michigan Press, 2017), noting that Fuchs "was among the first to characterize her works as self-mockery" (49).

## 3. Of Watchmen and Comedians: Jewish Jokes and Free Speech in Weimar Germany

Unless otherwise noted, all translations from the German are mine.

1. For a thorough review of the so-called cabaret-combat-campaign of the Centralverein, see Heidelore Riss, "'Unser Kampf gegen das mauschelnde Kabarett': Die *Kabarett-Kampf-Kampagne* des Centralvereins," in *Ansätze zu einer Geschichte des jüdischen Theaters in Berlin 1889–1936* (Frankfurt am Main: Peter Lang, 2000), 161–174. Riss summarizes the accusations: "In the opinion of the Centralverein, the Jewish artists were guilty of anti-Semitic utterances on stage and therefore stirred up anti-Semitic sentiment" (163).

2. Alfred Wiener, "Kabaretts, Witzbücher, heitere Wochenblätter, und die 'judische Witwe': Ein Ernstes Wort von Dr. Albert Wiener," *C.V.-Zeitung*, November 13, 1925.

3. Georg Kaiser, *Die jüdische Witwe: Biblische Komödie* (Berlin: S. Fischer, 1911) offers a comic interpretation of Judith's beheading of Holofernes. It was performed as a play in five acts in the early 1920s.

4. Thus, the relationship between the joke and the question was a regulative one for the watchmen whereas it was a much more open-ended one for the comedians.

5. Ludwig Holländer, "Gegen die Verzerrung des jüdischen Wesens," *C.V.-Zeitung*, April 30, 1926. This translation follows Peter Jelavich, "When are Jewish Jokes No Longer Funny?: Ethnic Humour in Imperial and Republican Berlin," in *The Politics of Humour: Laughter, Inclusion, and Exclusion in the Twentieth Century*, ed. Martina Kessel and Patrick Merziger (Toronto: University of Toronto Press, 2012), 34. I am greatly indebted to Professor Jelavich's publications on the debate over the limits of self-deprecating Jewish humor and the risks of anti-Semitism in Weimar Germany. However, Jelavich does not frame this particular debate in terms of the contrasting roles played by the watchman and the comedian.

6. The complaints against the harm spread by Little Moritz jokes continued with Arthur Schweriner, "Kabaretts und Film — Rückfall ins Unwürdige in Berliner Kabaretts," in *C.V.-Zeitung*, December 9, 1927.

7. Holländer, "Gegen die Verzerrung des jüdischen Wesens."

8. Freud takes up the triangulated method of smut that consists in its classic guise of two men telling (and getting excited by) tendentious jokes of a sexual nature directed at an absent woman. See Sigmund Freud, *Jokes and Their Relation to the Unconscious*, trans. James Strachey, in collaboration with Anna Freud (New York: W. W. Norton, 1960), 97–102.

9. Steven Aschheim has pointed out to me the similarity between Wiener's critique of the problems with Jewish cabaret and historian Walter Laqueur's criticism of the "questionable taste" exercised by Jewish-born and Christian-converted satirist Kurt Tucholsky in his essay, "The Tucholsky Complaint" (78). For Laqueur, the satirist's "indiscriminate" and purely negative criticism of all social and cultural institutions of the Weimar Republic (whether on the left or right) demonstrated a lack of good political judgment. Tucholsky's merciless mockery of the Jewish bourgeois businessman and parvenu figure is found in his character Herr Wendriner who also internalized a degree of anti-Semitism. Tucholsky wrote sixteen of these monologues between 1923 and 1930. See Walter Z. Laqueur, "The Tucholsky Complaint," in *Encounter* (October 1969): 76–80. Tucholsky's book of social criticism and complaints with several montages by John Heartfield was the ironically entitled *Deutschland, Deutschland über alles* (Berlin: Neuer Deutscher Verlag, 1929). Its witty mudslinging was aimed at the German military and patriotism among other targets.

10. Eduard Fuchs, *Die Juden in der Karikatur* (Munich: Albert Langen Verlag, 1921), 304.

11. Wiener, "Kabaretts, Witzbücher, heitere Wochenblätter, und die 'jüdische Witwe,'" *C.V.-Zeitung*, November 13, 1925.

12. Ernst Warlitz, *Lacht Euch Laune!:1000 Witze* (Berlin: Hesse, 1925).

13. Warlitz. For an example of a deceitful and cowardly friend, see Cohn's bad behavior toward Levi when he allows him to receive a second slap in the face instead of defending him against the non-Jewish brute (no. 485, 133). For an example of an immoral Jewish wife: "Kohn comes home and finds his wife with her lover. Kohn grabs his pistol in great excitement and wants to shoot the lover. But Mrs. Kohn covers him with her body and calls out: 'Izzy, you do not want to shoot the father of your children!'" (no. 923, 266). In another joke that Wiener would have found distasteful, a Jew makes his religion an object of haggling when he does not show gratitude for the kindness and charity of a rich coreligionist: "A poor Jew who has no money to buy himself Matzos writes a letter to the dear Lord with the request to send him money so that he can buy himself Matzos. He throws the letter out the window. A banker finds it, allows the Jew to be called to him and says, 'Here are five marks that I am supposed to issue to you on behalf of the dear Lord.' The Jew takes the

money and says: 'He should be struck down. Who knows how much he has earned on the deal!'" (no. 477, 130).

14. See, for example, Ernst Warlitz, *Purpurne Schmerzen* [Purple pains] (Zurich: Rutli Verlag, 1924) for the author's poetry that included a number of poems that are explicitly homoerotic.

15. Warlitz relates here a classic joke that recalls Ernst Simon's definition of the *Betonungswitz* (joke of accentuation) as a genre of Jewish wit derived from the lack of punctuation found in Hebrew. See Ernst Simon, "Zum Problem des Jüdischen Witzes," *Bayerische Israelitische Gemeindezeitung*, no. 20 (October 15, 1928): 314. But such formal and grammatical considerations give way in Wiener's negative analysis of the subject matter of Warlitz's jokes as he focuses instead on the disloyal Jew who seeks to sidestep his patriotic duty and service to the German nation: "'Private Cohen, why should the soldier sacrifice his life for his Fatherland?' asks the Sergeant. 'You are right, Herr Sergeant, why should he sacrifice himself'" (no. 296, 70). Interestingly, Simon's analysis also provides an example of a joke about a disobedient soldier, but his milder case involves a private strolling through the barracks yard with a burning cigar.

16. Warlitz, *Purpurne Schmerzen*, 142.

17. To give just one example, the previous joke about the questioning Jewish soldier is also found in T. L. Hirsch, *Jüdisches Witzbuch: Amüsante Witze, Humoresken und Anekdoten* (Berlin: Reform-Verlagshaus, 1913), 48.

18. Holländer, "Gegen die Verzerrung des jüdischen Wesens."

19. "Gegen die Auswüchse des Kabaretts," *Vossische Zeitung*, April 23, 1926, quoted in Jelavich, "Jewish Jokes," 35.

20. Holländer, "Gegen die Verzerrung des jüdischen Wesens."

21. Emil Faktor, "Das Mauscheln," *Berliner Börsen-Courier*, April 23, 1926. This line of reasoning foreshadows the exact rhetoric that was used by Siegfried Kadner to bolster his racist treatise in *Rasse und Humor* (1936).

22. Siegmund Feldmann, "Jeder Jude sein eigner Antisemit!," *Die Weltbühne* 22, no. 50 (December 14, 1926): 936.

23. In reading Holländer's overreaction, Riss points to the infiltration of Nazi and folk propaganda in the Centralverein's defense by the spring of 1926: "The last lines of the citation make clear to what extent folkish propaganda already had taken hold of the argumentation of the Centralverein because the statement that the Jews only pretended while cherishing very different intentions behind the 'mask of civilization' was derived from the anti-Semitic repertoire of *Volk* and NS circles" (168).

24. For a review of how the *Ostjuden* were often associated with the dirty and the primitive, see Steven E. Aschheim, *Brothers and Strangers: The East European Jew in German and German-Jewish Consciousness, 1800–1923* (Madison: University of Wisconsin Press, 1982). In the chapter "Ambivalent Heritage," Aschheim further recalls the preponderance of tendentious jokes directed against Eastern European Jews in the Viennese Jew Sigmund Freud's *Witz* book (50–51). But he also notes that

the "Eastern Jewish sense of humor" was often a source of admiration for German-speaking Jews: "Admiration for their wit, gall (*hutzpah*), and spirit in adversity was always a kind of hidden counter-theme in the Western Jews' regard for their Eastern brothers" (50).

25. Holländer, "Gegen die Verzerrung des jüdischen Wesens."

26. Robitschek spoke about this ideal in the KadeKo's comic journal, *Die Frechheit*. It is interesting how he incorporates the Jewish joke figure of the *schnorrer* in this excerpt: "My dream would have been a cabaret full of aggression, a cabaret of the satire of the day. But how many people are there who have appreciation of this ideal cabaret? Twenty journalists and 300 free ticket scroungers [*Freikartenschnorrer*]." See *Die Frechheit* 5, no. 12 (December 1929). Quoted in Marcus G. Patka and Albert Stalzer, eds., *Alles Meschugge?: Jüdischer Witz und Humor* (Vienna: Amalthea Verlag, 2013), 80–81.

27. Alan Lareau summarizes the typical fare at the KadeKo as follows: "The KadeKo offered a two-part program, combining a cabaret section of songs and specialty acts (with *conférence*) and a one-act musical, operetta, parody, or play in the second (ranging from Robert Stolz to Chekhov and Heinrich Mann, as well as many products from directors Paul Morgan and Kurt Robitschek). In format, then, it was more like the variety theater than the intimate literary cabarets. . . . The focus was clearly on humor and entertainment." See "The German Cabaret Movement during the Weimar Republic," *Theatre Journal* 43, no. 4 (December 1991): 482.

28. This politically pointed production that made the Nazis the butt of the joke speaks against Lareau's assertion that "politically, the programs [of the KadeKo] were noncommittal" (482). Marie-Theres Arnbom also asserts this political point of view: "For its political orientation, this cabaret was indebted to its founder Kurt Robitschek." See Arnbom, *War'n Sie schon mal in mich Verliebt: Filmstarts, Operettenlieblinge und Kaberettgrossen zwischen Wien und Berlin* (Berlin: Böhlau Verlag, 2006), 10.

29. For a review of this particular performance and for further background on the troupe, see "Kurt Robitschek und das 'Kaberett der Komiker,'" in Marie-Theres Arnbom, *War'n Sie schon mal in mich Verliebt*, 76–78. Meanwhile, Klaus Völker offers the standard history of the troupe in *Kabarett der Komiker Berlin 1924–1950* (Munich: Edition text + kritik, 2010).

30. Paul Morgan and Kurt Robitschek, *Die einsame Träne: Das Buch der guten Witze* (Berlin: Drei Masken Verlag, 1924), 99. This joke is accompanied by Paul Simmel's caricature that contrasts the hook-nosed Barches with the Aryan-passing blonde Jew.

31. Another self-mocking Jewish joke about not taking a bath (normally associated with East European Jews) is included in this collection. Titled "Ehrlich" ("Honest"), it reads: "'You are applying for the position of the night watchman. Can you bring me proofs of your honesty as well?' 'And how! For twenty years, I was a bath manager and I have never taken a bath!'" (73).

32. There are a few other jokes in the book that make the anti-Semites the butt of the Jewish humor, but this aspect of Robitschek's wit is not acknowledged in the accounts of the Centralverein watchmen. The most overt one included in the section "Philosophie des Humors" challenges the scapegoating of the Jews as responsible for the loss of World War I. This philosophical joke reads: "Political debate in the train compartment. A menacing-looking gentleman who is a retired officer and Ignaz Silberfaden are having a conversation. Finally, the martial says with certainty, 'For the evil outcome of the World War, only the Jews are to blame!' To which Ignaz Silverfaden concocts: 'And the cyclists!' 'Why the cyclists?' asks the former officer amazed. To which Ignaz replies: 'Why the Jews?'" (133). I will return to this famous joke and its transformation after the Holocaust in chapter 6.

33. Robitschek, "Der Standpunkt der Künstler," *C.V.-Zeitung*, April 30, 1926.

34. Holländer, "Gegen die Verzerrung des jüdischen Wesens."

35. Robitschek, "Der Standpunkt der Künstler."

36. "Jargon im Kabarett. Sturmszenen in einer jüdischen Versammlung," *Neue Berliner Zeitung — Das 12 Uhr Blatt*, April 23, 1926.

37. Robitschek, "Der Standpunkt der Künstler."

38. Robitschek.

39. Morgan and Robitschek, *Die einsame* Träne, 7.

40. Morgan and Robitschek, 5–8.

41. Morgan and Robitschek, 6.

42. An example of the former type is the case of the Kishinev Rabbi in an absurdly reasoned joke that also bears upon the dread of the anti-Semitic pogrom: "'Our Rabbi,' says Modche Gitterstab from Kishinev, 'literally can work miracles. Recently a mob came in front of his house and wanted to host a small pogrom. He merely raised his hands, an angel descended from the sky and flew with him straight to heaven from the midst of the crowd that wanted to kill him, and then sat him gently on a meadow outside of town.' 'I do not believe that,' said the skeptical Doctor Friedländer from Czernowitz. 'You do not believe it? You see indeed that the Rabbi liveth still . . . !'" (Morgan and Robitschek, 124–125). Here is an example of the latter type of joke and its ambivalent questioning of rabbinical authority: "Then one of the students came to the Talmudic scholar Rabbi one day and asked him: 'Great Rabbi, you know everything! Can you tell me when a person dies: does the soul go in from the outside or from the inside out?' The Rabbi pondered for some seconds, then he said slowly: 'If you ask me that, I have to tell you: Yes!'" (38–39). See also the "sophistical" joke of faulty reasoning recounted by Freud that mocks religious authority. In this Wonder Rabbi witticism, the far-sighted Rabbi N. of Cracow mistakenly announces the death of his colleague in Lemberg. Nevertheless, the telepathic view (*Kück*) from Cracow to Lemberg is said to matter much more than the fact that Rabbi N. was wrong about Rabbi L. See Freud, *Jokes*, 101–103. The Jewish joke folklorist Elliott Oring devotes a fascinating chapter to "The Kück" in *The Jokes of Sigmund Freud: A Study in Humor and Jewish Identity* (Northvale, NJ:

Jason Aronson, 1997), 79–90. Oring analyzes this joke in relation to Freud's belief in telepathy.

43. Morgan and Robitschek, *Die einsame Träne*, 93. "On the Day of Atonement, Tichowitz holds a particularly loud dialogue with God in a synagogue during the confession of his sins. In lamenting, he beats his chest so violently that one believes hearing his ribs crack. Then the temple servant taps him on his shoulder and says soothingly: 'With force, you will not prevail there!'"

44. Morgan and Robitschek, 105. "The old Meier, a *schnorrer* by profession, was very religious. And so one time, the archangel Gabriel appeared to him while he was in fervent prayers. 'Dear, Archangel,' Meier said, 'What is the time frame of a thousand years for the good Lord?' 'One minute!' the angel said. 'And what is one hundred thousand marks for the Master?' 'One penny!' 'Dear Master Archangel, please tell the good Lord that he should send me a penny!' 'Good!' said Gabriel, 'just wait a minute!'"

45. Morgan and Robitschek, 113.

46. In the Warlitz version, the freethinker who asks the sausage seller the price is named Samuel Jammermeier and, after the wrathful show of lightning and thunder, he looks to the heavens and remarks, "What — one is not even allowed to ask!" (*Nanana — fragen wird man doch noch können!*"). See Warlitz, *Lacht Euch Laune!*, 12.

47. For a joke about a cheap (and misogynist) Jew, see Mr. Pollitzer who would rather see his wife Rifke go to her grave than to give her a glass of wine as a last request on her deathbed (Morgan and Robitschek, 86). For a greedy Jew, there is the one about Strasser's son-in-law who wants to take advantage of the request from his observant father-in-law to close the business on Sabbath by asking him for more money to close down the business completely (159–160). For a deceitful Jew, we have the story of the man who is asked about how things are going after the fire that happened yesterday and then he tells his friend to be quiet since it is not scheduled to happen until the following week (141). There is even a joke about a shrewd Jewish convert to Christianity who still maintains the Jewish financial stereotype when he refuses to marry off his daughter to a Jewish family because they cannot provide a big enough dowry (160).

48. Morgan and Robitschek, 82. "After a long serious illness, Uncle Nathan is blissfully asleep with the Lord. The executor of his will is his nephew Ignaz Meier. And in the most important passage in the testamentary disposition, Uncle Nathan says: 'and from the rest of the 5,000, a beautiful stone should be purchased.' Since then, Meier wears a huge diamond in his tie." A similar version of this particular joke is included in Moszkowski's "segregated" chapter on "Entartete Sprossen" ("Degenerate sprouts") in *Der Jüdische Witz und seine Philosophie: 399 Juwelen echt gefaßt* (Berlin: Dr. Eysler, 1923), 130.

49. Morgan and Robitschek, 143.

50. Morgan and Robitschek, 94, 95, 142, and 145. As discussed already in the case of Eduard Fuchs, there was always the risk of provoking anti-Semitic stereotypes and

resentment when telling a joke involving the Rothschild banking family and their enormous wealth.

51. Morgan and Robitschek, 160.

52. Morgan and Robitschek, 7–8.

53. Alexander Moszkowski, *Die jüdische Kiste: 399 Juwelen echt gefaßt; Die Unsterbliche Kiste*, Zweiter Teil, (Berlin: Verlag der lustigen Blätter, 1911), 6–7.

54. Artur Schweriner, "Kabaretts und Film — Rückfall ins Unwürdige in Berliner Kabaretts," *C.V.-Zeitung*, December 9, 1927.

55. "Das Echo unseres Kampfes gegen würdelose Kabaretts" [The echo of our struggle against the undignified cabaret"], *C.V.-Zeitung*, January 6, 1928.

56. Jelavich, "When Are Jewish Jokes No Longer Funny?," 39.

57. "Die leidige Kabarettfrage: Vergleich Artur Schweriners mit Kurt Robitschek" [The vexing cabaret question: Artur Schweriner's settlement with Kurt Robitschek], *C.V.-Zeitung*, January 27, 1928.

58. Kurt Robitschek, "Sieg des Theaters über die Weltgeschichte" ["Victory of the Theater over World History"], *Die Frechheit* 7, no. 7 (July 1931), 1. In invoking Erik Charell, Robitschek refers to the legendary Jewish and queer Berlin stage director who brought the line-dancing Tiller Gills from Great Britain to Germany. This passage is also discussed and cited in Peter Jelavich, "Girls and Crisis": The Political Aesthetics of the Kickline in Weimar Berlin," in *Rediscovering History: Culture, Politics and the Psyche*, ed. Michael Roth (Stanford, CA: Stanford University Press, 1994), 236.

59. Kurt Robitschek, "Das siebente Jahr ["The seventh year]," in *Die Frechheit* 7, no. 6 (June 1931), 1. See Peter Jelavich, *Berlin Cabaret* (Cambridge, MA: Harvard University Press, 1993), 203. Robitschek elaborated his altered views in the May issue of his humor magazine: "The sharply politicized times have had other consequences . . . ; the public principally rejects all politics in the cabaret, be they left or right. The audience also rejects any art that tries to act serious. Only laughter interests people. . . . The lighter and shallower the entertainment, the more audience it finds." See "Randbemerkungen zum letzten Monat," *Die Frechheit* 7, no. 5 (May 1931): 2.

60. Holländer, "Gegen die Verzerrung des jüdischen Wesens." Ironically, Holländer views the antics of the Brothers Herrnfeld as palatable in this nostalgic commentary. In this way, he forgets that they were once considered deplorable and were denounced soundly by many Jewish cultural commentators, including Flaneur's "Die antisemitische Gebrüder *Herrnfeld*" ("The Anti-Semitic Brothers Herrnfeld") in 1908. In Holländer's selective memory: "They were mostly a harmless representation of occupational and human weaknesses, which were not put forward without intrinsic humor." Heidelore Riss comments on this altered state of political affairs: "True anti-Semitism which showed itself in ever new faces with the rise of National Socialism now rehabilitated the Herrnfelds retrospectively" ("Unser Kampf," 166).

61. See Ben Barkow, *Alfred Wiener and the Making of the Holocaust Library* (London: Vallentine Mitchell, 1997).

## 4. "Far from where?": Erich Kahler and the Jewish Joke of Exile

Unless otherwise noted, all translations from the German are mine.

1. The galley for the first edition of the book, published by Delphin-Verlag, is dated January 21, 1933; on January 30, 1933, Hitler was appointed chancellor of Germany. See Eric Kahler Collection; AR 2141/MF 755; box 1, folder 9, Leo Baeck Institute, Center for Jewish History, New York. For the digitized version, see reel 1, 927–930. These pages are found on-line at the Archive.org website, http://www.archive.org/stream/erichkahler_01_reel01#page/n927/mode/1up. The hand-written manuscript shows that Kahler also considered substituting "the Jewish question" instead of "the fate of Judaism" in the second sentence to denote the "fulcrum of history" for the Nazis. See reel 1, 940. The same first sentence is also found in the edition published in exile. See Erich Kahler, *Israel unter den Völkern* (Zurich: Humanitas Verlag, 1936), 11. Hereafter cited in text by page number in parentheses.

2. David Kettler and Volker Meja, "Karl Mannheim's Jewish Question," *Religions* 3 (2012): 244.

3. Steven E. Aschheim, "George Mosse at 80: A Critical Laudatio," *Journal of Contemporary History* 34, no. 2 (April 1999), 308. In reciting the key values of *Bildung*, Aschheim refers to George L. Mosse, "Jewish Emancipation Between *Bildung* and Respectability," in *The Jewish Response to German Culture*, ed. Jehuda Reinharz and Walter Schatzberg (Hanover: University of New England Press, 1985), 1–16.

4. See George L Mosse, *German Jews Beyond Judaism* (Bloomington: Indiana University Press, 1985). Mosse's central argument is that Jews in the post-emancipation period learned to become respectable and acceptable Germans by replacing traditional Judaism with the new humanist ideal of *Bildung* and that these newly bourgeois and upwardly mobile German Jews developed it into an ersatz religion and new Jewish identity. For Mosse, "The centrality of the word *Bildung* in German-Jewish consciousness must be understood from the very beginning . . . [as] fundamental to the search for a new Jewish identity after emancipation" (3).

5. Gerhard Lauer, "The Empire's Watermark: Erich Kahler and Exile," in *Exile, Science, and Bildung: The Contested Legacies of German Émigré Intellectuals*, ed. David Kettler and Gerhard Lauer (New York: Palgrave Macmillan, 2005), 64.

6. I thank Steven Aschheim for pointing out these aspects of the *Bildungsjude* and how they could apply to the case of Kahler.

7. Mosse, for instance, defined "the so-called 'mission of Judaism' with its emphasis upon *Bildung* as self-cultivation, cosmopolitanism, and a rational attitude towards life" (197). Kahler also spoke about the mission of diasporic Jews at the conclusion of *Israel unter den Völkern*. See George L. Mosse, "The End Is Not Yet: A Personal Memoir of the German-Jewish Legacy in America," *American Jewish Archives* 40, no. 2 (November 1988): 197.

8. Michael Brenner, *The Renaissance of Jewish Culture in Weimar Germany* (New Haven, CT: Yale University Press, 1996), 41. Werner Cahnmann to Erich von Kahler,

December 31, 1930, Erich Kahler Collection, LBI-AR, 3890. According to Brenner: "Influenced by the neo-Romantic ideas of the George circle, Kahler rejected Weber's liberal rationalism as well as that of the principal philosopher of Liberal Judaism, Hermann Cohen, and the founders of the CV [*Central Verein*]. Kahler believed that Jews should admit that they were a distinct tribe [*Stamm*], different from the German tribes" (41).

9. Kahler to Mann, letter, March 21, 1935, in *An Exceptional Friendship: The Correspondence of Thomas Mann and Erich Kahler* (Ithaca, NY: Cornell University Press, 1975), 11–12. For the original German, see Thomas Mann, *Briefe 1889–1936*, vol. 1 (Frankfurt: S. Fischer Verlag, 1961), 11.

10. Thomas Sparr writes: "The second, the published version that appeared in Switzerland in 1936, has remained essentially the same, but Kahler's expectation for salvation has given way to a realistic view of German-Jewish relations. Kahler refers to 'the persecution, the extermination of the Jews in Germany' by name, and in place of a pathetic concluding formula enters a citation from Hölderlin's *Hyperion*." See Sparr, "Verkannte Brüder": Jüdische George-Rezeption," in *The Jewish Self-Portrait in European and American Literature*, ed. Hans-Juergen Schrader, Elliott M. Simon, and Charlotte Wardi (Berlin: Walter de Gruyter, 1996), 52. According to Sparr, the book should be viewed as "the last attempt to reduce the negative relationship of Germans and Jews into conflicting symptoms of a shared nature, to an inner agreement which for Kahler — as a student of [Stefan] George — will serve as the *telos* of a redeemed world" (52).

11. Kahler, *Israel unter den Völkern*, 11.

12. The essay was published in the *Jüdische Revue* (June 1936): 41–45. For the author's own copy of the article, see Erich Kahler Collection, "Journal Contributions 1911–1955," AR 2141/MF 755, box 1, folder 24, Leo Baeck Institute, Center for Jewish History, New York, reel 3, 97–102. It is not clear whether Kahler selected this title or whether it was an editorial decision. This article is found on-line at the Archive.org website, http://www.archive.org/stream/erichkahler_03_reel03#page/n97/mode/1up.

13. Even though the American publication *The Jews Among the Nations* (New York: Frederick Ungar, 1967) appears to be only a slightly revised version of the earlier edition, it is a substantially different book. For instance, the discussion of Jewish wit that is the central subject of this chapter is reduced to a few lines in a couple of places at the beginning of the book. Here, Kahler stresses that Jewish wit is the cultural property of both religious and secular Jews but overlooks how the latter used it as a weapon to make fun of the former: "The distinct Jewish particularity is evidenced by innumerable stories, sadly funny stories, self-deriding stories, which, all of them, deal with the peculiar conditions, experiences, and attitudes of the Jewish people, not simply those who believe in Judaism" (6). The reference to "sadly funny stories, self-deriding stories" illustrates that Kahler embraces both the "laughter through tears" and "self-critical" hypotheses as rationales for understanding the sources of Jewish humor.

14. For example, Kahler already published "Juden und Deutsche," *Europäische Revue* 6, no. 10 (1930): 744–756.

15. Todd Samuel Presner, *Mobile Modernity: Germans, Jews, Trains* (New York: Columbia University Press, 2007), 4.

16. Presner, 4.

17. For Presner, the separatrix "refers to the line between the two words German and Jewish, the cut that separates them. The meaning of the separatrix is ambiguous; it may locate an opposition, as in German versus Jewish, it may signify simultaneity, as in both German and Jewish, and it may call upon a choice, as in German or Jewish" (3).

18. Blüher's phrase *"jüdisch-destruktiven Intellektualismus"* is cited in Otto F. Best, *Volk ohne Witz: Über ein deutsches Defizit* (Frankfurt am Main: Fischer Verlag, 1993), 153. See Hans Blüher, *Secessio Judaica: Philosophische Grundlegung der Historischen Situation des Judentums und der Antisemitischen Bewegung* (Berlin: Der Weisse Ritter Verlag, 1922). Meanwhile, Goebbels proclaimed the end of the era of an "exaggerated Jewish intellectualism" in his infamous speech to Nazi youth and students at the Berlin book-burnings on May 10, 1933. To recite the Nazi propaganda minister, "The era of extreme Jewish intellectualism has come to an end."

19. Sparr, "Verkannte Brüder," 52.

20. The handwritten manuscript of *Israel unter den Völkern* is found in Erich Kahler Collection; AR 2141/MF 755; box 1, folder 9, Leo Baeck Institute, Center for Jewish History, New York. The crucial section on Jewish wit can be found on manuscript pages 123 to 127.

21. For an excellent discussion of the history of this idea as crucial to an understanding of Jewish wit as a negating force in the context of modern German literary and political culture, see Best, "Vom 'Geist der Zersetzung': Jüdischer Witz," in *Volk ohne Witz*, 151–156.

22. Anna Kiel reviews this point in *Erich Kahler: Ein "uomo universale" des zwanzigsten Jahrhunderts* (Bern: Peter Lang, 1989), 188. Kiel compares Thomas Mann's interpretation of the Jewish joke with Kahler specifically. In contrast to Mann, "Kahler does not derive a metaphysical acceptance out of the Jewish joke; the background remains the dialogue between the individual and God that is characteristic for this tribe."

23. Kahler, *Jews Among the Nations*, 8.

24. See, for example, Sholom Aleichem, "Tevye Strikes It Rich," in *The Best of Sholom Aleichem*, ed. Irving Howe and Ruth R. Wisse (New York: Simon and Schuster, 1980), 137.

25. See the prefatory letter in Immanuel Olsvanger, *Contentions with God: A Study in Folklore* (Cape Town: T. Maskew Miller, 1921). Olsvanger warns, "In reading some grotesque anecdote you will with your deeper understanding not find it to accuse: 'How impious is this people who, even when speaking of God, see fit to jest.'"

26. Henri Bergson, *Le Rire: Essai sur la signification du comique* (Paris: Alcan, 1924).

27. This was the only phrase in the book that was not included in the publication of "Der Deutsche und der Galuthwitz" article in *Jüdische Revue*.

28. Steven E. Aschheim, *At the Edges of Liberalism: Junctions of European, German, and Jewish History* (New York: Palgrave Macmillan, 2012), 183–184. Aschheim's excellent discussion and analysis of the Herrnfeld Brothers allows us to see them as "the veritable distillation, the symbolic incarnations, of this underside" (184) of the striving for *Bildung* among respectable German Jews. Aschheim also likens their popularity as a reaction on the part of many Jews who frequented their performances (rather than anti-Semites) to an overly quick assimilation process and "too pressing a socialization" (184).

29. In referring to Kahler as a "conservative" thinker in this context, I follow his intellectual biographer Gerhard Lauer who situates him as allied to the so-called "conservative revolution" that began with Hugo von Hoffmanstahl and Stefan George. The young Kahler was influenced by George and his circle. See *Die Verspätete Revolution: Erich von Kahler; Wissenschaftsgeschichte zwischen konservativer Revolution und Exil* (Berlin: Walter de Gruyter, 1995). According to Lauer, Kahler's call for a "new man" insisted on the return to *Bildung* as a means of education and character formation where "the accumulations of knowledge could be compounded and transformed into a power to revolutionize life as a whole." From this perspective, Kahler seeks to bind Jewish wit not only to wisdom but also to these "accumulations of knowledge." See Gerhard Lauer, "The Empire's Watermark: Erich Kahler and Exile," in Kettler and Lauer, *Exile, Science, and Bildung*, 66.

30. In his *The Meaning of History* and in tandem with the corporeal thesis, Kahler would frame the Nazis in terms of a relapse into "human bestiality." Kahler writes, "Even Nazism, unprecedented as its mechanized atrocities are, can be traced back to centuries of an unfortunate German history, indeed Luther; and its particular novelty consists in the relapse, in an age of technological and collectivistic methods, into an always latently or patently existent human bestiality." See Kahler, *The Meaning of History* (New York: George Braziller, 1964), 202.

31. For his famous review of carnival in the context of the Renaissance, see Mikhail Bakhtin, *Rabelais and his World*, trans. Helen Iswolsky (Bloomington: Indiana University Press, 1984).

32. This language comes from the entry on the Deutsche Michel in the *Allgemeine Deutsche Real-encyklopädie für die Gebildeten Stände* (Leipzig: F. A. Brockhaus, 1846).

33. Tomasz Szarota, "Der Deutsche Michel," Haus der Geschichte, http://www.hdg.de/karikatur/view_content/class50_id4.html. For Szarota's thorough historical scholarship on the subject at hand, see his full-length study *Der deutsche Michel: Die Geschichte eines nationalen Symbols und Autostereotyps* (Osnabrück: Edition Fibre, 1998).

34. Erich Kahler, "The German Problem: Origins and Development," *Contemporary Jewish Record* 7, no. 5 (October 1944): 464–465.

35. Kahler, *Jews Among the Nations*, 117.

36. The original German caption reads: "*Und dann schrie der arme deutsche Michel so lange bis es all Welt glaubte: Zu Hilfe, zu Hilfe, Ich bin eingekreist!*"

37. Frazer Stephen Clark, *Zeitgeist und Zerrbild: Word, Image, and Idea* (Bern: Peter Lang, 2006), 222. The chapter is titled "Of Nightcaps and Nations."

38. Clark, 22.

39. Chayim Bloch, *Hersch Ostroploler* (Berlin: Benjamin Harz, 1921), 8. Bloch's earlier *Ostjüdischer Humor* (Berlin: Benjamin Harz, 1920) also references the connection between the two characters in a footnote on page 10.

40. See Heinrich Loewe, *Schelme und Narren mit jüdischen Kappen* (Berlin: Welt Verlag, 1920), 12. Loewe states: "Jewish humor even had its own special joy in retelling the German Eulenspiegel stories. But this was not enough for the cheerfulness of the Eastern European Jew. Just so, he therefore has his own funny figures to amuse himself and others, as he has admitted Till Eulenspiegel into his house." A book review framed Loewe's collection this way: "*Till Eulenspiegels Streiche im jüdischen Leben*" ("Till Eulenspiegel's antics in Jewish life"). It then went on to list the Jewish pranksters featured in the chapters of Loewe's book: "Efraim Greidiker, Mordche Rackewer, Schailke Feifer, und Herschel Ostropolier." See *Jüdische Volkstimme* 21, no. 13 (March 25, 1920): 6.

41. Lewis Browne, *The Wisdom of Israel: An Anthology* (New York: Random House, 1945).

42. The original German manuscript of Kahler's *Commentary* review can be found in digital format on pages 921–925, http://www.archive.org/stream/erichkahler _01_reel01#page/n921/mode/1up. The section dealing with Jewish wit is on page 924. There is no indication whether he translated the text into English himself. See "Book Review of *The Wisdom of Israel*," December 1945; Erich Kahler Collection; AR 2141/MF 755; box 1, folder 8, Leo Baeck Institute, Center for Jewish History, New York. For the English, see Erich Kahler, "Browne, Lewis (Ed.). *The Wisdom of Israel* (Book Review)." *Commentary* 1 (December 1, 1945): 88–89.

43. For Kahler's Certificate of Naturalization to the United States dated February 24, 1944, see Erich Kahler Collection; AR 2141/MF 755; box 2, folder 22, Leo Back Institute, Center for Jewish History, New York. Kahler officially lost his aristocratic title in the naturalization process. The back of the paper states: "Name changed, by Decree of Court from Erich Von Kahler, as a part of the Naturalization."

44. Richard Raskin, "'Far from where?': On the history and meanings of a classic Jewish refugee joke," *American Jewish History* 85, no. 2 (June 1997): 143–150. Raskin claims that the first publication of the joke in an anthology derives from Nathan Ausubel, *A Treasury of Jewish Humor* (New York, 1948) where the remote location is South Africa, but Browne's telling predates Ausubel's publication by three years. Given that the publication was not an anthology of humor but rather the "wisdom

of Israel," it was not on his radar. Raskin reviews two contrary interpretations of the joke — one "inspired by the eternal concept of the 'wandering Jew'" that is imbued with pathos and the other reflecting its "original historical context" and "at the time of Nazi domination" wherein the 'Far from where?' punch-line becomes "an indictment of a country in which Jews were offered little or no protection from the Nazis." While Brown's version places the anecdote in Czarist Russia, its actual publication in 1945 makes it a thinly veiled screen for the refugee situation during the Nazi era and this is the way that Kahler understood it. The joke (with Shanghai selected as "*Weit, von wo?*") also found its way into Salcia Landmann, *Jüdische Witze* (Olten: Walter-Verlag, 1962), 235–236.

45. Browne, *Wisdom of Israel*, 623.

46. Kahler, "Book review of *The Wisdom of Israel*," 89.

47. Franz Kafka's short and profound parable "My Destination" with the punchline "Away from here" constitutes his own Jewish joke of exile. It reads: "I gave orders for my horse to be brought round from the stables. The servant did not understand me. I myself went to the stable, saddled my horse and mounted. In the distance, I heard a bugle call, I asked him what this meant. He knew nothing and had heard nothing. At the gate he stopped me, asking: 'Where are you riding to, master?' 'I don't know,' I said, 'only away from here, away from here. Always away from here, only by doing so can I reach my destination.' 'And so you know your destination?' he asked. 'Yes,' I answered, 'didn't I say so? Away-From-Here, that is my destination.' 'You have no provisions with you,' he said. 'I need none,' I said, 'the journey is so long that I must die of hunger if I don't get anything on the way. No provisions can save me. For it is, fortunately, a truly immense journey.'" Franz Kafka, *Parables and Paradoxes*, ed. Nahum N. Glatzer (New York: Schocken Books, 1975), 189. Kahler addresses the importance and beauty of Kafka's prose in *Jews Among the Nations*: "Kafka's prose belongs to the most beautiful, classically beautiful, German prose ever written" (109).

48. Stephane Courtois and Mark Kramer, *The Black Book of Communism: Crimes, Terror, Repression* (Cambridge, MA: Harvard University Press, 1999), 317.

49. Erich Kahler, "Forms and Features of Anti-Judaism," *Social Research: International Journal of Political and Social Science* 6, no. 4 (November 1939): 483.

50. Kahler, "Book review of *The Wisdom of Israel*," 89.

51. For more on this point, see chapter 5 and the extensive discussion of Siegfried Kadner, *Rasse und Humor* (Munich: J. F. Lehmanns Verlag, 1936).

52. This view also needs to be placed in relation to the reverse idea that "German-Jewish self-satire disclosed a pathological internalization of the worst anti-Semitic stereotypes" putting Jewish abject self-mockery and anti-Semitism into a vicious circle of cause and effect. See Steven Aschheim, *At the Edges of Liberalism*, 183. For more on internalized Jewish self-hatred and self-directed satire, see Peter Gay, "Hermann Levi: A Study in Service and Self-Hatred," in *Freud, Jews and Other Germans: Masters and Victims in Modernist Culture* (New York: Oxford University Press, 1978), 209–210.

53. Freud, *Jokes and Their Relation to the Unconscious*, trans. James Strachey, in collaboration with Anna Freud (New York: W. W. Norton, 1960), 115.

54. Browne, *Wisdom of Israel*, 622–623.

55. Browne, 623.

56. In comparing *schnorrers* and *schlemiels*, Browne remarks: "He is as importunate as the other is easygoing, and as cunning as the other is slow-witted" (627). The anecdotes about the "Fools" of Chelm occupy the last part of the chapter. Browne notes, "The latter figure in a whole cycle of what would now be termed 'moron stories'" (630).

57. Letter from Erich Kahler to Thomas Mann, April 14, 1951, in *An Exceptional Friendship: The Correspondence of Thomas Mann and Erich Kahler*, trans. by Richard and Clara Winston (Ithaca, NY: Cornell University Press, 1975), 154. The earlier part of the letter reads: "Still: I hear, and your letter hints at it, that you are toying with the thought of moving to Europe, to Switzerland. Please don't do it! I cannot help warning you against it. You would gain nothing by it, for there is simply no escaping from what is going to happen this time. If we must suffer here from the delusions of stupid, perverted power, over there we will suffer from the unrelieved illusions of shameful impotence. And if what you fear really should prove to be inevitable, it would catch up with us there as well as here. So why go to all the effort and expose yourself to the harmful and spiteful misinterpretations your leaving would set off in this country? The only place to go that might serve a humane, a demonstrative purpose would be India. But of course that would be an excessive imposition upon both of you physically. It seems to me we must stay and resist where we are." For the original German, see Thomas Mann and Erich von Kahler, *Briefwechsel 1931–1955*, ed. Michael Assmann (Hamburg: Luchterhand, 1993), 124.

58. Salcia Landmann, "Jüdisches aus Israel," in *Jüdische Witze* (Munich: DTV, 1963), 244. Landmann also tells another version of Kahler's refugee joke in the chapter "Messianismus und Zionismus" that shifts the scene from the Atlantic to the Mediterranean and that turns the promised land into the contested destination: "In the Mediterranean Sea, two steamers encounter one other. The first is coming from Israel and the second is going there. Jews are standing on the decks of both steamers—immigrants to Israel on the one hand and emigrants from Israel on the other. As the passengers of both ships lean on the railing in sight of one another, they make the 'idiot sign' to each other by tapping a finger to their foreheads" (242).

59. Thomas Mann to Erich Kahler, letter, April 23, 1951, in *An Exceptional Friendship*, 156. For the original German, see Thomas Mann, *Briefe 1948–1955*, vol. 3 (Frankfurt: S. Fischer Verlag, 1965), 203.

60. Erich Kahler to Thomas Mann, letter, March 21, 1935, in *An Exceptional Friendship*, 12. For the original German, see Thomas Mann, *Briefe 1889–1936*, vol. 1 (Frankfurt: S. Fischer Verlag, 1961), 11.

61. Thomas Mann to Erich Kahler, letter, March 19, 1935, in *An Exceptional Friendship*, 10. For the original German, see Thomas Mann, *Briefe 1889–1936*, 1:10. The first part of the letter reads: "I read your proofs to the end day before yesterday

and am fascinated to the depth of my soul. The book is far and away the most elevating and penetrating thing I have seen dealing with this problem. Reading it, in fact, I had the feeling that it is precisely your characteristic fusion of Judaism with Georgian Germanism (*Deutschtum*), and no other combination existing today, which establishes your right and vocation to speak validly on all this—and by 'all this' I mean not only the German-Jewish question, but also the problem of Europe itself. The extended chapter on Germanism and Judaism is incontestably the truest and the psychologically keenest statement ever made on the subject—and I say that as a German with an overseas Latin admixture who in the course of time has grown more and more disgruntled living among Germans, and who cannot wholly forgive certain generous extenuations in your estimate of them."

62. Friedrich Nietzsche, *Die Geburt der Tragödie* (1886) was first translated into English as *The Birth of Tragedy, Or: Hellenism and Pessimism* by William A. Haussmann (London: George Allen W. Unwin, 1909). Nietzsche's notes from 1870/1871 already contain the suggestion of the title, "Die Tragödie und die griechische Heiterkeit" where *Heiterkeit* can be translated as serenity, cheerfulness, or gaiety.

63. Friedrich Nietzsche, *The Will to Power*, trans. Walter Kauffman and R. J. Hollingdale (New York: Vintage Books, 1967), 56. Nietzsche again refers to cheerful (*heiterste*) in this context.

64. Eleanor L. Wolff, ed. *Erich Kahler* (New York: Van Vechten Press, 1951), 37.

65. See Kettler and Lauer, *Exile, Science, and Bildung*, 63–73.

66. See David Kettler, *The Liquidation of Exile: Studies in the Intellectual Emigration of the 1930s* (London and New York: Anthem Press, 2011), 83–108.

67. Richard Raskin notes the first appearance of this Jewish refugee joke in Felix Mendelsohn, *Let Laughter Ring* (Philadelphia: Jewish Publication Society of America, 1941). However, it did not have "its definitive punch-line" until around 1960. In the first version, the final line reads, "Pardon me, have you anything else to offer?" (136).

68. Viktor Kellner, *Israel unter den Völkern* (Vienna: n.p., 1936), 2, 10.

69. Kellner, 10.

70. Kellner, 10–11.

71. The following sentence incensed Scholem: "The Jews did not live through two millennia of a world-scale destiny to end up within a tiny nationalistic framework" (Kahler, *Jews Among the Nations*, 112). In a letter dated August 17, 1967, Scholem wrote: "[This sentence] essentially echoes the anti-Zionist, cosmopolitan talk that all of the opponents of Zionism in my youth abandoned once they had their backs to the wall. I did not in fact expect to hear it from the mouth of Erich von Kahler." Kahler stood his ground in an undated reply: "Nevertheless, I refuse to accept the State of Israel as an end in itself or as the final aim of Judaism." See Gershom Gerhard Scholem, *A Life in Letters 1914–1982*, ed. and trans. Anthony David Skinner (Cambridge, MA: Harvard University Press, 2002), 424–425. Steven E. Aschheim also takes up Kahler's quotation and Scholem's rebuttal in "The

Metaphysical Psychologist: On the Life and Letters of Gershom Scholem," in *At the Edges of Liberalism: Junctions of European, German, and Jewish History* (New York: Palgrave Macmillan, 2012), 81.

72. Kahler, *Jews Among the Nations*, 109.

## 5. Of Jokes and Propaganda: The Mobilization of the Jewish Joke in the Nazi Era

Unless otherwise noted, all translations from the German are mine.

1. Jacques Ellul, *Propaganda: The Formation of Men's Attitudes*, trans. Konrad Kellen and Jean Lerner (New York: Alfred A. Knopf, 1966), 11–12.

2. See chapter 3, where I reviewed this point when dealing with the case of the Centralverein critics of "extreme" Jewish jokes who viewed them as a type of "self-hate" speech that required censorship. As Peter Jelavich frames the problem, the fear was that "some self-deprecatory jokes could be used as 'evidence' of anti-Semitic stereotypes, inasmuch as Jews themselves 'admitted' the faults of which they were accused." See "When are Jewish Jokes No Longer Funny?: Ethnic Humor in Imperial and Republican Berlin," in *The Politics of Humor: Laughter, Inclusion and Exclusion in the Twentieth Century*, ed. Martina Kessel and Patrick Merziger (Toronto: University of Toronto Press, 2012), 37.

3. Siegfried Kadner mobilizes this joke in *Rasse und Humor* (Munich: J. F. Lehmanns Verlag, 1936), 208. Rather than focusing on the logical twists of the "enemy supporter" embedded in this joke and its similarity to the propaganda techniques that he deploys in his own analysis, Kadner uses the joke instead to demonstrate disturbing racially determined Jewish characteristics.

4. For a critique of the theory of Jewish humor as self-critique, see Dan Ben-Amos, "The 'Myth' of Jewish Humor," *Western Folklore* 32, no. 2 (April 1973): 112–131.

5. Sigmund Freud, *Jokes and their Relation to the Unconscious*, trans. James Strachey, in collaboration with Anna Freud (New York: W. W. Norton, 1960), 157.

6. Kadner, *Rasse und Humor*, 208. Siegfried Kadner (1887–1949) received a degree in literary studies from the University of Kiel in 1919. In 1929, he was contracted to teach racial studies at Berlin University. However, Kadner did not become a member of the Nazi Party until 1933. He also joined the SS and he was listed as an expert speaker for race studies and genetics in the district training office. See Hans-Christian Harten, Uwe Neirich, and Matthias Schwerendt, *Rassenhygiene als Erziehungsideologie des Drittens Reichs: Bio-bibliographisches Handbuch* (Berlin: Akademie Verlag, 2006), 263.

7. Both the Nazi chief for psychological warfare Major Albrecht Blau and the communist critic and newspaper publisher Willi Münzenberg wrote books with the same title that stressed the role of propaganda as weapon — *Propaganda als Waffe*.

8. Christie Davies, *Ethnic Humor around the World: A Comparative Analysis* (Bloomington: University of Indiana Press, 1990), 117.

9. Davies, 124.

10. Davies, 124.

11. Hans Speier, *Witz und Politik: Essay über die Macht und das Lachen* (Zurich: Edition Interform, 1975), 70–71. Speier's position is the polar opposite of the view expressed by Eduard Engel on the joke as weapon of the weak discussed in chapter 2.

12. Eugen Hadamovsky, *Propaganda und nationale Macht: Die Organization der öffentlichen Meinung für nationale Politik* (Oldenburg: Verlag Gerhard Stalling, 1933), 18–19. The book was translated into English by Randall Bytwerk as *Propaganda and National Power: Organization of Public Opinion for National Politics*, http://research.calvin.edu/german-propaganda-archive/hadamovsky.htm.

13. For the political theorist Thomas Hobbes, "Sudden Glory, is the passion which maketh those Grimaces called LAUGHTER; and is caused either by some sudden act of their own, that pleaseth them; or by the apprehension of some deformed thing in another, by comparison whereof they suddenly applaud themselves." *Leviathan*, ed. Richard Tuck (Cambridge: Cambridge University Press, 1991), 43.

14. Freud, *Jokes*, 133.

15. The Nazi publishing house of Franz Eher in Munich published Goebbels and Schweitzer's successful book in 1928 and it reached its fifth edition by 1931. In the meantime, Goebbels edited a sequel under the title *Knorke: Ein Neues Buch Isidor für Zeitgenossen* (Munich: Franz Eher, 1929). This book included an extended anti-Semitic interpretation of the classic Jewish joke about the rich Jew (here, Rothschild) who refuses to give alms to the *Schnorrer* seeking charity ("Throw the bum out! He's breaking my heart!") in order to vilify both stereotypical Jewish characters. See Knipperdolling, "Aus der Asphaltwüste: Politische Ketzereien," in *Knorke*, 73.

16. Dietz Bering, *The Stigma of Names: Antisemitism in German Daily Life, 1812–1933* (Cambridge: Polity Press, 1992), 12.

17. *Die Brennessel* 4 (April 17, 1934): 247.

18. T. W. Adorno, Leo Löwenthal, and Paul W. Massing, "Anti-Semitism and Fascist Propaganda," in Theodor W. Adorno, *Gesammelte Schriften*, Bd. 8, *Soziologische Schriften* 1 (Frankfurt am Main: Surkhamp, 1972), 400.

19. Joseph Goebbels, *Kampf um Berlin: Der Anfang (1926–1927)* (Munich: Franz Eher, 1932), 203.

20. Ellul, *Propaganda*, 5.

21. For the direct links between Nazi propaganda and Freudian psychoanalysis, see the books on propaganda written (uncannily) by Freud's nephew Dr. Edward Bernays of whom Dr. Joseph Goebbels was an ardent admirer. Goebbels learned much from Bernays' classic *Propaganda* (New York: Horace Liverlight, 1928).

22. Freud, *Jokes*, 147.

23. Eduard Fuchs, *Die Juden in der Karikatur: Ein Beitrag zur Kulturgeschichte*, (Munich: Albert Langen Verlag, 1921), 303. In the most ironic of juxtapositions and as already discussed in detail in chapter 2, Fuchs placed the Hitler election poster above the title for chapter 11, "Die jüdische Selbstironie."

24. Christie Davies, "Exploring the thesis of the self-deprecating Jewish sense of humor," *Humor* 4, no. 2 (January 1991): 203.

25. Adolf Hitler, *Mein Kampf*, trans. Ralph Manheim (London: Pimlico, 1992), 287.

26. *Illustrierter Beobachter* 6 (1931): 3. For further details regarding the Nazi's use of caricature, see Gerhard Paul, *Aufstand der Bilder: Die NS-Propaganda vor 1933* (Bonn: Verlag Dietz, 1990), 143–145, and Dietrich Grünewald, "Bemerkungen zur nationalsozialistischen Karikatur," *Aesthetik und Kommunikation* 6 (1975), 865–890. Kadner's *Race und Humor* included an anti-Semitic caricature by Paul Schondorff originally published in *Die Brennessel* (October 22, 1935). According to Kadner, this "satirical note" illustrates the "racial background of the management of the League of Nations" (213).

27. According to Patrick Merziger, "*Brennessel* was closed down in 1938 because of dwindling sales and a lack of new subject matter" (284). It is Merziger's contention that political satire had its limits in Nazi Germany and that it gave way to a form of "German Humour" that represented "the all-embracing laughter of the *Volksgemeinschaft*" at that time. He writes: "In the specific public sphere of National Socialism, a laugh that attempted to exclude could not be tolerated because to be shut out of the *Volksgemeinschaft* meant total exclusion" (289). Merziger omits the Jewish joke and the Jewish question entirely from this analysis. But this analytical exclusion makes sense if we consider that the Jew functioned as the totally excluded other on which the Nazi utopia was to be founded. In this way, Jews could function either as the targets of political satire or as the racial other for the new "German Humour" that brought the *Volk* together. See Merziger, "Humour in Nazi Germany: Resistance and Propaganda? The Popular Desire for an All-Embracing Laughter," *International Review of Social History* 52 (2007): 275–290.

28. This propagandistic title was published in Dresden by NS.-Verlag für den Gau Sachsen.

29. Adorno, Löwenthal, and Massing, "Anti-Semitism and Fascist Propaganda," 406. Gerhard Paul has referred to the same murderous death drive expressed in Nazi caricatures as "*Vernichtungswillen*" (will to extermination). See Paul, *Aufstand der Bilder*, 145.

30. Adorno, Löwenthal, and Massing, "Anti-Semitism and Fascist Propaganda," 401.

31. The other side of this joke warfare on the part of the Nazis was the censorship of the Jewish joke, exemplified by the title of an article in the exile newspaper *Pariser Tagezeitung*: "Der Nazikrieg gegen den Witz" (The Nazi's war against the joke), February 4, 1939. The article reviewed the Nazi regime's eradication (*Ausrottung*) of the Berlin-based Kaberett der Komiker (Cabaret of Comics) detailing how comedian Werner Finck had angered Dr. Goebbels with his anti-Nazi jokes and how the Minister responded with the iron fist of political censorship. The article goes on to paraphrase Goebbels's justification that was published as the lead article in the *Voelkische Beobachter*: "There he declared these jokes as a remnant of the

liberal epoch and a phenomenon of degeneration that would have to eradicated immediately because the Nazi regime would create a system of two thousand years duration in the same way as the Catholic Church." See "Der Nazikrieg gegen den Witz," *Pariser Tageszeitung*, February 5–6, 1939, 2.

32. Kadner, *Rasse und Humor*, 10.

33. Kadner, 11. Compare the Nazi *Totlachen* strategy with the joyfully masochistic response of Salomo Friedlaender (aka Mynona) who published his grotesque *Der Lachende Hiob* (Paris: Éd. Du Phénix, 1935) in Parisian exile. Insisting on the transmutation of Jewish suffering into laughter, Mynona's grotesque prescribes comic inversion—and perversion—as the only way for the victims to deal with Nazi persecution. As the tickled Mynona outlined his project: "In fact, I envision these days the grotesque motif of a joyful Job, a laughing Job! Who considers the blows of fate as attempts to tickle him pleasantly. Thus, the anti-Semite tickles the Jews." See Mynona, "Letter to Salomon Samuel and Family" (December 4, 1933), in *Salomo Friedlaender/Mynona, Briefwechsel 3: Mai 1931–Dezember 1934* (Heersching: Waitawhile, 2012), 291.

34. Kadner, *Rasse und Humor*, 219.

35. Marcus G. Patka, *Wege des Lachens: Jüdischer Witz und Humor aus Wien* (Vienna: Bibliothek der Provinz, 2011), 37. Kadner's criticism of Bergson's book stresses how "mixed up" it is in terms of its racial attributes rather than in terms of its conceptual rigor: "The French Jew Henry Bergson has written a philosophical study about laughter, in which, in fact, it is difficult to distinguish to what extent it is dictated by Jewish thought processes and to what extent by French ones (i.e., Celtic = Romanesque nature of a Western stamp)" (17).

36. The one major addition to the second edition was the inclusion of Wilhelm Busch's anti-Semitic caricature of Schmulchen Schivelbeiner composed in 1882 (225). Kadner added this commentary: "Like in so many phenomena of existence, Wilhelm Busch also understands how to bring the Jews into word and image via the fastest and most comprehensible satirical formula" (225–226). On the other hand, a few images found in the first edition were dropped from the second edition, including Hans Schweitzer's "Monte Zion." See Siegfried Kadner, *Rasse und Humor* (Munich: J. F. Lehmanns Verlag, 1939), 215–230.

37. Kadner, *Rasse und Humor*, 208. Kadner is intent on making a rigid binary opposition here between Nordic and Jewish self-irony. While the Nordic humorist shows a "preference to make fun of his own style and his own nature," this partakes of the "cool distancing of the ego" and strikes one as "ego-averse." This is in stark contrast to Jewish self-irony that involves "taking intimate pleasure in himself and his kind and striving to remove racially conditioned seriousness into the harmless light of drollery." Coincidentally, Kadner's reference to Jewish intimacy recalls Theodor Reik's essay on the subject of intimacy and aggressiveness in Jewish wit published just a few years earlier, "Die Intimität im Judenwitz," in *Nackdenkliche Heiterkeit* (Vienna: Internationaler Psychanalytischer Verlag, 1933), 70–90.

38. Ellul, *Propaganda*, 58.

39. This infamous diary entry dated March 27, 1942, is also where Goebbels makes explicit reference to the liquidation of the Jews. The German text reads: "Das Judentum hat nichts zu lachen." See Elke Fröhlich ed., *Die Tagebücher von Joseph Goebbels* (Munich: K. G. Saur, 1994), 3.2:561.

40. See Jefferson S. Chase, *Inciting Laughter: The Development of "Jewish Humor" in 19th Century German Culture* (Berlin: Walter de Gruyter, 2000).

41. Mel Gordon also takes up and mocks this racialist valuation of humor in Kadner: "Unsurprisingly, the Germans came out as the comic superstars of the civilized world and the Jews the most inferior" (98). See Gordon, "Nazi 'Proof' that Jews Possessed the Worst Humor in the World," *Israeli Journal of Humor Research* 1, no. 2 (2012): 97–100.

42. Kadner, *Rasse und Humor*, 202. In addition to possessing no humor at all, the denigrating propagandist also maintains that the Jewish joker's laughter is stunted and unnatural. Therefore, he writes later about "the Jew, to whom a free roaring laughter [*freies schallendes Gelächter*] is alien in general" and insists that "crafty, winking eyes and smirks [*Grinsen*] are more to his nature" (233).

43. Kadner, 201–202. In contrast, the work of the Jewish folklorist Rabbi Chayim Bloch contests Kadner's contention that the Jews possessed no humor in *Ostjüdischer Humor* (Berlin: Benjamin Harz, 1920).

44. Anonymous, "Rasse und Humor," *Das Schwarze Korps*, April 9, 1936, 10.

45. Anonymous, "Rasse und Humor." Chase also analyzes this citation in the form of an extended footnote in chapter 5 of *Inciting Laughter* to "illustrate the direct influence of the nineteenth century *Judenwitz* discourse on Nazi attitudes" and the dichotomization of Jewish *Witz* versus German *Humor* along strictly racialist lines (219–220). This citation from *Das Schwarze Korps* concludes with aspersions cast against Saphir and Heine as two cynical Jewish exemplars (". . . for example, Saphir in Vienna, or in part also Heine, whose vein of anti-German satire only began to flow after he entered the paid service of the French government"). Nevertheless, Chase does not allude to Kadner's book directly.

46. Günther's books were published by J. F. Lehmanns Verlag in Munich — the same publisher of Kadner's *Rasse und Humor*. In fact, some of these works receive promotional consideration in the back pages of Kadner's book.

47. Hans F. K. Günther, *Kleine Rassenkunde des deutschen Volkes* (Munich: J. F. Lehmanns Verlag, 1929), 9.

48. Kadner, *Rasse und Humor*, 233.

49. Kadner's appropriation of Goethe as anti-Semitic thinker — even though he lived in an era that was "not yet ripe to apply the standard of race to human relationships" (233) — relies on Goethe's infamous letter to Friedrich Heinrich Jacobi on January 12, 1785, after reading Moses Mendelssohn's "Morgenstunden": "'Oh, you poor Christian!' Goethe exclaimed. 'What will happen to you [*wie wird es dir ergehen*] when by and by the Jew will have spun his web around your humming wings.' This is not the only place where he deals with Judaism, and the racial defenses awaken in him every time" (233). Surprisingly, Kadner cited a milder

version of the quotation that actually begins: "*Wie schlimm wird es dir ergehen* [How badly will you fare]."

50. Kadner, 234. Günther's racist book that laid the groundwork for "Nordic thinking" and that exposed the eugenic risks posed to the "Nordic race" was published by J. F. Lehmann Verlag in 1920 and reached its fourth printing by 1935.

51. Alexander Moszkowski entitles one chapter of his classic Jewish joke collection "*Schlagfertig und Spitzfindig*" [Quick-witted and hairsplitting]. See *Der jüdische Witz und seine Philosophie: 399 Juwelen, echt gefaßt* (Berlin: Dr. Eysler, 1923), 90–96.

52. Kadner, *Rasse und Humor*, 203.

53. Kadner, 204.

54. Gershom Scholem, *Lamentations of Youth: The Diaries of Gershom Scholem, 1913–1919*, trans. Anthony David Skinner (Cambridge, MA: Harvard University Press, 2005), 286.

55. Ernst Simon, "Zum Problem des Jüdischen Witzes" was first published in the *Bayerische Israelitische Gemeindezeitung* (no. 20) in Munich on October 15, 1928. The quotation appears on page 315. In the edited version published in English twenty years later at the time of the founding of the State of Israel in 1948, Simon also praises the "mental calisthenics" (44) of Talmudic thought. This phrasing uncannily parallels Kadner's reference to the "mental gymnastics" (*Geistesgymnastik*) that pervade the Lemberg-Warsaw lying joke in the Nazi propagandist's version. See Ernst Simon, "Notes on Jewish Wit," *Jewish Frontier* 15, no. 10 (October 1948): 42–48.

56. Kadner, *Rasse und Humor*, 203.

57. Kadner, 204.

58. Freud, *Jokes*, 147.

59. Kadner, *Rasse und Humor*, 202–203. Kadner continues his mudslinging campaign against Freud by mocking the psychoanalyst's scatological association of money and dirt to be discussed later in this chapter.

60. See Kadner, 209. Cf. Moszkowski's earlier version in *Die Jüdische Kiste* (Berlin: Dr. Eysler, 1911). The Jewish satirist tells this joke with the Jew testifying on the witness stand (38–39). In contrast, Kadner puts his "Jewish vagrant" into the accused role of the defendant.

61. Kadner, *Rasse und Humor*, 204. While Kadner's version has Warsaw as the contested destination, Freud's version has the character travel to Cracow.

62. Freud, *Jokes*, 161. Freud's version of the joke in translation reads as follows: "Two Jews met in a railway carriage at a station in Galicia. 'Where are you going?' asked one. 'To Cracow,' was the answer. 'What a liar you are!' broke out the other. 'If you say you're going to Cracow, you want me to believe that you are going to Lemberg. But I know that in fact you're going to Cracow. So why are you lying to me?'"

63. Freud, 161. Freud's original German is quite clear in marking out the skeptical

space that questions both belief ("*dass ich glauben soll*") and knowledge ("*nun weiss ich aber*"). See Sigmund Freud, *Der Witz und seine Beziehung zum Unbewußten* (Frankfurt am Main: Fischer, 1960), 94.

64. Sigmund Freud, "Character and Anal Erotism," in *The Freud Reader* (New York: W. W. Norton and Company, 1989), 297.

65. Kadner, *Rasse und Humor*, 214.

66. Kadner, 205. The original caricature was published in living color in *Simplicissimus* on September 16, 1907, 390. While the journal was forced to shut down by the Nazis in 1933, Thöny fared much better during the Third Reich. The Nazis lauded him and he was the recipient of honors including a professorship awarded to him by Hitler.

67. Marcus G. Patka, *Wege des Lachens*, 37. This is reminiscent of the pithy joke recounted by Freud: "Two Jews met in the neighborhood of the bath-house. 'Have you taken a bath?' asked one of them. 'What?' asked the other in return, 'is there one missing?'" (*Jokes*, 49). This classic joke allows the Western European Jew to mock the *Ostjude* on two counts—hygiene and honesty. Thanks to Norman Kleeblatt (and his *Yekke* sensitivity) for reminding me of the double abuse heaped upon the Eastern European Jew in this joke.

68. Elvira Bauer, *Trau keinem Fuchs auf seiner Heid und keinem Jud bei seinem Eid* (Nuremberg: Stürmer Verlag, 1936).

69. Kadner, *Rasse und Humor*, 208.

70. Kadner, 209.

71. Moszkowski, "Die Philosophie des jüdischen Witzes," in *Der jüdische Witz und seine Philosophie*, 24.

72. Moszkowski, 24.

73. Kadner, *Rasse und Humor*, 209.

74. Siegfried Kadner, *Die Prosaschmiede: Vom Richtigen Lesen Sprechen/Schreiben; Ein Buch vom deutschen Stil* [The prose-smith: proper reading speaking and writing; a German style book] (Berlin: Deutsche Buch-Gemeinschaft, 1932).

75. Kadner, *Rasse und Humor*, 209. Kadner already mocks the German-Jewish dialect of Yiddish as a mongrel language issuing from a hybrid race in chapter 3, "Gebärde und Sprache" (Gesture and Language), when he writes that "the origin of the Jews . . . stems from ancient, inharmonious racial crossings" that result in "*das Mauscheln*" (26).

76. For a perceptive article on the anti-Semitic attack on Yiddish dialect and Jewish accentuation of German in the form of "*mauscheln*," see Sonia Gollance, "Using Yiddish to Teach About German Antisemitism," *In geveb*, June 2019, https://ingeveb.org/pedagogy/using-yiddish-to-teach-about-german-antisemitism. Gollance discusses how the pejorative term is "likely derived from the name 'Mausche' (Moses or the Hebrew version Moshe, as pronounced by German Jews)" and that it "means to speak German like a Jew." She also refers to Jeffrey Grossman's scholarship on the farcical performances of the Berlin comedian Albert Wurm (1794–1834) and his

uncanny ability to "mock the Yiddish speech of Jews" as well as their body language. See Jeffrey Grossman, *The Discourse on Yiddish from the Enlightenment to the Second Empire* (Columbia, SC: Camden House, 2000), 150.

77. Kadner, *Rasse und Humor*, 26.

78. Patka, *Wege des Lachens*, 37–38. The use of *mauscheln* as a hidden and corrupt language of the Jews has been taken up in several of Sander Gilman's writings, most notably in *Jewish Self-Hatred: Anti-Semitism and the Secret Language of the Jews* (Baltimore, MD: Johns Hopkins University Press, 1986), 140–144.

79. Gilman, *Jewish Self-Hatred*, 145.

80. Gilman, 146. Gilman explores not only the career of Moritz Saphir (145–148) but also that of Ludwig Börne (148–167), and Heinrich Heine (167–188). All three Jewish writers are at the center of Chase's *Inciting Laughter*.

81. Kadner, *Rasse und Humor*, 214.

82. Kadner, 210.

83. Paul Nikolaus, *Jüdische Miniaturen* (Hannover: Paul Steegemann Verlag, 1925), 27.

84. Kadner, *Rasse und Humor*, 217.

85. Kadner, 218.

86. Kadner, 211. Moreover, Kadner turns to a joke whose punch line alludes to the doubtful success of a proposed baptism thereby driving home the point that Jewish-Christian religious difference cannot be bridged because of physical and racial differences: "That Pastor to whom Counsel Veilchenfeld comes also has similar doubts about mutual understanding: 'Mr. Superintendent, I would like to be baptized.' The pastor, after close scrutiny: 'Well, good. I will try it.'"

87. Davies, *Ethnic Humor around the World*, 124.

88. See, for example, the caricature by "Fips" (Philipp Rupprecht) in *Der Stürmer* (no. 37 [1932]) that depicts a Jew who is about to crush a flea and that thinly veils the Nazi's "will to extermination" in the form of black humor. Before being sent off to flea heaven, the cartoon parasite pleas for a reversal of the death sentence: "I will be destroyed [*kaput gemacht*] and he shall live, the Jew, even though he is the bigger blood sucker of the two of us."

89. Keeping this in mind, Art Spiegelman's *Maus* with its transformation of the tragic history of the Holocaust into a cartoon struggle of cat and mouse makes perfect sense as a counter-discursive response to the Nazi's staging of the Jew in parasitic and animalistic fashion by means of caricature.

90. Several compilations of *Flüsterwitze* (whisper jokes) and assessments of their role in the Nazi era have been published: Hans-Jochen Gamm, *Der Flüsterwitz im Dritten Reich* (Munich: List Verlag, 1963); Ralph Wiener, *Als das Lachen tödlich war* (Rudolstadt: Geifenverlag, 1988); Alexander Drozdzynski, *Das verspottete Tausendjährige Reich* (Düsseldorf: Droste, 1978); Max Vandrey, *Der politische Witz im Dritten Reich* (Munich: Goldmann, 1967); and Kathleen Stokker, *Folklore Fights the Nazis: Humor in Occupied Norway, 1940–1945* (Madison: University of Wisconsin Press, 1997).

91. S. Felix Mendelsohn, *Let Laughter Ring* (Philadelphia: Jewish Publication Society of America, 1941).

92. Drozdzynski, *Das verspottete Tausendjährige Reich*, 77.

93. Mendelsohn, *Let Laughter Ring*, 43.

## 6. Jewish Joke Reparations and Mourning in Post-Holocaust Germany

Unless otherwise noted, all translations from the German are mine.

1. Indeed, the view that the more "sacred, taboo, or disgusting" the topic is, the more often it becomes "the principal grist for humor mills" is taken up by folklorists Alan Dundes and Thomas Hauschild in their study of the "cycle of sick jokes" known as "Auschwitz Jokes," *Western Folklore* 42, no. 4 (1983): 249–260.

2. In this quotation from *Maximen und Reflexionen*, Goethe also points out the wonderful powers of divination in Lichtenberg's jests: "Lichtenberg's writings can serve us as the most wonderful divining rod: where he makes a jest [*Spass*], there a problem lies concealed." Richard Dobel, *Lexikon der Goethe Zitate* (Zurich: Artemis, 1968), 526. Similarly, this chapter posits the discourse in and on the Jewish joke as a wonderful way to divine the problems of cultural and intellectual *Wiedergutmachung*. While Goethe focuses on *Spass* (joke or jest) in this passage, he refers to the *jüdische Witz* by name in his Karlsbad diaries. For a discussion and a recitation of the specific jokes that found favor in Goethe's eyes, including one where the problem of jokes and mourning lurks in the background, see Chajim Bloch, *Das jüdische Volk in seiner Anekdote: Ernstes und Heiteres* (Berlin: Verlag für Kulturpolitik, 1931), 7–8, 327–328.

3. For a discussion of the "question of taboos which the new German society was trying to forget at all costs" (188), see Jean-Paul Bier, "The Holocaust, West Germany, and Strategies of Oblivion, 1947–1979," in *Germans and Jews Since the Holocaust: The Changing Situation in West Germany*, ed. Anson Rabinbach and Jack Zipes (New York: Holmes and Meier, 1986), 183–207.

4. Salcia Landmann, *Der jüdische Witz: Soziologie und Sammlung* (Olten and Freiburg im Breisgau: Walter Verlag, 1960). Hereafter cited as *DJW* followed by the year of the edition and page number.

5. Landmann's dissertation *Phänomenologie und Ontologie: Husserl, Scheler, Heidegger* (Leipzig: Heitz, 1939) was published under her maiden name of Salcia Passweg. The juxtaposition of the future Yiddish jokelorist Landmann studying the Nazi philosophical sympathizer Heidegger as a graduate student makes for an intriguing and ironic image. Landmann claimed that she was led to the study of Jewish jokes when noticing their similarity in nature to Kant's undecidable treatment of "aporias" and the impossibility of determining "whether space and time are finite or infinite . . . in a philosophical seminar of Professor Hermann Schmalenbach in Basel." Salcia Landmann, letter to author, February 10, 1995.

6. The staging of Anne Frank in Germany is discussed in Anat Feinberg,

*Wiedergutmachung im Programm: Jüdisches Schicksal in deutschen Nachkriegsdrama* (Cologne: Prometh Verlag, 1988), esp. 20–24. The subsequent proliferation of media relating to Anne Frank's memory is pursued in Barbara Kirshenblatt-Gimblett and Jeffrey Shandler, eds., *Anne Frank Unbound: Media, Imagination, Memory* (Bloomington: Indiana University Press, 2012).

7. As Landmann states: "It became possible with this introduction to turn to the Jewish joke after the Shoah and to laugh again [*wieder zu lachen*] in connection with the Jews." Salcia Landmann, letter to author, February 10, 1995.

8. The critics of Landmann's book who accused it of spreading anti-Semitism charged that it was only a "laughing at." See, for example, Edwin Hartl, "In Sachen erklärter Widersprüche: Friedrich Torberg als Satiriker und Polemiker," in *Und Lächeln ist das Erbteil meines Stammes: Erinnerung an Friedrich Torberg*, ed. David Axmann (Vienna: Edition Atelier, 1986); Hartl writes: "it easily allowed the remaining unchristian part of Christendom to laugh *at* the Jews instead of *with* them" (44).

9. For an extended analysis of mourning and nostalgia in relation to the Holocaust in Syberberg, see Eric Santner, "Allegories of Grieving: The Films of Hans Jürgen Syberberg," in *Stranded Objects: Mourning, Memory and Film in Postwar Germany* (Ithaca, NY: Cornell University Press, 1990). Santner also quotes Syberberg's provocative remarks demanding restitutions from America on account of the film, *Holocaust*: "America now has its own reparations to pay [*hat einiges wiedergutzumachen*] after this *Holocaust* from Hollywood in the German media" (104).

10. Theodor Reik, "Zur Psychoanalyse des jüdischen Witzes," in *Lust und Leid im Witz* (Vienna: Internationaler Psychoanalytischer Verlag, 1929), 33–58. Cf. Reik, *Jewish Wit* (New York: Gamut Press, 1962), which does not reference his earlier work on the theme of wit and melancholy.

11. Sigmund Freud, *Jokes and their Relation to the Unconscious*, trans. James Strachey, in collaboration with Anna Freud (New York: W. W. Norton, 1960), 156.

12. Santner, *Stranded Objects*, 12.

13. James Joyce, *Finnegans Wake* (London: Penguin, 1992), 6.

14. Georges Bataille, "Hegel, la mort et le sacrifice," *Oeuvres completes*, vol. 12, *Articles 2, 1950–1961* (Paris: Gallimard, 1988), 341.

15. The difficulties of how to read joke mourning—or of not reading its message, as the following mourning joke makes clear—are enacted in the adventures of Moses Steinpilz. Here, the realm of sensual pleasures stands in for the joke that defers the work of mourning until the next morning. Nevertheless, from another perspective, the satirical thrust of this joke might be directed toward the need for better respecting the dead: "On his business trip, Moses Steinpilz had taken a loose woman with him to his hotel room. He had hardly entered the room together with the girl when there is a knocking and the manager hands him a telegram. Steinpilz rips open the envelope, casts a quick glance at its contents, and sees that the sudden

death of his wife is reported in it. Startled he puts the telegram aside and says: 'Oh, how mournful and tearful I will be tomorrow when I read the telegram!'" (*DJW* [1960], 385).

16. Salcia Landmann, "Zum jüdischen Witz," in *Neues* (Munich: F. A. Herbig, 1972), 7.

17. Salcia Landmann, "*Vorwort: Jüdischer Humor aus Amerika*," in *Das grosse Buch des jüdischen Humors*, eds. William Novak and Moshe Waldoks (Königsberg: Athenäum Verlag, 1982), 9.

18. Salcia Landmann, letter to author, February 10, 1995.

19. See Landmann, "Glossar," in *DJW* (1962), 657.

20. Landmann, *DJW* (1962), 434.

21. Landmann comments about this trend in her publications record: "The Jewish joke was for me the entry point to other publications in which I represent the Jews to the Gentiles." Salcia Landmann, letter to author, February 10, 1995.

22. Immanuel Olsvanger, *Röyte Pomerantsen or How to Laugh in Yiddish* (New York: Schocken Books, 1947), xvii.

23. Landmann, "*An Alle Liebhaber und Verächter des jüdischen Witzes*," in *Jüdische Witze* (Munich: DTV, 1963), 13. This foreword was written for the publication of the mass market paperback edition.

24. The Nobel Prize–winning Yiddish author Isaac Bashevis Singer took issue with this aspect of Landmann's project in his fabulous and humorous book review, "The Everlasting Joke." Singer wrote the following witty rejoinders: "Miss Landmann clearly intends, with this book, to erect a monument to the Jewish joke. But the body is not quite in its grave. It is still very much alive and busy turning out new jokes in New York, Tel Aviv, Buenos Aires, and even Moscow." He later focuses on the case for the American revivification of the Jewish joke that includes a joke that mocks Landmann's theorizing: "To paraphrase Mark Twain, the death of the Jewish joke is grossly exaggerated. It reminds me . . . of the anecdote about the doctor who had completely given up on a patient, and when the patient came to visit him, vigorous and healthy, the doctor ordered him, 'Get out of here. Theoretically, you're a corpse.'" Isaac Bashevis Singer, "The Everlasting Joke," *Commentary Magazine*, May 1, 1961, 458–462.

25. Landmann, *DJW* (1960), 105.

26. Landmann, 111. This reiterates the earlier passage on Jewish joke extinction in the Holocaust: "With the exception of mass extermination by the Hitler thugs, the Jewish joke has really overcome (*überdauert*) it all" (102).

27. This leads to a rather ambivalent passage that recommends both a mourning of the Jewish joke *and* a good riddance to it because it suggests that it is rooted in Jewish weakness and bitter conditions. This is perhaps the closest that Landmann came to endorse the "*Witz aus Trauer*" hypothesis: "In Israel, the Jewish joke is already extinct because it has no vital function there anymore. But around the world, it is going to meet its exit. Too bad for it! It had—and has—no equal. Indeed, when one considers to what bitter terms and conditions it is attached, and that it would

awaken itself back to life again in Israel only in connection with a second Jewish Holocaust specifically, one can mourn it, but one would not wish it any resurrection. It belongs irrevocably to the past along with European Judaism." Salcia Landmann, "Der Jüdische Witz und Sein Tod," unpublished manuscript, 9. While Landmann informed me in 1995 that this article was forthcoming in Die Welt, I have not been able to locate it in print.

28. This returns to the inscription of Landmann's "Requiem" and the question of timing in relation to joke mourning. If Landmann's requiem over the Jewish joke was written in 1960, then what on earth is she doing in 1982 as the invited guest eulogist at Novak and Waldoks's Jewish joke revival? She herself seems to be asking this same question in the section called "Ende des jüdischen Witzes?" This strange contradiction reveals the pattern of production in the discourse of post-Holocaust Jewish joke mourning and reparations that consists of a series of eulogies that are converted into resurrections and revivifications.

29. Jürg Ramspeck, "Ein ungewöhnlicher Bestseller," Die Weltwoche, December 30, 1960, 15.

30. For a further development of the thesis, see Elliott Oring, "The People of the Joke: On the Conceptualization of a Jewish Humor," Western Folklore 42, no. 4 (1983), 261–270. Oring traces the thesis back to B. Rohatyn, "Die Gestalten des Jüdischen Volkshumor," Ost und West 11 (1911) in which Rohatyn asks rather rhetorically: "Can one better overcome sorrow and gnawing pain than by laughing them away?" (267).

31. Elisabeth Petuchowski, Das Herz auf der Zunge: Aus der Welt des Jüdischen Witzes (Freiburg im Breisgau: Herder, 1984), 53.

32. Jonas Kreppel, "Einführung," Wie der Jude Lacht: Anthologie jüdischer Witze, Satiren, Anekdoten, Humoresken, Aphorismen — Ein Beitrag zur Psychologie des jüdischen Witzes und zur jüdischen Volkskunde (Vienna: Verlag "Das Buch," 1933), vi.

33. Freud, "The Purposes of Jokes," in Der Witz, 111–112. Freud's thesis reads in part: "The occurrence of self-criticism as a determinant may explain how it is that a number of the most apt jokes (of which we have given plenty of instances) have grown up on the soil of Jewish popular life. . . . Incidentally I do not know whether there are many other instances of a people making fun to such a degree of its own character."

34. Landmann's ethnocentric Jewish joke defense reads as follows: "However, the success of the book is explained not only in terms of the current political and psychological situation in Central Europe. The Jewish joke is superior to any other ethnic joke in terms of form and content" ("Zum jüdischen Witz," 9).

35. In the context of intercultural reconciliation and understanding, Carlo Schmid also delivered a radio lecture on January 1, 1961, entitled "Wir Deutschen und die Juden." An edited version is reprinted in Carlo Schmid, Politik als geistige Aufgabe (Munich: Knaur, 1976). This includes the following blanket affirmation (with the emphasis on "good") regarding Jewish publishing in the era

of *Wiedergutmachung*: "Of course, many books in the German language by Jewish writers also appear in our days that find their way to us. It is good that we read them; we can have a lot of them and learn a lot about the world and about ourselves" (263).

36. Carlo Schmid, "*Geleitwort*," *DJW* (1960), 9.

37. Schmid, 12.

38. Fritz Muliar, "*Nachwort*," in Novak und Waldoks, *Das grosse Buch des jüdischen Humors*, 312.

39. J. Klein-Haparash, *Krug und Stein: Jüdische Anekdoten* (Munich: Piper Verlag, 1961), 7.

40. Schmid, "*Geleitwort*," *DJW* (1960), 11.

41. J. G. Burg, *Jüdische Anekdotiade* (Munich: C. Ederer, 1977).

42. Erich Lüth, *Durch Wahrheit zum Frieden: Aktion "Friede mit Israel"* (Hamburg: Gesellschaft für christlich-jüdische Zusammenarbeit, 1952), 20.

43. Landmann, "*Zum jüdischen Witz*," 17.

44. For these definitions, see Freud, introduction to *Jokes*, 11.

45. The latter view is expressed by the controversial figure J. G. Burg in the final remarks to his postwar collection of Jewish jokes, *Jüdische Anekdotiade*. Burg believes: "Truthful anecdotes also will contribute more to understanding between Jews and Germans than those grossly overblown (*groß aufgebauschte*) and superficial weeks of 'brotherhood' that recur regularly on the calendar can do" (225).

46. Friedrich Torberg, "'Wai geschrien!, oder Salcia Landmann ermordet den jüdischen Witz," *Der Monat* 14, no. 157 (October 1961): 64.

47. Josef Müller-Marein, "*Die Waffe der Wehrlosen: Ein Buch, das helfen könnte, die deutsche Verkrampfung zu lösen*" [The weapon of the defenseless: A book that could help to solve German tension], *Die Zeit*, May 5, 1961.

48. Torberg, "Wai geschrien!," 64. The argument and its unpacking of the terms of indebtedness continues: "From this willingness to take sentiment for quality, character for talent, or suffering for performance, no bad book with so much injustice has yet profited like the book of the Switzerland-based Jewess Salcia Landmann which expressed neither sentiment nor quality, neither character nor talent, and can make no further claims for itself than the choice of a rewarding theme for two reasons: rewarding not only because it is a Jewish theme, and thus a priori had its share of the tabooed *Wiedergutmachung* for sure, but also because this *Wiedergutmachung* was accomplished in a particularly easy [*bequem*] and catchy way in reference to the Jewish joke — one of the few bright spots that one accorded to the Jews in general" (64).

49. Neumann refers to Torberg's review as "superb criticism" ("*grossartige Kritik*"). See *Vielleicht das Heitere: Tagebuch aus einem anderen Jahr* (München: Verlag Kurt Desch, 1986), 310. Neumann also wrote two pieces in *Die Zeit* (December 20, 1963, and January 3, 1964) on the theme of Jewish joke narration under the title of "Über das Erzählen von Witzen" (On telling jokes).

50. Neumann, *Vielleicht das Heitere*, 311.

51. At this juncture, it does well to recall the Auschwitz joke recited by avant-

garde theater director George Tabori in an interview. As one of the most important breakers of taboos in German theater in the post-Holocaust era, Tabori's black humorous witticism gives food for thought. In contrast to Neumann's abreactive image, Tabori's punchline is additive: "G. T. Ich gebe Ihnen ein Beispiel. Kennen Sie den kürzesten deutschen Witz überhaupt? [I give you an example. Do you know the shortest German joke of them all?]/H. K. Nein. [No.]/G. T. Auschwitz." Tabori defines this as a German rather than as a Jewish joke because this lethal joke was in reality played on the Jews. Following the post-Holocaust script of laughter out of mourning, Tabori defines the Jewish joke as making the unbearable bearable and calls attention to how it springs out of a collective experience of pain and suffering. See Herlinde Koelbl, *Jüdische Portraits* (Frankfurt am Main: Fischer, 1989), 236–237.

52. Torberg, "Wai geschrien!," 65.

53. Torberg, 64–65.

54. For a thorough review of the wave as a multisided political conflict, see Werner Bergmann, "Antisemitismus als politisches Ereignis: Die antisemitische Welle im Winter 1959/1960," in *Antisemitismus in der Politischen Kultur nach 1945*, ed. Werner Bergmann and Rainer Erb (Opladen: Westdeutscher Verlag, 1990), 253–275.

55. Landmann sets up this joke with a sociocultural commentary of her own that displays another error in historical accounting (1959 – 1945 = 14). She writes: "Twenty years after the end of the Nazi era, rowdies desecrated the walls of synagogues in some German towns with Swastikas and anti-Semitic slogans. The desecraters were severely punished. At that time, the following joke arose" (*DJW* [1976], 575).

56. This story goes back to medieval times. See Julius H. Schoeps, "*Sepulcra hostium religiosa nobis non sunt*: Zerstörung und Schändung jüdischer Friedhöfe in der Bundesrepublik Deutschland seit 1945," in *Antisemitismus nach dem Holocaust: Bestandsaufnahme und Erscheinungsformen in deutschsprachigen Ländern*, eds. Alphons Silbermann und Julius H. Schoeps (Cologne: Verlag Wissenschaft und Politik, 1986), 33–39.

57. Peter Schönbach, *Reaktionen auf die Antisemitische Welle im Winter 1959/1960* (Frankfurt am Main: Europäische Verlagsanstalt, 1961), 82.

58. In reviewing Torberg's accusations against her book, Landmann tries to personalize the attack and categorically dismisses the charge that her book spread anti-Semitism as pure nonsense: "He burst with envy over my success and wrote a multipage pamphlet in his journal, in which he accused me of spreading anti-Semitism with my book and of not formulating some jokes perfectly. The former is nonsense." Salcia Landmann, letter to author, February 10, 1995.

59. Torberg, "Wai geschrien!," 62.

60. Torberg, 62–64.

61. Theodor Adorno, "Zur Bekämpfung des Antisemitismus heute" (1962), *Vermischte Schriften 1*, in *Gesammelte Schriften*, ed. Rolf Tiedemann (Frankfurt am Main: Suhrkamp, 1986), 20.1:368. According to Paul Stöcklein's hearsay, Adorno

was not at all pleased with Landmann's book, but he never put this in writing: "By the way, Adorno rejected the collection passionately without expressing himself in public unfortunately." See Franz-Heinrich Hackel, "Mittel der Sprach- und Inhaltsanalyse am Beispiel des Essays über Salcia Landmann," in *Zur Sprachkunst Friedrich Torbergs Parodie—Witz—Anekdote* (Frankfurt am Main: Peter Lang, 1984), 87.

62. Nietzsche poses this double play in the form of a questioning equation: "Have these genealogists of morals had even the remotest suspicion that, for example, the fundamental moral concept of 'guilt' [*Schuld*] had its origin in the very material concept of 'debts' [*Schulden*]?" Friedrich Nietzsche, *Zur Genealogie der Moral: Eine Streitschrift* (Leipzig: C. G. Naumann, 1900), 66.

63. Jan Meyerowitz, *Der echte jüdische Witz* (Berlin: Colloquium Verlag, 1971), 13.

64. Landmann replicates a joke that appeared in *Brennessel* verbatim. It is a satirical reading of Zionism that puts the Jew in the role of interminable meddler and middleman: "What is Zionism? If a Jew contracts a second one to collect money from a third one with which one can send a fourth one to Palestine." Landmann, "Messianismus und Zionismus," in *DJW* (1960), 483.

65. The argument of repressed aggressions links up with Henryk Broder's provocative catchphrase: "There is anti-Semitism not *in spite*, but rather *on account of* Auschwitz." Broder, *Der Ewige Antisemit: Über Sinn und Funktion eines beständigen Gefühls* (Frankfurt am Main: Fischer, 1988), 11.

66. Alexander Mitscherlich and Margarete Mitscherlich, *Die Unfähigkeit zu trauern: Grundlagen kollektiven Verhaltens* (Munich: Piper, 1967), 40. The original German reads: "Reaktionsformen, mit denen die Einsicht in die überwältigende Schuldlast ferngehalten wird."

67. Mitscherlich and Mitscherlich, 60.

68. Torberg, "Wai geschrien!, 48.

69. Landmann, *DJW* (1960), 193.

70. Sander L. Gilman, *Jewish Self-Hatred*, 345–354. This is from chapter 6, "The Ashes of the Holocaust and the Closure of Self-Hatred."

71. For a close reading of the means and content of Torberg's polemic paragraph by paragraph, see Hackel, "Mittel der Sprach- und Inhaltsanalyse," 87–118.

72. Torberg, "Wai geschrien!," 54.

73. See Lutz Röhrich, *Der Witz*, 284. Miming Torberg, Röhrich's accounting reviews how Landmann's intended good mourning (*"eine Art Ehrenrettung"*) conceals bad mourning: "Although the book was written by a Jewish woman and thought of as a kind of vindication of Jewish humor, it has experienced angry criticism. . . . In S. Landmann, the punchlines are often bent or killed. Friedrich Torberg blames the dismal pallor of the joke versions, their humorlessness and lack of punchlines, their dilettantish narrative style, their lack of feeling and lack of instinct. In addition, there are repetitions, misleading definitions, ignorance of historical and theological presuppositions, the unsystematicity and superficiality

of the commentary, misquotations and false literary information. Due to all of the above errors, Torberg attacks the book as un-Jewish and therefore of a necessarily anti-Jewish character."

74. Torberg, "Wai geschrien!," 56.

75. Hartl, "In Sachen erklärter Widersprüche," 43.

76. Harry Zohn, *Wiener Juden in der Deutschen Literatur: Essays* (Tel Aviv: Edition "Olamenu," 1964), 104–105.

77. Landmann, letter to author, February 10, 1995.

78. Freud, *Jokes*, 212.

79. Landmann, letter to author, February 10, 1995.

80. Landmann stresses this in the same letter: "There were, as stated, only enthusiastic reviews from the newspapers and magazines and electronic media of non-Jews [*Nichtjuden*]."

81. Nevertheless, the claim to having knowledge of Jewish tradition may not have convinced no less an authority on these matters than Gershom Scholem. Even though he is not referring to Landmann's edition by name, one can infer that it is the direct referent in his negative appraisal of contemporary Jewish joke books in comparison with those of his youth, given his specific reference to Manuel Schnitzer, *Das Buch der jüdischen Witze* published in 1907 which "towers in superiority over some of today's horrible [*greulichen*] products in these genres in which a reader who is familiar with Jewish things will not overcome his astonishment and anger." See *Von Berlin nach Jerusalem: Jugenderinnerungen* (Frankfurt am Main: Jüdischer Verlag, 1982), 45. I thank Jacob Hessing for this fabulous reference.

82. Landmann, "Zum jüdischen Witz," 7.

83. Landmann, *DJW* (1962), 645. The original reads: "Alexander Moszkowski hat die jüdische und goische Witzreaktion in Versform zusammengefasst:/E jüdischer Witz/Mit e jüddisch Akzent:/Was e Goi nicht versteht/Und e Jüd immer schon kennt."

84. Landmann, *DJW* (1962), 645. The original reads: "Erzählt man aber einem Juden einen Witz, so sagt er: 'Den kenn' ich schon!' und erzählt einen noch besseren."

85. Präger and Schmitz, eds., *Jüdische Schwänke* (Vienna: R. Löwit Verlag, 1928), 3. The original reads: "Erzählst du aber einem Juden einen Witz, so unterbricht er dich: 'Ach was, ein alter Witz!' — und er kann ihn dir besser erzählen.'"

86. Frank Stern reviews the transformation of philo-Semitism into official state policy as follows: "With reparations then, philo-Semitism transformed from an ambivalent sociopsychological element of the German postwar period to an integral part of the ideological legitimacy of the Federal Republic. It became politically instrumentalized philo-Semitism." See Stern, *Im Anfang war Auschwitz: Antisemitismus und Philosemitismus im deutschen Nachkrieg* (Gerlingen: Bleicher Verlag, 1991), 300.

87. This follows again Stern's analysis of the postwar admixture of manifest philo-

and latent anti-Semitic elements: "The pro-Jewish and philo-Semitic statements and behaviors, in so far as they are public, often take place via a deeper level of opinions and attitudes that represent a conglomeration of traditional and new anti-Jewish or anti-Semitic elements" (330).

88. Landmann, *Jüdische Witze*, 240.

89. Freud, *Jokes*, 121. The "Wiederjudmachungswitz" resembles a rather ambivalent Jewish self-critical/anti-Semitic joke in form and content that, as Freud relates, plays between a slight modification of two vowels. This turn of phrase as narrated by Herr N. is turned against an anonymous Jewish convert and turncoat: "He heard of a gentleman who was himself born a Jew make a spiteful remark about the Jewish character. 'Herr Hofrat,' he said, 'your ant*e*semitism was known to me; your ant*i*semitism is new to me'" (33).

90. This is played out in a dictionary of Berlin wit published just a few years before Landmann's book. It contains the following anecdote about the good Egon Schulze under the entry "JUT": "JUT. Herr Egon Schulze stellt sich vor. Berliner: Sehr anjenehm! (Für sich): Ejon? Ejon is jut." (Mr. Egon Schulze presents himself. Berliner: Very pleased! (To himself): Ejon? Ejon is good.") See Alfred Mühr, ed., *Berliner Witz ABC* (Berlin-Grunewald: Non-Stop Bücherei, 1957), 60. Utilizing the same interplay between the *g*, *j*, and its absence, a Jewish joke from around the turn of the century on the theme of Jewish suffering and God's absence makes the same basic linguistic point in the transformation from *Gott* to *Jot*: Frage: "*Was sind die 'Uden?*" (What are the Jews?) Antwort: "*Ein Jottverlassenes Volk.*" (A God-forsaken folk, as well as one lacking the letter "J" in this joke.)

91. Adorno's spreading of the nasty rumor is bracketed as follows: "(ich habe einmal gesagt, der Antisemitismus sei das Gerücht über die Juden)" ("Zur Bekämpfung des Antisemitismus heute," 363).

92. On a related note, the word also appears in a letter that none other than Friedrich Torberg sent to Paul Celan in the hope of reversing Celan's decision to resign from the PEN Club of Austria in March 1964 on account of two anti-Semitic slurs made against him by Paula Ludwig. The self-ironic humorist puts the pejorative in quotation marks in referring to himself and his own Jewish credentials: "In my capacity as 'Jew on duty' ['Jud vom Dienst'] and thus, as a militant defender of precisely that position which is also your own." But, alas, the attempt to re-enlist Celan into the PEN Club failed. See Letter, Torberg to Celan, March 24, 1964, in Friedrich Torberg, *In diesem Sinne . . .* (München: Langen Müller, 1981), 80.

93. Stéphane Moses, "'Wege, auf denen die Sprache stimmhaft wird': Paul Celans 'Gespräch im Gebirg,'" in *Argumentum e Silentio: Internationales Paul Celan-Symposium Seattle 1984*, ed. Amy D. Colin (Berlin: Walter de Gruyter, 1987), 50.

94. It is not as if Landmann in *Der jüdische Witz* was unfamiliar with this term. The sixth edition of the book contains a post-Holocaust Jewish joke (with the capitalized title: "ENTNAZIFIZIERUNG") that mocks the bureaucratic travesty of Nazi rehabilitation that always seems to come at the expense of skeletons hiding

in the closet, or in this case, the cellar: "The officer is trying to denazify regular party member Müller: 'Were you locked up under Hitler? Did you hear about the resistance movement? Did you otherwise suffer under Hitler?' 'No,' admits Müller, 'Things went very well for me. I always had enough to eat and even had a lot of very good wine hidden in the cellar.' The Officer: 'Excellent! Miss, you write that regular party member Müller kept hidden in his basement during the whole time of Hitler a certain 'Oppenheimer' [known German wine].'" Landmann, *Der jüdische Witz* (Frankfurt am Main: Büchergilde Gutenberg, 1976), 574.

95. Alexander Drozdyznski, *Das verspottete Tausendjährige Reich* (Düsseldorf: Droste, 1978), 219.

96. Frank Stern, *Im Anfang War Auschwitz*, 356.

97. For a critical assessment and a multifaceted array of contemporary documentation, see Siegfried Zielinski, *Veit Harlan, Analysen und Materialien zur Auseinandersetzung mit einem Film-Regisseur des deutschen Faschismus* (Frankfurt am Main: Rita G. Fischer Verlag, 1981).

98. The twists and turns of the trial are recounted in Wolfgang Benz, "Postwar Society and National Socialism: Remembrance, Amnesia, Rejection," in *Tel Aviver Jahrbuch für deutsche Geschichte* (Gerlingen: Bleicher Verlag, 1990), 19:3–5. Harlan's self-styled philo-Semitism can be found in his autobiography, Veit Harlan, *Im Schatten meiner Film: Selbstbiographie* (Gütersloh: H. C. Opfermann, 1966).

99. Salcia Landmann, "On Jewish Humour," *Jewish Journal of Sociology* 4, no. 2 (December 1962): 199.

100. The strategy of identification with the victim, according to the Mitscherlichs, goes something like this: "The substitution of mourning through identification with the innocent victims often happens; it is above all a logical defense of guilt [*Abwehr der Schuld*]. . . . The past represents itself in the consciousness as follows: There were many victims who suffered in the war. One has been discriminated against long afterwards although he was innocent because he had indeed been ordered to do everything to which he now stands accused" (Mitscherlich and Mitscherlich, *Die Unfähigkeit zu trauern*, 60).

101. Although the lecture "Zur Bekämpfung des Antisemitismus heute" was delivered at the end of 1962, it was not published until two years later in *Das Argument* 6, no. 29 (1964): 88–104. See Adorno, *Gesammelte Schriften*, 20.1:372.

102. Slavoj Žižek, *Tarrying with the Negative* (Durham, NC: Duke University Press, 1993), 244. The same joke is repeated in *Žižek's Jokes: Did You Hear the One About Hegel and Negation?* (Cambridge, MA: MIT Press, 2014), 117.

## Conclusion: Final Thoughts and Last Laughs

1. Hans Speier, *Witz und Politik: Essay über die Macht und das Lachen* (Zürich: Edition Interform, 1975), 16–17; translation mine. Speier's source is R. F. Pauls, "Der neue Beginn in Israel," *Das Parlament* 22, no. 45 (November 1972): 9.

2. The phrasing of the young Israeli industrialist recalls the imperative plea

for laughter delivered by Nietzschean gay scientist Zarathustra in *"Von höheren Menschen"* (chap. 73, no. 20): *"Das Lachen sprach ich heilig; ihr höheren Menschen, lernt mir—lachen!* [I pronounced laughter holy. Learn from me, you higher men—laugh!]" See *Also Sprach Zarathustra: Ein Buch für Alle und Keinen* (Stuttgart: Alfred Kröner Verlag, 1950), 328; translation mine.

3. This scene also recalls the ambivalence inscribed in the Yom Kippur (Day of Atonement) joke narrated by Theodor Reik and analyzed by Jacques Derrida where an act of forgiveness is always already contaminated with enmity and broken promises: "Two Jews, longtime enemies, meet at the synagogue, on the Day of Atonement [*le jour du Grand Pardon*]. One says to the other [as a gesture, therefore, of forgiveness—J.D.]: 'I wish for you what you wish for me.' The other immediately retorts: 'Already you're starting again?'" Derrida goes on to call this "an unfathomable story" that carries forgiveness "to the abyss of impossibility." Jacques Derrida, "Hostipitality," in *Acts of Religion*, ed. Gil Anidjar (New York: Routledge, 2002), 381.

### Afterword: The Jewish Joke in Trump's America

1. Jonathan Greenblatt quoted in Debra Birnbaum, "Larry David Criticized for 'SNL' Jokes About Holocaust," *Variety*, November 5, 2017, https://variety.com/2017/tv/news/larry-david-snl-monologue-holocaust-1202607500/.

2. Jeremy Dauber, "Why Larry David's Holocaust Joke Was So Uncomfortable," *Atlantic*, November 7, 2017.

3. Kurt Robitschek, "Der Standpunkt der Künstler," *C.V.-Zeitung*, April 30, 1926; translation mine.

4. Sander Gilman, "Jewish Humor and the Terms by Which Jews and Muslims Join Western Civilization," in *Leo Baeck Institute Year Book* 57 (2012): 65.

5. Joel Stein, "Milo Yiannopoulos Is the Pretty, Monstrous Face of the Alt-Right," *Bloomberg*, 15 September 15, 2016, https://www.bloomberg.com/features/2016-america-divided/milo-yiannopoulos/.

6. Quoted in Tabatha Southey, "Neo-Nazis Are No Joke—They Just Want You to Think They Are," *MacLeans*, December 15, 2017, https://www.macleans.ca/opinion/neo-nazis-are-no-joke-they-just-want-you-to-think-they-are/.

7. Aja Romano, "YouTube's Most Popular User Amplified Anti-Semitic Rhetoric. Again," *Vox*, December 13, 2018, https://www.vox.com/2018/12/13/18136253/pewdiepie-vs-tseries-links-to-white-supremacist-alt-right-redpill.

8. Jason Wilson, "Hiding in Plain Sight: How the 'Alt-Right' Is Weaponizing Irony to Spread Fascism," *Guardian*, May 23, 2017, https://www.theguardian.com/technology/2017/may/23/alt-right-online-humor-as-a-weapon-facism. Wilson continues: "Experts say that the 'alt-right' have stormed mainstream consciousness by weaponizing irony, and by using humour and ambiguity as tactics to wrong-foot their opponents."

9. *The Daily Stormer* Style Guide, quoted in Southey, "Neo-Nazis Are No Joke."

10. Gavriel D. Rosenfeld, "Digital Anti-Semitism: From Irony to Ideology," *Jewish Review of Books* (Winter 2019), https://jewishreviewofbooks.com/articles/4963/digital-anti-semitism-from-irony-to-ideology/. See also Gavriel D. Rosenfeld, *Hi Hitler! How the Nazi Past is Being Normalized in Contemporary Culture* (New York: Cambridge University Press, 2014), chap. 6.

11. Joshua Barajas, "Nazi salutes 'done in a spirit of irony and exuberance,' alt-right leader says," PBS NewsHour, November 22, 2016, https://www.pbs.org/newshour/politics/white-nationalist.

12. Jeet Heer, "Ironic Nazis Are Still Nazis: Hatred Often Hides Behind a Mask of Jokiness," *New Republic* (online), November 25, 2016, https://newrepublic.com/article/139004/ironic-nazis-still-nazis.

13. Southey, "Neo-Nazis Are No Joke."

# Index

*"Die Abtrünnigen"* ("The apostates"), 35–36
Adorno, Theodor, 160, 202, 212, 216–18, 291n61, 294n91
Aleichem, Sholem, 93–94, 125–26, 263n83
*Alle Meschugge?*, 14, 249n53
Allen, Woody, 258n41
alt-right, 15–16, 224, 227–29, 296nn5,8, 297n11
Aly, Götz, 242n60
amusing contradictions *(heiterer Gegensätzlichkeit)*, 56
*Der Angriff* (The attack), 157
Anti-Defamation League, 15, 225–26, 240n40
anti-Jewish terror, 13
anti-Semitism, 1; Adorno on, 202, 212, 216–17; alt-right antics of, 228–30; in America, 15, 224–30; anachronism, 11; Ascher collection and, 16, 240n45; Bebel on, 89, 262nn75,76; of Borat, 14–15, 227, 240n40; campaign poster of, 87; capitalist basis, 66; caricature of, 100–1; Centralverein and, 96–97, 100, 108, 116; classification, 237n23; collusion with, 15; contemporary, 67–68, 224, 227; and contingency, 216–18; conversion of, 15; culture of, 24–25; cyclist joke and, 216–17, 242n60; defusing of, 9; digital, 229; dogs of, 40, 247n46; economic, 77, 89, 257n38; end of, 93; Fuchs and, 65–68, 75, 89, 91–92, 255n15, 257n38; Germanic, 130; of Herr Wendriner, 264n9; Herrnfeld Brothers and, 258n46, 261n67, 269n60; Hitler's views about, 202; Jewish, 24–25, 247n139; KadeKo controversy and, 95–118; Kahler on, 127, 129–30; lack of causality, 22; Landmann accused of, 199–204, 291n58; latent, 63–65, 91, 200, 212, 215, 293n87; linguistic antagonism, 41–42; of Marx, 76–77, 255n15; militant, 35; mockery of, 14–15; Moszkowski on, 113–14; movement for, 5, 68; Nazi, 105, 107, 179, 221, 269n60; parrot joke about, 100; post-Holocaust, 182–83, 199–200, 202, 212, 216–18, 292n65; provocation of, 15; racial, 57–58, 86, 89, 91, 114, 227, 257n38; reactionary brand of, 68–69; reinforcement of, 11; relationship with self-irony, 4–12, 16, 21, 37, 67–68, 75, 113–16, 127, 143, 219–21, 236n13, 239n33, 240n45, 256n35, 263n15, 275n52; religious, 57–58, 91, 114; roots of, 64–67; Social Democratic Party and, 259n50; on social media, 228; and social tensions, 66, 89, 91–92; state-sanctioned, 20; truth of, 67; visual, 77, 88; weapons of, 8; during and after World War I, 5–6; Žižek on, 217–18

*Apikoires* (Jewish free thinker), 51–52, 110, 268n46
"The apostates" ("Die Abtrünnigen"), 35–36
Aryan cranium, 30, 245n24
Ascher, Judas, 16, 240n45
Ascher, Solomon, 16
Aschheim, Steven, 74, 237n17, 250n66, 257n40, 258n42, 259n46, 264n9, 265n24, 270nn5,6, 273n28, 275n52, 277n71
The attack *(Der Angriff)*, 157

The audacity (Die Frechheit), 115–16
Austria, 5, 14, 25, 59, 88, 206, 294n92
Austrian Republic, 13
authenticity, 35–38, 247n41

Bakhtin, Mikhail, 130–31
Baron Cohen, Sacha, 14–15; Anti-Defamation League letter to, 240n40; Dauber on, 15; political satire of, 226–28; on Trump, 226–27; warning for, 15
Bataille, Georges, 186, 189
Bebel, August, 89, 262nn75,76
Benjamin, Walter, 60–61, 91–92, 186, 253n2, 255nn19,22, 262nn79,81,82
Bergson, Henri, 125–26, 162, 273n26, 281n35
Berlin anti-Semitism conflict (Berliner Antisemitismusstreit), 5
Berliner Börsen-Courier, 102–3
Bermann, Heinrich, 1, 11–12, 18, 19, 242n5
Bernstein, Elias, 110–11
Beweglichkeit (mobility), 25–27, 34, 37, 48–49, 54–56, 73, 244n9
Bible, 70–71,173
Bildung (education), 119, 121, 127, 129, 143–44, 152, 243n67, 270nn3,4,5,7, 273nn28,29
Bildungsjude (Jewish man of culture), 6–7, 121, 127, 139, 145–46, 220, 270n6
Bloch, Chayim, 8, 37–38, 139, 237nn21,22, 246n36, 274n39, 282n43, 286n2
Bloch, Joseph S., 8, 37
Blüher, Hans, 124, 257n40, 272n18
Bois, Curt, 104–5
Bolshevik Revolution, 92–93
Bolshevism, 202
The book of Jewish jokes (Das Buch des jüdischen Witze) (Schnitzer), 83–84, 261nn65,67
Börne, Ludwig, 14–17, 26, 163–64, 176, 260n62, 285n80
Bourke, John Gregory, 241n53
Bramson, Dovidl, 35–36
Brenner, Michael, 121, 243n3, 270n8
Broder, Henryk, 292n65
Brömsel, Sven, 29, 245n22
Brothers Herrnfeld, 9, 11, 75, 127, 238n25, 258n46, 269n60
Browne, Lewis, 276n56; Kahler on, 140–46; self-irony and, 140–46
Brumlik, Micha, 14, 63, 67, 255n16
Das Buch des jüdischen Witze (The book of Jewish jokes) (Schnitzer), 83–84

Burg, J. G., 250n65, 290nn41,45
Busch, Wilhelm, 281n36
Büschenthal, Lippman Moses, 16–17, 22, 241nn46,48

Cabaret of Comics (Kabarett der Komiker) "KadeKo," 7–9, 11–13, 102–5, 107–8, 110, 115–6, 118, 225, 237n24, 266n26
Cahnmann, Werner, 121, 270n8
capitalism: Bebel on 89, 262n76; condemnation of, 77–78; critique of, 75–80; Fuchs on, 63, 66–67, 71; growth of, 65, 89; as Judaism, 77, 90
caricatures: and anti-Semitism, 5, 53, 95, 280n29; concept of, 67; Fuchs on, 60–61, 62–67, 69, 89, 91–93, 220, 240n37, 254n3, 255n20, 261n71; Hitler on 159; of Michael the German,137; Nazis on, 173, 179; perception of, 67; of Rothschild, 77–81; by Simmel, 111
Caricatures of European Peoples (Die Karikatur der europäischen Völker) (Fuchs), 60–61, 254n3
Celan, Paul, 212–13, 294nn92,93
censorship, 9, 95, 101, 109–10,115; comic, 226; of Nazis, 121–22, 278n2, 280n31
Central Association of German Citizens of Jewish Faith (Centralverein deutscher Staatsbürger jüdischen Glaubens), 6–7, 95–96, 116
Centralverein, 8–9, 75, 91–92, 95–98, 100–2, 107–12, 118, 121, 208, 220, 263n11, 265n23, 267n32, 278n2; complaints of, 116; leaders of, 115
Centralverein deutscher Staatsbürger jüdischen Glaubens (Central Association of German Citizens of Jewish Faith), 6–7, 95–96, 116
Central-Verein Zeitung (CVZ), 96–97, 101–3, 114–15
Chamberlain, Houston Stuart, 30, 48–49, 245n22
Charlottesville Unite the Right race riot, 224–26
Chase, Jefferson S., 16–17, 41, 163–64, 236n6, 241nn49,50, 242n60, 282nn40,45, 285n80
circumcision, 105–6
Citron, Simon, 253n90
Clark, Frazer Stephen, 137–38
class, 16, 32, 64, 70, 76, 80, 89–90, 163, 257n38, 262n76

clueless *(ratlos)*, 127–28
Cold War, 146
comic spin *(Dreh)*, 20, 39, 107, 220
comic unmasking, 27, 83–86, 158
commercial trading practices, 54–55
Communism: anti-, 24; Communist Party, 76; Fuchs on, 92, 220
contemporary currents, 12–15
*Contentions with God* (Olsvanger), 125
contingency affirmation, 217–18
counterpropaganda, 179–81
crude jokes *(Lozale)*, 8, 37
Cuddihy, John Murray, 250n69
cultivated discourse, 18–19
cultural consciousness, 183
cultural memory, 183, 185
culture: of anti-Semitism, 24–25; European Jewish, 26–27; of Germany, 164–65; modernity of, 1, 4, 57; popular, 225–28; of visual media, 60; of wandering Jew, 26–27. *See also* modern culture
*Curb Your Enthusiasm*, 226
CVZ. *See Central-Verein Zeitung*

d'Ache, Caran, 257n44
*The Daily Show*, 14–15
*The Daily Stormer*, 228
Dauber, Jeremy, 4–5, 14–15, 226–27
Daumier, Honoré, 60–61
David, Larry, 225–26
Davies, Christie, 155–56, 159, 165, 179–80
Day of Atonement *(Yom Kippur)*, 11–12, 46, 107, 110, 238n29, 296n3
death: of Jewish jokes, 190–91; of Landmann, 188; laugh oneself to, 160; laughing to *(Totlachen)*, 161; of Trebitsch, 24–25
deconstruction, 123, 242n63
"dejokification," 13–14
denazification *(Entnazifizierung)*, 214
denial of exile *(Galuthbejahung)*, 150–52
Derrida, Jacques, 123–24, 242n63, 296n3
*Der Deutsche Michel. See* Michael the German
Deutsches Literaturarchiv, 121–22
*Deutsche Stilkunst* (Engel), 70
*Deutschtum*, 11, 18–19, 123, 127, 129–30, 134, 276n61
*Deutschvölkischer Schutz- und Trutzband* (German Nationalist Protection and Revenge League), 90–91
*The Diary of Anne Frank* (Frank), 205–6

Diasporism, 150
Dinter, Artur, 100
dirt *(Schmutz)*, 170–71
donors list *(Spenderliste)*, 195–96
Douglas, Mary, 12–13, 241n50
*Dreh* (comic spin), 20, 39, 107, 220
droll story *(Schwank)*, 20, 37, 139, 238n28, 247nn40,46
*Duckmäuser* (hypocrites), 97

Eastern European Jews *(Ostjuden)*, 103, 121, 171–73, 236n12, 250n66, 265n24
Edel, Edmund, 1–4, 2–3, 17, 230, 235n1; on comic spin, 20, 220; on Itzig Feitel Stern, 256n35; on Jewish humor, 5–6; on motivation, 20; Patka on, 6; on persecution and laughter through tears, 22; on pun, 248n47; on self-irony, 4–6; speculation of, 18; Trebitsch compared to, 248n47
education *(Bildung)*, 121, 143–44, 243n67, 273n29
Eher, Franz, 159–60
Eichmann, Adolf, 184–85
*Einfalt (naiveté)*, 50
*Die Einsame Träne (The lonely teardrop)* (Morgan and Robitschek), 105, 107–10
Elders of Zion, 80
Ellul, Jacques, 153, 158–59, 162–63, 180
Engel, Eduard, 70–72, 256n29, 279n11
Enlightenment, 57, 121, 125–26, 212, 215
*Entnazifizierung* (denazification), 214
*The Erotic Element in Caricature* (Fuchs), 60–61
*Ersparnis* (saving), 183–84
*Ethnic Humor Around the World* (Davies), 155–56
Eulenspiegel, Till, 139, 274n40
Europe: oppression in, 7–8; wandering Jews of, 64–65
European Jewry, 21, 182, 187, 189–90
evolutionary biology, 73–74
exile *(Galuth)*: chosen for, 149–52; jokes of, 6–7, 119–52, 273n27; Mann on, 149–52

facial physiognomy, 50
Factor, Emil, 102–3
*Faust* (Goethe), 165
Federal Compensation Law, 183–84
Federal Republic of Germany. *See* Germany
Feldmann, Siegmund, 102–3
Fiedler, Friedrich Kurt, 10

Final Solution, 21,169, 180
fixed gaze, 49–50
Flaneur, 9, 238n26, 258n46, 261n67, 269n60
fleeting gaze, 49–50
*Die Fliegende Blätter*, 5–6, 32
Fliess, Wilhelm, 19
*Flüsterwitze* (whisper jokes), 180–81, 285n90
folklore, 18, 29, 67, 139, 183
Foxman, Abraham, 15
Frank, Anne, 184–85, 205–6, 286n6
Frankfurt School, 161, 216–17
*Die Frechheit* (The audacity), 105, 114–16, 266n26, 269nn58,59
free speech, 7–8; on limits of, 115, 220; Robitschek on, 109, 115–18, 220; in Weimar Germany, 95–118
French patriotism, 145
Freud, Anna, 235n4
Freud, Sigmund, 1, 2–3, 144–45, 154, 185, 208, 211, 241n53, 283n62, 294n89; on aggressive jokes, 157–58, 168; on anal character, 170–71; Chase on, 17; on comic unmasking, 85; on communication, 158–59; condensation technique of, 211–12; contradictions to, 249n60; on democratic mode of thinking, 48; on dreams and jokes, 242n56; on Eastern European Jews, 265n24, 284n67; Fuchs compared to, 63–64, 258n45; ghostwriting of, 43–48; Gilman on, 63–64; goals of, 17–18; Goebbels compared to, 157, 181; on good joke, 212; interpretations of, 236n14; on joke science, 17–19, 43; on joking brevity, 186; on *Judenwitz*, 17; Kadner on, 168–71, 283n59; Lacan compared to, 28, 244n112, 253n89; Landmann on, 192, 237n19, 238n28; Laqueur on, 35, 245n35; on laughter, 72, 158–59, 181; on money, 170–71; Oring on, 235n4, 238n28, 251n74, 267n42; psychoanalysis by, 19–20; on puns, 42–43; on schadchen jokes, 44–45, 249n60; on self-criticism, 4, 30, 47–48, 154, 192, 235n4, 255n18, 289n33; on skeptical jokes, 144–45, 169–70, 283nn62,63; on smut, 264n8; Trebitsch compared to, 42–48; on truth, 170; Wisse on, 238n29; on *Wunderrabbi*, 45, 267n42; on Yom Kippur joke, 238n29
Freytag, Gustav, 208–9
Fuchs, Eduard, 13; on anti-Semitism, 65–68, 71–72, 75, 77, 86–89, 91, 262n80; arrests of, 61–62; background of, 60–61; on Bebel, 262n75; Benjamin on, 60–61, 91–92, 254n2, 255nn19,22, 262n82; Brumlik on, 14, 63, 67, 91, 240n37, 254n10, 255n16; on capitalism, 65–67, 71, 77; on caricatures, 60–61, 63–67, 77–80, 254n13, 255n20, 258n44; case of, 60–94; as collector, 61, 262n82; contradictions in, 63, 65; on Daumier, 61; on Engel, 71–72; Gilman and, 8, 63–64; on Heine, 68, 255n22; on Herrnfeld Theater, 75, 258n46; and Hitler, 86–89, 262n73, 279n23; on Holzschuher, 71, 256n35; on "How They Laugh" joke, 80–83; Hounker on, 255n15, 262n72; innovations of, 61; on intellectualism, 73; intention of, 66–67; irony in, 220; on Jew as actor, 259n48; Kadner on, 88–89; Kahler compared to, 127; on language, 257n38; on laughter and suffering, 85–86, 261n71; marriage of, 83, 261n66; on Marxism, 61–62, 90, 92, 94; on mimicry, 73–75; on mobility, 73; reflections on, 91–94; on Rothschilds, 63, 75–80; on Schnitzer, 84–85; on self-esteem, 70, 74, 83; on self-irony, 8, 62, 64, 67–75, 83–84, 91–94, 210–11, 256n36; shortcomings of, 61, 80, 89, 92, 262n73; on social tension, 64–66; and Sombart, 66, 73, 77, 254n14, 257n38, 262n77; success of, 254nn3,9; on Tang Dynasty, 91–92; on Treitschke, 63, 68–70, 260n62; on truth, 66–67; Weissberg on, 63, 254n9, 257n38, 261n66; on wordplay, 75–76

Galician Jews (*Galizien*), 171–73, 172
*Galuth. See* exile
*Galuthbejahung* (denial of exile), 150–52
*Galuthswitz* (the joke of exile), 6–7, 119–52, 273n27
*Geist und Judentum* (Spirit and Judaism) (Trebitsch), 7, 24–27, 37, 43, 49, 50, 244n7, 248n52, 249n54, 251n70, 252n80; analysis of, 31–35; anecdote of, 30–32
*Geld* (money), 32, 53, 56, 58, 63, 66, 72, 77–79, 99, 110, 121, 168, 170–71, 173, 204, 208–9, 252n84, 258nn44,46, 264n13, 268n47, 283n59
Geller, Jay, 74, 257n40
gender, 16
*Die Generalpumpe*, 77, 78
George, Manfred, 122–23
German Communist Party (KPD), 92–93

German corporeality, 148
*German History in the Nineteenth Century* (Treitschke), 68–69
German-Jewish symbiosis, 127, 129, 134, 148
German maiden, 86, 88–89, 159
German Nationalist Protection and Revenge League *(Deutschvölkischer Schutz- und Trutzband)*, 90–91
Germany, 59, 102, 145, 151, 203; anti-Semitism in, 199, 216, 255n15; cabaret in, 98; crisis of Jews in, 18; criticism of, 37–38; culture of, 121, 164–65, 215; defeat of, 25, 100, 134,194; expulsion from, 151; flight from,118; graveyard desecration in, 199–204; humor of, 17; intercultural dialogue with, 178–79, 196; intercultural relations with, 12–13, 18, 68, 152; intercultural success with, 134–35, 195; Israeli relationship with, 222–23; Jews in, 183, 271n10; Jewish joke in, 13–14, 16, 20, 96, 152, 163, 169, 182, 199, 228; Jewish question in, 31; Kadner on, 165; Kahler on, 121–22, 124–25, 131, 135, 137, 146, 151–52; Landmann and 183, 196–97, 208: nationalism of, 5–6, 16–17, 137, 139; Nazi, 169, 178, 215, 280n27; philo-Semitism in, 211; politics of, 88,165; press in, 196–97; racism in, 80, 89, 119; reparation from, 13; return to, 151, 214; Second Reich in, 5–6; self-irony in, 72–73; threats to,164–65. *See also* Holocaust; Weimar Germany
Gerron, Kurt, 103–4
*Geschlecht und Charakter (Sex and Character)* (Weininger), 48–49
Gilman, Sander, 4, 14, 16, 236n12, 285n80; on Baron Cohen, 14, 227; on Frank, 205–6; Fuchs and, 8, 63–64; on Jewish self-hatred, 244n9, 292n70; on *mauscheln*, 176, 256n33, 287n78; on Schnitzer, 84–85; on Trebitsch, 25, 40–41, 244n11, 245n28; Wiener and, 97–98
Gitterstab, Modche, 267n42
Gluck, Mary, 6, 12–13, 19, 236n13, 239n33, 241n50
God: absence of, 294n90; comic, 194; Jewish saying about, 257n39; Kahler on, 121, 125–26, 128, 272n22; Olsvanger on, 272n25; omnipotence of, 52–53; Robitschek on, 109–10, 226; Tevye and, 125; Torberg on, 196–97. *See also* Jewish Creator
Goebbels, Joseph, 15, 21, 95, 124, 165, 176, 178, 180, 215, 228, 272n18, 279n15, 280n31,

282n39; background of, 157; Freud, S. compared to, 158, 181, 279n21; joke about, 181; mission of, 157–58; and tendentious jokes, 157–58
Goethe, 17, 165, 182, 282n49, 286n2
Goi (non-Jew), 70, 82–83, 167–68, 260n61, 293n83
Gollance, Sonia, 284n76
Gordon, Mel, 282n41
Graeber, Isacque, 244n15
graffiti wave *(Schmierwelle)*, 199–200
Greek culture, 70–71
Greenblatt, Jonathan, 225–26
Grossman, Jeffrey, 284n76
Grotjahn, Martin, 257n37
*Guardian*, 229
Günther, Hans F. K., 164–65
Guttenbrunn, R., 246n33

Hadamovsky, Eugen, 156–57, 279n12
Hansen, Mac, 103–4
Hapsburg Empire, 5–6, 25
Harlan, Veit, 214–15, 295nn97,98
Hartl, Edwin, 207–8, 287n8
hate speech, 4–6, 21, 95, 100–1
Heartfield, John, 137, 138, 264n9
*Heeb Magazine*, 14–15
Heer, Jeet, 229–30
Heine, Heinrich, 14, 16–17, 38, 68,163–64, 176, 246n31, 255n22, 260n62, 282n45, 285n80
*heiterer Gegensätzlichkeit* (amusing contradictions), 56
"Help Sigi, the ship is going down!" ("Hilfe Sigi, das Schiff geht unter!"), 177
Herrnfeld Brothers, 9, 11, 75, 127, 238n25, 258n46, 269n60
Herrnfeld Theater, 258n46, 261n67
"Hilfe Sigi, das Schiff geht unter!" ("Help Sigi, the ship is going down!"), 177
Hirsch, Eike Christian, 237n19
history: of anti-Semitism, 40; art, 60–61; cultural, 262n82; of German language debates, 175; of Holocaust, 285n89; of ideas, 38; irony of, 59, 182–83, 245n15; of Jewish joke books, 112;of Jewish jokelore, 210, 212; of Jewish wit, 1, 4, 272n21; of oppression, 7–8; philosophy of, 149; social, 60, 253n1; of Viennese cabaret, 249n53
*History of Erotic Art* (Fuchs), 60–61
*History of European Caricature* (Fuchs), 78

Hitler, Adolf, 262n72; actions of, 159–60; Adorno on, 201–2; anti-Semitic election poster by, 86–89, 88, 159, 262n72, 279n23; being at wit's end, 20–21, 242n60; on caricature, 159; Fuchs on, 89, 262n73; funding for, 24–25; and ironic Nazism, 229, 297n10; Landmann on, 188–89, 294n94; mockery of, 104–5, 116; National Socialism and, 86–91; rise of, 20–21; threat of, 9; Torberg on, 201–2; and Trebitsch, 24–25; writings of, 159–60
*Hitler Tells Fairy Tales II* (Heartfield), 137, 138
Hobbes, Thomas, 156, 279n13
Hofmann, Walter, 160, 160–61
Holländer, Ludwig, 9, 11, 75, 97–98, 101–3, 107, 112, 115–16, 265n23, 269n60
Holocaust, 12–13, 21, 118, 141, 154, 223, 285n89, 288n26; anti-Semitic jokes about, 15, 224, 228; genocide during, 213–14; Jewish jokes about, 225–26, 228; Jewish jokes after, 11, 14, 182, 191–95, 242n63, 260n61, 289n28, 294n94; media of, 184–85; mourning after, 182–218, 287n9, 289nn27,28; post-, 13, 21–22, 89, 182–218, 221, 291n51
*Holocaust* (1979), 185
Holzschuher, Heinrich, 71, 256n35
humor: ancient Greek, 70–71; Bergson on, 125, 162; Bloch, C. on, 282n43; congenial national, 48–49; Douglas on, 241n50; Freud, S. on, 212; German, 17, 41, 127–28, 139, 164, 241n51, 255n22, 282n45; Holocaust, 224; illustrated, 246n29, 252n84; Kadner on, 162–65; Kahler on, 127–28, 139; magazines, 5, 53, 61–62, 79, 96–97, 131, 269n59; Nordic, 168, 281n37; pseudo-, 98; in propaganda, 155, 159, 179; racial doctrines of, 154, 161–65, 281n37, 282nn41,42,45, 285n88; scatological, 171, 226; self-ironic, 258nn41,45, 294n92; Weininger on, 48–49
humorist-scientist *(Witzenschaftler)*, 42–43
Huonker, Thomas, 255n15, 262n72
hypochondria, 44
hypocrites *(Duckmäuser)*, 97

ideological prisms, 12–15
ideology, 48, 62, 89, 129, 155, 162–63, 165, 217, 229
*Ihr Recht! (Their Right!)*, 133
*Im Anfang war Auschwitz* (Stern, F.), 214–15, 293n86

*Im Bade (In the Bath)*, 105–7, 106
*The Inability to Mourn, 1967 (Die Unfähigkeit zu trauern)* (Mitscherlich, A. and Mitscherlich, M.), 203–4, 216
*Infragestellung* (putting-into-question), 57
inner ambiguity *(innere Vieldeutigkeit)*, 49–51
Institute for Social Research, 200
intellectualism *(Intellektualismus)*, 32, 73, 124–25, 128, 219, 257n38, 272n18
interpretation *(Midrash)*, 166–67
In the Bath (Im Bade), 105, 105–6
*The Invisible Jewish Budapest* (Gluck), 6, 236n13, 239n33, 241n50
Israel, 15, 80, 147, 150, 51, 190, 195, 221–22, 227, 240n43, 276n58, 277n71, 283n55, 288n27
*Israel among the nations (Israel unter den Völkern)* (Kahler), 119–21, 120, 131, 135, 142, 148–52, 248n51, 270n7, 272n20
Israeli Anti-Semitic Cartoon Contest, 240n44
*Israel unter den Völkern (Israel among the nations)* (Kahler), 119–21, 120, 131, 135, 142, 148–52, 248n51, 270n7, 272n20
Itler, H., 9–11, 10

Jean Paul, 196
Jelavich, Peter, 115–16, 263n5, 278n2
Jellinek, Adolf, 75–76, 259nn47,48,49
Jew *(Jud)*, 211–13
Jewish Anti-Defamation League, 15, 225, 240n40
Jewish Central Information Service, 118
Jewish character *(jüdische Charakter)*, 27
*Jewish Comedy* (Dauber), 4–5, 15, 236n8
Jewish Creator, 53
Jewish difference, 31–32, 107
Jewish disease *(Morbus judaicus)*, 251n77
Jewish Emancipation, 8, 16, 51–52
Jewish financial model, 54
Jewish free thinker *(Apikoires)*, 51–52, 110, 268n46
Jewish intellectual characteristic *(jüdischen Geisteseigenschaft)*, 73–74
Jewish joker *(Judenwitzler)*, 4, 11, 16–17, 69, 72, 98, 124–25, 163–64, 176, 209, 227–28
Jewish jokes: analysts of, 11, 14, 219; and anti-Semitism, 11, 21, 91, 199–203, 220–21; and business practices, 53–56; Büschenthal on, 22; censurable, 102; classification of, 37–38, 237n23; comic instability of, 28, 48, 221–22; context of, 247n39; deadly discourse on, 21,161–79; death of, 190–91;

defense of, 225–26; disagreements over, 8; Edel on, 1, 6, 22; folklorists on, 8; Engel on, 71; in Freud, 19, 85; Fuchs and, 62–67, 76, 83–84, 89, 91, 93, 220; heart of, 37–38; hierarchies in, 74–75; about Holocaust, 225–26, 228; after Holocaust, 11, 14, 22,182–83,191–95, 213–14, 242n63, 260n61, 289n28, 294n94; homonymic, 41; idealization of, 183–84; as intercultural bridge, 221–22; Kadner on, 144, 155, 161–80, 278n3, 281n36, 283n50, 285n86; Kahler on, 127, 129, 140, 144, 152, 221; Landmann and, 183–218; and laughter through suffering, 22; in literary productions, 14; mobilization of, 153–81; Moszkowski on, 113–14; mourning in, 185–88, 206; during Nazi era, 20–21,153–81; as pay back, 211–18; perception of, 45–46; reparations for, 182–218; resistance of, 19; Robitschek on, 105, 107, 109–13, 115, 118, 267nn32,42, 268nn43,44,47,48; self-critical, 30; and self-irony, 6, 8, 37, 82, 85, 95–96, 113, 115, 118, 154; significance of, 19, 21, 219–20; spirit of, 39; Trebitsch and, 7, 24–59; Treitschke on, 68–69; Trump and, 224–25; as venting repressed aggression, 203–4; in Weimar Germany, 95–118; Wiener on, 97–99

*Jewish Jokes* (Levi), 22, 243n64

"Jewish joke science," 4, 16–20, 43

Jewish man of culture *(Bildungsjude)*, 6–7, 121, 127, 139, 145–46, 220, 270n6

Jewish matchmaker *(Shadchenit)*, 195–96

Jewish names, 15

Jewishness and Germanness *(Judentum und Deutschtum)*, 122–23, 127, 139, 149

Jewish question, 1, 4, 12, 18–23, 31–32, 35, 57, 63–64, 76, 86, 89, 91, 115, 149, 162, 169, 180, 183, 217, 219, 236n10, 245n26, 255n20, 258n44, 259n50, 270n1

Jewish Renaissance movement, 8

*Jewish Self-Hatred* (Gilman), 205–6

Jewish self-hatred *(jüdische Selbsthaß)* (Lessing), 27–29, 243n5

Jewish spirit *(jüdische Geist)*, 27

*Jewish Wit (Der Witz der Juden)* (Edel), 1–4, 2–3, 250n60

Jewish Wit: Sociology and Collection (Landmann), 202–3

Jewish wit/joke. See *Judenwitz*

*The Jews Among the Nations* (Kahler), 125, 134–35, 151, 271n13

*The Jews and Modern Capitalism* (Sombart), 63

*Jews in caricature (Die Juden in der Karikatur)* (Fuchs), 62–64, 67, 76–81, 85–86, 87, 93–94, 159, 254n9

*The Jews in Modern Capitalism* (Sombart), 63

joke appropriation, 4–5, 180

joke authenticity, 35–38

jokelore, 46, 52, 55, 99, 186, 210, 212–15

joke mourning, 182, 185, 187, 191–94, 221, 223, 242n63; and anguished gaiety, 186, 189; as diversionary tactic, 193, 198, 205; doubts about, 190–91,198; good riddance and, 288n27; interpretation of, 287n15; in Joyce, 186–87, 189, 191; Landmann on, 190–91, 195–99, 204–11; as linguistic shifter, 185–86; and mourning joke example, 204–7; Neumann and, 197–98; Olsvanger and, 189; philo-Semitic, 198–99; possibilities for reception of, 187–89; as reversible strategy, 187, 194, 205; revivals of, 190–91, 289n28; Schmid and, 193–94; Torberg on, 198–99, 204–11; *Wiedergutmachung* and, 213–14

the joke of exile *(Galuthswitz)*, 6–7, 119–52, 273n27

*Jokes and Their Relation to the Unconscious (Der Witz und seine Beziehung zum Unbewussten, 1905)* (Freud, S.), 1, 2–3, 4, 19, 42, 144–45, 154, 235n4

joke reparations, 182–218, 221, 223

"joke science," 4, 16–20, 43

"joking business," 53–57

joking separatism, 41

"jokologist," 112–13

*Die Journalisten* (Freytag), 208–9

Jud (Jew), 211–13

Judaism: and *Bildung*, 270nn4,7; as capitalism, 63, 77; crisis of, 57; death of, 190–91; defamation of, 9, 100; diasporic, 38; European, 289n27; exiting from, 35; Goebbels on, 163; Goethe and, 282n49; and Jewish self-firony, 6–7; Kadner against, 89; Kahler on, 119, 126, 270n1, 271n13, 276n61, 277n71; Landmann on, 190–91; as malaise, 192; and Marx, 255n16; Petuchowski on, 191–92; threat of, 7; as tragicomedy,1, 18, 242n54; Trebitsch against, 28–29, 31, 34, 245n17, 246nn33,35; vacillating spirit of, 28

Judaization *(Verjudung)*, 214

*Die Judenfrage* (d'Ache), 257n44

*Der Judenfreund* (Ascher, S.), 16, 240n45

*Die Juden in der Karikatur (Jews in caricature)* (Fuchs), 62–64, 67, 76–81, 85–86, 87, 93–94, 159, 254n9

*Judentum*, 9, 11, 18–19, 282n39
*Judentum und Deutschtum* (Jewishness and Germanness), 122–23, 127, 139, 149
*Judenwitz* (Jewish wit/joke), 6, 8; appropriation of, 19; authenticity of, 37–38; Benjamin and, 255n22; Chase on, 16–17, 41, 163, 282n45; congenial national humor compared to, 48–49; deconstructive potential of, 65; discourse on, 16–17, 163, 282n45; evolution of, 21; Fuchs on, 66, 260n62; Gluck on, 12, 19, 239n33, 241n50; history of, 1, 4; intellectualization of, 18–19; irony in, 175; and Jewish question, 12; Kadner on, 162, 176; as necessity, 20–21; in psychoanalysis, 17–18; reflection of, 219–20; resistance to, 19–20; Röhrich on, 237n22; as scientific knowledge, 17–18; self-directed, 103–14; self-irony in, 4, 162; spirit of, 41–42; Trebitsch on, 25, 41; Weininger on, 48
*Judenwitzler* (Jewish joker), 4, 11, 16–17, 69, 72, 98, 124–25, 163–64, 176, 209, 227–28
Judeophobia, 24–25, 34
*jüdische Charakter* (Jewish character), 27
*jüdische Geist* (Jewish spirit), 27, 244n9
*Jüdische Miniaturen* (Nikolaus), 177–78
*jüdischen Geisteseigenschaft* (Jewish intellectual characteristic), 73–74
*Jüdische Selbsthaß* (Jewish self-hatred) (Lessing), 27–29, 243n5
*Jüdische Revue*, 122–23, 149, 273n27
*Jüdische Schwänke* (Schmitz), 37, 80, 247n37, 293n85
*Das Jüdische Volk in der Anekdote* (Bloch, C.), 37
*Der jüdische Witz* (Landmann), 13, 183–85, 187–88, 190, 192, 195–201, 203–5, 209, 211, 236n16, 238n28, 243n67, 294n94
*Jüdische Witze* (Itler), 9–11, 10
*Jud Süss*, 178, 212, 214–15

*Kabarett der Komiker* (Cabaret of Comics) "KadeKo," 7–9, 11–13, 102–5, 107–8, 115–16, 118, 225, 237n24, 266n26
Kabbalah, 237n18
*Kaddisch*, 188–89
*Kaddish* (Robitschek), 107–8
Kadner, Siegfried, 6–7, 13, 15–17, 19, 49, 144, 278n6; accusations by, 173; and alt-right, 228; analysis of, 162–64, 178, 282n42, 285n86; anti-Semitic discourse in, 162–63, 169–73, 178; *aporia* of, 221; binary opposition of, 163, 165, 281n37; on belief, 170–71; on Bergson, 162, 281n35; on Busch, 281n36; and caricature, 171; and cynicism, 158, 162–64; deadly discourse of, 161–80; on Freud, S., 168–71, 283n59; comparison with Freud, 154, 283n61; on Fuchs, 88–89; on German-Jewish dialogue, 178–79; Germany, 165; on Goethe, 165, 282n49; on Günther, 165; on humor 161–64; on Jewish joke, 161–80, 278n3, 281n36, 283n50, 285n86; on *Mauscheln*, 175, 284n75; mission of, 221; and Nazi party, 278n6; and Nazi propaganda, 154–55, 169–70, 172–74, 176, 178–79, 221; on Nordic humor, 162–64, 168; on oaths, 173; outrage of, 173–74; racialist views of, 161–66, 170–71, 178, 180, 228, 265n21, 278n3, 280n26; on self-irony, 162–63, 221, 281n37; on sophistry, 165–66; stereotype in, 170, 173; style of, 169–70; on Talmud, 165–68
Kafka, Franz, 57, 141–42, 275n47
Kahler, Erich, 6–7, 13, 17, 248n51, 271n8, 273n30; analysis by, 128–29; on anti-Semitism, 122, 124, 129–30, 134, 140, 143, 152; approach of, 123–24; background of, 119–21; on Bergson, 125–26; as *Bildungsjude*, 6, 119, 121, 127, 139, 145, 220, 270n6; on Browne, 140–46; Certificate of Naturalization to the United States for, 274n43; censorship of, 121–22; confession of, 148; as conservative thinker, 273n29; on corporeality, 124, 127, 129, 135, 137, 219, 248n51; criticism of, 125, 139; defense of, 139; on Diaspora, 149–51; on exile, 140–42, 149–52; failure of, 220–21; on faith, 128–29; Fuchs compared to, 127; on German-Jewish relations, 122–23, 127–30, 134–35, 139, 152, 271n10; on *Germanismus*, 129–30; on Germany, 124–25, 135, 137; on intellectualism, 124–25, 248n51; on Jewish exile joke, 6, 119–52, 274n44; on Jewish self-irony, 142–43, 220; on Jewish wit, 121, 123–29, 134, 140–44, 148, 151–52, 271n13, 271n20, 274n42; judgment of, 143–44; on Kafka, 275n47; Kellner on, 150; Landau on, 276n58; compared to Landmann, 276n58; and Mann, 122, 142, 146–49, 272n22, 276n57,61; on Michael the German, 128, 132–39; mission of, 119; on Nazism, 273n30; on neo-romanticism, 121–22, 241n52, 270n8; reflections of, 219–20; on

INDEX

refugee, 141; responsibility of, 126–27; and Scholem, 150, 277n71; self-identification of, 141, 147–48; on skepticism, 128–29; on stereotypes, 124; style of, 143; on tribe, 121, 150, 270n8; writing talent of, 148–49
Kahler-Kreis, 146
Kaiser, Georg, 96, 263n3
*Kalauer* (pun), 40–43, 75–76, 84, 211, 248nn47,48, 256n27
*Die Karikatur der europäischen Völker (Caricatures of European Peoples)* (Fuchs), 60–61, 67, 254n13, 258n44, 261n71, 262n71
Katznelson, Siegfried, 261n66
Kellner, Viktor, 150
Kettler, David, 119, 149
Kiel, Anna, 272n22
*Kikeriki*, 5–6, 32, 33, 201, 236n12
Kishinev, 140, 267n42
Kjellberg, Felix "PewDiePie," 228–29
*Kladderadatsch*, 5–6
*Klangwitz* (sound joke), 40–41
Kleeblatt, Norman, 284n67
KPD. *See* German Communist Party
Kraus, Karl, 14, 249n56
Kreppel, Jonas, 192
Kunze, Richard, 99–100

Lacan, Jacques, 28, 58, 244n12
*Lacht Euch Laune!: 1000 Witze (Laugh yourself happy!: 1000 jokes)* (Warlitz), 99, 264n13, 268n46
*Lacht ihn tot!* (Waldl), 160–61
La Fontaine, Maurice, 157–58
Landau, Paul, 249n53
Landmann, Salcia, 11–14, 22, 147, 183–85, 184, 203, 220–22, 275n44, 276n58, 286n2, 288n21, 289n34, 291n58; anti-Semitism, 199–203, 213, 287n8; background of, 188, 286n5; controversy of, 209, 221–22, 239n36; convictions of, 190–91; criticism of, 209–11; death of, 188; on death of Jewish joke, 190–91; on Freud, S., 192, 237n19, 238n28; on Hitler, 188–89; and Holocaust, 182–88, 190–91,196–98, 206–7, 209, 287n7, 288n26, 289n27; on joke mourning, 185–92, 195–99, 204–11, 289n28; on joke reparations, 205, 207, 211, 213, 214, 221; on nonreligious Jews, 236n16; and philo-Semitism, 195–99, 213, 215, 293n80; and post-Holocaust, 182–218; Röhrich on, 292n73; and Schmid, 192–93; on self-criticism, 236n16; Singer on, 288n24; sociocultural commentary of, 291n55; success of, 195–99; Torberg compared to, 204–11, 220, 292n71; Torberg on, 201–3, 208–9, 230n36, 290n48, 291n59; *Wiedergutmachung* jokes of, 213–16, 218; on Zionism, 292n64

language: body, 285n76; Celan on, 212–13; critical, 45; of dreams, 171; Fuchs on, 257n38; German, 1, 4, 19, 56–57, 71, 131, 175–76, 290n35; Gilman on, 176, 244n11, 285n78; house of, 38–40; ironic, 176; of Jews, 68–69, 71, 83, 175–76, 235n1, 285n78; metaphysics of, 38, 40, 53; misuse of, 41; mongrel, 175, 284n75; nimble space of, 28; perception of, 12; prejudice of, 71; primacy of, 39; psychology of, 244n11; scientific, 32, 242n60; secret, 175; strategic, 154; Trebitsch on, 38–40, 42; and warfare, 160; word inversion in, 39–41, 43
Laqueur, Walter, 35–36, 246n35, 264n9
Lareau, Alan, 266n27, 266n28
Lauer, Gerhard, 149
*Laugh yourself happy!: 1000 jokes (Lacht Euch Laune!: 1000 Witze)* (Warlitz), 99, 264n13, 268n46
laughter through suffering, 22–23, 128, 191–95
laughter through tears, 20–23, 141, 271n13
laughter with heartache, 192
Léandre, Charles Lucien, 79
Lessing, Theodor: approach of, 27–30; on Trebitsch, 28–30, 243n5, 244nn15,17,18
*Let Laughter Ring* (Mendelsohn, S.), 180–81, 277n67
Levi, Calman, 22, 243n64
Levin, Meyer, 205–6
Little Moritz, 97–98, 112
Loewe, Heinrich, 139, 274n40
Lohse, Theodor, 24
*The lonely teardrop (Die Einsame Träne)* (Morgan and Robitschek), 105, 107–10
Loucheur, Louis, 90–91
*Lozale* (crude jokes), 8, 37
Lüth, Eric, 195
Luther, Martin, 173, 273n30

Mann, Thomas, 122, 142; on exile, 149–52; Kahler on, 146–48, 272n22, 276nn57,61
marriage broker *(schadchen)*, 44–45, 232, 249nn58,60
Marx, Karl, 63, 76–77, 80, 90, 220, 254nn10,11, 255n16, 259n50

Marxism, 8, 13, 54, 76–77, 257n38; Fuchs on, 61–64, 72, 77, 80, 89–92, 94; neo-, 14, 60, 89–90; on value, 54
Marxist-Leninist fantasy, 94
mask of civilization *(Zivilisationsmaske)*, 102–3
*Maus* (Spiegelman), 285n89
*mauscheln* (Yiddish accent), 71, 85, 101,171, 175–76, 256n33, 284nn75,76, 285n78
Mauthner, Fritz, 256n29
*Maximen und Reflexionen* (Goethe), 286n2
*The Meaning of History* (Kahler), 273n30
Mehring, Franz, 76, 259n50
*Mein Kampf* (Hitler), 159–60
Meja, Volker, 119
Mendelsohn, Erich, 103–4
Mendelsohn, S. Felix, 180–81, 277n67
Mendes-Flohr, Paul, 18
Merziger, Patrick, 280n27
Messianic Christ, 35
metajoke, 80–83
Meyerowitz, Jan, 202–3, 247n41
Meyer-Sickendiek, Burkard, 14, 239n36
Michael the German *(Der Deutsche Michel)*, 131, 136, 273n33; analysis of, 132, 134; Kahler on, 132–39
*Midrash* (interpretation), 166–67
Mies van der Rohe, Ludwig, 61–62
*The Mirror of the Jews* (Pfefferkorn), 245n26
Mitscherlich, Alexander, 203–4, 216, 292n66, 295n100
Mitscherlich, Margarete, 203–4, 216, 292n66, 295n100
*Mobile Modernity* (Presner), 123–24
mobility *(Beweglichkeit)*, 25–27, 34, 37, 48, 54–56, 73, 244n9
mobilization, 153–81
modern culture, 1, 4
modernization, 57
money *(Geld)*, 32, 53, 56, 58, 63, 66, 72, 77–79, 99, 110, 121, 168, 170–71, 173, 204, 208–9, 252n84, 258nn44,46, 264n13, 268n47, 283n59
Morad, Erran, 227
*Morbus judaicus* (Jewish disease), 251n77
Morgan, Paul, 103, 107–14, 111, 266n27, 266n30, 268nn43,44,48
Moses, Stéphane, 57, 212–13, 237n18
Mosse, George, 121, 270nn3,4,7
Moszkowski, Alexander, 11, 13, 35–36, 70–71, 82–83, 252n85, 253n88, 256n31; citation of, 112–13, 210, 293n83; logic of, 113–14; on

Treitschke, 256n27; *Tristan and Isolde* joke, 174–75
mourning joke *(Trauerwitz)*, 204–5
mourning orator *(Trauerredner)*, 205
MS *St. Louis*, 142
Muliar, Fritz, 193–94
Müller-Marein, Josef, 196–97

*naiveté (Einfalt)*, 50
nationalism: of Germany, 5–6, 16–17; mainstream, 17
National Socialism, 12, 86–91, 95, 124, 269n60, 280n27
National Socialist Party, 24–25, 86, 95–96
Nazi era, 22, 40, 88, 153–81, 187, 203, 214, 275n44, 285n90, 291n55
Nazification, 156
Nazis, 13, 40, 59; censorship of, 119, 121–22, 280n31; defeat of, 211; eugenics of, 161–62, 165; Final Solution, 180; Freud, S. on, 246n35; Fuchs and, 87–88, 92; influence of, 153–54; ironic, 228–30; in jokes, 147, 158, 174; Kahler on, 121, 129, 144, 151, 270n1, 273n30; Landmann on, 188; legacy of, 220; and Michael the German, 131, 135; mockery of, 104–5, 108, 110, 116, 118, 154, 266n28; neo-, 15, 224, 226, 228–29; practice of, 155–61; propaganda of, 144, 153–54, 162, 169, 173–74, 179–180, 203; racist doctrine of, 107; themes of, 169–70; theory of, 155–61; victims of, 183, 214; Wiener on, 96–97, 101, 114–15, 118
Neumann, Robert, 197–98, 290n49
*Nicht so heftig! (Not so hard!)*, 111
Nietzsche, Friedrich, 175, 202–3, 292n62, 296n2
Nietzschean tradition, 148
Nikolaus, Paul, 177–78
*No Joke* (Wisse), 4, 82, 238n29, 260n60
non-Jew *(Goi)*, 70, 82–83, 167–68, 260n61, 293n83
*Not so hard! (Nicht so heftig!)*, 111
Novak, William, 40, 247n45, 289n28

Och, Gunnar, 14, 239n35
Olsvanger, Immanuel, 80–82, 125, 189–90, 211, 242n58, 247n37, 272n25
*On the Genealogy of Morals* (Nietzsche), 202–3
oppression, 7–8, 16, 70, 256n36
"ordeal of civility," 11–12, 250n69
Organization Consul, 90–91

INDEX 309

Oring, Elliott, 241n46, 289n30; on Freud, S., 235n4, 238n28, 251n74, 267n42; on Weininger, 49
*Ostjuden* (Eastern European Jews), 103, 121, 171–73, 236n12, 250n66, 265n24
Ostropoler, Hersch, 139, 274n39
*Otto Weiningers Tod* (Swoboda), 49
*Our Hitler* (1977), 185

Panofsky, Erwin, 146
Patka, Markus, 6–7, 14, 162, 171, 173, 176, 235n5, 249n53, 281n35, 285n78
peppering *(Pilpul)*, 167
persecution, 7, 20–22, 40, 99, 140, 151, 195, 271n10, 281n33
Petuchowski, Elizabeth, 191–92
Pfefferkorn, Johannes, 91, 245n26
*Phänomenologie und Ontologie* (Landmann), 286n5
philo-Semitism, 88, 183, 197, 211–12, 220, 293n86, 295n98
*Pilpul* (peppering), 167
Pittsburgh Tree of Life synagogue massacre, 224
Polish Jews, 142, 145, 169, 181, 257n39
"political correctness," 15, 158
post-Enlightenment assimilation, 212
*Pranksters and fools with Jewish caps (Schelme und Narren mit jüdischen Kappen)* (Loewe), 139
prejudice: danger of, 100–2; of language, 71; in tendentious jokes, 200; against women, 48–49
Presner, Todd, 123–24, 272n17
Prince, Cathryn J., 240n43
Princeton University, 146
Princeton University Library, 121–22
*Propaganda and National Power* (Hadamovsky), 156
pseudo-art *(Scheinart)*, 101–2
psychoanalysis, 17–19, 43, 168, 171, 183–84, 190–92, 249n56
pun *(Kalauer)*, 40–43, 75–76, 84, 211, 248nn47,48, 256n27
putting-into-question *(Infragestellung)*, 57

questionable practices: in business, 53–57; Trebitsch on, 55

*Race and humor (Rasse und Humor)* (Kadner), 17, 49, 88–89, 144, 154, 161–64

racial defilement *(Rassenschande)*, 86–87, 178
racism, 58–59, 80, 87; contemporary, 224, 229; ideology of, 129–30. *See also* anti-Semitism
*Raisins and almonds (Rosinkes mit Mandlen)* (Olsvanger), 80, 242n58
Ramspeck, Jürg, 191
Raskin, Richard, 56, 140–41, 274n44, 277n67
*Rassenschande* (racial defilement), 86–87, 178
*Rasse und Humor (Race and humor)* (Kadner), 17, 49, 88–89, 144, 154, 161–64
Rathenau, Walter, 90–91
rationalization, 18, 241n52
*ratlos* (clueless), 127–28
*Real-Encyclopedia of 1846*, 131–32
Reik, Theodor, 13, 185, 239n31, 250n67, 281n37, 287n10, 296n3
religion: hatred of, 57–59, 114; stereotypes of, 90
religious conversion, 84, 253n92
Relink, Karel, 260n56
Remarque, Erich Maria, 151
*The Renaissance of Jewish Culture in Weimar Germany* (Brenner), 121
reparation *(Wiedergutmachung)*, 13, 21–22, 182–218
"reparations jokes," 211–18
Robey, Ken, 118
Robitschek, Kurt, 7–8, 13, 103, 104, 118, 226, 266nn26,29, 269n59; audience of, 105; behavior of, 109–10; defense of Jewish wit in, 103–14, 118; and *Die Einsame Träne*, 105–12; on free speech, 7, 107, 109, 114–16, 118, 220; and Jewish jokes, 105, 107, 109–13, 115, 118, 267nn32,42, 268nn43,44,47,48; on Moszkowski, 112–14, 118; Nazi satire by, 103–5,116, 266n28, 269n58; rally speech of, 107–8; rationale of, 103–4; respectability of, 108–9; and Schweriner libel case, 115–16; and self-censorship joke, 110
Röhrich, Lutz, 8, 247n40, 248n4, 292n73
*Le Roi Rothschild* (Léandre), 79, 79–80
Romano, Aja, 229
Rosenduft (Rose-scent), 22–23
Rosenfeld, Gavriel D., 229, 297n10
*Rosinkes mit Mandlen (Raisins and almonds)* (Olsvanger), 80, 242n58
Rothschild, Amsel (Amschel), 76–82, 78–79, 81, 262n77, 269n50, 279n15

Rothschild joke, 63, 66, 75–80, 112
Rupprecht, Philipp, 285n88

Sagdiyev, Borat, 227
Sanders, Bernie, 226
Sandy, Amitai, 240n44
Santner, Eric, 186, 287n9
Saphir, Moritz, 16–17, 163–64, 176, 248n47, 282n45
*Saturday Night Live*, 225
saving *(Ersparnis)*, 183–84
*schadchen* (marriage broker), 44–45, 232, 249nn58,60
*Scheinart* (pseudo-art), 101–2
*Schelme und Narren mit jüdischen Kappen (Pranksters and fools with Jewish caps)* (Loewe), 139, 274n40
Schmid, Carlo, 192–94, 289n35
*Schmierwelle* (graffiti wave), 199–200
Schmitz, Siegfried, 37–38, 247n37
*Schmutz* (dirt), 170–71
Schnitzer, Manuel, 9, 83–85, 238n26, 247n43, 261n67, 293n81
Schnitzler, Arthur, 1, 11–12, 238nn29,31, 242n54
Scholem, Gershom, 7, 150, 166–67, 237n18, 277n71, 293n81
Schönbach, Peter, 200
Schreber, Daniel, 29, 245n20
*Schwank* (droll story), 20, 37, 139, 238n28, 247nn40,46
*schwankhaftig* (vacillating), 20, 37
Schweitzer, Hans "Mjölnir," 176–78, 177
Schweriner, Arthur, 115–16
*Secessio Judaica* (Blüher), 257n40, 272n18
"secondary moves," 29, 43, 59, 219
*The second encounter (Die zweite Begegnung)* (Torberg), 205–7, 206
Second Reich, 5–6
secularization, 57
self-criticism, 4, 11–12, 37, 47, 134, 153–54, 162, 170, 173–74, 180, 192, 221, 235n4, 236n16, 238n28, 247n39, 289n33
self-expression, 127
"self-hate" speech, 6, 12, 15, 96, 101–2, 108, 113, 115–16, 278n2
self-hatred: dynamics of, 212, 244n11; Lessing on, 28–30; self-irony or, 5–6, 239n33, 275n52; theory of, 30–31; and Trebitsch, 27–31, 58
self-irony: anti-Semitism and, 4–12, 16, 21, 37, 86–87, 91, 114, 220, 239n33, 240n45, 261n67;

Browne and, 140–46; and caricature, 254n10; as defense mechanism, 71–75; Edel on, 4–6; Fuchs on, 8, 62, 64, 67–76, 82–4, 91–94, 210–11, 256n35, 258n46; German, 72–73; in *Judenwitz*, 4, 235n5; Kadner on, 162–63, 221, 281n37; neo-Nazi, 230; reflection on, 7; and self-criticism, 154, 200; self-hatred or, 5–6, 239n33, 275n52; as self-protection, 73; as strength, 8; symbolic significance of, 7–8; understanding, 67–71
*Sex and Character (Geschlecht und Charakter)* (Weininger), 48–49
*Shadchenit* (female Jewish matchmaker), 195–96
Sherman, Rick, 227–28
Simon, Ernst, 13, 167, 265n13, 283n55
Singer, Isaac Bashevis, 260n63,288n24
skepticism, 50–51, 124, 128–29, 252n80
Social democracy in the 'mirror of truth' *(Die Socialdemocratie im Spiegel der Wahrheit)*, 32–34, 33
Social Democrat, 61–62, 89–91, 131, 193
*Die Socialdemocratie im Spiegel der Wahrheit* (Social democracy in the 'mirror of truth'), 32–34, 33
social humiliation, 72–73
Sombart, Werner, 63, 66, 73–74, 76–77, 254n4, 255n16, 257nn38,39
sophistry, 45, 163, 165–66, 238n28
sound joke *(Klangwitz)*, 40–41
Southey, Tabatha, 229–30
Sparr, Thomas, 124, 271n10
*Speak German! (Sprich Deutsch!)* (Engel), 71
Speier, Hans, 155–56, 222–23
Spencer, Richard, 229–30
*Spenderliste* (list of donors), 195–96
*The Spider's Web (Das Spinnennetz)* (Roth), 24–25
Spiegelman, Art, 285n89
*Das Spinnennetz (The Spider's Web)* (Roth), 24–25
Spirit and Judaism. See *Geist und Judentum*
*Sprich Deutsch! (Speak German!)* (Engel), 71
Stalzer, Alfred, 14
Steiner, George, 38
stereotypes: of corruption, 170–71; as deceiver, 74; of dogs, 247n45; on hygiene, 105, 167–68; of Jewish joker, 124–25; of Jews, 50; Kahler on, 124; of money, 170–71; on oaths, 173; of religion, 90; tribal, 124. *See also* anti-Semitism

Stern, Frank, 214–15, 293n86
Stern, Itzig Feitel, 71, 256n35
Stewart, Jon, 14–15
Streicher, Julius, 95, 173
*Struggle for Berlin* (Goebbels), 158
*Der Stürmer*, 95, 179–80
*Stürmer* tradition, 5
Swoboda, Hermann, 49
Syberberg, Hans-Jürgen, 185
Szalit-Marcus, Rachel, 92–94, 93

Tabori, George, 290n51
Talmud: interpretation of, 7; Kadner on, 165–68, 179, 283n55
Temple Mount, 38
*Their Right! (Ihr Recht!)*, 133
Third Reich, 13, 15, 17, 21, 59, 153, 155, 180, 195; fall of, 142–43; German-Jewish estrangement in, 122
Thöny, Eduard, 171–72, 284n66
Tobia, P. J., 229–30
Torberg, Friedrich, 11, 14, 22, 188–89, 206, 294n92; claims of, 220; criticism of Landmann, 201–3, 208–9, 230n36, 290n48, 291n59, 292n73; image of, 209, 291n58; on joke mourning, 198–99, 204–11; Landmann compared to, 204–11, 220, 292n71; Neumann on, 290n49; on philo-Semitic joke reparations, 196–99
totalitarian principles, 213–14
*Trauerredner* (mourning orator), 205
*Trauerwitz* (mourning joke), 204–5
Trebitsch, Arthur, 5–7, 13, 19, 26; accusations of, 25; analysis of, 27–28, 55–56, 220; and anti-Semitism, 31–32, 35, 40–41, 57–59; on Aryan primary spirit, 25–26, 41–42, 59, 249n54, 251n77; and authenticity search, 36–38; career of, 35–36; on Chamberlain, 29–30; character of, 24–25; conceptual framework of, 27–28; conclusion of, 37–38, 47; confession of, 42; contradictions of, 25, 55, 253n92; as court jester, 30; criticism of, 248n47; death of, 24–25, 59; dichotomy of, 34; doubts of, 249n56; Edel and, 248n47; on fixed gaze, 26, 49–50; on fleeting gaze, 26, 49–50; Freud, S. compared to, 42–48, 249n56, 254n89; Gilman on, 25, 40–41, 233n11, 245n28; Graeber on, 244n15; Hitler on, 24–25; idols of, 30; image of, 35–36; impact on, 36; influences on, 43–49; on "inner ambiguity," 49–50; interpretation of, 46–47; Jewish conspiracy and, 25, 29–30, 40, 244n17, 245nn20,24, 248n52; Jewish joke and, 7, 24–59; Jewish secondary spirit, 25, 27–28, 32, 34, 36, 38–39, 43, 45–46, 50, 54, 57, 59, 244nn9,10, 248n50, 249n54; Jewish self-hatred and, 7, 24, 27–28, 30; joke analysis of, 39–40, 45–47, 51–56; on *Judenwitz*, 25; on language, 38–40, 42, 55; lectures from, 30; Lessing on, 28–30, 253n5; life of 24, 244n17; on linguistic performance, 36–37; messianism of, 246n33; mission of, 30–31, 35, 57; narrative of, 31–35; Nazis and, 24–25, 35, 59; obsession of, 245n24; paranoia of, 29, 244n15, 246n31, 251n77; perception of, 30, 34–35, 57–58; philosophy of, 26–27; on puns, 40–42, 248n50; on questionable Jewish business practices, 53–57; racialist views, 24, 57–58, 250n66, 253n92; research of, 36; on secondary moves, 27, 29, 43, 59, 219; on skepticism, 51, 251n80; speech of, 44–45; Steiner compared to, 38–39; story of, 29–30; success of, 248n52; and Weininger, 48–57, 251nn70,77; word play of, 51–52
Trebitschean mirror stage, 31–35
Treitschke, Heinrich von, 5, 63, 68–70, 74, 236n10, 255n23, 256n27, 260n62
*Tristan and Isolde* (Wagner), 174–75
trouble *(Tsuris)*, 147
Trump, Donald, 224–27
*Tsuris* (trouble), 147

*Die Unfähigkeit zu trauern (The Inability to Mourn, 1967)* (Mitscherlich, A., and Mitscherlich, M.), 203–4, 216

vacillating *(schwankhaftig)*, 4, 20, 28, 54, 57–58, 244n12
Valley, Eli, 15, 240nn42,43
values: democratic, 7–8; ethical, 110–12; Marxism on, 54; relativization of, 57, 253n88; "transmitted values," 57
Veilchenduft (Violet-scent), 22–23
*Verjudung* (Judaization), 214
Verlag, Delphin, 119
Verlag, J. F. Lehmanns, 162
Verlag, Schocken, 122
Viennese strudel, 57–59
"the vigilant one" ("*der Wachsame*"), 207–8
Vischer, Theodor, 196
*Vossische Zeitung*, 101–2

*"der Wachsame"* ("the vigilant one"), 207–8
Wagner, Richard, 135, 174
Waldoks, Moshe, 40, 247n45
Warlitz, Ernst, 99–100, 111, 264n13, 265n15, 268n46
Wassermann, Henry, 5, 246n29, 247n46, 252n84
*The Way into the Open* (Schnitzler), 11–12, 14, 238n31
Weber, Elizabeth, 242n63
Weber, Max, 63, 241n52, 271n8
Weimar Germany: free speech in, 95–118; Jewish jokes in, 95–118
Weimar Republic, 7–9, 12–13, 21; collapse of, 130–31; evolution of, 24–25, 62–63; landscape of, 89–90
Weininger, Otto, 35, 246n34; on character, 48–49; on humor, 48–49; on knowledge, 51; Oring on, 49; Trebitsch on, 48–57; on women, 48–49
Weinstein, Harvey, 225
Weiss, Bernhard, 157
Weissberg, Liliane, 63, 254n10
Wergenthin, Georg von, 12
Western civilization, 8
West German Bundestag, 193
whisper jokes *(Flüsterwitze)*, 180, 285n90
*Why the Germans? Why the Jews?* (Aly), 242n60
Wickberg, Daniel, 237n24
*Wiedergutmachung* (reparation), 13, 21–22, 182–218
*Wiederjudmachung*, 211–18
Wiener, Alfred, 6–9, 75, 117, 226; background of, 95–96; Centralverein and, 95–103; defense of, 98–100; Gilman on, 97–98; morality of, 98–99; on Nazis, 96–97, 114–15; warnings from, 100–1
Wiener Library for the Study of the Holocaust and Genocide, 118
Wilhelm, Kaiser, III, 112–13
Wilson, Jason, 229
*The Wisdom of Israel* (Browne), 140, 142–43
Wisse, Ruth R., 4, 14, 82, 238n29
*Wissenschaft*, 19

*Der Witz der Juden (Jewish Wit)* (Edel), 1–4, 2–3, 250n60
*Witzenschaft*, 16–20
*Witzenschaftler* (humorist-scientist), 42–43
*Witz und Politik* (Speier), 155–56
*Der Witz und seine Beziehung zum Unbewussten*, 1905 *(Jokes and Their Relation to the Unconscious)* (Freud, S.), 1, 2–3, 4, 19, 42, 144–45, 154, 235n4
women: defense of, 98–99; prejudice of, 48–49; Weininger on, 48–49
wonder rabbi *(Wunderrabbi)*, 45, 267n42
wordplay *(Wortwitz)*, 42, 51–52, 75–76
World War I: aftermath of, 13; anti-Semitism during, 5–6
*Wortwitz* (word play), 42, 51–52, 75–76
*Wunderrabbi* (wonder rabbi), 45, 267n42

xenophobia, 224–25

Yiannopoulos, Milo, 228–29
Yiddish, 20, 22, 28, 71, 80, 83, 85, 105, 146, 175–76, 188–89, 192, 242n58, 243n66, 247n37, 256n33, 263n83, 284nn75,76, 286n5,
Yiddish accent *(mauscheln)*, 71, 85, 101, 171, 175–76, 256n33, 284nn75,76, 285n78
Yiddishisms, 36, 71, 84–85
*Yom Kippur* (Day of Atonement), 11–12, 110, 296n3
YouTube, 228–29

*Zelig*, 258n41
Zentnerschwer, Effze, 52–53
Zionism, 227, 256n36, 277n71, 292n64
Zionist, 13, 80, 92, 150, 167, 178, 227, 248n52, 277n71
Zionist movement, 150
*Zivilisationsmask* (mask of civilization), 102–3
Žižek, Slavoj, 217–18, 243n65, 295n102
Zohn, Harry, 207–8
Zusman, Eyal, 240n44
*Die zweite Begegnung (The second encounter)* (Torberg), 205–7, 206

Louis Kaplan is professor of Visual Studies and Art History and an affiliated faculty member at the Centre for Jewish Studies at the University of Toronto. He is the author of *Photography and Humour*; *The Strange Case of William Mumler, Spirit Photographer*; *American Exposures: Photography and Community in the Twentieth Century*; and *László Moholy-Nagy: Biographical Writings*.

www.ingramcontent.com/pod-product-compliance
Lightning Source LLC
Chambersburg PA
CBHW030434300426
44112CB00009B/1000